BEYOND SENSATION

Mary Elizabeth Braddon in Context

joint introduction

edited by

Marlene Tromp, Pamela K. Gilbert, and Aeron Haynie

+ her essay

foreward & afterwrd by very distinguished scholars (Kincaid & Pykett)

State University of New York Press

collections of essays - peer reviewed

Cover photograph of M. E. Braddon
courtesy of the Harry Ransom Humanities Research Center,
The University of Texas at Austin

Published by
State University of New York Press, Albany

For information, address State University of New York Press
State University Plaza, Albany, New York 12246

Production by Dana Foote
Marketing by Dana Yanulavich

Library of Congress Cataloging-in-Publication Data

Beyond sensation : Mary Elizabeth Braddon in context / edited by
Marlene Tromp, Pamela K. Gilbert, and Aeron Haynie.
p.   cm.
Includes bibliographical references and index.
ISBN 0–7914–4419–8 (alk. paper). — ISBN 0–7914–4420–1 (pbk. :
alk. paper)
1. Braddon, M. E. (Mary Elizabeth), 1837–1915—Criticism and
interpretation.   2. Braddon, M. E. (Mary Elizabeth), 1837–1915. Lady
Audley's secret.   3. Psychological fiction, English—History and
criticism.   4. Women and literature—England—History—19th century.
5. Domestic fiction, English—History and criticism.
6. Sensationalism in literature.   I. Tromp, Marlene, 1966–   .
II. Gilbert, Pamela K.   III. Haynie, Aeron, 1964–   .
PR4989.M4Z53 2000
823'.8—dc21   99–37009
CIP

10   9   8   7   6   5   4   3   2   1

BEYOND SENSATION

CONTENTS

FIGURES AND TABLES

FOREWORD

James Kincaid

This volume explores not simply Mary Elizabeth Braddon's novels but their contexts: what they tell us about the social and discursive world they helped form, our own habits of reading and professional practices, and how we might most interestingly and generously construe a writer so shrewd, popular, various, and enigmatic as Mary Elizabeth Braddon. This remarkably sharp-edged and plain-speaking collection maintains as high a level of sophistication as I've seen, while wrestling directly with a range of central questions, perhaps most centrally with the issue caught by Laura Goodlad, the dilemma of "a popular writer whose works dramatize ('sensationalize,' 'gothicize') women's lives without articulating any obvious 'feminist' position." How do we deal with a writer who, on one hand, was able to sniff out new trends and models, new modes, in order to keep up with and slightly ahead of, public taste; and, on the other, often write against the models she was using? The Braddon presented here is a writer of great range and variety, both acquiescent and resistant, lurid and playful, a combination of Larry Flynt, Gloria Steinem, Henry James, "Days of Our Lives," Charlotte Perkins Gilman, "Cops," and Joan Didion.

The collection is remarkable in presenting to us an opportunity to read into Braddon, the "Braddon problem," and modern approaches by charging straight through the volume, beginning, as the Red King says, at the beginning, going on till we come to the end, and then stopping. So assured are these essays that there is nothing of the over-inflated or the defensive here, no mention of "strangely neglected topics" or of the unaccountable idiocy of others who have gone on ignoring Braddon. Perhaps no novelist has been more dramatically or successfully rediscovered, and this volume builds on that strength, both demonstrating it and providing the finest body of work on the novelist we have, a model for vital and illuminating criticism.

The rediscovery of Braddon has, however, been sharply limited to the glorious Lady Audley's Secret—a novel that, until I read this volume, formed the limits of my own experience with Braddon. Recognizing this, the scholars here, all of whom seem to know virtually all of Braddon, lead us into the subject by way of five initial, slam-bang essays on the one well-known novel, so as not to frighten us. The first two essays, by Elizabeth Langland and Gail Turley Houston, both employ new-historical cultural analysis to suggest how the novel demystifies public culture: Langland shows how the discourse of the enclosure of land swept onward to secure women within a symbolic architecture of penetrable, scrutinized childishness, linked both to incapacity and to madness; Houston explores the way in which the law, rooted in Blackstone, maintained a series of distinctions fundamental to male privilege, distinctions subjected to radical revision in the novel.

Using the Sepoy Rebellion as a model, Lillian Nayder argues that the novel is, for all that, marked by "a deeply conservative bent," finally supporting the "patriarchal norms and traditions" it can sometimes criticize but in a fairly superficial way. It's a strong corrective and fun reading, also allowing Katherine Montwieler to argue the reverse case and chart the novel's "subversive political vision." Aeron Haynie's concluding essay to this section is a poised and delicately articulated study of the very ambiguity implicit in the case-making of the previous two essays. Using the image of the decaying country estate, both threatening and threatened, Haynie suggests the "troubled" class and readerly relations between the heart of the novel and those penetrating it.

I see I have fallen into the ghastly trap of offering one-sentence summaries of each of the essays. I can't go on with that, so let me just point: to Toni Johnson-Woods's engaging study of how Braddon used Australia and was used there; to Law and Carnell's brilliant and convincing study of Braddon and the marketplace and, surprisingly, how her rapid writing "was not necessarily in her own best economic interests, nor necessarily detrimental to the literary value of her writing"; to Pamela Gilbert's sly and masterful deconstruction of the realist/sensational binary in the context of male anxieties and jealousies and the imperial expansion of the seventies. The essays on Aurora Floyd, on Braddon and the theater, the other novels, the ghost stories, the detective fiction: ditto. They give superb evidence of the great range and variety of a writer who has been tied to tag lines for some time. They fill me with embarrassment at not having read more of her work, and they make me determined to be a better person and a better scholar. What else can one ask from a volume such as this one? Even if you aren't as interested in self-improvement as I am, you are about to enter as fine a set of essays on a puzzling and powerful writer as any I have read.

ACKNOWLEDGMENTS

The editors would like to express their sincere gratitude to Kathy Boyer, David Eisenhauer, Ceara Flake, Tamar Heller, Aphrodite Keil, Elizabeth Langland, Teresa Reed, Roena Haynie-Reitz, George Suttle, Eileen and Hans Tromp.

INTRODUCTION

Marlene Tromp, Pamela K. Gilbert, and Aeron Haynie

> What is silenced within discourses—and what remains
> unprinted, untaught, and virtually unread within
> institutions—is inseparable from what is written and from
> what remains "real and remembered" within a canon.
> —Tricia Lootens, *Lost Saints*

> She is a part of England, she has woven herself into it;
> without her it would be different.
> —Arnold Bennett

For the past several years, Victorian studies conferences have prominently featured the name of Mary Elizabeth Braddon in their programs.
Indeed, it was following a panel on Braddon's novels that the three of us
began to discuss the ways in which Braddon had become increasingly
important to our research and, as we believed, to a rich understanding of
the latter half of the nineteenth century. One of the most popular and
prolific novelists of the period,[1] her evident significance to the Victorians
themselves—and to the market economy that made *Lady Audley's Secret*
the bestselling novel of the period and kept Braddon in business producing an abundant variety of fiction until the turn of the century—
necessitates an examination of the role she played in literary history and
culture. Braddon's fiction, through which she offered a revisioning of
Victorian codes of behavior and narrative, along with her unorthodox
life, attracted the attention of the public and contemporary scholars
alike. W. Fraser Rae lamented, in an early review of Braddon, that despite

the "low type of female characters" depicted in her novels she might *still* "boast, without fear of contradiction, of having temporarily succeeded in making the literature of the kitchen the favourite reading of the Drawing room" (Wolff 196–7).[2]

Rae's commentary suggests a variety of tensions that make the study of Braddon's work rich and provocative. Her career not only spanned the century, making her writing a far-reaching presence in the period, but crossed boundaries in readership, style, and the politics of socioeconomic identity. Popularized when Mudie's circulating library had established itself as an arbiter of middle-class morality, even Braddon's most "shocking" fiction was packaged and regularly delivered to the homes of those middle-class readers whose attitudes, writings, and behaviors we have studied for decades—and, as Rae's remarks claim, Braddon's was writing that somehow seemed to reflect an intimate appeal to those who labored in those households, a suggestion that begs for analysis. In addition, though known today as primarily a sensation novelist, after establishing her reputation and generating a stable income, Braddon secured the freedom to experiment with other stylistic approaches, to create the "art" in addition to the "sensation" that had inaugurated her career.[3] The discursive diversity that appears in this movement across so many fields of significance has provided Braddon scholars with multiple points of entry for analysis.

Though there have been critics who have questioned the legitimacy and significance of Braddon's work, we have often found, in their dismissals, fertile ground for inquiry as well. Some critics have suggested that Braddon's historical marginalization derives from the concerns expressed in foregoing decades about Charles Dickens: her productivity. She simply generated "too many" novels to seem worthy of serious academic consideration. Joseph O'Mealy, in his examination of Margaret Oliphant, argues that "Steeped as we are in the late-twentieth century belief that less is more, and conditioned by the modernist examples of lapidary and or slowly gestated novels, [voluminous publication] not only discourages the modern reader but probably gives rise to a mild contempt for the author of such excess" (65). Further, this "excess" may explain some of the contemporary and Victorian attention to Braddon's life that has led to her neglect. Tricia Lootens suggests that a woman writer's sullied social reputation may have been constituted, in part, in her literary success, arguing that "female aspirants to literary genius tend to be cast in particularly humiliating sexual or somatic terms" (49).[4] These patterns and their often gendered nature, however, pose intriguing questions for the student of the period and have already begun to generate inquiry like that contained in this collection.

Another source of criticism (ironically countering the charge of "sensationalism," which implies resistance to accepted codes of narrative) has concerned Braddon's "conventionality." Ellen Miller Casey suggests that, in her concern for maintaining Victorian codes of propriety, Braddon sacrificed the possibility of political inquiry and "feminine rebellion," "succumb[ing] to the pressure of other people's prudery and [producing novels] which [are] therefore less interesting as a finished work[s] of art than for what [they] reveal about [their] age" (81). We would argue that although many of Braddon's novels may seem to capitulate to normative Victorian standards of morality in their closing moments, the resistance depicted throughout the novel as a whole provides a form of "revelation" other than the one Casey identifies here—a subversive variety of revision that allows figures like the infamous Lady Audley to confound and, thus, call into question notions of gendered identity and the domestic order. Indeed, Lynda Hart finds this complexity in the presence of these tensions and the "pathological repetition [in *Lady Audley's Secret*] of a profoundly paranoid culture that ironically displays what it suppresses" (22).[5] Increasing numbers of critics have found the questions produced by the irony of Lady Audley's placid execution of profoundly non-Victorian and unwomanly crimes, and, the final "recuperation" of the Audley home and her formerly wayward nephew by her interment in a Belgian *maison de santé* a fruitful sites for investigation, and we would argue that their reexamination of this novel provides an apt model for the study of Braddon's life and the corpus of her work.

In the face of various forms of resistance, we have discovered, in our preparation for this collection, many devoted Braddon scholars pursuing these and other lines of inquiry. The public's voracious desire for an engagement with Braddon's work during her own lifetime was evidenced by the widespread, and often unauthorized, reproduction of her novels in various forms (*Aurora Floyd,* for example, immediately appeared on stages all over London, produced by at least four different companies); likewise, intellectual conversations concerning Braddon and her work—which have been taking place for decades—have often been staged outside the powerfully legitimated realms of academic discourse. The enthusiasm with which analysis has continued in the hallways at conferences, even after the doors to the session have closed, bespeaks the demand for accessible, current research on Braddon. The dearth of resources on Braddon has not silenced her voice in the active scholarship of literary and cultural critics and historians, whose interests include a range of issues as rich and diverse as economics, sexuality, madness, art, identity, imperialism, canonization, social policies, publication history, theater, and the law—explorations that attest to the complexity of her work and the importance it has in our study of the period. As Tricia Lootens suggests in the epigraph to this introduction, the previous lack of critical attention does not indicate insignificance, nor can it serve as a continuing justification for her neglect.

Although we wish to strongly argue that Braddon cannot be satisfactorily summed up simply as a sensation novelist, it may be useful to recall that the reason for that insistence is precisely because that is how she is usually identified. Critical and cultural ambivalence about the sensation genre and its gendered implications at the time of its production have done much to contribute to Braddon's obscurity, and it is important to be aware of the reasons for this. As most of the essays in the collection either assume familiarity with this information, or ignore it in favor of other approaches, it seems useful to briefly review the history of reception of the sensation genre itself.

Braddon's earliest, and perhaps greatest public impact was as a sensation novelist, the author of *Lady Audley's Secret* and *Aurora Floyd*. That typecasting was early on injurious to Braddon—the sensation novel, a genre category of the 1860s, was thought of as a diseased, feminine genre, relying more on plot complications than on artistry, and more on shock potential than on any solid ethical foundation. Interestingly, for many years in the late twentieth century, Wilkie Collins was the only representative of the genre in print, though the Victorians considered the genre itself to be feminine, and certainly the great bulk of sensation novels were produced (and consumed) by women. Victorian critics responded with alarm to what seemed to them a frightening new manifestation of female aggression and cultural decay.

Victorian anxiety about the sensation novel tended to be articulated in terms of the sexual and economic improprieties of the women they depicted. Mrs. Oliphant's condemnation is the best known:

> Now it is no knight of romance riding down the forest glades, ready for the defence and succour of all the oppressed, for whom the dreaming maiden waits. She waits now for flesh and muscles, for strong arms that seize her, and warm breath that thrills her through, and a host of other physical attractions, which she indicates to the world with a charming frankness . . . were the sketch made from the man's point of view, its openness would at least be less repulsive. The peculiarity of it in England is, that it is oftenest made from the woman's side—that it is women who describe these sensuous raptures—that this intense appreciation of flesh and blood, this eagerness of physical sensation, is represented as the natural sentiment of English girls. (259)

The physicality of the women described in sensation novels certainly was disturbing to many critics. But even more disturbing was the answering physical response in its readers. The sensation novel, as the name implies, was defined by its ability to cause a physical sensation in the reader—a thrill, a gasp, a creeping of flesh. The *Quarterly Review* defines sensation novels as novels that produce "excitement, and excitement alone" by "preaching to the nerves," "There are novels of the warming pan, and others of the galvanic battery type—some which gently stimulate a particular feeling, and others which carry the whole nervous system by steam" (Mansel 481, 487). Many critics were also distressed by the blatant commercialism of the sensation novel. Henry Mansel characterized the sensation novel as a diseased product incident to degenerate mass production: "A commercial atmosphere floats around works of this class, redolent of the manufactory and the shop. . . . There is something unspeakably disgusting in this ravenous appetite for carrion, this vulture like instinct which smells out the newest mass of social corruption, and hurries to devour the loathsome dainty before the scent has evaporated" (483–506). For these critics, the sensation novel was dangerous in its evocation of corrupt mass tastes, and the fear that those tastes would in turn corrupt the upper classes who shared the "appetite" for sensation with their social "inferiors."

In the twentieth century, with the exception of those critics—most notably Audrey Peterson—who positioned Braddon firmly at the foundation of the Victorian detective novel, though as a "minor writer," and of enthusiasts such as Sadleir and the collector, Robert Lee Wolff, whose biography of Braddon remains the *vade mecum* of Braddoniana, Braddon was virtually neglected, her readership limited to two main groups: feminists in search of a female literary tradition, such as Showalter, and those interested in sensation fiction itself. To Showalter and others who worked in her mode, we owe an incalculable debt of recovery. These scholars were followed by feminist critics (and others) interested in revising—or dispensing with—canonical modes of aesthetic evaluation, and that influence is very evident in the current "Braddon explosion," including most of the work included here. In tandem with this trend was a reevaluation of "minor genres." Early on, this discussion acceded to the general opinion of the low aesthetic value of sensation and treated it as a topic primarily of historical importance. By the 1980s, however, scholars such as Winifred Hughes, Jonathan Loesberg, and Thomas Boyle came to see it as increasingly central to an understanding of the period and were more interested in how the aesthetics of sensation worked culturally than in evaluating it against dominant realist aesthetics.

Hughes argued that sensation was a truly new genre, "What distinguishes the true sensation genre, as it appeared in its prime during the 1860s, is the violent yoking of romance and realism, traditionally the two contradictory modes of literary perception" (16). Its appeal, she contends, was based in part on the setting, which was contemporary and domestic (18). Hughes believes that the sensation novel is a response to the stringencies of Victorian respectability. Boyle, however, finds little difference between sensation fiction and Victorian life described in other genres. He notes that the average Victorian newspaper "was sensational to say the least, [and] certainly not supportive of an image of domestic tranquility" (3). Boyle, therefore, opens up the study of sensation discourse to extend over a wide range of texts, of which the novels are only a part. Other studies of sensation tend to focus on gender and class implications of apprehensions about their production and reception. Jonathan Loesberg argues that the defining characteristic of sensation fiction is anxiety over the loss of class identity, which he relates to the debates over the second Reform Bill. Most recent studies of sensation have particularly concerned themselves with gender issues. In her excellent 1988 study of Wilkie Collins, Jenny Bourne Taylor notes that the appetite for sensation was linked to anxieties about cultural degeneration, observing that the physiological referents of "sensation" operated "to articulate anxiety about imminent cultural decline by referring to an image of an explicitly 'feminine' body that was at once its product and metonymic model" marked by a neurotic susceptibility to excitement that was a reaction to modernity (4). Kate Flint argues that the primary source or anxiety about sensation novels has to do with their primarily female audience, but notes that the female author is implicated in this equation as well, and observes the special hostility shown toward female authors with sexually aggressive female characters. Lyn Pykett's recent work compares the cultural production of sensation to the more explicitly feminist production of New Woman fiction at the end of the century, and focuses also on the role of readers. She argues that, "By being positioned as the spectator (especially of a female character) the female reader is offered a culturally masculine 'position of mastery' . . . [I]n sensation fiction this mastery is also an effect of the specularity of the melodramatic style [which offers the female body as object while simultaneously inviting an identification of reader and protagonist]. . . . It is this contradictory process . . . which opens a space for oppositional readings" (80). Ann Cvetkovich's excellent book is also concerned with the female reader, and the offer of emotional relief from a possibly transgressive expression of affect, a "telling" of pain that might seem to offer ways to effect social change, although she sees that "relief" as often illusory. She positions the sensation novel firmly back in the mainstream of Victorian literary development, moving seamlessly from Braddon to Eliot in her exploration of sensational discourse. Examining the icon of the transgressive or suffering woman that pervades sensational literature, Cvetkovich traces the construction of affect as both natural and particularly female, and as therefore potentially transgressive, requiring regula-

check this book out for Hardy cook

tion and control. The political potential of sensation lies in the way affect (e.g., readers' sympathy) generated by the sensational representation of power relations can be mobilized, as, for example, Marx attempts to direct readers' energies. Pamela Gilbert continues the focus on the body as the locus of the construction of sensation, and examines the way in which sensation is constructed as a genre out of anxieties about the grotesque and permeable body of culture, a body literalized in the body of the middle-class woman reader. Examining the way in which reading, ingestion, and sexual penetration are metaphorically aligned in critical discourse of the period, she seeks to position sensation as a genre constructed by its readers within a larger network of cultural discourse and historical circumstance. The work of these critics suggests that the study of the "minor" genre of sensation has become an important part of the scholarly discourse on Victorian cultural issues as a whole.

However, despite this newfound interest that has revived scholarship on Braddon, it is important to realize that Braddon's production extended beyond the sixties and beyond the conventional understanding of the sensational. Although few critics today remain unaware of *Lady Audley's Secret,* we believe this collection can diversify the study of this complex and often controversial author. It explodes the predominating conception that Braddon's work is summed up in this single novel. In offering this broad foray into her work, representing many texts and theoretical approaches, we hope not only to furnish some response to the enthusiasm for Braddon that already exists, but generate fertile ground for future study.

In 1867, at the height of an astounding popularity that would last almost forty years, Mary Elizabeth Braddon found herself the target of a series of stinging reviews that condemned both her "sensation" novels and her life. Although Braddon was neither glamorous nor criminal, reviewers assumed that the attractive and unconventional heroines/ villains of Braddon's sensation novels were based on the author's own experiences and character. Even Robert Wolff, her biographer, claims that, "the story of her life [was] as sensational in its way and for its time as any novel she ever wrote" (3). The most famous of her contemporary reviewers, Margaret Oliphant, suggested that the author of *Lady Audley's Secret* has "brought in a reign of bigamy . . . and it is an invention that could only have been possible to an Englishwoman knowing the attraction of impropriety, and yet loving the shelter of the law" (203). This was clearly an attack on Braddon's adulterous relationship with the publisher John Maxwell, who published reports of his "marriage" to Braddon in 1864 while his own wife was in an insane asylum in Ireland. Although Braddon lived with Maxwell for thirty-four years (they were married in 1874) and eventually established a rather conventional middle-class domestic arrangement, Braddon suffered from a taint of disreputability that took years to dispel.

Who was this woman, the author of over eighty novels, who elicited such violent condemnation from many reviewers and staunch and affectionate support from fellow writers such as Dickens, Thackeray, Robert Louis Stevenson, and Henry James? She is still known primarily as the author of her first bestseller, *Lady Audley's Secret* (1862), which ran through eight editions in three months, was a staple of Victorian theater, and was even made into a musical comedy in the United States in the 1970s. However, the fierce popularity of this early novel tends to overshadow the growth and development of her later fiction.

Mary Elizabeth Braddon was born in London in 1835, the third child of "a failed Cornish solicitor of good family" and an Irish Protestant mother. In her unpublished memoir, *Before the Knowledge of Evil,* Braddon remembers her father as a shadowy figure, a "well-groomed," handsome man who was "nobody's enemy but his own" (Wolff 22). Braddon found out later, after her beloved mother's death, that her father had been an unfaithful husband; whatever the motive, her parents separated when Braddon was five, and she and her mother lived in reduced circumstances, eventually moving to a poorer suburb of London and taking lodgers.

After her brother, Edward, left the family to make his fortune in the Indian civil service, and her sister, Margaret, married an Italian and moved to Naples, Mary became the sole provider for her mother and decided to supplement her mother's meager income by going on stage, "a thing to be spoken of with bated breath, a lapse of a lost soul" (45). From 1857 to 1860, Mary Braddon, as "Mary Seyton," played a number of minor roles in the theater, usually middle-aged women—an aunt, a spinster, or a wife. This experience fueled her descriptions of theatrical life in her later novels.

In 1860 Braddon secured the patronage of a Yorkshire squire, Gilby, who paid her to complete a long epic poem in Spenserian meter. However, Mary Braddon soon began writing for half penny journals in London and from 1862 to 1866 had published nine three-volume novels. She continued to write virtually nonstop through the 1880s, always concerned that her haste might damage the literary quality of her novels. In her correspondence with her literary mentor, Edward Bulwer-Lytton, she offered self-deprecating evaluations of her work: "I have learned to look at everything in a mercantile sense, & to write solely for the circulating library reader whose palette [sic] requires strong meat, and is not very particular as to the quality. . . . Can the sensation be elevated by art, & redeemed from all its coarseness?" (155). One wonders about the sincerity of her disparagements of her work, since these seem to be the terms upon which her friendship with Lytton depended. In any case, Braddon was supporting the Maxwells: William, his five children by his first marriage, and their own growing family. In addition to managing a large family and producing a steady stream of best-sellers, in 1866 Braddon became editor of Maxwell's magazine, *Belgravia*. Her life during this period was marked by an intense, driven productivity that left little time for the typical leisure pursuits of an upper-class Victorian woman: "[I have] little inclination for spending money & positively no time to be extravagant, if I wished to be so. I go nowhere where I require fine dress—I can't drink wine. I am not able to stir from London, or would spend my money in traveling; but am altogether bound hand and foot by hard work" (134). In 1868, after the birth of her fourth child and the death of her mother, Mary Braddon suffered a nervous breakdown. This occasioned the only nonproductive period in her adult life: for the next two years, she ceased writing. Yet she recovered, gradually resumed writing, and published a book, *Fenton's Quest*, in 1871, after which her pace never again flagged.

In 1874, after the death of his wife, Maxwell and Mary Braddon were finally legally married. However, despite attaining this formal seal of respectability, Braddon again faced the condemnation of public opinion: when her servants found out that their employers had been unmarried, many of the staff left the house. Yet, other than this slight upset, Mary Braddon began her life of respectability and entered what Wolff has termed "the years of fulfillment." Between 1875 and 1885 Braddon became the *grande dame* of her social circle and Lichfield House became a social center for many writers and intellectuals, including Robert Browning, Oscar Wilde, Whistler, the du Mauriers, Henry Irving, and Bram Stoker. In addition to her social duties, she published twenty-one books and studied French, German, and Italian, and Greek literature. In fact, Braddon studied the French realist writers—Flaubert, Balzac, and Zola—extensively and wrote a long critical essay on Émile Zola that was never published (Wolff 317–20). Critics such as Ellen Miller Casey see the 1870s as a transition period for Braddon's novels: she moved from the "sensation" novel to producing more "novels of character," or realist novels. Robert Wolff claims that, "from the early sixties to the early nineties the trajectory of her writing was generally upward," and claims that her literary masterpieces were her later novels: *Joshua Haggard's Daughter* (1876) and *Ishmael* (1884) (Wolff 8).

Braddon's diaries during this period record her social engagements, but not her thoughts. Much of what we know about the later part of Braddon's life comes from the biography of her son, William Maxwell, and from the comments of her contemporaries. Despite her reputation as a writer of scandalous books, her adulterous affair with Maxwell, and her humble background in the theater, the lasting image that many had of Braddon is of a comfortably established matron. Ford Maddox Ford, describing an eighty-year-old Braddon at her home in Richmond, likens Braddon to Queen Victoria: "The good sea-coal fire shone on the gleaming steel and gilt accoutrements. So there you had the clean fire, the clear hearth, and the vigor of the Victorian game" (in Wolff 11). Braddon seemed to have finally inhabited those country estates that her novels were so adept at portraying. As Arnold Bennett describes them: "Let us have riches and bright tempers, and eat and dress well, and live in glorious old mansions. The life of the English country house, with its luxurious solidity—with what unaffected satisfaction she describes it!" (in Wolff 14).

In 1895 William Maxwell died, ending their thirty-four years together and four years later, in 1899, Braddon's daughter Rose died. Despite these personal tragedies, Braddon remained very active, traveling abroad and continuing to write until her stroke in 1908. This grande dame of the Victorian era became a citizen of the twentieth-century: she bought an automobile, saw an aeroplane, and even saw the film version of *Aurora Floyd* in 1913. Mary Elizabeth Braddon died in 1915. Her last book, *Mary,* was published posthumously in 1916.

During the course of editing this collection, we have become aware of the work of an astonishing number of impressive scholars; regrettably, only some of that work can be represented here. We have arranged the collection with an eye toward indicating the variety and richness of Braddon scholarship. Often, that richness results in contradictory readings; we have made a special effort to respect the diversity of positions articulated by the scholars whose work appears here, choosing to highlight disagreements by juxtaposing opposed arguments rather than seeking to smooth over differences. Because *Lady Audley's Secret* is now the "canonical" Braddon novel, we begin with a series of essays modeling a range of approaches to this well-known text. The extant scholarship suggests that Braddon's work is particularly crucial for understanding the representation of domesticity in the middle-class family and the idealized country house. Elizabeth Langland begins by reading *Lady Audley's Secret* against the other best-known sensation novel of the period, Wilkie Collins's *Woman in White.* Using the Enclosure Acts as a point of departure, Langland explores the way in which Braddon's "more morally ambiguous" tale highlights the gendering of enclosed domestic space. Enclosure's use to display wealth, she argues, paradoxically necessitated that the domestic woman's privacy also be put on display, made visible and penetrable. Improprietous "secrets" are concealed by the seamless transfer of the Lady from one kind of enclosure to another, "asylum" having an ironic double meaning. Gail Turley Houston is interested in the novel as a commentary on the inequities in the legal status of married women. Examining Blackstone and Dicey, she reads the "trial" at Audley Court as a commentary on this legal debate and critique of the inadequacies of the prevailing system. Lillian Nayder, on the other hand, reads the novel as a conservative affirmation of the rights of men under the marriage laws, examining the novel's use of racial and national imagery associated with the so-called Indian Mutiny of 1857, in order to expose the novel's endorsement of a backlash that compares disobedient wives to rebellious sepoys. Katherine Montwieler is also interested in the interpenetration of contemporary cultural discourses with the novel. Attentive to the genre's display of anxieties about class, she surveys the place of material culture in the advertising of commodities and the way in which novels became conduct books in the training of socially ambitious women to utilize commodities "properly." Aeron Haynie examines the most significant and vexed of those status symbols, the country estate itself. Placing Audley Court in the contexts of the picturesque tradition and Victorian tourism, she discusses the import of the declining fortunes of the Audley family and its relevance to the symbolism of the English country house in this period, evoking some aspects of a potential nineteenth-century reader response that have been overlooked.

Aurora Floyd, Braddon's "other" best-selling sensation novel was serialized and released contemporaneously with *Lady Audley's Secret*. It is Braddon's second-best-known work, and one often contrasted with its better-known sister. Jeni Curtis and Marlene Tromp both concern themselves with the representation of the woman's body in this novel, with its constant theme of violence, both suppressed and enacted. Curtis discusses the construction of the woman's body as vegetative, and the gendered tropes of control that eventually turn the eponymous protagonist into an "espaliered girl." Tromp traces the novel's veiled treatment of male violence and spousal abuse, its persistent representation of Aurora as erotically orientalized, and considers the discourse surrounding the disciplining of "aberrant" women through the Contagious Diseases (CD) Acts in relation to Aurora's "domestication."

As an extremely professional and prolific author, Braddon and her work provide fertile ground for studies of the history of publishing; part III of this volume attends to those issues. Toni Johnson-Woods explores the roots of Braddon's immense popularity among the colonial readership in Australia. Drawing on both publication history and the history of her reception, she identifies thematic and material elements that made Braddon the undisputed Queen of the Antipodean market for British novels. Graham Law and Jennifer Carnell, similarly, are engaged by Braddon's remarkable career for the insights it gives into Victorian publishing. Looking at the relationship of Braddon and her husband with the

Tillotson publishing couple, their work gives new insights into Victorian book marketing and the role of women within it, in addition to its detailed study of aspects of Braddon's publishing history. Heidi Holder sheds light on an area of Victorian culture both central to an understanding of the period and often neglected by scholars, tracing Braddon's relationship to the stage, recuperating and reading several of her plays within the contexts of their production.

Our fourth and longest section broadens the focus of the collection to include other texts, contexts, and approaches to Braddon's work. Pamela Gilbert and Tabitha Sparks both address Braddon's work as a realist author, and both wish to complicate the apparently simple dichotomy between sensation and realism, although they disagree about the status of sensational discourse itself within Braddon's work. Gilbert examines a later realist novel, *Joshua Haggard's Daughter,* observing the ways in which Braddon takes up the question of generic difference, exploiting references to sensation novels, including her own, to position her realist text as a text that eschews the use of a woman's body as a sensational focus and examines the male body and male anxiety directly. Sparks examines Braddon's first and most famous realist novel, *The Doctor's Wife.* Sparks sees the evidence of "competing epistemologies" of gender in the melange of narrative genres brought together in this novel, and uses that confusion productively, to open to examination the emergence of conflicting models of femininity in fiction of this era.

Lauren Goodlad, Eve Lynch, and Heidi Johnson are all interested in other examples of what might, like sensation, be termed "genre fiction": Braddon's vampire story, her ghost stories, and her tales of detection. All three use these foci as starting points to discuss larger issues than are often admitted of in discussions of these popular and enduring forms. Goodlad examines Braddon's short vampire tale, "Good Lady Ducayne," and finds in it a carefully textured consideration of capitalism and the places of professionalism and femininity within it. Within the reliably saleable form of the ghost story, Eve Lynch argues, Braddon found the perfect platform upon which to explore issues of social critique and reform that the public sometimes shied away from in realist novels. Lynch surveys several of the ghost stories to trace Braddon's interest in a number of social issues. Heidi Johnson surveys the rich and largely untapped vein of Braddon's later detective fiction, and pursues a detailed analysis of Braddon's recurrent theme of the daughter's need to overcome inappropriate attachment to the father. The essays collected here clarify the unique gift of Braddon's work. They also help us to understand the England that, as Arnold Bennett stated, without Mary Elizabeth Braddon, would have been quite different.

NOTES

1. Robert Wolff indicates in his biography of Braddon, *Sensational Victorian*, that she published over eighty novels and that the sales of *Lady Audley's Secret* outnumbered those of any other novel in the period.

2. One of her most prominent reviewers, Margaret Oliphant, described sensation fiction like Braddon's as potentially "dangerous and foolish work, as well as false, both to Art and Nature" (567) in her 1867 essay, "Sensation Novels." She also defined serial publication, the format in which most of Braddon's novels appeared, as a "violent stimulant . . . with [a] necessity for frequent and rapid recurrence of piquant situation and starling incident" (568), a stylistic choice that might excessively stimulate an unsuspecting reader and lead him or her into moral turpitude. Most of Braddon's critics took up this kind of moral standard in their critiques of her work, a trend in contemporary criticism we discuss below.

3. Her letters, particularly those to Edward Bulwer-Lytton, one of her most important mentors, indicate that this was a concern of Braddon's throughout her career. As the Oliphant review indicates, critics and writers alike have traditionally seen these categories, "art" and "sensation," as mutually exclusive. Some of the arguments in this collection call that dichotomy into question, positing additional bases for the study of sensational fiction, as well as Braddon's later work.

4. Lootens points out that, in the blurred line between woman and devil that both she and Nina Auerbach discuss, the woman writer as a Victorian ideal was always in danger of collapse into her opposite. Thus, they note, the apotheosis of a literary career for a woman is death, what Lootens calls a "punitive" form of canonization, an argument also advanced by Angela Leighton's discussion of Victorian women poets. The evacuation of the woman writer in "everything and nothing" may help explain the "invisibility" of significant writers, like Braddon.

5. Beginning with Elaine Showalter's 1976 discussion of *Lady Audley's Secret*, "Desperate Remedies," feminist critics have grappled with the political "subversions" of Braddon's writing.

WORKS CITED

Boyle, Thomas. *Black Swine in the Sewers of Hampstead: Beneath the Surface of Victorian Sensationalism*. New York: Viking, 1989.

Braddon, Mary Elizabeth. *Aurora Floyd*. Ed. Richard Nemesvari and Lisa Surridge. Peterborough, Ontario: Broadview P, 1998.

Casey, Ellen Miller. "'Other People's Prudery': Mary Elizabeth Braddon." *Sexuality and Victorian Literature*. Ed. Don Richard Cox. Knoxville: U of Tennessee P, 1984. 72–82.

Cvetkovich, Ann. *Mixed Feelings: Feminism, Mass Culture and Victorian Sensationalism*. New Brunswick, N.J.: Rutgers, 1992.

Flint, Kate. *The Woman Reader, 1837–1914*. Oxford: Clarendon P, 1993.

Gilbert, Pamela K. *Disease, Desire and the Body in Victorian Women's Popular Novels.* Cambridge: Cambridge UP, 1997.

Hughes, Winifred. *The Maniac in the Cellar: Sensation Novels in the 1860s*. Princeton, N.J.: Princeton UP, 1980.

Loesberg, Jonathan. "The Ideology of Narrative Form in Sensation Fiction." *Representations* 13 (1986): 115–38.

Lootens, Tricia. *Lost Saints: Silence, Gender, and Victorian Literary Canonization.* Charlottesville: U of Virginia P, 1996.

Mansel, H. L. "Sensation Novels." *Quarterly Review* 113 (1863): 481–515.

Oliphant, Margaret. "Novels." *Blackwood's* 102 (1867): 257–80.

O'Mealy, Joseph. "Mrs. Oliphant, *Miss Marjoribanks*, and the Victorian Canon." *The New Nineteenth Century: Feminist Readings of Underread Victorian Fiction*. Ed. Barbara Leah Harman and Susan Meyer. New York: Garland, 1996: 63–76.

Peterson, Audrey. *Victorian Masters of Mystery: From Wilkie Collins to Conan Doyle.* New York: Frederick Ungar, 1984.

Pykett, Lyn. *The "Improper" Feminine: The Women's Sensation Novel and the New Woman Writing*. London; New York: Routledge, 1995.

Showalter, Elaine. "Desperate Remedies." *The Victorian Newsletter* 49 (1976): 1–5.

Taylor, Jenny Bourne. *In the Secret Theater of Home: Wilkie Collins, Sensation Narrative and Nineteenth Century Psychology*. London: Routledge, 1988.

Wolff, Robert Lee. *Sensational Victorian: The Life and Fiction of Mary Elizabeth Braddon*. New York: Garland, 1979.

PART I

Lady Audley's Secret

ONE

Enclosure Acts:
Framing Women's Bodies in Braddon's
Lady Audley's Secret

Elizabeth Langland

In the late eighteenth and early nineteenth centuries, a new series of enclosure acts allowed landowners progressively to annex public lands, the commons, producing a proportionately small number of wealthy country estate owners and a larger number of the landless and disinherited. In this essay I explore the relationship between the enclosure of lands and the enclosure of bodies reflected in descriptions of the country houses, which are architectural, domestic sanctuaries that function as visible signs of the social order. In the process of enclosure, upper-middle-class women were positioned unevenly; on the one hand, they enjoyed certain class and gender privileges, on the other, as symbols of those privileges, they found themselves confined and circumscribed by their demands. Whereas domestic novels governed by the conventions of realism often obscure the resulting tensions, the very sensationalism of sensation fiction allowed it to expose not only the conflicting passions of middle-class women but the dark side of domesticity itself. And Mary Elizabeth Braddon's pioneering sensation novel, *Lady Audley's Secret*, took the lead in foregrounding this dialectic between freedom and enclosure, privilege and confinement that structures the lives of upper-middle-class women.

Although Wilkie Collins's *Woman in White,* 1860, preceded and has generally been credited with influencing Braddon's 1862 *Lady Audley's Secret,* the relationship between them cannot be reduced to simple influence on the one hand and borrowing on the other. Although Braddon took key plot elements from Collins, such as the conflated identities of two women, one living and one dead, she reconceives both characters and events to produce a more morally ambiguous tale than Collins's. And although Braddon ostensibly produces the conventional conclusion of evil punished at the end of her story, the representation of Lady Audley complicates a traditional reading of that conclusion. Indeed, in *Lady Audley's Secret* Braddon carried out a significant revision of Collins's novel, a revision that allowed Braddon to solidify interest in this new subgenre while subtly expanding and redirecting its focus to illuminate further the persistently troubling links between country house and madhouse and to expose the connections between the ideal upper-middle-class lady and childishness associated, on the one hand, with asexuality and, on the other, with madness.

Collins's novel illuminated for Braddon the suggestive connection between country house and asylum. *The Woman in White* focuses on the attempts of an impoverished baronet, Sir Percival Glyde, to procure a wealthy wife in Laurie Fairlie and then to appropriate her fortune to his own uses by substituting her identity for that of Anne Catherick, a woman for many years confined to an asylum and, therefore, certified as "mad." Anne, who closely resembles Laura, suffers from a heart condition, and her escape, recapture, and timely death allow the baronet and his ally, Count Fosco, to replace her with Laura, announce Laura's death, and confine the real Laura in the asylum as Anne Catherick. Although Laura's release is procured and her identity ultimately restored, she retains traces of the imbecility she has suffered as a result of her incarceration in the asylum. Collins thus foregrounds the relationship between the country house and the asylum, and he is astute about the ease with which upper-class men can confine women in both country houses and asylums.[1]

In playing on the double and conflicting meanings of asylum, Collins further exposes the way in which the country house can be a place of confinement.[2] In its positive connotations, an asylum is a sanctuary, a place of refuge from oppression, providing safety from threatening forces without. This is, in fact, the meaning that the novel first employs when Hartright reveals that his Italian friend Pesca has adopted, as "the ruling idea of his life," the belief that "he was bound to show his gratitude to the country which had afforded him an asylum and means of subsistence, by doing his utmost to turn himself into an Englishman" (3).[3] A scant few pages later Hartright meets the woman in white, whom, he is told, has just escaped from an Asylum, and he confesses to the horror, "the idea of absolute insanity which we all associate with the very name of an Asylum" (22). This is, of course, the alternative meaning of the word, associated now with confinement of those who pose a danger to the safety of others. The country house and the insane asylum, the lady and the madwoman, are syntactically linked when Hartright realizes the "ominous likeness between the fugitive from the asylum and my pupil at Limmeridge House" (51).[4] The country house cycles back and forth between asylum as confinement and asylum as refuge, and Laura's experiences as wife and inmate do not differ materially. In both spheres she is deprived of her freedom and wits. However, Collins's novel retreats from the implications of these connections by concluding with Laura's seemingly joyous restoration to Limmeridge House, where she and her half-sister, Miriam, serve as vessels and props for the new heir of Limmeridge. But it looks suspiciously like the old order, and, arguably, the asylum of Limmeridge House remains as much a confinement as a sanctuary.[5]

Braddon's *Lady Audley's Secret* refuses to mystify this dialectic that is obscured in the closing pages of Collins's novel.[6] Whereas Collins retreats from his initial insights, leaving them ultimately unexplored, Braddon pursues the connections through representing the subtle parallels in the position of both country house and asylum.

Analyzing briefly the impact of those Enclosure Acts passed principally in the last half of the eighteenth and first quarter of the nineteenth century begins to illuminate Braddon's achievement.[7] Although enclosure had been part of the sociopolitical landscape of Britain since early modern England, the later acts gave a distinctive character to the landscape of Victorian England, a subject usefully addressed by Raymond Williams in *The Country and the City*. Williams illuminates the effect of concentrating "nearly a quarter of the cultivated lands" in the hands of four hundred families, in conjunction with other processes like rack-renting, on the class configuration of nineteenth-century England. Just as the appropriation of surviving open field villages and common rights put general economic pressure on small landowners and eliminated marginal lands on which lower classes could eke out an independent livelihood, so, too, that appropriation set in motion new ways of symbolizing power through possession of land, crowned by the English country house, which focalized the possession and power. Williams comments that, "What had happened was not so much 'enclosure'—the method—but the more visible establishment of a long-developing system . . . a formal declaration of where the power now lay" (107). That "formal declaration" was most manifest in the country house. Williams elucidates:

> What these "great" houses do is break the scale, by an act of will corresponding to their real and systematic exploitation of others. . . . These were chosen for more than the effect from the inside out. . . . They were chosen . . . for the other effect, from the outside looking in: a visible stamping of power, of displayed wealth and command: a social disproportion which was mean to impress and overawe. (106)

Whereas Williams brilliantly illuminates the effect of enclosure on class configurations, he does not turn his lens on the way that enclosure impacted the position and representation of upper middle-class women, who functioned centrally in the process of signifying wealth and class. And, ironically, often the owners' coffers were emptied not in developing the lands, which could have produced greater profits, but in augmenting the size and grandeur of the house, which could yield no profit.

Thus, enclosure in nineteenth-century England was as much about signifying wealth as producing it, and women played a key role in that process of signification. In Austen's *Pride and Prejudice,* written in 1813, Elizabeth Bennet recognizes that displayed wealth and command, that "social disproportion," when she views Darcy's estate for the first time and acknowledges that, "to be mistress of Pemberley might be something!" (167). Later, in responding to Jane's inquiry about when she began to love Darcy, Elizabeth laughingly punctures the social grasping after position that would lead many women to accept the man to get the estate—"I believe it must date from my first seeing his beautiful grounds at Pemberley" (258). Despite Elizabeth's self-irony or, we might say, because of her self-irony, we discover that the social motive can never be wholly discounted, even for the most disinterested young lady.

Indeed, to become mistress of an estate like Pemberley, or Limmeridge House, or Audley Court *is* something. But the role brings with it explicit social expectations, which are given full development in Braddon's novel. Mark Girouard's *Life in the English Country House* lays out the implications of country house life in the Victorian era. Girouard entitles his chapter on that period "The Moral House: 1830–1900," and argues that "an essential part of the new image cultivated by both new and old families was their domesticity; they were anxious to show that their houses, however grand, were also homes and sheltered a happy family life" (270). To this end, the mistress was essential; she was the *primum mobile* of that self-contained world, and her values and their successful embodiment in organization and decor were on display for the world.[8] Indeed, in this regard, the country house functioned as would have Bentham's prospective Panopticon, a space in which one could be under continuous anonymous surveillance. The house metaphorically and metonymically stood for power and one's moral entitlement to that power. Because it operated most effectively through its continual visibility, it was thus open to random visitors and even its most intimate spaces could be penetrated with impunity, as we will see. And at the center of that visible structure stood the lady of the house, whose motions were precisely regulated by etiquette practices such as morning calls, afternoon teas (instituted in the 1840s), and elaborate dinners that put her continually on display.[9]

Recent studies in the history of architecture suggest that the gendering of space and the spatializing of gender is not new. Drawing on Alberti's classic and canonical fifteenth-century treatise, *On the Art of Building in Ten Books,* Mark Wigley argues that its fifth book, "discussing the delight of 'private' houses, contains an overt reference to architecture's complicity in the exercise of patriarchal authority by defining a particular intersection between a spatial order and a system of surveillance which turns on the question of gender" (332). He continues,

> Women are to be confined deep within a sequence of spaces at the greatest distance from the outside world while men are to be exposed to that outside. The house is literally understood as a mechanism for the domestication of (delicately minded and pathologically embodied) women. (332)

Wigley cites Alberti, who clarifies that, "The woman, as she remains locked up at home, should watch over things by staying at her post, by diligent care and watchfulness. The man should guard the woman, the house, and his family and country, but not by sitting still" (334). And, as Wigley notes, Alberti's text is closely following Zenophon's fifth-century treatise *Oeconomicus.* This long architectural history provides the foundation for Wigley's claim that "the house is involved in the production of the gender division it appears to merely secure," and "the role of architecture is explicitly the control of sexuality" (336). One might argue that *plus ça change, plus c'est la même chose.*

Wigley focuses his argument almost exclusively on gender questions and on the relationship of partriarchal control to household architecture. But the class implications of these architectural treatises are equally available for analysis and provide us with a model for thinking about the crucial intersections of class and gender constraints in the architecture of the English country house. With the advent of enclosure in England, domestic architecture increasingly secured class as well as gender relations, allowing a growing gentry, or upper middle class, to define itself apart from the prosperous merchant and professional middle classes immediately beneath it and the poor, far below. It is true of class as well as gender to say that the wife "is one of the possessions whose status the house monitors and is exposed by the structure of the house she maintains. It is this exposure by a system of classification, rather a simple enclosure by walls, that entraps her" (Wigley 341). The lady of a house is trapped within interlocking systems of sexual and class management.

But the logic of class demands the visibility of even private spaces, so the lady, like the house with which she is identified, is subject to continual scrutiny. It is Braddon's astute articulation of this relationship between lady and country house that is remarkable in *Lady Audley's Secret*. Present are all the key architectural elements: enclosure securing wealth and power; the maintenance of wealth and power demanding continual visibility; continual visibility justifying the penetration of even private spaces; and private space gendered feminine so that the woman who is most protected by the architecture is also most exposed by it.

Lady Audley's Secret opens with an extensive description of Audley Court, which emphasizes exclusiveness tied to exclusion:

> It lay down in a hollow, rich with fine old timber and luxuriant pastures; and you came upon it through an avenue of limes, bordered on either side by meadows, over the high hedges of which the cattle looked inquisitively at you as you passed, wondering, perhaps, what you wanted; for there was no thoroughfare, and unless you were going to the Court, you had no business there at all. (1)

Everything about the house bespeaks enclosure. Its wall "bordered with espaliers . . . shut out the flat landscape, and circled the house and gardens with a darkening shelter," and "the principal door was squeezed into a corner of a turret at one angle of the building, as if it were in hiding from dangerous visitors, and wished to keep itself a secret" (1). Described as a "glorious old place," its glory seems to consist in the yearning wish it provokes "to have done with life, and to stay there forever" (2). However, the very seclusion of the spot, which allows it to function as a sanctuary, also and ominously facilitates its function as confinement: "A noble place: inside as well as out, a noble place—a house in which you incontinently lost yourself if ever you were so rash as to attempt to penetrate its mysteries alone" (2). Braddon has picked up on the dual meanings of asylum and bodied both forth in Audley Court, at once sanctuary and confinement. The avenue that heralds approach to the house, is "so shaded from the sun and sky, so screened from observation by the thick shelter of the over-arching trees that it seemed a chosen place for secret meetings or for stolen interviews; a place in which a conspiracy might have been planned or a lover's vow registered with equal safety; and yet it was scarcely twenty paces from the house" (3). The narrator continues throughout this descriptive balance of a seclusion at once protective and ominous: "The very repose of the place grew painful from its intensity, and you felt as if a corpse must be lying somewhere within that gray and ivy-covered pile of building—so deathlike was the tranquillity of all around" (17). George Talboys shortly thereafter echoes this description in remarking of the approaching avenue that "it ought to be an avenue in a churchyard. . . . How peacefully the dead might sleep under this somber shade!" (44).

Despite the seclusion provided by ancient trees and walls, Lady Audley's private spaces are curiously vulnerable to penetration. Audley Court provides her with little protection, as it both limits her range of motion and opens to visibility all of her activities, much like a Panopticon. Even those things that Lady Audley tries to hide from prying eyes are almost immediately exposed to view. Within the first few pages of the novel, Lady Audley's maid has invited her brutish lover to "see my lady's rooms" and offered to show him her jewels. They penetrate her jewel casket even to the secret drawer and discover sufficient evidence of her past to blackmail her during the remainder of the novel.

But it's not only her maid, with her legitimate access to her lady's chambers if not to her jewelry casket, who can penetrate those seemingly private spaces and her very identity. To avoid exposing her face to George Talboys's view, Lady Audley cleverly evades the social etiquette that demands she invite her nephew and his friend to dinner. However, she cannot prevent their illicit entry to her private chambers or keep their prying eyes from viewing her portrait. The secret passages and chambers that formerly hid suspect persons and activities from view, now lead straight to Lady Audley's exposure. Sir Michael Audley's daughter, Alicia, confides to her cousin, "if you don't mind crawling upon your hands and knees, you can see my lady's apartments, for that passage communicates with her dressing-room. She doesn't know it herself, I believe" (45). Ironically, the locks and keys, secret passages and drawers that should secure her secrets from penetration, prove no defense against the social expectation of continual and invited visibility.

What we discover is the seamless interpenetration of the house and its lady. Ironically, Phoebe does not intend to expose her mistress, and it is not Alicia's intention to expose her new stepmother; they assume, as does everyone else, that there can be nothing to expose, that both Lady Audley and Audley Court are available for public viewing, part of that economy that Williams identified in which the house and its occupants stand in for social power and moral entitlement to that power. Operating most effectively through continual visibility, the house and its lady secure the economic status quo.

More than being simply available to viewing, Lady Audley is herself decked out to invite scrutiny, her garments and jewels metonyms for class privilege, luxury, and idleness. As she plays the piano, Robert Audley lingers by her side:

> he amused himself by watching her jeweled, white hands gliding softly over the keys, with the lace sleeves dropping away from her graceful, arched wrists. He looked at her pretty fingers one by one; this one glittering with a ruby heart; that encircled by an emerald serpent; and about them all a starry glitter of diamonds. From the fingers his eyes wandered to the rounded wrists: the broad, flat, gold bracelet upon her right wrist dropped over her hand, as she executed a rapid passage. She stopped abruptly to rearrange it; but before she could do so Robert Audley noticed a bruise upon her delicate skin. (59)

Because everything about her is structured to invite the gaze that secures class standing, she becomes, in spite of herself, a constantly available text as Robert sets out to penetrate the mystery of George Talboys's disappearance. His licit scrutiny allows him to discover the signs of her illicit activity.

Further, the confinement of the lady's legitimate activities within a limited sphere keeps her virtually under continual surveillance. When she will be away from home, she must declare where she is going, how long she will be absent, and when she will return. She cannot move without accounting for her whereabouts. The surveillance under which she lives in her role as lady contrasts most dramatically with the virtual invisibility of George Talboys. He enters Audley Court, departs, sets out for Liverpool with the intention of returning to Australia and ends up in America, but his tracks are impossible for Robert Audley to trace. His very invisibility allows him to be presumed dead and therefore justifies the relentless pursuit of a highly visible Lady Audley.

There is, readers will note, a tension between the very visibility of a lady and her sexualized, because privatized, body. If we return now to Wigley's argument about gendered space, we can appreciate the significance of these interlocking systems of surveillance by following through the connections he lays out between architecture and gender. Domestic space, Wigley argues, produces "sexuality as that-which-is-private" (346), so that a "privacy within the house developed beyond the privacy of the house" (347). Hence, the logic of separate bedrooms/chambers for the master and mistress.

Indeed, one would expect a lady's chambers to be penetrable, like her body, only by the master. How can her private spaces be penetrable by the public if what they produce and secure is her sexualized body? In a gendered scheme, as we have seen above in the architectural treatises, the private spaces should be inviolate. But once visibility is necessary to the logic and economy of enclosure, then that class discourse must (re)produce the Victorian lady as asexual.

Thus, Braddon's novel enables us to revise radically our understanding of Victorian prudishness, produced less it would seem, *pace* Foucault, by the discourse of sexuality than by the discourse of class. Of course, Foucault does recognize the way that sexual discourse flows from the upper middle classes down to the lower middle and lower classes throughout the nineteenth century, but what his analysis misses is the extent to which class claims demand the continually visible and, therefore, asexual or sexually immature female body.

It is this logic that ties enclosure and visibility to the childishness that marks both Collins's Laura Fairlie and Braddon's Lady Audley. Class visibility requires that their bodies be produced as asexual or sexually immature, belonging to a child. The child woman can have nothing to hide. Walter Hartright's early impression on viewing Laura of "something wanting," expresses not only her "ominous likeness" to the woman from the asylum but also confirms her childishness and asexuality. In the sexuality that marks Miriam's face and form, Hartright had already found, and been repulsed by, the something he had wanted. And the childishness that characterizes Laura's behavior marks her off-limits as an object of Hartright's *sexual* interest. She exists as an embodiment of an ideal, and Walter's determination to have her recognized again as an heiress suggests that she is a locus for his class ambitions rather than his sexual desires.

Just as Laura's childishness is tied to the mental vacuity of madness, so, too, her detention in the insane asylum produces a further infantilization and seems further to equip her for her future life as mistress of Limmeridge. The "quaint, childish earnestness" that was initially only a part of her character becomes, after her incarceration, its defining feature: "She spoke as a child might have spoken; she showed me her thoughts as a child might have shown them" (43, 403).

Like Laura Fairlie, Lady Audley is defined by her idealized asexual beauty and her childishness. Despite having married her and fathered her child, George Talboys recalls leaving "my little girl asleep with my baby in her arms" (12). As Lady Audley, she is described as "irretrievably childish," acting in her own "childish, unthinking way," as possessing a "winning childish smile," as speaking in a "pretty musical prattle" (32, 37, 43, 58). Even her penmanship is childish, as are her every whim, mood, desire, and motivation.

And Lady Audley, like Laura, is found to have "something wanting," ominously linked to madness. Robert concludes of his uncle's passion for his wife: "I do not believe that Sir Michael Audley had every *really* believed in his wife. He had loved her and admired her; he had been bewitched by

her beauty and bewildered by her charms; but that sense of something
wanting . . . had been with him" (232). Just as Collins set up a relationship between childishness and madness, so does Braddon. Although we
are tantalized with the prospect that Lady Audley's "secret" focuses on
illicit behavior—she is a bigamist, a murderess, an arsonist—in fact, she
is hiding from the world a tendency to madness inherited from her
mother. It is that which has caused her to flee her father and child to
pursue employment as a governess after her husband has abandoned her
to pursue wealth in Australia. What is infantile is also, potentially, mad.
That is what she confesses when Robert Audley confronts her as "the
demoniac incarnation of some evil principle" (227). She taunts him: "It is
a great triumph, is it not—a wonderful victory? You have used your cool,
calculating, frigid, luminous intellect to a noble purpose. You have
conquered—a MAD WOMAN!" (227). She continues: "When you say that I
killed George Talboys, you say the truth. When you say that I murdered
him treacherously and foully, you lie. I killed him because I AM MAD! . . .
Bring Sir Michael; and bring him quickly. If he is to be told one thing let
him be told everything; let him hear the secret of my life!" (227). Ironically, of course, Lady Audley has not killed her first husband; he has
survived his tumble down the well with only a broken arm and absconded
for America. And one might argue that she is more sinned against that
sinning in taking Sir Michael Audley for her husband after George Talboys abandoned her with no prospect of returning unless he struck gold.
But Talboys is absolved of guilt whereas Lady Audley must play out the
play. Her mother was mad and institutionalized, and, under duress, she,
too, is destined for a similar fate. That this is to be her fate is written in
her childish aspect. Although Lady Audley fears to find her mother a
"distraught and violent creature," she discovers instead "no raving,
straight-waist-coated maniac, guarded by zealous jailers, but a golden-
haired, blue-eyed, girlish creature, who seemed as frivolous as a butterfly,
and who skipped toward us with her yellow curls decorated with natural
flowers, and saluted us with radiant smiles, and gay, ceaseless chatter"
(230).

The relationships between asexual childishness and the ideal lady
of the house and between childishness and madness underscore the
homology between country house and Panopticon, between country
house and madhouse, the juxtaposition with the latter calling into question the freedoms of the former. Both Laura Fairlie and Lady Audley can
be transferred against their wills from their estates to asylums. And the
very qualities that have led to their idealization as ladies facilitate their
condemnation as madwomen. And if Lady Audley is not the innocent she
pretends to be—if, if fact she has a past to hide—then her visibility

becomes a liability rather than an asset, and she must be transferred without a ripple from public view.

D. A. Miller perceptively notes in *The Novel and the Police* that madness as a diagnosis "lies in wait to 'cover'—account for and occlude—whatever behaviors, desires, or tendencies might be considered socially deviant, undesirable, or dangerous" (169). he continues:

> The "secret" let out at the end of the novel is not, therefore, that Lady Audley is a madwoman but rather that, *whether she is one or not,* she must be treated as such. . . . The doctor's double-talk ("the cunning of madness, with the prudence of intelligence") will be required to sanction two contradictory propositions: 1) Lady Audley is a criminal, in the sense that her crimes must be punished; and 2) Lady Audley is not a criminal, in the sense that neither her crimes nor her punishment must be made public in a male order of things. (169–70)

However, it is not specifically or singly a "male" order of things; it is also a class order of things that facilitates this seamless transfer from country house to madhouse. Robert Audley wants to avoid at all costs "the necessity of any exposure—any disgrace" (250). The class entitlement of a Sir Michael rests on his visible presence, as Girouard argues, of the moral order. It is thus extraordinarily convenient that the lady who fails that moral order should be susceptible to private "burial" from sight instead of the public exposure of a trial. Lady Audley claims that she goes to a "living grave," a sentiment confirmed by the doctor's promise to Robert that, "If you were to dig a grave for her in the nearest churchyard and bury her alive in it, you could not more safely shut her from the world" (256, 250). That we should have been prepared from the beginning for this transfer is suggested by the way Braddon's description of the *"maison de santé"* at the end ironically echoes the early descriptions of Audley Court, with its darkening shelter, its intensely painful repose, and its deathlike tranquillity provoking a "yearning wish to have done with life" (1, 2, 16, 17).

In conclusion, the lurid sensationalism of this new subgenre facilitated Braddon's articulating the subtle connections between country house and madhouse and disclosing how the class and gender position of the upper-middle-class lady might simplify her private transfer from one sphere to the other. By returning Laura Fairlie to Limmeridge House and her senses at the end of *The Woman in White*, Collins ultimately deranges the archaeology through which we expose knowledge of those connections. Mary Elizabeth Braddon, however, lets the logic of asylum and Asylum play itself out in Lady Audley's fate. Moreover, she exposes how the lady's mandatory visibility secures the class system and thus requires that her deviance be marked as madness and the lady be buried alive.

NOTES

1. This connection, which may be otherwise formulated as the connection between country house and madhouse, is early suggested in Mary Wollstone-craft's *Maria of The Wrongs of Woman*, in which the wife is drugged and transferred to a madhouse so her husband can seize her property, and in Charlotte Brontë's *Jane Eyre*, a novel whose gothic influences make it a kind of precursor to sensation fiction. Here, the connection emerges in the relationship between Jane Eyre, the would-be mistress of Thornfield, and Bertha Mason, the actual mistress of Thornfield, who is mad and confined to its upper quarters. The relationship between Jane and Bertha was early adumbrated in Elaine Showalter's *A Literature of Their Own: British Women Novelists from Brontë to Lessing*. The motif of the female carceral in nineteenth-century literature was identified by Sandra Gilbert and Susan Gubar in *The Madwoman in the Attic*.

2. Insofar as Collins's novel explored these relationships between women and madness, that exploration has been nicely adumbrated by D. A. Miller in *The Novel and the Police*. However, Miller's focus on gender issues leads him to ignore significant class issues that also haunt Collins's novel, so that he notices but does not analyze the allusions to Limmeridge as an "asylum." Nonetheless, Miller gives a fine analysis of female confinement in Collins's novel: "Male security in *The Woman in White* seems always to depend on female claustration" (166). Miller also observes that, "the suitably feminine wife must have been schooled in a lunatic asylum, where she is half cretinized" (166).

3. It is not only women alone who are imaged in terms of confinement. Collins begins his novel with the arrival of middle-class Walter Hartright at Limmeridge House, where he has been hired as a drawing master for the ladies. His inferior class status allows his employer, Philip Fairlie, to frame his position as a kind of possession. He welcomes Hartright to his employment with the words, "So glad to possess you at Limmeridge" (33), and Hartright picks up the verb when he reflects later that, "Throughout the whole of that period, Mr. Fairlie had been rejoiced to 'possess' me, but had never been well enough to see me for a second time" (96). What Hartright fails or refuses to recognize is that having bought and possessed him, Mr. Fairlie need not give him a second thought. More ominously, having possessed his nieces at Limmeridge, Mr. Fairlie sees them no more often; after all, they have nowhere else to go.

4. Subsequently, when Laura is married to Sir Percival Glyde, Miriam queries him: "Am I to understand . . . that your wife's room is a prison, and that your housemaid is the gaoler who keeps it?" He responds that, "Yes; that *is* what you are to understand. . . . Take care my gaoler hasn't got double duty to do—take care

your room is not a prison, too" (267). Prompted by this outrage, Miriam urges her reluctant uncle to "turn Limmeridge House into an asylum for [his] niece and her misfortunes" (316).

5. See my book *Nobody's Angels: Middle-Class Women and Domestic Ideology in Victorian Culture* for an analysis of the conclusion of *The Woman in White*, 233–38.

6. Again, D. A. Miller's analyses of the rhetoric of madness lead him to a similar conclusion: "The achievement of blowing this cover belongs to *Lady Audley's Secret* (1862), the novel where, writing under the ambiguous stimulus of *The Woman in White*, Mary Elizabeth Braddon demonstrates that the madwoman's primary 'alienation' lies in the rubric under which she is put down" (169). Miller does not take up the emerging meanings of the country house in the nineteenth century that are producing these connections. His gendered analysis thus leads him to conclude that Lady Audley is mad, then, only because she must not be criminal. She must not, in other words, be supposed capable of acting on her own diabolical responsibility and hence of publicly spoiling her assigned role as the conduit of power transactions between men" (170–71).

7. The enclosure of common lands had been going on for a couple of centuries by the dawn of the nineteenth century, and critics are beginning to analyze questions of enclosure and sexuality. Specifically, *Enclosure Acts: Sexuality, Property, and Culture in Early Modern England*, edited by Richard Burt and John Michael Archer, emphasizes the "figure of enclosure itself as the uneven ground on which sexuality and politics meet in the cultural study of early modern England" (2). The collection's essays, like mine, "deal variously with bodily enclosure and the enclosure of property" (2).

8. See my *Nobody's Angels*, 1–61, for an extended discussion of the role of the middle-class woman as household manager.

9. Girouard notes the institution of afternoon teas in the 1840s (280). I discuss these etiquette practices in chapter 2 of *Nobody's Angels*.

WORKS CITED

Austen, Jane. *Pride and Prejudice*. New York: Norton, 1966.

Braddon, Mary Elizabeth. *Lady Audley's Secret*. New York: Dover Publications, Inc., 1974.

Brontë, Charlotte. *Jane Eyre*. Ed. Richard J. Dunn. New York: Norton, 1971.

Burt, Richard and John Michael Archer, eds. *Enclosure Acts: Sexuality, Property, and Culture in Early Modern England*. Ithaca and London: Cornell UP 1994.

Collins, Wilkie. *The Woman in White*. New York: Oxford, 1973.

Colomina, Beatriz, ed. *Sexuality and Space: Princeton Papers on Architecture*. New York: Princeton Architectural Press, 1992.

Foucalut, Michel. *The History of Sexuality, Vol. 1*. Trans. by Robert Hurley. New York: Vintage Books, 1980.

Gilbert, Sandra, and Susan Gubar. *The Madwoman in the Attic: The Woman Writer and the Nineteenth-Century Literary Imagination.* New Haven: Yale UP, 1979.

Girouard, Mark. *Life in the English Country House.* New Haven: Yale UP, 1978.

Langland, Elizabeth. *Nobody's Angels: Middle-Class Women and Domestic ideology in Victorian Culture.* Ithaca and London: Cornell UP, 1995.

Miller, D. A. *The Novel and the Police.* Berkeley: U of California P, 1988.

Wigley, Mark. "Untitled: The Housing of Gender." in Colomina 327–89.

Williams, Raymond. *The Country and the City.* New York: Oxford UP, 1973.

Wollstonecraft, Mary. *Maria or the Wrongs of Woman.* New York: Norton, 1975.

Two

Mary Braddon's Commentaries on the Trials and Legal Secrets of Audley Court

Gail Turley Houston

> It is not a matter of indifference whether a body elected to
> adjudicate . . . consists of males solely, or females solely, or of
> both combined. As it consists of one, or the other, or of both,
> so not only will the answers vary, but, in some cases, will they
> be completely diverse. . . . [H]ere one sex cannot
> adequately represent the other.
> —Olive Schreiner, *Women and Labour*

> The stories told within jurisprudential and legal argument can
> be read as literature, and as therefore rooted in our dreams
> and nightmares regarding the role of authority in our lives,
> as well as in our analytic assessments of law's legitimacy.
> —Robin West, *Narrative, Authority, and Law*

In his retrospective on nineteenth-century English law, jurist Montague
Lush cites the novel as evidence of the effects of legislation regarding
women's rights. In the eighteenth century, he asserts, "you find no trace
in the ordinary literature" of women's "position in point of law," and that
"when they entered into the marriage relation" their legal status "became

one of almost absolute subjection." Lush then refers his reader to an expert witness: "Read for example the novels of Miss Austen and you could scarcely suppose that they reflected a state of things in which a woman on her marriage became unfit, in the view of the law, to enjoy rights over property or to enter into contracts on her own behalf" (Lush 349). Given Lush's erroneous remarks about Austen's ostensibly apolitical novels to prove his point that women's changed legal status was a major example of how nineteenth-century law had evolved from the brilliant if antique Commentaries on the Laws of England (1758) by William Blackstone, Lush almost seems to imply that Victorian women writers were a constitutive element in constitutional changes regarding "the sex." In this essay, I want to outline the ways one Victorian woman novelist did underwrite evolving British discussions about women and the law.

If it can be argued that of all literary genres the sensation novel was most concerned with Victorian laws about women, Mary Braddon's bestseller *Lady Audley's Secret* stands out as a commentary on the law's machinations. Indeed, electrifying the reading public with her shrewd subversion of the chief witness in the case, gentleman barrister Robert Audley, Braddon cross-examines the mystification of women inscribed in the law, and, using cultural circumstantial evidence, proves the self-interestedness of the law and male lawmakers. Thus, juxtaposing Mary Braddon's sensational rewrite of domestic fiction with Blackstone's Commentaries and Victorian revisions of the law is a helpful way to show how the sensation novel caused readers to listen to if not immediately formulate more progressive opinions about women's rights. I will begin, then, by briefly tracking the evolution of some important legal views of men and women from the eighteenth to the nineteenth century and then examine how *Lady Audley's Secret* incorporates and sustains that trajectory.

First of all, it is important to note that Blackstone's Commentaries were originally presented in a series of lectures in 1758 as a means of fostering "the infancy of a study, which is now first adopted by public academical authority"—the study of law (Blackstone, vol. 1, 9). Authorizing law as a "science," Blackstone reifies the English version, concluding that it is the "pitch of perfection" and the world's legal ur-text (vol. 1, introduction, sec. 1, 23). Defining law as "a rule of action dictated by some superior being," Blackstone asserts that since man is a "creature," he "must necessarily be subject to the laws of his Creator" (vol. 1, introduction, sec. 2, 34). Nevertheless, in this benevolent universe, man had the "faculty of reason to discover the purport of those laws" (vol. 1, introduction, sec. 2, 35). Mystifying the law as unbiased and divinely sanctioned and man as the universal generic subject, Blackstone also mystifies the kind of men he considers best able to administer God's laws.

If God is an Englishman, in Blackstone's eighteenth-century worldview, an Englishman is a gentleman (vol. 1, introduction, sec. 1, 10, 11, 12, 13, 15).

Blackstone's treatise, then, contains a fundamental tautological, even monomaniacal, argument. To begin with, Blackstone asserts that those who legislate should remember that "the whole should protect all its parts, and that every part should pay obedience to the will of the whole" (vol. 1, introduction, sec. 2, 42). But since Blackstone assumes that gentlemen should make the laws because they are the most rational and noble of subjects, he also concludes that by virtue of being the best representative of the whole, what is best for the gentleman is what is best for the body politic. Not surprisingly, then, just as "man" is an all-purpose term designating the whole but privileging gentlemen, "man," is also assumed to be interchangeably—as needed—a generic and gender-specific term. Thus in appearance "man" is objective and disinterested, but in practice serves the interests of men.

This becomes clear in Blackstone's section on domestic relations. Noting that one of "the three great relations in private life" is "That of husband and wife" (vol. 1, bk. 1, chap. 14, 358), Blackstone asserts the legal concept of coverture:

> By marriage, the husband and wife are one person in law: that is, the very being or legal existence of the woman is . . . incorporated and consolidated into that of the husband; under whose wing, protection, and cover, she performs everything; . . . and her condition during her marriage is called her coverture. (vol. 1, bk. 1, 442)

Erasing the woman's legal identity, Blackstone concludes that coverture shows that the "female sex" was a "great . . . favorite" of "the laws of England" (vol. 1, bk. 1, chap. 5, 387). But Blackstone's chivalry only barely conceals the fact that eighteenth-century law rationalized bringing women to court—covering the woman's legal identity with that of her husband—through courtliness—expressing its love and concern for women as the reason for such legal erasure.

Producing more legal scholarship than ever before, nineteenth-century students of the law focused heavily on the legal status of women. One jurist, for example, gloated that Victorian jurists had moved from the "dark ages" of woman's subordination, predating the Victorian period, to the enlightened changes that occurred in the nineteenth century.[1] Lush asserts that shifts in public opinion brought about nineteenth-century reforms in divorce and property law. Noting that "this branch of the law, which depends on questions of public policy, is always and necessarily undergoing changes," Lush explains that "some of these changes in the law owe their existence to the change that has come over the public sense and feeling with regard to the proper relations between the husband and wife" (344). Thus, in the last fifty years of the nineteenth century, "married women have been emancipated and set free from the restraints imposed upon them by the common law" (378).

According to jurist A. V. Dicey, the law's complexity, inconsistency, and instability—its bricolage—can only be made sense of by examining the multiplicitous effects of public opinion upon the law. "Permanent currents of opinion," he argues, directly influence "the mass of irregular, fragmentary, ill expressed, and as it might seem, illogical or purposeless enactments" (Dicey vii). By "permanent," Dicey means that changing, diverse public opinion is always an influential part of the legal as well as social climate. Thus, for Dicey, to be a lawmaker is to be an ethnographer. As Dicey assesses the cultural climate, "there exists at any given time a body of beliefs, convictions, sentiments, accepted principles, or firmly-rooted prejudices, which, taken together, make up . . . the reigning or predominant current of opinion" which "determine[s], directly or indirectly, the course of legislation" (19–20). In England, he notes, public opinion, and, consequently, legislative opinion, develops gradually but continuously (27), and always through the "cross-current" of minority opinions (41). As I will show, these "cross-current[s]" of minority opinion are crucial to the powerful political narrative of *Lady Audley's Secret*.

Explicit about the interestedness of law, Dicey assumes that the law is not some tablet of rules brought down from deity as Blackstone would have it. As Dicey opines, "men legislate, it may be urged, not in accordance with their opinion as to what is a good law, but in accordance with their interest" (12). In fact, this is so true "that from the inspection of the laws of a country it is often possible to conjecture . . . what is the class which holds, or has held, predominant power at a given time" (12). In contrast to Blackstone, then, Dicey recognizes that, "individuals, indeed, and still more frequently classes, do constantly support laws or institutions which they deem beneficial to themselves, but which certainly are in fact injurious to the rest of the world." Likewise, men, he argues, mystify their own conduct, as they "come easily to believe that arrangements agreeable to themselves are beneficial to others" (14).

Also important to my discussion of *Lady Audley's Secret* is Dicey's assertion that "the true importance, indeed, of laws lies far less in their direct result than in their effect upon the sentiment or convictions of the public" (41–42). For example, noting that the implementation of law produces attitudinal shifts and establishes norms of behavior, Dicey suggests that the actual allowance of divorce by the Divorce Act of 1857 was less important than the Act's influence on public perception. As he explains, the Divorce Act supported the notion that "women ought, in the eye of the law, to stand substantially on an equality with men, and have encouraged legislation tending to produce such equality." Dicey concludes that the divorce "laws have deeply affected not only the legislative but also the social opinion of the country as to the position of women" (43).

Oppositional legal and social opinions about women's rights and roles are central to the sensation novel *Lady Audley's Secret*. Filled with these cross currents of opinion, Braddon's novel illustrates and impels the transition of public beliefs about women's rights from Blackstone's way of thinking to Dicey's. Braddon also deftly shows how the seemingly private, social nature of courting is ingrained with the judicial concerns of the court. Just as Collins begins *Woman in White* with Hartright laying out his story as though it were a court case, in *Lady Audley's Secret*, the narrator's description of the setting places the reader in the position of "going to the [Audley] Court" (1). In this punning jest based upon the multiple meanings of court, Braddon implies the collusion between man-made courts of law and male property rights. As a matter of law, one of the hidden motivations for the hero's relentless legal pursuit of Lady Audley is that he stands to lose the property of Audley Court if he cannot prove that she is an outlaw. Also men's self-interested legislative power is figured in the fact that the court to which Robert Audley brings Lady Audley is a court of his own making.

A visual double entendre, then, Audley Court is the arena for Lady Audley's case, for almost immediately after Lucy is courted and becomes the ruler of the private domicile, Audley Court then becomes a legal court pitting Robert Audley versus Lady Audley. Critiquing the court system and courting as constituted in the nineteenth century, the setting places the reader in the position of "going to the [Audley] Court," which refers both to legal and domestic spheres (1). Further establishing a juridical atmosphere, the narrator consistently refers to the hero, Robert Audley, as "the barrister." Instituting himself as detective, judge, prosecutor, and prison guard of Lady Audley (122, 115, 131, 145, 167, 216, 233, 315, 323), Robert calls Lucy the most "demoniac" of criminals and concludes that "there are some crimes that can never be atoned for, and [Lucy's] is one of them" (292, 324).

The narrator's description of Audley Court also graphically illustrates Dicey's point that the law is a "mass of irregular, fragmentary, ill expressed," or "purposeless enactments" (vii). If the reader assumes that she will find self-consistent legal codes at Audley Court, she is quickly disabused of such an expectation: "A house in which you incontinently lost yourself if ever you were so rash as to go about it alone," it is a "house that could never have been planned by any mortal architect." Rather, as with all legal formulae, it is a domicile created over time, its owners:

> adding a room one year, and knocking down a room another year, toppling
> over now a chimney coeval with the Plantagenets, and setting up one in the
> style of the Tudors, shaking down a bit of Saxon wall there, and allowing a
> Norman arch to stand here, throwing in a row of high narrow windows in
> the reign of Queen Anne, and joining on a dining-room in the time of
> George the Third to a refectory that had been standing since the Conquest.
> (2)

Thus Braddon describes the architectonics of Audley Court—like Dicey's architectonics of public opinion vis-à-vis legislation—as hardly consistent because the structure itself is always both antiquated and in process.

Within that legal architecture, the reader immediately feels plaintive/plaintiff. At the outset of Braddon's novel, the narrator subverts the primacy of law and its ostensible foundation in the laws of nature, for though the initial description of the setting takes on legal as well as architectural connotations, going to Audley Court is a humanly constructed activity, not a natural undertaking. Thus, in contrast to Blackstone's view that the law was based upon natural principles, at Audley Court, humans, the narrator warns, are out of their element in the natural world: "you came upon [Audley Court] through an avenue of old oaks, bordered on either side by meadows, where the cattle looked inquisitively at you as you passed, wondering, perhaps, what you wanted" (1). Interpreting the law of Audley Court from this description, "what you wanted" rather than what is good for the community is seen to be the motivation behind man-made laws and institutions. In the contest over getting what one wants, in contrast to Robert, as a woman Lucy is legally handicapped. Indeed, although Robert is the epitome of Blackstone's gentleman lawyer, his moral handicaps do not impede his legal potency.

Juxtaposing Robert Audley's idealistic statements about the law's sacredness with his increasingly lawless behavior, the narrator, however, influences public opinion about such a double standard. On the one hand, Robert meditates about entering "the ranks of a profession, the members of which hold solemn responsibilities, and have sacred duties to perform" (103). But Robert's view of himself as the law is meant to be troubling. As the narrator remarks, when he becomes "a pitiless embodiment of justice, a cruel instrument of retribution," he is filled with "a cold sternness that was so strange to him as to transform him into another creature" (232). Likewise, after a brutal interrogation of his quarry, Lucy, Robert "wonder[s] if the judges of the land feel as I do now, when they put on the black cap and pass sentence of death upon some poor, shivering wretch who has never done them any wrong" (233).

To the attentive reader/juror, in this statement, Robert undermines his whole legal case, for his formulation of the "chain" of "evidence" convicting Lucy is very often wrong. With a "JOURNAL OF FACTS" (86) full of inaccuracies, Robert obsessively "forge[s]" together links in his "chain of circumstantial evidence" against Lady Audley (214, 222, 44). Most importantly, Lucy has not murdered George Talboys, nor is he dead. She has broken the law by committing bigamy, but only after being deserted for three years. In Robert's scheme of things, à la Blackstone, the culpability for murder must be cross-examined with class in mind, for, to this barrister, to attempt murder of a gentleman is more heinous than to actually murder a member of the lower class. The death of the working-class character Luke Marks, resulting from Lucy's deliberate pyrotechnics, means nothing to Robert, the novel's chief representative of the law. Instead, Robert is more upset about Lucy's attempt to murder himself and the trouble she has caused George, his gentleman friend (365).

Perhaps as subliminally shocking for the reader is the realization that Robert's misogynist private opinions affect his practice of the law. Robert, it will be remembered, has "outbursts of splenetic rage against the female sex" (282). "What a wonderful solution to life's enigma there is in petticoat government!" says the sarcastic barrister, who imagines that "man might lie in the sunshine and eat lotuses, and fancy it 'always afternoon,' if his wife would let him! But she won't, bless her impulsive heart and active mind! She knows better than that" (177). It is, for a while, amusing to consider Robert's opinion that "to do away with the tea-table is to rob woman of her legitimate empire" (190). But his private opinions directly influence his leanings in legislative matters, for immediately after he fantasizes relegating women to the tea-table, he concludes, "better the pretty influence of the teacups and saucers gracefully wielded in a woman's hand, than all the inappropriate power snatched at the point of the pen from the unwilling sterner sex" (190–91).

Such defects in the individual barrister can scarcely be explained away in the law in general, for in this culture Robert becomes a reputable lawyer after having tried, convicted, and incarcerated a woman totally out of his official jurisdiction. Thus when the hero maniacally argues for and against the incarceration of women in general, the reader is put in a position of having to make a legal judgment about his professional objectivity:

> The Eastern potentate who declared that women were at the bottom of all mischief, should have gone a little further and stated why it is so. It is because women are never lazy. They don't know what it is to be quiet. They are Semiramides, and Cleopatras, and Joan of Arcs, Queen Elizabeths, and Catherine the Seconds, and they riot in battle, and murder, and clamour, and desperation. If they can't agitate the universe and play at ball with

hemispheres, they'll make mountains of warfare and vexation out of domestic molehills, and brew social storms in household teacups. (177)

Dramatically undercutting his own position that men should rule in the public sphere and women remain protected in the private, Robert asserts women's full capacity to perform in the political arena and points out the destructive impulses that occur when they are forced by legal coverture to remain in the private sphere. Thus, at this point, the barrister bizarrely speaks the crosscurrents to his own opinions.

Braddon also creates an uncomfortable position for the English reader when Robert invades the shabby quarters of Lucy's father to interrogate him. Though Robert has no official capacity, he feels no compunction about violating Mr. Maldon's private abode. Hence, in this scene, the reader is compelled by the assumption that a man's home is his castle, even if that man is a woozy, lower-class alcoholic and the intruder a gentleman. As Mr. Maldon vigorously asserts to Robert, the law gives a man fair warning:

> The—the—law, sir, has that amount of mercy for a—a—suspected criminal. But you, sir, you—you come to my house, and you come at a time when—when contrary to my usual habits—which, as people will tell you, are sober—you come, and perceiving that I am not quite myself—you take—the—opportunity to—terrify me—and it is not right, sir—it is—. (145)

Mr. Maldon's inebriated declaration rings true to an English audience inculcated with the right of privacy, and, as a result, in this scene the attractive hero's use of the law comes to seem more abusive than the repulsive Maldon's abuse of liquor.

In a later scene, Maldon's daughter also asserts her right to privacy, and, in doing so, the rights of the accused. As Lucy announces, "if I were placed in a criminal dock, I could, no doubt, bring forward witnesses to refute your absurd accusation. But I am not in a criminal dock, Mr. Audley, and . . . I tell you that you are mad!" (234). Later when Robert rids England of her crime that he, not a jury, decides cannot be forgiven, Lady Audley tells him "you have used your power basely and cruelly, and have brought me to a living grave" (330). Indeed, when Robert conjectures, "If there were any secret tribunal before which you might be made to answer for your crimes, I would have little scruple in being your accuser; but I would spare that generous and honourable gentleman upon whose stainless name your infamy would be reflected," his aristocratic self-interest is clearly implied. But it is also apparent that Robert has already subjected Lady Audley to a "secret tribunal" without official sanction, and the reader cannot help but feel the old boy network asserting its claims (291).

Curiously, both *Lady Audley's Secret* and *Woman in White* represent a blatant masculinist sub-rosa rationale to man-made law. Known in both novels as the Brotherhood, this network of men compels feminine submission to the fissured patriarchal order that asserts the superiority of the universal man but must conceal the self-interested trajectory of that project even from itself. In *Woman in White* this organization, the members of which are not known to each other, "are identified with the Brotherhood by a secret mark, which we all bear, which lasts while our lives last" (Collins 596). The Brotherhood ensures that those who bear the secret signifying mark (the phallus) act as individual links in a subliminal network of patriarchal rule. As the narrator notes of the relationship between Madame and Count Fosco, "The rod of iron with which he rules her never appears in company—it is a private rod, and is always kept upstairs" (244). Thus, formed ostensibly to assert the rights of Man, the universalizing Brotherhood, like the Commentaries, erases, in courtly fashion, the rights of women.

Audley Court also carries the traces of this male priesthood: in one of its secret passageways there is a "hiding-place in which was found a quaint old carved oak chest half filled with priests' vestments that had been hidden there" (3). Moreover, the narrator refers to a contemporary brotherhood that institutes its own legalistic gaze. As Braddon describes the stylistic monomania of the Pre-Raphaelite Brotherhood (PRB), it becomes clear that Robert, who is captivated by one of the PRB's portraits of Lucy, is an honorary member of the Brotherhood. The PRB's meretricious authorization of its works as exact depictions of nature, like Robert Audley's inaccurate if obsessively meticulous "JOURNAL OF FACTS," are illustrated in Braddon's extensive descriptions of the PRB portrait of Lucy:

> The painter must have been a pre-Raphaelite. . . . No one but a pre-Raphaelite would have so exaggerated every attribute of that delicate face as to give a lurid brightness to the blonde complexion, and a strange, sinister light to the deep blue eyes. No one but a pre-Raphaelite could have given to that pretty pouting mouth the hard and almost wicked look it had in the portrait.
>
> It was so like, and yet so unlike; it was as if you had burned strange-coloured fires before my lady's face, and by their influence brought out new lines and new expressions never seen in it before. . . . [I]t seemed as if the painter had copied mediaeval monstrosities until his brain had grown bewildered, for my lady, in his portrait of her, had the aspect of a beautiful fiend. (60)

Suggesting the "exaggerated" agenda behind the Pre-Raphaelite framing of Lady Audley, this passage is associated with the framing that Robert also performs on Lucy. As Braddon implies, insanity is incipient in the painter (equivalent to Robert) more than the model (equivalent to Lady Audley) because, like "the young man" who "belonged to the pre-Raphaelite brotherhood," the painter/Robert "spent a most unconscionable time upon the details of this picture" and thus the painter's "brain had grown bewildered" (59, 60).

It seems, then, that to become an official member of the courts of law, Robert must first become a member of the clandestine Brotherhood by simultaneously pursuing the monomaniacal intentions of the law while mystifying the law as universal in its intents and its beneficiaries. As Martin Danahay argues, because of the forms of patriarchal law in nineteenth-century Britain the male sex could virtually only structure experience as autonomous and separatist. Danahay adds that, as a result, nineteenth-century British male writers often inscribe a monolithic monologism that verges on solipsism (Danahay 5). In *Lady Audley's Secret,* Robert's investigation of Lucy's crimes is repeatedly described as bordering on monomania (228, 180, 217, 125, 236, 246, 339). For example, the hero himself worries, "Am I never to get any nearer to the truth; but am I to be tormented all my life by vague doubts and wretched suspicions, which may grow upon me till I become a monomaniac?" (125). The reader also cannot help but be affected by Robert's own persistent self-doubts intermingled with his moments of self-righteous authority: "What if this edifice of horror and suspicion is a mere collection of crotchets—the nervous fancies of a hypochondriacal bachelor?" he wonders, and suddenly realizes, "Oh, my God, if it should be in myself all this time that the misery lies!" (218).

Thus, if there is a madness in the novel, it is masculine, as Lucy keeps testifying. But not only is it the man who is mad in this novel, he is the one who makes the rules. With this in mind, the reader is faced with the fact that the female protagonist's ambiguous inherited feminine madness is bland, to a certain extent, when compared with the solipsism that is passed on from fathers to sons and from uncles to nephews. In an outlandish conspiracy theory, Harcourt—hard court— Talboys, for example, believes that his son has deliberately disappeared in order to counteract being disinherited by his father. The epitome of phallogo-centric thinking, Talboys Sr.'s "mind ran in straight lines, never diverging to the right or the left." Harcourt also displays the solipsism that underlines his rule of law, concluding that George has deliberately disappeared "for the purpose of influencing me." "Taking a stand upon his own self-esteem," this father "traced every event in life from that one centre, and resolutely declined to look at it from any other point of view" (155, 162, 163). Like his father, presuming that his wife Lucy will mirror back his own self-absorbed identity as her husband, George Talboys assumes that her feelings for him will not change, even though, after abandoning her, he neglects to correspond with her for over three-and-a-half years and the first person he contacts when he returns is his friend Robert instead of his wife. These forms of masculine monomania act as potent crosscurrents to Robert's aspersions against the madness of women.

Furthermore, described in terms of the mythical brotherhood of Damon and Pythias, Robert's friendship with George causes his heightened sensations when Talboys institutes a crisis—not because he leaves his wife and child stranded—but, rather, because he mysteriously leaves Robert. In addition, the narrative continually implies that Robert falls in love with Clara because she is George's sister and bears a striking resemblance to him. Presumably, then, marrying Clara is the closest Robert can come to the secret of monomaniacal homosocial desire—and not all homosocial desire is monomaniacal—impelling patriarchal law (31, 130, 13, 173, 221, 171, 339, 314, 370). Robert agonizes at one point "To think" that "it is possible to care so much for a fellow!" (76). Thus Robert's obsessive desire to capture, incarcerate, and bury Lady Audley's body covers his other monomaniacal impulse to find and re-immerse himself in the missing body of his erstwhile brother, George Talboys. As Braddon suggests, then, man-made laws naturally degenerate from the ostensibly objective aims of the generic universal man into solipsistic narcissism.

Referring to the implicit violence that underwrites Robert's illicit legal shenanigans, Braddon squarely counters the "physical force" argument that explicitly or implicitly underwrote Victorian opinions about women's suffrage. Essentially this view held that "because the security of the state rested on the ability of men to defend it physically, men were entitled, through their vote, to participate in matters of national concern" (qtd. in Kent 180). According to this reasoning, the supposedly weaker sex was not capable of political action. Furthermore, the "physical force" argument implied that if women defied men's will, men would force them to submit. Victorian Harry Thurston Peck illustrated the consequences of feminine crosscurrents of opinion: Man, he said, "has the physical power to work his will, and this alone is a lasting badge of his superiority." Hence, Peck warned the New Woman that if she "should ever bring about a state of things where man collectively begins to be uncomfortable," "the remedy" for disruption would be "swift," "certain," and "brutal" (Peck 161, qtd. in Marks 3–4).

If the physical force argument has implicit effects upon Lady Audley's case, it has explicit repercussions on her maid Phoebe. Believing that her fiancé Luke will kill her if she refuses to marry him, Phoebe tells Lucy that he often threatens her with violence. Asserting, that "I daren't refuse to marry him," she notes that

> "I've often watched him as he has sat slicing away at a hedge-stake with his great clasp-knife, till I have thought that it is just such men as he who have decoyed their sweethearts into lonely places, and murdered them for being false to their word. When he was a boy he was always violent and revengeful. . . . I tell you, my lady, I must marry him." (93)

An astute lay student of the law, Lucy replies, "You think he'll murder, you, do you? Do you think, then, if murder is in him, you would be any safer as his wife?" (93). Pinpointing the inherent flaws in the "physical force" argument, Lucy graphically exhibits the double bind women were in as its result.

If Robert does not physically abuse Lucy the way Luke abuses Phoebe, his taking of the law into his own hands to pursue her is analogous to Luke's brutal courting. At the end of the novel, when Robert and his friends and family enjoy their idyllic, private social world, the reader knows it is the result of physically confining "the wretched woman who was wearing out the remnant of her wicked life in the quiet suburb of the forgotten Belgian city" (373). It must be remembered, too, that with this confinement, Robert ensures his own inheritance of what would have been Lady Audley's estate after Michael Audley's death. Cruelly forcing Lucy into confinement for her sins against men, Robert never mentions or conducts an unofficial legal investigation of Michael Audley's offense of expecting a young wife's absolute devotion, and George's transgression, desertion of both wife and child. Nor does he question the legal position a married woman was put in when her husband deserted her. Indeed, the male self-interest upon which the laws are made rationalizes George's behavior toward his wife as for the good of the whole, sets aside Talboys's obsessive rejection of his son as mere idiosyncrasy, and allows Robert's fears about his own possible madness to recede as Lucy's are magnified.

Likewise, the system of man-made law firmly places the aggressive ingenue Clara in the domestic domicile. Hence, just as Robert has doubly "courted" Lady Audley, he has simultaneously successfully "courted" Clara, for he sets her aside as chief investigator of the ostensible crime against her brother while romantically courting her and thereby confining her in the private sphere. The successful conclusion of both of these unofficial court cases against women results in Robert's official entrance into the official practice of law. The other—clandestine—reward is that George, Clara's brother, is now truly Robert's blood brother, "the one subject which was always a bond of union between" Robert and Clara (370). This union suggests that Robert takes more pleasure in proving his love for Clara by asserting that he will go to Australia to find George (and not return until he does), than he does in asking Clara to marry him. Clara insists upon an explicit heterosexual match by telling Robert that they can both go to "bring our brother back between us" as the central focus of their "honeymoon trip" (372). But, obviously, the ménage àtrois looms in her future married life.

At the conclusion of the novel, Audley Court is abandoned, but it is with the assurance that another case of courting will turn into a court case. Robert's first brief as a real lawyer is "in the great breach of promise case of Hobbs Nobbs, wherein he convulsed the Court by his deliciously comic rendering of the faithless Nobbs's amatory correspondence" (375). A seemingly minor plot point, this court case actually highlights the basis of Robert's double courtly success. First of all, Robert's inaugural official legal case indicates his continued callousness to women and his implicit acceptance of the sexual double standard that inherently favors men. To Robert, that is, women's rights and men's sexual peccadilloes are merely the occasion to make jokes and to make a living in doing so. This case also shows that men in Victorian society continued to get away with breaking the very laws they themselves made about courting and marriage and that Robert literally defends those infractions.

Finally, that the formerly engaged couple, Hobbs and Nobbs, separate also hints at the ways the laws covering English marriages did not encourage economic or political equality or social intercourse between the sexes. As Braddon shows in *Lady Audley's Secret,* this kind of disengagement of the sexes in legal terms also constituted them as separate in social terms, a situation hardly conducive to the heterosexual love story that British legal experts like William Blackstone purportedly endorsed. Rather, in the Victorian legal code, forever locked in a battle of the sexes, men and women, who should be hobnobbing, are not allowed by the law to share the emotional intimacy that only results from equality before the law. That emotional intimacy is enabled, instead, between men, who form a brotherhood of which they themselves are unaware. Hence, even that intimacy is estranged and alienated.

Thus the ending of *Lady Audley's Secret* graphically represents the intertextuality of the court and courting, implying that Victorian men's pursuit of the law would always be tainted with the desire to legislate "in accordance with their interest" (Dicey 12). The happy ending is haunted by the illegal incarceration of the novel's title character who insisted, in futility, that the barrister Robert Audley was mad. But, by subliminally putting the reader in the position of the jurist, Braddon brilliantly creates a space for the interaction and evaluation of crosscurrents of public opinion about women's rights and roles, including Blackstone's "courtly" testimony as well as the testimony of juridical scholars she would preempt and make possible. Indeed, A. V. Dicey and Montague Lush, among other scholars who lauded the enlightened changes in laws regarding women, could not self-reflexively confer these kudos until the early years of the twentieth century, forty years after Braddon's novel was published.

NOTES

1. See Lush, *A Century of Law Reform.*

WORKS CITED

Blackstone, Sir William. "Introduction: Of the Study, Nature and Extent of the Laws of England." *Commentaries on the Laws of England.* 4 vols., 1758; Chicago: Callaghan, 1899.

Braddon, Mary E. *Lady Audley's Secret.* New York: Penguin, 1987.

Collins, Wilkie. *Woman in White.* New York: Penguin, 1974.

Danahay, Martin. *A Community of One: Masculine Autobiography and Autonomy in Nineteenth-Century Britain.* Albany: State University of New York P, 1993.

Dicey, A. V. *Lectures on The Relation between Law and Public Opinion in England during the Nineteenth Century.* London: Macmillan, 1905.

Kent, Susan Kingsley. *Sex and Suffrage in Britain, 1860–1914.* Princeton, N.J.: Princeton UP, 1987.

Lush, Montague. "Changes in the Law Affecting the Rights, Status, and Liabilities of Married Women." *A Century of Law Reform: Twelve Lectures on the Changes in the Law of England during the Nineteenth Century.* London: Macmillan, 1901.

Marks, Patricia. *Bicycles, Bangs, and Bloomers: The New Woman in the Popular Press* Lexington: U of Kentucky P, 1990.

Peck, Harry Thurston. "For Maids and Mothers: The Woman of Today and of Tom-Morrow." *Cosmopolitan.* (June 1899).

Schreiner, Olive. *Woman and Labour.* London: T. F. Unwin, 1911.

West, Robin. *Narrative, Authority, and Law.* Ann Arbor: U of Michigan P, 1993.

THREE

Rebellious Sepoys and Bigamous Wives: The Indian Mutiny and Marriage Law Reform in *Lady Audley's Secret*

Lillian Nayder

Addressing the House of Lords in December 1857, six months after the Hindu and Muslim sepoys in India had begun to rebel against their British officers, Lord Campbell used the Indian Mutiny and its suppression as a metaphor for events much closer to home—to describe the "war" he was helping to wage against prostitution in London. Drawing an analogy between London's "red-light" districts and the city of Delhi, retaken from the Indian mutineers in September, Lord Campbell compared the "seige of Holywell Street . . . to the seige of Delhi": "The place was not taken in a day, but repeated assaults were necessary, and at last . . . it was now in the quiet possession of the law."[1]

In his address, Lord Campbell views domestic affairs through the imperial lens provided by the Indian Mutiny. His remarks support Patrick Brantlinger's claim that British Victorians were virtually obsessed with the Indian Mutiny, and that "no episode in British imperial history raised public excitement to a higher pitch" (199). At the same time, however, Lord Campbell's remarks also suggest the particular usefulness of the Indian Mutiny and the British Empire to those anxious about the changing status and the political demands of women in Victorian England. While Lord Campbell compares English prostitutes to rebellious sepoys in order to convey his sense of their sexual deviance and otherness, and

31

to justify his "seige" against them, many of his contemporaries develop such metaphors to similar social ends. The "sexual science" of Victorian anthropologists as well as the literary representations of Victorian novelists often conflate the sexual "inferiority" of Englishwomen with the racial "inferiority" of colonized peoples. Drawing an analogy between restless savages and discontented Englishwomen agitating for their legal and political rights, these writers discredit the cause of female emancipation. As Cynthia Eagle Russett explains, this analogy was particularly appealing at mid-century, when "women were exhibiting a disturbing propensity to challenge long-established social arrangements with respect to their rights and duties," and could be conveniently dismissed and discredited as " 'flat-chested, thin-voiced Amazons . . . pouring forth sickening prate about the tyranny of men and the slavery of women' " (Allan, qtd. in Russett 27).

One might expect Mary Elizabeth Braddon, a Victorian novelist whose work was perceived as subversive, "unnatural," and "diseased" by contemporary reviewers,[2] to challenge the image of the English "Amazon" demanding her rights, and to question the analogy between sexual and racial inferiority. As E. S. Dallas complained in 1862, the heroines of Braddon's sensation fiction are active and manly rather than passive and womanly; as members of "the fair sex," they "would have made our fathers and grandfathers stare" (8[c]). Yet in *Lady Audley's Secret* (1861–62), Braddon herself compares these unconventional and defiant Englishwomen to mutinous sepoys, recalling Lord Campbell's 1857 address, and using the imagery of the Indian Mutiny and the racism it generated to defend the social status quo. Suggesting that mutinous wives and daughters, like rebellious sepoys, are "unnatural" and ungrateful creatures who should be punished for their transgressions and returned to their "proper place," Braddon responds to those seeking to gain legal and political rights for Englishwomen in a notably reactionary way. Her use of the Mutiny in *Lady Audley's Secret* calls into question her status as a feminist writer, and lends force to those critics who feel that her subversive qualities are, at best, heavily qualified and contained.[3]

I

In the consciousness of many Victorians, 1857 was the year of the Indian Mutiny—the year in which myths of imperial progress, and the willing subservience of the colonized, received their first major check. The Hindu and Muslim sepoys employed by the British had a number of economic and political grievances against their colonizers, but the immediate cause of their mutiny was religious. The British had introduced

Enfield rifles into the army, and the new cartridges had to be bitten off before they were loaded. Acting under the belief that these cartridges were greased with cow and pig fat—and hence that they were being forced to commit sacrilege in loading their weapons—the sepoys rebelled, killing their officers as well as English women and children. Accounts of Indian atrocities and examples of British martyrdom were reported daily in the British press: the rape and murder of Englishwomen, for example, and their sale to Indians in the streets of Cawnpore. Predicably enough, these accounts elicited "calls for repression and revenge" (Brantlinger 199), and were used to fuel and justify the genocidal reprisals of the British in putting down the revolt.[4]

While 1857 was the year of the Indian Mutiny, it was also the year in which the Divorce and Matrimonial Causes Act was passed by Parliament, creating a civil divorce court in England, and altering the law in such a way that divorce was no longer solely a male prerogative. The culmination of nearly a decade of political debate, the Act allowed husbands to divorce their wives on the grounds of adultery, and granted wives the right to divorce adulterous husbands if their adultery was compounded by cruelty, bigamy, incest, or bestiality.[5] The Act also stipulated that wives legally separated from their husbands were entitled to the same property rights as single women, qualifying the common law doctrine of *coverture* in their particular case. Thus at the same time in which imperial rule was threatened in India, the sanctity of the marriage bond and its patriarchal privileges were challenged at home, as advocates of women's rights questioned the justice of English common law and the doctrine of *coverture*, which deprived women of property rights and legal identity upon marriage.

In the year of the Indian Mutiny and the Matrimonial Causes Act, Mary Elizabeth Braddon began her professional career. Supporting herself and her mother by becoming an actress on the provincial stage, Braddon was among those Victorian women who understood the importance of female employment opportunities and property rights, and had witnessed the inequities of Victorian marriage law at first hand. Braddon's mother separated from her adulterous husband in 1840, but only after she had lost all the property she brought to the marriage because of her husband's financial incompetence. After two years of acting in Yorkshire, the twenty-four-year-old Braddon began writing fiction to make money. Her first novel, *Three Times Dead,* appeared in 1860, and her second, *Lady Audley's Secret,* from 1861 to 1862. Braddon's first, illegitimate child—by her publisher John Maxwell—was born in March 1862, as the serialization of *Lady Audley's Secret* drew near its end.

With her knowledge of marital inequities and her willingness to defy Victorian sexual conventions, Braddon seems likely to champion marriage law reform in her novels. Yet her fictional treatment of such issues proves to be much more conservative than her own experiences might lead us to expect. Her decision to have six children out of wedlock may seem inherently subversive, and express her desire to retain her legal rights as a single woman, regardless of scandal. But her behavior was partly based on circumstances beyond her control. Indeed, she and John Maxwell married as soon as they legally could—after the death of the first Mrs. Maxwell in an Irish insane asylum—and Braddon largely defends the institution of marriage against subversion and reform in her novel.

II

Lady Audley's Secret tells the story of a beautiful young governess named Lucy Graham, who has the good fortune to marry the wealthy baronet, Sir Michael Audley, nearly forty years her senior. Living at Audley Court with her elderly husband and his eighteen-year-old daughter, Alicia, the child of his first marriage, Lucy delights those around her with her childlike and angelic charm. "The innocence and candour of an infant beamed in [her] fair face," we are told (52). Yet Alicia remains jealous and aloof, expressing "undisguised contempt for her step-mother's childishness and frivolity" (52).

We soon learn that Alicia has good reason to object to her step-mother, whose assumed innocence masks a fallen and heartless nature. After Alicia's cousin Robert visits Audley Court with his friend George Talboys, a widower and ex-dragoon, George disappears, last seen asking for Lady Audley at the mansion house. Assuming the role of amateur detective, Robert Audley learns that his uncle's beautiful wife is, in fact, a bigamist. Uncovering "Lady's Audley's secrets," Robert identifies her as Helen Talboys, the wife of his friend George, who left her and their infant son to seek his fortune in Australia. Learning of his imminent return to England soon after her bigamous marriage to Sir Michael, Helen Talboys falsifies her death and advertises it in the *Times*, in an attempt to throw her first husband off the scent. When George discovers his wife in Lady Audley, confronts her, and threatens her with exposure, she attempts to kill him. She removes the rusty spindle from the windlass of the old well at Audley Court, on which her husband leans during their confrontation, and he falls to the bottom. "Sink[ing] with one horrible cry into the black mouth of the well" (393–94), George Talboys is left for dead. Although he miraculously survives, climbs out of the well, and secretly leaves England for America, Lady Audley presumes that she has killed him, and is blackmailed by Luke Marks, the husband of her maid Phoebe, who witnessed the scene by the well. After Lady Audley attempts to murder

Robert Audley and Luke Marks by burning them in their beds, Robert forces her to confess her crimes. In the process, she discloses her *deepest* secret, the madness she inherited from her mother. Protecting the Audley family name, Robert conveys Helen Talboys to a Belgian asylum rather than bringing her to trial. The novel ends soon after George's return to London, and the celebration of two marriages—that of Robert Audley to George's sister Clara; and that of Alicia Audley to a young baronet, Sir Henry Towers.

Like the other sensation novels of the early 1860s (Wilkie Collins's *The Woman in White,* for example), *Lady Audley's Secret* responds to the ongoing debates over marriage law reform by exposing marital conflict and deception within middle- and upper-class homes. At various moments in her novel, Braddon acknowledges the need for marriage law reform by dramatizing the oppression and powerlessness of English wives, subjected to the mistreatment and brutality of their husbands, and perceived as a lucrative source of income to the impoverished or greedy men who marry them for their money. Phoebe Marks is continually subject to the threats and violence of her alcoholic husband Luke, and believes him capable of murdering her out of jealousy or greed (105–6); and her experience as a working-class wife is shared by some of her social superiors. In the view of sympathetic acquaintances and family members, for example, Helen Talboys is "cruel[ly]" deserted (41) by her husband George before she begins life again as the governess Lucy Graham. The respectable governess Miss Maldon, returning to England from Australia, worries that her fiancé will only "welcome [her] for the sake of [her] fifteen years' savings" (16). Even the "kind" Sir Michael conceives of his first marriage as a "bargain" made "to keep [an] estate in the family" (6), and for all the splendor in which she lives as Sir Michael's wife, the second Lady Audley remains financially dependent and propertyless, "rich in a noble allowance of pin-money" (53).

In light of such dependence, we can understand why Alicia Audley names her beloved horse "Atalanta" (64), after the Greek maiden who outran her suitors in the hopes of remaining unmarried. Nonetheless, matrimony seems the sole expedient for genteel women in the novel, who are taught, as schoolgirls, that their "ultimate fate in life depended upon . . . marriage" (350). Braddon repeatedly notes the limited opportunities for "respectable" female employment, as Lady Audley recounts her "dull slavery [as] a governess" (353), and the narrator remarks on the "poor salary" she received in the home of her employer, where she dressed in "shabby clothes, . . . worn and patched, and darned, and turned and twisted" (5, 27).

Responding to Braddon's representations of gender inequities and the sufferings and dependence of English wives, some literary critics have characterized *Lady Audley's Secret* as a deeply subversive novel, one that calls into question "the social and economic dominance of men" (Skilton viii). Emphasizing what he sees as Braddon's subversive subtext, David Skilton argues for the *sanity* of Braddon's heroine, who "commits crimes only in order to ensure her own survival and prosperity in her male-dominated world" (xvi). In similar terms, Elaine Showalter asserts that "Lady Audley's real secret is that she is *sane,* and, moreover, representative" ("Desperate" 4). According to these critics, we must read between the lines of Braddon's novel, and question her explicit moral aims. Although Braddon "would have us . . . accept that all is for the best in the ending she provides," Skilton asserts, "we are made to know that it is not so" (xvi).

Yet such readings downplay the conservative bent of Braddon's novel, and her willingness to support the patriarchal norms and traditions that she criticizes in certain portions of her work. In *Lady Audley's Secret,* Braddon responds to the issue of marriage law reform, but does so in a deeply divided way. While she acknowledges the need for marriage law reform, she simultaneously criminalizes it. Rather than celebrating the newly won right of Englishwomen to sue their husbands for divorce under certain circumstances, or of legally separated wives to possess their own property, Braddon tells a story about a wife's bigamy and greed, associating such rights with female lawlessness.[6]

Describing "woman's hellish power of dissimulation" (274), Braddon depicts Helen Talboys as a modern-day Eve, and indicts female nature in the process. In his conflict with the wife of Sir Michael, Robert Audley "remember[s] the horrible things that have been done by women, since that day upon which Eve was created to be Adam's companion and help-meet in the garden of Eden" (273–74). Despite the presence of the abusive Luke Marks in the novel, Braddon's generalizations about marriage and adultery always cast husbands as the injured party. "Ah, Heaven help a strong man's tender weakness for the woman he loves," the narrator tells us:

> Heaven pity him when the guilty creature has deceived him and comes with her tears and lamentations to throw herself at his feet. . . . Pity him, pity him. The wife's worst remorse when she stands without the threshold of the home she may never enter more is not equal to the agony of the husband who closes the portal on that familiar and entreating face. The anguish of the mother who may never look again upon her children is less than the torment of the father who has to say to those children, "My little ones, you are henceforth motherless." (284)

Embracing the sexual double standard and insisting that men who cast out their wives are the *real* victims, Braddon associates marriage law reform with a wife's bigamy, and Lady Audley with Eve, and treats adultery as if it were solely a female transgression. At the same time, she casts her antiheroine as a female "traitor" (200) and "arch conspirator" (253) whose crimes against her husband recall those committed by the murderous Indian sepoys against the British. While Braddon acknowledges the exploitation of women by connecting the poor English governess to the African slave (353), she more insistently compares the bigamous wife to the rebellious sepoys. Drawing on the inflamatory language used to describe these Indian "devils" in the English press, she discredits the cause of female emancipation, reinforcing the patriarchal anxieties of her readers with the imperial fears generated by the Indian Mutiny.

III

Braddon fills her novel with references to India and the Indian Mutiny. While Robert rides the train in the company of "an elderly Indian officer" (161), Lady Audley serves tea from "a marvellous Indian tea-caddy of sandal-wood and silver" (223) and "wrap[s] herself in an Indian shawl; a shawl that had cost Sir Michael a hundred guineas" (373), and Audley Court is cluttered with valuable objects from the British colony (295). Sir Michael and Alicia discuss the Mutiny and the "fighting in Oudh" at the beginning of volume 3 (329), immediately after Lady Audley exhibits her "demoniac force" (324) by burning down the Castle Inn at Mount Stanning. This "deed of horror" reveals her "as the demoniac incarnation of some evil principle" (345) and implicitly connects her to the mutinous sepoys, who repeatedly set fire to buildings in the course of their revolt.

Braddon ties Lady Audley to the sepoys more directly when she describes the psychological wound that the bigamous wife inflicts on George Talboys in 1857—the year of her marriage to Sir Michael—an injury that George compares to those received by his comrades in India. One year after seeing the advertisement of his wife's death in the *Times,* and shortly before he discovers her treachery, the ex-dragoon speaks metaphorically of the bullet wound that afflicts him. "Do you know, Bob," he tells Robert Audley, when his friend congratulates him on his apparent health, "that when some of our fellows were wounded in India, they came home bringing bullets inside them": "They did not talk of them, and they were stout and hearty, and looked as well, perhaps, as you or I; but every change in the weather, however slight, every variation of the atmosphere, however trifling, brought back the old agony of their wounds as sharp as ever they had felt it on the battle-field. I've had my wound, Bob; I carry the bullet still, and I shall carry it into my coffin" (49). When Lady Audley attempts to murder her husband at Audley Court,

Braddon strengthens the analogy between the treacherous wife and the rebellious sepoy. She does so by drawing on one of the most notorious images of the Mutiny, one that was often used by British Victorians to epitomize the hellish barbarism of the Indian race—the image of the well at Cawnpore.

In late June 1857, after nearly a month of bombardment, the British survivors of the deadly seige at Cawnpore were promised that they could travel safely to Allahabad by Nana Sahib, a local Indian leader and the adopted son of a dethroned Mahratta ruler. After they accepted his offer, and began their exodus, he ordered their massacre by the nearby river. Men, women and children were shot, clubbed, burned to death, and mutilated with swords. All the men were murdered, and the surviving women and children, about 125 in number, were then incarcerated in a small house without furniture or bedding. On 17 July, those who had not yet died were attacked and murdered with swords at close quarters. The next morning, those few women who were still alive were dragged out of the house along with the dead bodies of their companions, stripped of clothing, and dropped into the well. Soon after the arrival of the British forces in Cawnpore, the well became a public symbol of British martyrdom and Indian atrocity—a sight to which British officers and soldiers flocked, gathering locks of the dead women's hair from nearby bushes, and often "burst[ing] into tears" (Hibbert 214). "The '*poor poor* creatures,'" Major Bingham wrote in his diary, after he looked down the well at the mutilated remains. "'It was a sight I wish I had never seen, but once seen never to be forgotten.'"[7] As Christopher Hibbert explains in his history of the Mutiny, the well at Cawnpore filled its British visitors with both pity and rage. Symbolizing "a crime of unspeakable, blasphemous enormity" (Hibbert 210), it was used by the British to justify the torture and execution of Indians without trial in the months following the Cawnpore massacres.

In *Rule of Darkness,* Brantlinger entitles his chapter on Mutiny literature "The Well at Cawnpore" because the so-called well of evil fame (Trevelyan 228) is the "one spot" on which this literature converges (203). Invited by such writers as Sir George Trevelyan to "look . . . into the depths of the well," Brantlinger explains, "the reader is meant to understand the absolute villainy of the Mutineers and the heroic purity of their victims" (203). In *Lady Audley's Secret,* Braddon invokes the familiar image of the Cawnpore well, but relocates it in the beautiful English countryside. Like the well at Cawnpore in Mutiny literature, the well at Audley Court is the spot on which Braddon's narrative persistently converges. Again and again, Braddon directs us—and her characters—to the old well, "half buried" in shrubbery (3). Inviting us to look down "the long green vista" to "the broken well at the end" (4), she evokes its imperial counterpart, the ruined condition of which came to represent the heroic martrydom of the British, even before it became a mass grave. Stories of the self-appointed "Captain[s] of the well," and their courageous attempts to supply women and children with water from it, circulated widely back home (Hibbert 184). The well was their only source of water, and many soldiers and officers were killed at the spot. "The creaking of the tackle would usually call forth a storm of musketry," Hibbert explains, and its machinery and masonry were soon "shot away" (184).

In Braddon's novel, the ruined well is not under seige—its crumbling brickwork and its broken machinery mark its antiquity (272), like that of the manor house itself. Nonetheless, its "rusty iron wheel and broken woodwork seem as if they were flecked with blood" (24), Braddon tells us, and although we do not hear the story ourselves, Alicia tells George and Robert a "legend connected with" the "ruined well": "some gloomy story . . . of sorrow and crime" (66).

In *Lady Audley's Secret,* this legend both is and is not that of the well at Cawnpore. Having invoked the well-known imperial image, Braddon domesticates it, reworking the murderous drama enacted by its side. While Braddon retains the sense of Gothic horror associated with Mutiny legends of Cawnpore as well as their stark moral polarities, she redefines the agents of villainy and heroic purity to suit her particular ends. Conflating the threat of native insurrection with that of feminist revolt, Braddon displaces the fiendish Indian sepoy with the seemingly innocent Englishwoman. As Lady Audley forces George Talboys down the well, the rebellious sepoy of Mutiny fame is transformed into the treacherous wife, and the martyred Englishwomen of Cawnpore into her victimized husband.

By means of this racial and sexual inversion, Braddon suggests that the real threat posed to the British empire in the 1860s does not come from unruly natives in the colonies but from Englishwomen agitating for their rights, and empowered to divorce their husbands and reclaim their property rights. Defusing this threat at the conclusion of her novel, Braddon stages the "conquest" of the independent Englishwomen who figure in it by the newly strengthened male characters. Not only does Robert Audley incarcerate Helen Talboys in a Belgian asylum; he also marries Clara Talboys, whose financial autonomy and willingness to act as the novel's detective threaten to emasculate and "conquer" him (258): "I will travel from one end of the world to the other to find the secret of [George's] fate," she tells him. "I am of age; my own mistress; rich, for I have money left me by one of my aunts. . . . Choose between the two alternatives, Mr. Audley. Shall you or I find my brother's murderer?" (199). By the end of the story, however, the would-be female detective and world traveler is the happy mother of Robert's child, her independent fortune the property of her husband under common law, and her "petticoat government" defeated (206). At the same time, Alicia Audley, a "strong-minded" young woman (127) who wants to excerize male prerogatives (61), is returned to her proper place as a dutiful daughter and a faithful wife and mother. Like the Hindus and Muslims of British India, these ambitious women wish to establish their own "dynasty" and rule (293)—a regime distinct from what many perceive to be their "legitimate empire" over "the tea-table" (222). But while his experience among these women convinces Robert Audley that females rather than males are "the stronger sex" (207) and are capable of becoming "lawyers, doctors, preachers, teachers, soldiers, legislators" (207) and even "empress[es]" (305), their mutiny—like that of the colonized Indians—is successfully put down.

NOTES

1. *Hansard's Parliamentary Debates,* vol. 148, third series, 7 December 1857, col. 227; quoted by Nead (85).

2. See Rae (187) and Mansel (482–83).

3. See, for example, Ann Cvetkovich, "Detective in the House: Subversion and Containment in *Lady Audley's Secret,*" in *Mixed Feelings: Feminism, Mass Culture, and Victorian Sensationalism* (45–70). In arguing that Braddon's representation of Lady Audley confirms "a masculine fantasy about women's hidden powers" (48) and "consolidates the patriarchal family" (50), Cvetkovich usefully complicates the view of Elaine Showalter, who sees Braddon as a writer who rebels against social convention and creates "a new kind of heroine, one who could put her hostility toward men into violent action." See Showalter, *A Literature of Their Own* 160.

4. For discussions of the Indian Mutiny from different vantage points, see Wayne G. Broehl Jr., Pratul Chandra Gupta, Christopher Hibbert, Thomas Metcalf, and Vinayak Savarkar.

5. While the 1857 Act registered the sexual double standard of Victorian England, and the belief that wives should forgive the adultery of their husbands while husbands should not forgive their adulterous wives, it also reflected a compromise between those who felt that divorce should be a male prerogative that defended husbands against wives who threatened to produce "spurious" heirs, and those who believed that married women were entitled to the same legal protection as married men. For discussions of Victorian marriage and divorce law, and the debates over married women's property, see Lee Holcombe, Mary Poovey (51–88); Mary Lyndon Shanley, and Lawrence Stone.

6. A number of critics have attributed the interest in bigamy displayed by sensation novelists to the debates over the Divorce and Matrimonial Causes Act,

and to the cultural and political anxieties the Act generated. See, for example, Jeanne Fahnestock and Patrick Brantlinger ("What is 'Sensational'").

7. General G. W. Bingham, diary, Bingham papers, National Army Museum; quoted by Hibbert, p. 209.

WORKS CITED

Allan, James McGrigor. "On the Real Differences in the Minds of Men and Women." *Journal of the Anthropological Society of London* 7 (1869): ccxii.

Bingham, General G. W. Diary. Bingham papers. National Army Museum. NAM. 1959-03-105.

Braddon, Mary Elizabeth. *Lady Audley's Secret.* Oxford: Oxford U P, 1992.

Brantlinger, Patrick. "What is 'Sensational' about the 'Sensation Novel'?" *Nineteenth-Century Fiction* 37 (June 1982): 1–28.

Brantlinger, Patrick. *Rule of Darkness: British Literature and Imperialism, 1830–1914.* Ithaca, N.Y.: Cornell U P, 1988.

Broehl, Jr., Wayne G. *Crisis of the Raj: The Revolt of 1857 through British Lieutenants' Eyes.* Hanover, N. H.: U P of New England, 1986.

Cvetkovich, Ann . "Detective in the House: Subversion and Containment in *Lady Audley's Secret,*" *Mixed Feelings: Feminism, Mass Culture, and Victorian Sensationalism.* New Brunswick, N.J.: Rutgers U P, 1992.

[Dallas, E. S.] "Lady Audley's Secret." *Times* (18 November 1862), 8(c).

Fahnestock, Jeanne. "Bigamy: The Rise and Fall of a Convention." *Nineteenth-Century Fiction* 36 (June 1981): 47–71.

Gupta, Pratul Chandra. *Nana Sahib and the Rising at Cawnpore.* Oxford: Clarendon, 1963.

Hansard's Parliamentary Debates. London: Printed for H. M. Stationery Office by Harrison and Sons. 1803–1908.

Hibbert, Christopher. *The Great Mutiny: India 1857.* New York: Penguin, 1980.

Holcombe, Lee. *Wives and Property: Reform of the Married Women's Property Law in Nineteenth-Century England.* Toronto: U of Toronto P, 1983.

[Mansel, H. L.] "Sensation Novels." *Quarterly Review* 113 (April 1862): 481–514.

Metcalf, Thomas. *The Aftermath of Revolt: India, 1857–1870.* Princeton: Princeton U P, 1964.

Nead, Lynda. *Myths of Sexuality: Representations of Women in Victorian Britain.* Oxford: Basil Blackwell, 1990.

Poovey, Mary. *Uneven Developments: The Ideological Work of Gender in Mid-Victorian England.* Chicago: U of Chicago P, 1988.

[Rae, W. F.] "Sensation Novelists: Miss Braddon." *North British Review.* n.s. 4 (1865): 180–204.

Russett, Cynthia Eagle. *Sexual Science: The Victorian Construction of Womanhood.* Cambridge: Harvard UP, 1989.

Savarkar, Vinayak. *The Indian War of Independence, 1857*. Bombay: Phoenix, 1947.

Shanley, Mary Lyndon. *Feminism, Marriage, and the Law in Victorian England*. Princeton: Princeton UP, 1989.

Showalter, Elaine. *A Literature of Their Own*. Princeton: Princeton UP, 1977.

Showalter, Elaine. "Desperate Remedies: Sensation Novels of the 1860s." *Victorian Newsletter* 49 (Spring 1976): 1–5.

Skilton, David. Introduction. *Lady Audley's Secret*. Oxford: Oxford UP, 1992.

Stone, Lawrence *Road to Divorce: England, 1530–1987*. Oxford: Oxford UP, 1990.

Trevelyan, G. O. *Cawnpore*. London: Macmillan, 1865.

FOUR

Marketing Sensation:
Lady Audley's Secret and Consumer Culture

Katherine Montwieler

Lady Audley's Secret (1862), the sensation novel exemplar, contains a wealth of physical objects, a savvy, powerful heroine, and a telling story of the encroachment of the working class. Mary Elizabeth Braddon's attention to the trappings of prosperity and her valorization of Lady Audley work in tandem to create a subversive political vision that belies the novel's superficial condemnation of class transgressions. If contemporary conduct books taught women to be happy in their station in life, contemporary advertisements taught women that happiness could be acquired through the purchase of material possessions. Braddon borrows from both strategies to show poor women how to affect gentility, and once they have accomplished this goal, how to perfect it. Lady Audley's (Helen Maldon's) secret is Braddon's complicity in a radical discourse that undermines social stratification. Through the variety of cultural artifacts that appear in the novel, Braddon teaches women readers how to pretend to be members of a class into which they were not born. Ultimately, it is in Braddon's interest to invest energy in detailing commodities, since sensation novels themselves were as much commodities as the "inlaid cabinets, bronzes, cameos, statuettes, and trinkets" (Braddon 20) that clutter Audley Court. Indeed mid-nineteenth-century reading practices were intimately related to the marketing of the gentrification of society. Advertisements of books and things overwhelmed those with purchasing power and tempted those without it. Braddon's canny recognition of her culture's materialism is manifest in the sheer number of objects at Audley Court, which so vividly depicts the Victorian obsession with acquisition. Through an examination of Lady Audley and the artifacts of Audley Court (after an introduction to Victorian consumer culture and reading practices), I intend to show how Braddon constructs her subversive domestic manual and how that manual participates in the general discourse of the rise of capitalism and commodification of Victorian England.

VISUALIZING VICTORIANS

After all, the publication of *Lady Audley's Secret* coincided with the development of the modern department store. Eleven years earlier, the Great Exposition of 1851 had set a precedent for department stores that presaged the capitalist marriage between spectacle and commercial expansion. The seven-thousand-item collection was staggering, including such disparate exhibits as raw goods, machines, textiles, and metal, glass, and ceramic objects. These items were not for sale, but rather, representatives of quality. All spectators had the ability to look; no one had the ability to purchase. But in spite of the variety of objects paraded before the Exposition's visitors, the Crystal Palace, with "its 293,655 panes of glass, its 330 standardized iron columns and its 24 miles of guttering, was the biggest and most extravagant [attraction of all]" (Briggs 54). The palace—a new schoolroom that taught its students a lesson of channeling desire toward the same objects housed within it—prophesied a moment of the capitalist mass market. Over 6 million people toured the Palace, including Queen Victoria "on more than forty separate occasions" (Morse 33). Thus, for all the wondrousness of the edifice and of the items within its glass walls, the Crystal Palace was a people's palace, where those from all classes converged in a moment of shared spectatorship.

In the years that followed, department stores took their cue from the Great Exposition. Shared spectatorship was the first step toward shared desires and mass consumerism. Just as the presentation of items in the Exposition was significant, so commodities in department stores "were put on show in an attractive guise, becoming unreal in that they were images set apart from everyday things, and real in that they were there to be bought and taken home to enhance the ordinary environment" (Bowlby 2). An object's value lay in its ornamental properties, not in its usefulness. And so, the Victorian home became glutted with ornaments, large and small, flat and shapely, hard and soft, domestic and exotic. If portraits, pictures, and papers covered walls, so rugs, parquet, and carpets covered floors, and curtains, drapes, and leaded glass covered windows. Fruit bowls, clocks, and pillows adorned tables, mantles, and sofas, and vases, plants, and curios decorated buffets, cabinets, and desks. Of course, the flaunting of this materialism acquired some critics. The nineteenth-century *Hints on Household Taste,* for example, complained of "far too many knick-knacks (advertised as 'articles of vertu') and 'fancy things' from glass shades and paper weights to wax flowers and scrapwork screens. There were also far too many 'what-nots', specially carved for displaying them" (quoted in Briggs, sic 226). Yet such knick-knacks, fancy things, and what-nots were indications of the material democratization of society (as well as [or at least marketed as] signifiers of moral worth, exemplified in "articles of virtue"). Consumers could purchase the correct signs of good taste, which would ideally correlate with the correct signs of moral distinction. In other words, certain props—now available for the first time to many because of the new phenomenon of mass production—indicated both middle-class taste and middle-class morality. By the late nineteenth century, women were generally responsible for shopping for the home, the new chore of creating a domestic tableau of wealth and respectability. As a result, manufacturers began targeting women as purchasers in the new medium of advertisements.

Victorian advertisements ranged from home improvement to personal beauty. According to Lori Anne Loeb, to transform a home into "a hub of warmth and familial entertainment," one could simply buy a piano, a gramophone, or a stove (13). And "with the acquisition of creams to whiten the complexion, fringes to improve the coiffure, and corsets to mold the female figure it was possible to create the 'perfect lady,' a beacon of Victorian affluence" (10). By 1850 the display advertisement that originally only appeared in working-class periodicals began to appear in the middle-class press as well. Publishers were "confronted with pressure from advertisers, the promise of financial gain, and the attraction of political independence" (5). The enormous variety of items for sale underscores the demographic spread of Victorian advertising. Objects included "floral mantillas, cod liver oil, cutlery, camomile pills, pocket sophonias (raincoats), respirators (anti-allergic masks), patent self-adjusting shirts, patent barley and groats (invalid fare), invisible ventilating perukes (gentlemen's wigs)" (Altick, *Presence* 227). Yet by far the majority of advertisements were directed toward and depicted women, who were quickly becoming the primary consumers in (and of) English society. The women pictured in Victorian advertisements, rather than being embodiments of evangelical piety, are interested in pleasure, leisure, and beautification. Even in domestic scenes, they play, relax, and primp. Working women do not sell products. Rather, the seductresses of display advertisements beckon with the lure of languor, beauty, and sexual potency. In the world of the advertisement, all women have physical beauty and time to pamper themselves.

READING MATERIALS

The rise of commodification was paralleled by the rise in literacy. Like shopping, reading moved from being an elite to a majority practice. In 1840, 50 percent of England's population could read. By 1900, the rate had risen to over 95 percent, almost doubling in sixty years (Mitch xvi). This explosion in literacy demanded an explosion in reading materials. The market responded with a huge increase of novels published in the form of serials. At the same time, the price of these publications dropped to fall within the budget of working-class readers. In 1870, Anthony Trollope maintained, "We have become a novel-reading public. Novels are in the hands of us all; from the Prime Minister down to the last-appointed scullery maid" (108). Books thus became accessible commodities, both constructors and constructions of consumer culture. As early as 1827, William Hazlitt noted the connection between consumerism and novel-reading, assessing, "You dip into an Essay or a Novel, and may fancy yourself reading a collection of quack or fashionable advertisements:— Macassar Oil, Eau de Cologne, Hock and Seltzer Water, Otto of Roses, *Pomade Divine*, glance through the page in inextricable confusion and make your head giddy" (quoted in Altick, 1991, 214).[1] Furthermore, novels were sold in the same stores that sold the products the books "advertised," whether literally with advertisements in the front and back, or covertly, in "hidden" messages. Wilkie Collins wrote of popular novels, "Day after day, and week after week, the mysterious publications haunted my walks, go where I might. . . . There they were in every town, large or small. I saw them in fruit-shops, in oyster-shops, in cigar-shops, in lozenge shops" (quoted in Cvetkovich 18). The ubiquity of novels points to their popularity—but also to their successful marketing. Both the novels' self-awareness as and privileging of material objects—regardless of whether they contained actual advertisements or not—highlight the authors' complicity in the creation of a consumer culture.[2] The word "Victorian," Asa Briggs points out, "can be applied with equal justice to . . . wallpapers and . . . tapestries . . . books and . . . stained glass" (53).

And just as consumer culture was associated with femininity, so was leisure reading. Women's magazines, domestic guides, and fiction proliferated in the nineteenth century. Like the advertisement, the magazine directed toward the middle-class woman was "an important element in a wider process of re-defining leisure or pleasure in terms of the rational and the private, or domestic, as distinct from the public" (Ballaster et al.

76). A number of fronts identified women's work of relaxing. "Conduct manual" magazines such as *Lady's Magazine* and *Englishwoman's Domestic Magazine* fostered the middle-class ideal of domestic femininity. Other magazines, including *The Gentlewoman* and *Queen,* focused on the bourgeois home, another manifestation of a woman's social and moral status. Such magazines often highlighted descriptions of aristocratic mansions and "articles and advertisements in which, either in high quality pictures or in print, furniture, pictures, books and other cultural objects were paraded before the readers as indicators of taste, culture, and (implicitly) wealth" (Ballaster et al. 94). Theoretically, (some) didactic fiction, instructional articles, and advice manuals countered the materialistic vision of these magazines, promoting a feminine ideal of submission, docility, domesticity, and repression of desires (whether for objects or for persons). Still other books straddled both the moralistic and the materialistic camps and spoke of the importance of household management. Briggs observes that *The Complete Home* was vastly popular, partially because of "the increase in the number of things in the home and the number of things about which the housewife had to know" (220). Didactic novels often imparted similar lessons, and could therefore be just as edifying as conduct books.

Sensation novels, however, were another issue entirely. The heroines of such novels challenged the domestic middle-class ideal of a passionless, devout, submissive daughter/wife. Accordingly, Richard Altick understands the major charge leveled against sensation novels as the fact that they were "written for, and devoured by, a middle-class clientele whose literary taste should be the exemplar of wholesomeness, proof against the seductions of romancers" (*Deadly Encounters* 153). Wholesomeness, apparently, could not stand up to the power of sensationalism. Indeed, the genre itself may be a reaction against repressive Victorian punctilio. Furthermore, "respectable" classes feared the invasion of their spheres by this lower-class literature, as Fraser Rae notes: Mary Braddon "'may boast without fear of contradiction of having temporarily succeeded in making the literature of the kitchen the favourite reading of the Drawing-room'" (quoted in Flint 278). Winifred Hughes goes so far as to claim the sensation novel's origins "in penny dreadfuls and other working-class entertainments" and its success in upper-class spheres made it the first undisputed example of democratic art (9). Reading such novels thus becomes a subversive pursuit as "it brings the middle and lower classes together over [and in] the same printed pages" (42). The department store and the advertisement fostered the dream of material democratization with the illusion that working-class people could buy their way into English society. Conversely, the popularity of working-class literature in upper-class homes signaled another leveling of class stratification.

VICTORIAN SENSATION

Mary Elizabeth Braddon's *Lady Audley's Secret* was the first mainstream and most infamous sensation novel.[3] The prototypical sensation novel is preoccupied with materialism, spectacle, and the rise of the working class—all phenomena significant to the Victorian age. Regarding the novel's attention to mass culture, Henry James noted, "The intense probability of the story is constantly reiterated. Modern England—the England of to-day's newspaper—crops up at every step" (112–113). *Lady Audley's Secret* is as timely as a newspaper article—or as an advertisement.[4]

While Hughes reads the hallmark of the sensation novel as "the violent yoking of romance and realism" (16), I am less concerned with "the romance" of *Lady Audley's Secret* and more concerned with its realism or representations thereof. Invested in the sensations of Victorian culture, the novel participates in the discourse of consumerism outlined above, the discourse Henry James called "knowing English" (115). Further underscoring the link between consumerism and sensation novels was their very name, called so because of their massive popularity. *Lady Audley's Secret* is loyal to its status as a product of mass culture, referring constantly to similar products. Rather than attempting to dissociate the novel from current popular fads, Braddon overtly revels in the products she names.

This attention to conspicuous consumption embodies the novel's subversive politics. Braddon follows the strategy of domestic manuals to relay the message of advertisements: if you look like this, act like this, buy these things, you will become genteel. *Lady Audley's Secret* is a tell-all manual that instructs poor young women how to charm everyone, how to win rich husbands, and how to create a home. Jill Matus speaks for many critics when she observes that what "seems primarily to be the matter with Lady Audley is that she threatens to violate class boundaries and exclusions, and to get away with appropriating social power beyond her entitlement" (335). But, not only does Lady Audley threaten class boundaries, her creator shows her readers how they can as well. The novel, then, is an alternative domestic economy manual that teaches women how "to live correctly and especially to demonstrate taste" (Loeb 120). Lady Audley's final institutionalization and death also serve as a warning, indicating that she did not follow the rules successfully in not ridding herself of all of the evidence of her former life (the ring, the baby's bootie, the stickered trunk) as Helen Maldon Talboys. If she had completely destroyed "the circumstantial evidence" that Robert Audley finds, Braddon suggests, the actress could have pulled off her starring role as the ideal Victorian wife. But if Helen Maldon Talboys finally fails as Lady Lucy Graham Audley, her creator leaves in clear relief the reasons for both her temporary success and her failure. In the developing commodification of Victorian culture, the covetous young Helen represents the woman to whom advertisements were addressed, while Lady Audley represents the woman of advertisements.[5]

LADY AUDLEY

Braddon presents Lady Audley in two fundamentally different ways: as a childlike beauty and as a powerful, self-interested woman. Both figures were popular tropes within the literature of the day. And, like any good woman, Lucy cultivates her childlikeness. In the first extended description of her, the narrator relays:

> The very childishness had a charm which few could resist. The innocence and candor of an infant beamed in Lady Audley's fair face, and shone out of her large and liquid blue eyes. The rosy lips, the delicate nose, the profusion of fair ringlets, all contributed to preserve to her beauty the character of extreme youth and freshness. She owed to twenty years of age, but it was hard to believe her more than seventeen. Her fragile figure, which she loved to dress in heavy velvets, and stiff, rustling silks, till she looked like a child tricked out for a masquerade, was as girlish as if she had just left the nursery. (35)[6]

Lady Audley's beauty is centered in her infantilism and girlishness. If George Talboys, Sir Michael Audley, and Robert Audley find this woman attractive, Alicia Audley does not: to her cousin, she says, "'I'm sorry to find you can only admire wax dolls'" (37) and later, to her father: "'You think her sensitive because she has soft little white hands, and big blue eyes with long lashes, and all manner of affected, fantastical ways, which you stupid men call fascinating'" (69). The real lady—who sports the blood of the Audleys in her veins—recognizes an imposter (a woman tricked out for a masquerade) when she sees one.[7] And a minor character admits grudgingly that although Lady Audley is "'very, very pretty,'" she is "'rather a childish beauty though'" (172). Lady Audley's childlike attributes are much less intriguing to the female characters than to the male ones. Yet at least two male readers of the novel were troubled by the substitution of "characteristics for character" and Lady Audley's status as "non-entity, without a heart, a soul, a reason" (Hughes 26). The very production of Lady Audley's affect manifested the Victorian concern with representation. Affect, Braddon shows, can be learned; interiority is another issue. But affect, of course, is the lesson that Braddon can teach her readers. Lucy's child-wife persona is a performance and the fact that it is an impersonation is crucial to the subversive message of the book. For all women can dress up in heavy velvets or marry into wealthy families in order to become the next lady of a household. Childlikeness is only one of the attributes that can be learned.

Braddon alternatively represents Lady Audley as "a beautiful fiend" in the portrait that discloses her villainous inclinations:

> No one but a pre-Raphaelite would have so exaggerated every attribute of that delicate face as to give a lurid brightness to the blonde complexion, and a strange, sinister light to the deep blue eyes. No one but a pre-Raphaelite could have given to that pretty pouting mouth the hard and almost wicked look it had in the portrait. (47)

Kate Flint regards Braddon as drawing "on the moral equivocation of art critics commenting on the unorthodox attractions of Pre-Raphaelite female models" (283). Although Braddon might simply be flaunting her familiarity with the contemporary art scene and her opinion of art critics, I recognize the portrait's debt to the Pre-Raphaelites as a mark of Lucy's erotic power. For unlike many contemporary critics, I read Lucy as an erotic figure, particularly because of her hair, which recalls Milton's Eve. Lady Audley's characteristic feature is her "shower of curls . . . . the most wonderful . . . in the world—soft and feathery, always floating away from her face, and making a pale halo around her head when the sunlight shone through them" (6). If Lucy Audley is an angel, she is a sensuous one, and her power over the men of Audley Court is erotic, as the painter has recognized. Such power, Bowlby and Loeb claim, is another aspect of Victorian consumer discourse. Lady Audley is like the women of advertisements who urge consumers "to procure . . . luxurious benefits and purchase sexually attractive images for themselves" (Bowlby 11). Rather than being the secret underside of domesticity, this representation of femininity was publicly marketed, as contemporary advertisements "presented an aggrandized portrait of feminine power that was . . . aggressive and sexual" (Loeb 10–11). Helen Maldon is aware of the power of "her lovely face, her bewitching manner, her arch smile, her low, musical laugh" (203). And Lady Audley is quite conscious of her self-image, as well. Whether she trips around the house playfully wearing clothes that imply a game of dress-up or majestically dons "her most gorgeous silk, a voluminous robe of silvery, shimmering blue, that made her look as if she had been arrayed in moonbeams" (22), Lucy is involved in a project of self-fashioning. Thus, although the men of Audley Court see Lucy as recovering "her beauty and joyousness in the morning sunshine" (51), Phoebe, Lucy, and the female reader know she is a craftswoman constructing an elaborate identity—a living, breathing, display-window doll.

And as Lady Audley's physique is consistent with two of the bodies marketed by the press, so does her behavior follow cultural guidelines. She acts both the angel in the house and the self-indulgent consumer of advertisements. Before Lucy Graham marries Sir Richard Audley to become his Lady, she is a loved and respected member of the community who visits the poor, attends church "three times every Sunday," and teaches her young charges the finer arts of watercolor and piano, in addition to academic subjects (6). Graham's active involvement in and acceptance by the community bode well for her tenure at Audley Court, perhaps with the exception that the Lady is a trifle too intimate with the servants.[8] Still, while at the Court, Lady Audley is the perfect mistress with the house firmly under her control (including that troublesome first husband whom she at least attempted to tidy up nicely). The domestic angel beautifies the house, "sitting down to the piano to trill out a ballad or the first page of an Italian bravura, or running with rapid fingers through a brilliant waltz—now hovering about a stand of hot-house flowers, doing amateur gardening with a pair of fairy-like, silver-mounted embroidery scissors" (52). Lady Audley is an active decorative object, a mechanical doll who knows how to act appropriately in any given scene. Her movements are impeccable. The angel in the house, Braddon shows her readers, is an elaborate theatrical performance—and a performance that men might not necessarily understand. As Lucy prepares tea—that activity that sets women to their best advantage—Braddon comments on the rituals of daily life, their significance, and their possible cover-ups: this

> most feminine and most domestic of all occupations imparts a magic harmony to her every movement, a witchery to her every glance. The floating mists from the boiling liquid in which she infuses the soothing herbs; whose secrets are known to her alone, envelope her in a cloud of scented vapour, through which she seems a social fairy, weaving potent spells with Gunpowder and Bohea. (146)

When performing idealized domestic tasks, women seem supernatural creatures, more powerful than mere mortals. Whether Lady Audley acts the angel or the fairy, her male audience views her as greater than human. Such power, Braddon shows, is to be cultivated and not to be underestimated.

Certainly Lady Audley's most important activity, then, is her self-production—the decorating of her own body. Helen Maldon, no doubt delighted to be Lady Audley, savors self-indulgence, wallowing in the luxuriousness (if not decadence) of her position. Just so did the subjects of advertisements for soaps, body creams, and colognes. The personal nature of these products required that the subject "be pictured in isolation. Alone, perfumed and exquisitely costumed, the consumer, however responsible to cultural expectations and the pressures of social emulation, seemed hedonistic and self-absorbed" (Loeb 131). Lady Audley similarly basks in her sensuality, most often when she is alone, although sometimes with Phoebe. Exemplifying narcissism, Lucy consoles herself in her boudoir, "in that half-recumbent attitude, with elbows resting on one knee supported by her hand, the rich folds of drapery falling away in long, undulating lines from the exquisite outline of her figure, and the luxurious, rose-colored fire-light enveloping her in a soft haze" (194). Loeb emphasizes that such self-pampering is an essential component of certain subjects of nineteenth-century advertisements: "in recline or eyes veiled, she reveals not her weakness, but her potent temptation. . . . Superficially, at least, her thinly disguised sensuality suggests a hedonistic interest in gratification" (42). And although we never see Lady Audley in the bath, as we see the woman Loeb describes, we do see her in autoerotic activities, such as snuggling into bed alone, "curling up cozily under the eiderdown quilt and burying herself in soft wrappings of satin and fur" (39). Lady Audley's self-absorption is further manifested in her vanity. After her confession to Robert Audley, she stares into her cheval glass, thinking, "whatever they did to her, they must leave her her beauty" (245)—completely blind to the possibility that she will be locked up and that her beauty will no longer serve her. Both display window doll and ideal consumer, her punishment is that she will no longer be seen and that she will no longer be able to shop. Lady Audley's narcissism is inextricably linked to her consumerism. She is vain about her sexual power and aware of the objects she must obtain to maintain it. But by spending a little extra time on your body, Lucy shows, you will later have more time to pamper yourself. If, as Loeb suggests, "the advertiser acknowledged the potent force of feminine sexuality and the desire of women for sensual pleasures" (62), so, clearly, did Braddon. Braddon markets self-indulgence.

AUDLEY COURT

The writer markets more tangible items as well. The conspicuous consumption at Audley Court is a verbal picture of the fantasies of mid-century advertisements. Home products advertised for sale ranged from linoleum underfoot to light fixtures overhead and included everything in between: sofas, pillows, portraits, china, silver, curtains, drapes, knickknacks. All these items can be found within the pages of *Lady Audley's Secret*. If gentility is expressed exclusively in material terms, Sir Michael and Lady Audley have acquired it. Audley Court is full of signs of domestic bliss: Lady Audley plays the piano throughout the novel,[9] purebred dogs run through the mansion, Sir Michael recovers in a luxurious bedchamber, clocks tick, music stools twirl, fires burn, illuminating statues, mirrors reflect and multiply, Wedgewood ornaments adorn chimneypieces, cigars and meerschaum pipes smoke, tea brews, portraits amuse, telegrams arrive. Although some items are more valuable as cultural capital than others, it is the cornucopia of items that I want to emphasize. The excessiveness of the number of things in Audley Court draws our attention to Braddon's catalog. Not only does the writer prove herself to be knowledgeable about the artifacts of gentility, but she lets the reader know what she must buy to affect that gentility. Braddon leaves her props in clear sight of the audience. Furthermore, with the "circumstantial evidence" that Robert Audley finds, Braddon shows her readers just how much they must rid themselves of in order to jump classes. Class-shifting necessitates tracks-covering. Helen Maldon has not effectively buried her past.

Those remnants of her former life, the baby bootie and hair hidden in "a secret drawer, lined with purple" in "the massive walnut-wood and brass inlaid casket in her boudoir," are all too tangible reminders of Lady Audley's origins and of her interiority. Helen does not don the mask perfectly. The build-ups toward both invasions of Lady Audley's boudoir (the first by Luke and Phoebe Marks, the second by Robert Audley and George Talboys) are clearly presented as metaphorical rapes that function as violations of Lady Audley's identity. For at the heart of the secret drawer in the woman's boudoir is the key to who she is, and the secret of the title. Braddon surrounds the drawer with other significant secrets as well. The reader gets to the dressing room through a circuitous route including an octagonal outer chamber, a second passage way, and a hidden "fairy-like boudoir" (20). Luke Marks is "bewildered by the splendor of the room" (20) and George Talboys is similarly displaced by the femininity of the apartments where

> the whole of her glittering toilette apparatus lay about on the marble dressing-table. The atmosphere of the room was almost oppressive for the rich odors of perfumes in bottles whose gold stoppers had not been replaced. A bunch of hot-house flowers was withering upon a tiny writing-table. Two or three handsome dresses lay in a heap upon the ground, and the open doors of a wardrobe revealed the treasures within. Jewelry, ivory-backed hair-brushes, and exquisite china were scattered here and there about the apartment. (46)

The men have entered a women's place. With their wonder "at how out of place [they] seemed among all these womanly luxuries" (46), Braddon addresses the position of the male reader and those female readers not privy to scenes of such luxury. These voyeuristic looks into a woman's secret chambers titillate. Paradoxically, the increased market for personal belongings necessarily led to their increased visibility in shop windows and advertisements; they become public secrets. Lady Audley's secret rooms are similarly set up to be shown to valued guests and readers.

TELLING SECRETS

Yet the women's rooms of Audley Court are also its secret rooms because it is in these rooms where Lady Audley takes Phoebe (and the reader) into her confidence, proclaiming to her maid: "'You *are* like me. . . . Why, with a bottle of hair-dye, such as we see advertized in the papers, and a pot of rouge, you'd be as good-looking as I, any day, Phoebe'" (39). Anyone can become Lady Audley. The actress must simply apply her makeup correctly and perform impeccably. Advertisements, conduct books, and that new, dangerous literary form that combines both methodologies to produce a stunning concoction—the sensation novel—will show one how. Mary Elizabeth Braddon, through Lady Audley nee Helen Maldon, already has. The reader need only be open to Helen Maldon's lesson to learn from her example. Throughout *Lady Audley's Secret*, Braddon drops hints about Helen's ambitious social-climbing desires. Helen's drive, coupled with the lessons she has learned about manners and beauty, has led her to become Lady Audley. If other poor women wish to get ahead, they must adopt her strategy, and not make her mistakes. Lucy's revelation to Phoebe Marks articulates Braddon's secret: the novel includes the proper recipe—instructions and ingredients—needed to become the next Lady Audley.

The most important ingredient is the desire and the drive to marry wealth and respectability. As Helen Maldon, Lucy Graham, and Lady Audley, the heroine has always been honest about her social-climbing aspirations. To her first husband, she explains: "'Girls always want to marry dragoons; and tradespeople always want to serve dragoons; and hotel-keepers to entertain dragoons. . . . Who could have ever expected that a dragoon would drink sixpenny ale, smoke bird's-eye tobacco, and let his wife wear a shabby bonnet?'" (120). Marriage is an economic contract. Years later she is just as materialistic and just as forthright about it, when upon Sir Michael's proposal to her, she stammers compulsively,

> Remember what my life has been; only remember that! From my very babyhood I have never seen anything but poverty. . . . Poverty—poverty, trials, vexations, humiliations, deprivations. *You* cannot tell; you, who are

among those for whom life is so smooth and easy, you can never guess what
is endured by such as we. Do not ask too much of me, then. I *cannot* be
disinterested; I cannot be blind to the advantages of such an alliance. I
cannot, I cannot! (8)

The consummate actress never lies about her motivations. Sir Michael
eventually settles for the language of a business deal for his proposal, "'Is
it a bargain, Lucy?'" (8), and she accepts. The woman's desire for the
good life has led her to it. She has learned "that which in some indefinite
manner or other every school-girl learns sooner or later— . . . that [her]
ultimate fate in life depended upon [her] marriage" (281). Helen Maldon's covetousness has paid off. The only way for an ambitious young
woman to obtain wealth (since gold-mining in Australia is out of the
question) is through marriage.

But motivation without proper knowledge is useless. Throughout the
text Braddon's allusions to products of quality act as advertisements for
good taste. The shrine of Lady Audley's boudoir shows readers the proper
objects to desire, the items one must possess in order to affect gentility:

> Drinking-cups of gold and ivory, chiseled by Benvenuto Cellini; cabinets of
> buhl and porcelain, bearing the cipher of Austrain [sic] Marie-Antoinette,
> amid devices of rosebuds and true-lovers' knots, birds and butterflies,
> cupidons and shepherdesses, goddesses, courtiers, cottagers, and milk-
> maids; statuettes of Parian marble and biscuit china; gilded baskets of
> hothouse flowers; fantastical caskets of Indian filigree-work; fragile tea-cups
> of turquoise china, adorned by medallion miniatures of Louis the Great
> and Louis the well-beloved, Louise de la Valliere, Athenais de Montespan,
> and Marie Jeanne Gomard de Vaubernier. (195)

Part of ladydom is appreciating the proper things, particularly the proper
ornaments. Real taste can be learned and collected. At the same time,
Braddon also contrasts the decor of Audley Court with that of less affluent
homes. As she demonstrates good taste to the reader, she also warns of
bad taste. The home of Mrs. Vincent, Lucy's first employer, possesses "an
aspect of genteel desolation and tawdry misery not easily to be paralleled
in wretchedness by any other phase which poverty can assume" (153). The
chipped, broken, oversized piano that dominates the parlor is an aesthetic faux pas. Instead of outfitting her home in a style appropriate to her
means, Mrs. Vincent has proven herself to be a fallen member of the
upper class—a mistake as tasteless as cheap copies of expensive objects.
Phoebe Marks's home is another warning to readers of poor executions.
To compensate for the shabby furniture, Phoebe hung cheap chintz
"from the tent-bedstead; festooned drapery of the same material shrouded

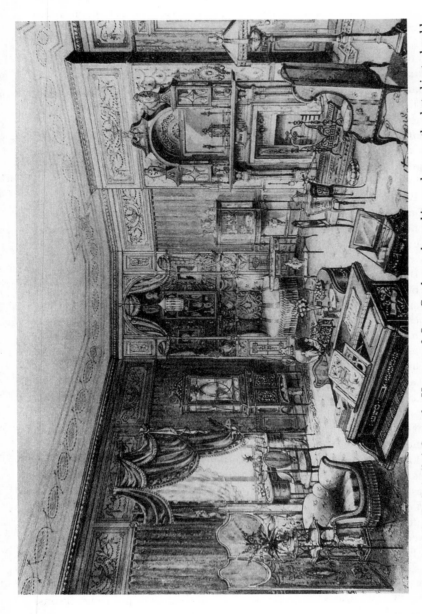

Figure 4.1 Like *Lady Audley's Secret*, the Hampton & Sons Catalogue showed its readers exactly what objects should be displayed in ladies' boudoirs. *The Victorian Catalogue of Household Furnishing.* (Studio Editions, Random House.)

the narrow window shutting out the light of day, and affording a pleasant harbor for tribes of flies and predatory bands of spiders" (212). The former maid's emulation of her mistress's bedroom is a macabre failure. But Phoebe's attempt indicates that she has learned from Lady Audley—and that she is a quick learner, if not initially as successful as her mistress is.

Phoebe and Helen are similar, however, and Braddon underscores their similarities. Although the two women don't possess a striking physical likeness, "there were certain dim and shadowy lights in which, meeting Phoebe Marks gliding under the shrouded avenues in the garden, you might have easily mistaken her for my lady" (71). These dim lights harbor the most danger, making it impossible to tell whom one is addressing. And Phoebe and Helen's similarity is not even so much physical as temperamental. Phoebe recognizes their likeness early on, asking her roughneck fiancé, "'What was she but a servant like me? Taking wages and working for them as hard, or harder, than I did?'" (18). But in addition to working hard for goals they want, both women also act craftily, unethically to further their own materialistic desires through bigamy or blackmail. Lady Audley recognizes the "sympathies between her and this girl, who was like herself, inwardly as well as outwardly—like herself, selfish, and cold, and cruel, eager for her own advancement, and greedy of opulence and elegance; angry with the lot that had been cast her, and weary of dull dependence" (198). Through Helen Maldon and Phoebe Marks, Braddon shows us that women who plan can get ahead. A lady may actually be a lady's maid in disguise. For a lady's maid (like an avid magazine reader) knows a lady's secrets:

> That well-bred attendant knows . . . when the ivory complexion is bought and paid for—when the pearly teeth are foreign substances fashioned by the dentist—when the glossy plaits are the relics of the dead, rather than the property of the living; and she knows other and more sacred secrets than these; she knows when the sweet smile is more false than Madame Levison's enamel, and far less enduring—when the words that issue from between gates of borrowed pearl are more disguised and painted than the lips which help to shape them. (221)

A lady's maid knows that being a lady is a performance. Indeed she helps to construct it. Like advertisements, Braddon's novel moves the secrets of the boudoir into the public eye. Anthea Trodd reads the secret of the title as "the fact that [Lady Audley] is not a lady at all, but really rather common like Phoebe" (64). I suggest the secret is the strategy—knowledge and know-how—included in the novel about the means to becoming that lady. If Helen Maldon has become Lady Audley, Phoebe Marks is next in line.

"Mamma, shall I have beautiful long hair like you when I grow up?"
"Certainly, my dear, if you use **'Edward's Harlene'**."

Figure 4.2 Edward's Harlene Hair Tonic delivers the same message that Mary Elizabeth Braddon does: Showers of golden curls sometimes need help (*Illustrated London News*, 1896. From the collection of the University of Georgia Library.)

Helen Maldon, the exemplary gold digger, is an enterprising, poor, young woman who invades two wealthy homes and families. She is nearly successful in her attack (and perhaps her son's success indicates that a de-stratification between the upper and lower classes is inevitable). I propose that *Lady Audley's Secret* functions the same way conduct books do, but toward a different end: You, too, can become Lady Audley. Let me show you how.

The insidious invasion of the upper-class sphere by poor women in *Lady Audley's Secret* parallels the invasion of serious literature by the sensation novel. Indeed, at least one contemporary critic of Braddon's appears to have collapsed himself with the sleuth, Robert Audley, and the novelist with her heroine: "[Braddon] has bewitched so many persons that those who have the misfortune to be blind to her charms have had small chance of being listened to when pronouncing an adverse judgment" (quoted in Cvetkovich 15–16). Literary history has borne his assessment out. For although Helen Maldon was not ultimately successful, the success of *Lady Audley's Secret* was phenomenal, demanding eight editions in the first three months, numerous theatrical adaptations, a film, a musical, and sales of more than one million copies. In a novel as rooted in mass culture as *Lady Audley's Secret* is, it seems appropriate that it would subsequently play a defining role in mass culture. If Lady Audley is dead, her secret endures.[10]

NOTES

Many thanks to Roxanne Eberle, Tricia Lootens, Anne Williams, and Mark Boren for their gracious assistance with and pointed criticism on various drafts of this project.

1. *Lady Audley's Secret* abounds with brand names as well. For example, when Phoebe attempts to blackmail Lady Audley, her mistress responds, "'What can I do to appease you? Shall I sell my Marie Antoinette cabinet or my pompadour china, Leroy's and Benson's ormolu clocks, or my Gobelin tapestried chairs and ottomans? How shall I satisfy you next?'" Phoebe emits a piteous cry, so clearly Lucy is suggesting a huge monetary sacrifice. And Braddon is suggesting to her readers a list of objects that signify gentility.

2. Judith Rowbothan writes that the silver fork novels addressed to the social elite, "were also closely read by 'manufacturers who made fortunes moving to the capital from the industrial north' and by City bankers and merchants already on the fringes of that elite. For aspiring social entrepreneurs the detailed realms of these books made them 'compulsive reading with their intimate portrayal of the world they hoped to enter'; initially through the marriage of a suitable daughter" (sic 14).

3. Certainly there were many sensation-style novels before the publication of *Lady Audley's Secret*. According to Hughes, two direct antecedents include *Eugene Aram* (1832) by Edward Bulwer-Lytton and *Jane Eyre* (1847) by Charlotte Brontë (8). But the popularity of *Lady Audley's Secret* was unprecedented.

4. Ellen Miller Casey follows Richard Altick in claiming that Braddon is one of those minor novelists "who can be examined 'with profit to our understanding both of the nature of popular literature itself and of the frustrations and conflicts that were at work in the ordinary Victorian's subconscious' " (72). Although one can take issue with Casey's reading of Braddon as "a minor novelist," I support her position of the significance of popular literature.

5. I generally refer to Helen Maldon Talboys or Lucy Graham Audley or Mrs. Taylor as Lucy or Lady Audley. When I refer to the character as Helen Maldon, I'm referring to her premarried life. I've chosen to call the woman Lucy or Lady Audley because these are the names she has chosen for herself. (Her other representation of herself as Lucy Graham is not as interesting to me, although it is important if we see her as participating in the popular *Jane Eyre*/governess myth about the poor, young, educated woman who marries the master of the house).

6. Of course the narrator also emphasizes the performative aspect of Lady Audley. She is not a one-dimensional character, but a character actress.

7. The position of "Lady Audley" is, however, one of marriage anyway. That is, since Robert Audley is the heir apparent to Audley Court, the next Lady Audley will be another woman who marries into the family (presumably Clara Talboys). Braddon suggests that there is no authentic Lady Audley then—that any woman can substitute for another.

8. Lucy's ease with Phoebe is another indication of her posturing and the difference between one born into society and one who pushes her way into it. When Alicia comes into her stepmother's "dressing-room to bid her good-night, and found the maid and mistress laughing aloud over one of the day's adventures, Alicia, who was never familiar with her servants, withdrew in disgust at my lady's frivolity" (39). Since Braddon does not treat Alicia very kindly, the author's sympathies may lie with Lucy.

9. Yet, Clara Talboys's instrument of choice, the organ, is "a symbol of Christian virtue and wholesome entertainment as well as grand cathedral celebrations" (Loeb 90).

10. We see similar, albeit perhaps more innocuous stories, in such recent productions as *My Fair Lady* and *Pretty Woman*. Their representations of the permeability of the wealthy class connects them to *Lady Audley's Secret*.

WORKS CITED

Altick, Richard D. *Deadly Encounters: Two Victorian Sensations*. Philadelphia: U of Pennsylvania P, 1986.

———. *The Presence of the Present: Topics of the Day in the Victorian Novel.* Columbus: Ohio State UP, 1991.

Ballaster, Ros, Margaret Beetham, Elizabeth Frazer, and Sandra Hebron. *Women's Worlds: Ideology, Femininity, and the Woman's Magazine.* Hong Kong: Macmillan Education Ltd., 1991.

Bowlby, Rachel. *Just Looking: Consumer Culture in Dreiser, Gissing, and Zola.* New York: Methuen, 1985.

Braddon, Mary Elizabeth. *Lady Audley's Secret.* Intro. Norman Donaldson. New York: Dover, 1974.

Briggs, Asa. *Victorian Things.* Chicago: U of Chicago P, 1988.

Casey, Ellen Miller. "'Other People's Prudery': Mary Elizabeth Braddon." In *Sexuality and Victorian Literature.* Ed. Don Richard Cox. Knoxville: U of Tennessee P, 1984. 72–82.

Cvetkovich, Ann. *Mixed Feelings: Feminism, Mass Culture, and Victorian Sensationalism.* New Brunswick, N.J.: Rutgers UP, 1992.

Flint, Kate. *The Woman Reader, 1837–1918.* Oxford: Clarendon P, 1993.

Hughes, Winifred. *The Maniac in the Cellar: Sensation Novels of the 1860s.* Princeton, N.J.: Princeton UP, 1980.

James, Henry. *Notes and Reviews.* Cambridge, Mass.: Dunston, 1921.

Loeb, Lori Anne. *Consuming Angels: Advertising and Victorian Women.* New York: Oxford UP, 1994.

Matus, Jill L. "Disclosure as 'Cover-Up': The Discourse of Madness in *Lady Audley's Secret.*" *University of Toronto Quarterly* 62.3 (Spring 1993): 334–55.

Mitch, David F. *The Rise of Popular Literacy in Victorian England: The Influence of Private Choice and Public Policy.* Philadelphia: U of Pennsylvania P, 1992.

Morse, David. *High Victorian Culture.* New York: New York UP, 1993.

Rowbothan, Judith. *Good Girls Make Good Wives: Guidance for Girls in Victorian Fiction.* Oxford: Basil Blackwell, 1989.

Trodd, Anthea. *Domestic Crime in the Victorian Novel.* New York: St. Martin's, 1989.

Trollope, Anthony. *Four Lectures.* Ed. Morris L. Parrish. London: Constable & Co., 1938.

FIVE

"An idle handle that was never turned, and a lazy rope so rotten": The Decay of the Country Estate in *Lady Audley's Secret*

Aeron Haynie

> [Audley Court was] a place that strangers fell into raptures
> with; feeling a yearning with it to have done with life . . . a
> spot in which Peace seemed to have taken her abode. . . . [It
> contained] the stagnant well . . . with an idle handle that was
> never turned, and a lazy rope so rotten that the bucket had
> broken away from it, and had fallen into the water.
> —M. E. Braddon, Lady Audley's Secret

Mary Elizabeth Braddon's novel *Lady Audley's Secret* (1862), follows the formula of the "sensation novel," presenting the reader with an elaborate plot of bigamy, attempted murder, and romance. In this "sensation novel," a dilettantish young barrister, Robert Audley, discovers that his ravishing young aunt, Lucy Audley, has lied about her past and is hiding a former marriage, a child, and the attempted murder of his missing friend, her first husband, George Talboys. The bulk of the novel charts Robert Audley's dawning suspicions of his aunt and his accumulation of evidence against Lady Audley (all of which results in her confinement in a Belgian *maison de santé*). While the overt focus of the novel is the seemingly angelic "Lady Audley," the book begins and ends with descriptions of Audley Court, the contested site of power in the novel and the symbol of the health and integrity of the Audley family. One of the central anxieties in the novel is voiced by Robert Audley when he asks, "'Would other people live in the old house, and sit under the low oak ceilings in the homely familiar rooms?'" (Braddon 183). Braddon's novel illustrates mid-Victorian concerns over the sanctity of the aristocratic country estate, the fear that it could be metaphorically invaded and contaminated by the middle class. I wish to focus on the representation of the landscape of Audley Court, and the ways that the novel negotiates issues of class within its representation of the "picturesque" landscape.

Coming after the heyday of the picturesque movement, *Lady Audley's Secret* employs easily recognizable elements of the genre and, much like picturesque guidebooks, offers its middle-class readers a glimpse into the life of the country estate. Yet Braddon's novel also presents a veiled critique of the system of the country estate. *Lady Audley's Secret* illustrates the confrontation between the landed gentry and the frightening specter of the "mobile poor" and "wandering strangers" (Helsinger 107) and envisions a tragic ending for both.

The threat to the Audley estate comes from Lucy Graham/Helen Maldon, a member of this "wandering poor" who refashions herself with a false genteel identity. After her first husband deserts her (to seek his fortune in the Australian gold mines) Helen Maldon fakes her own death, abandons her son, creates a new identity as Lucy Graham, a refined governess, and marries the wealthy widower, Lord Audley. The plot of the novel traces Robert Audley uncovering Lady Audley as an imposter, and exposing her claims to the Audley estate as illegitimate.

We discover that Lady Audley's bloody and bigamous secret is concealed within the tranquil gardens of Audley court; thus, the novel subverts the usual formula of Victorian crime novels, which place violence and lawlessness within an urban setting. Yet Lady Audley's "crime"—the attempted murder of her first husband, George Talboys—overshadows her true crime: her fraudulent social identity and artificial femininity. Lady Audley/ Lucy Graham/Helen Maldon is a usurper who invades and appropriates Audley Court because she is able to reproduce, on her own body, the appearance of upper-class femininity and beauty. Lady Audley's irresistible femininity is based on a hyperconsciousness of her lack of status : her charm is in her self-conscious role as dependent child. On one hand, Lady Audley 's effect on others is described as a result of an organic phenomenon, her beauty; yet Lady Audley's beauty—like her alleged madness—is hereditary and is marked as both genuine and contrived, organic yet constructed. She describes her marriage to Lord Audley as a calculated campaign to improve her social status by manipulating her beauty: "[Lord Audley] made me an offer, the acceptance of which would lift me at once into the sphere to which my ambition had pointed ever since I was a school-girl, and heard for the first time that I was pretty" (Braddon 299). Lady Audley herself suggests that both her childlike beauty and her social identity are self-constructed when she tells her maid, Phoebe, "Why, with a bottle of hair dye, such as we see advertised in the papers, and a pot of rouge, you'd be as good-looking as I any day" (49).

The tension of the novel—does Lady Audley belong in Audley Court?—mirrors the situation of the middle-class reader who reads in order to enter into the country estate. Braddon's novel illustrates the complicated relationship between the middle-class reading public and the upper-class "taste" that they wanted to see represented. As Linda Brodkey notes in her autobiographical essay, readers are fascinated by the novel's representation of the interiors of homes; through these textual renderings, readers can gain access to the complicated system of taste (Brodkey 41). By reading *Lady Audley's Secret* middle-class readers gain access to the myriad details about the interior and external grounds of the Audley estate. The interior of the estate, particularly Lady Audley's boudoir, is described from the point of view of intruders (Luke Marks, Robert Audley, and George Talboys) and the reader becomes a voyeur. Like Luke Marks, the reader can creep into Lady Audley's boudoir and fondle her clothes and jewels.

The falseness of Lady Audley's beauty, social status, and identity can be read as implicating the aesthetic value of the estate itself; just as the estate constructs Lady Audley's social class, so too is the value of the estate linked to the genteel femininity of its mistress, Lady Audley. However, the character of Lady Audley serves a dual function: on the one hand, she symbolizes the aesthetic values of the landed gentry, yet on the other hand she is represented as an outside invader, a contamination: "'I [Robert Audley] will go straight to the arch-conspirator, and will tear away the beautiful veil under which she hides her wickedness . . . and banish her forever from *the house which her presence has polluted*" (Braddon 217, emphasis mine). Yet despite the novel's villainizing of Lady Audley, the estate itself is described as somehow culpable in its own demise.

On page one of the novel Audley Court is described as unwelcoming and impregnable: "the cattle looked inquisitively at you as you passed, wondering, perhaps, what you wanted; for there was no thoroughfare, and unless you were going to the Court, you could have no business there" (1). As the novel progresses, however, the sanctity of Audley Court has been so "polluted" by the presence of an alleged murderess and a lower-class con artist—Helen Maldon—that at the conclusion of the novel, Audley Court has become a local tourist attraction: "The house is often shown to inquisitive visitors, though the owner is not informed of that fact" (376). By the conclusion of the novel the Audleys are scattered and seem to have relinquished their rights to the estate. Although the Audley family is rescued from the threat of Lady Audley, there exists a prevailing tone of nostalgia and loss. After Lady Audley has been revealed as an imposter and expurgated, Lord Audley leaves for an extended tour of the continent and the manor is deserted: "Audley Court is shut up, and a grim old housekeeper reigns paramount in the mansion" (Braddon 376). Even though Lady Audley has been defeated, the briefly described conventional romantic resolution at the novel's end does not dispel the sense of loss.

My reading of the novel proposes that Lady Audley's success in penetrating the estate results from a weakness in the Audley family and their estate: a lack of productivity. The estate is described as "neglected," "stagnant" and in "disuse." Robert Audley—the heir apparent of the estate until his uncle remarried—is presented as an indolent bachelor, engaged in the feminine pursuits of reading novels. Even Robert's cousin, Alicia, is described as an inefficient, comical housekeeper. This lack of productivity—and the artificial naturalness of the Audley estate—designates their gentility and places them within the tradition of the "picturesque" aesthetic movement.

THE PICTURESQUE AESTHETIC

The "Picturesque" was an aesthetic movement and a category in painting, literature, and landscaping in the late eighteenth and early nineteenth centuries. Despite the wealth of current and contemporary debates over the picturesque, there remains no fixed definition, possibly because eighteenth-century aestheticists presented a rather circular argument in which a landscape should be judged by how well it conformed to certain paintings (particularly the Continental landscape paintings by Nicolas Poussin, Savator Rosa, and Claude Lorraine) and painting should be praised for representing "nature." Picturesque theorists and practitioners, such as Uvedale Price and R. P. Knight, urged fellow landowners to "improve" their estates, eschew the formal, symmetrical French gardening styles, and the fashionable smoothness and conformity of "Capability" Brown, and instead use "Nature [as] . . . the great model of imitation" (Price 275). They defined "nature" as a "wild," "irregular" landscape, perhaps overgrown, and the picturesque scene included gnarled trees, old mills, worn-out cart horses, ruins, gypsies, beggars, banditti, and rustic hovels. Paradoxically, this "natural," landscape was often manipulated into a pleasingly "wild" prospect or view from which the landowner could survey his property. Thus, nobility is linked with the possession of a "natural" view, one that appears rambling and decayed, and one that shows the passage of time.[1] Looking at a picturesque scene was not a passive activity; the artist or viewer could not just gaze upon a preexisting scene, he must position himself so as to achieve the best possible view. While no new objects should be added to the scene, viewers were advised to move or adjust objects in order to create a "natural" look. Therefore, nature was not necessarily what one sees before one in the countryside, but what constitutes a "picturesque" scene. In one instance those desiring a picturesque prospect were advised to take a mallet to a piece of Palladian architecture in order to create the desired appearance of ruins (Hussey 195).

The picturesque emphasis on ruins privileges the old, and valorizes the landscape mellowed by time: "what time only and a thousand lucky accidents can mature" (Price 68). Equating old with "natural" can be read as a reaction on the part of the landed gentry to the nouveau riche and to the gentry who abandoned their estates to seek commercial wealth in the expanding cities. However, some of the gentry were themselves involved in improving the agricultural yield of their estates though enclosures and therefore held an ambivalent attitude toward the pastoral, pre-enclosed landscape: at the same time as they were increasing the productivity of their estates, the picturesque style of landscaping depended upon the appearance of large pre-improved vistas. Ironically, picturesque views were most popular during the time of the Enclosure Acts (1750–1815) which privatized common lands and transformed open vistas into improved agricultural fields. The Enclosure Acts also created a mass of dispossessed rural workers, and these "mobile poor" were a source of anxiety for the landed gentry (Helsinger 107).

The theories of the picturesque developed by landowners Price and Knight valorized the taste of the landed gentry since only they were "disinterested" enough and had a knowledge of the classic paintings from their Grand Tours of Europe. However, the travel guide books of William Gilpin (1724–1804) packaged picturesque views of Wales, Scotland, and the Lake District and sold them to the emerging middle-class tourists.[2]

> The picturesque became a popular mode of consumption, a leisure activity in which the middle classes were able, by enjoying their native land as a series of rustic scenes at little financial or social cost, to show that they too could afford and enjoy the disinterested view which had been a criteria for the exercise of cultural and political power by the landed class. (Fulford 117)

Gilpin's guidebooks, which became popular in the 1770s, offered a middle-class tourist very prescriptive, structured directions about how best to appreciate popular sites, such as the Lake District. These guidebooks contained sketches of picturesque views, showing the traveler what to look at and exactly where to position himself: "Britain became . . . a spectacle to be consumed. . . . With Gilpin in hand, one could be sure not only that one was seeing the proper spot from the proper vantage point but also that one was having the proper aesthetic response" (Bermingham, "The Picturesque" 86). This commodification of the landscape became so enforced that in Thomas West's Guide to the Lakes the reader is encouraged to purchase a "Claude Lorraine glass," a portable mirror that would literally frame the view of the landscape, turning it into a continental painting (Buzzard 21).

Although these early middle-class tourists supported a growing market of travel guidebooks and paraphernalia, they were still a relatively small group when compared to the boom in the mid-nineteenth century after the expansion of the railway. Critics have explored the profound impact of the railroad on British conceptions of time, space, and regional identity. However, the expansion of the railway also opened up new landscapes to tourism and provided access to members of the lower middle class and working class. One man who capitalized on these new developments was Thomas Cook, founder of the first comprehensive tourist industry who coined the phrase, "traveling made easy." Cook's company started by providing day excursions for working-class families (he originally marketed his trips as part of the temperance movement) and by the 1870s his company ran trips to international locations. Suddenly, groups of working-class tourists, "day-trippers," materialized in what had been the exclusive landscapes of the gentry. Cook facilitated his tours; he selected appropriate sites, arranged all of the minute details and made landscapes accessible for middle- and lower-class tourists. In some sense, Cook helped to create what we now think of as the modern tourist.

The specter of middle- and working-class tourists and their ability to infiltrate the property of the landed gentry was a threatening notion. These new tourists threatened the singularity, rarity, and inaccessibility of the picturesque views that had formerly been the domain of the landed gentry.

In aestheticising the natural and often commonplace scenery of Britain,

> the Picturesque awakened a large segment of the population to the realization that aesthetic judgment was not the gift of the privileged few but could be learned by anyone and applied to just about anything. The Picturesque's most important and abiding effect was that it encouraged the

middle classes to aestheticise their lives. (Bermingham, "The Picturesque" 86–87)

The picturesque aesthetic, originated by the landed gentry as a defense of elitism and class snobbery, was popularized by guide books for middle-class tourists and eventually was adopted by middle-class readers of popular fiction as a way to designate upper-class taste.

Thus the picturesque aesthetic—which was a fashionable and elite aesthetic movement in the late seventeenth century—lingered on in a popularized form as a signifier of a defunct country estate ethos. Between 1730 and 1830 the picturesque aesthetic "became the universal mode of vision" (Ross 271). However, the Picturesque as an aesthetic category and marker of genteel taste, persisted well into the nineteenth century. I would argue that although the picturesque movement was no longer at its height of popularity in the 1860s, it continued to be used as a signifier of aristocratic taste and gentility. For example, the heroine of Elizabeth Gaskell's novel, *North and South* (1854–55), establishes her true gentility when she admires the "picturesqueness" of an unimproved rural scene (Gaskell 25).

THE REPRESENTATION OF THE PICTURESQUE AESTHETIC IN *LADY AUDLEY'S SECRET*

In her descriptions of Audley Court, Braddon uses coded language that would be recognized as designating the picturesque: the emphasis on old architecture; the pleasing prospect; the lack of productivity. In keeping with the rhetoric of the picturesque, the design of the landscape is agentless; it is the "handiwork of . . . Time" (Braddon 2) and thus encoded as natural. The language of the landscape implicitly links the "noble" with the irregularity and decay of the picturesque.

> A noble place . . . a house in which you incontinently lost yourself . . . a house that could never have been planned by any mortal architect, but must have been the handiwork of . . . Time, who—adding one room a year . . . a chimney coeval with the Plantagenets, . . . the Tudors . . . a Saxon wall . . . Norman arch . . . Queen Anne, . . . George the Third. (2)

In the above passages Audley Court is described as containing and encompassing different styles and periods of English history—old to "modern"—from "the Plantegenets" to the architectural style of George III. The Audley family is linked with the continuance of English history and represents a kind of permanence and continuity. However, this idyllic representation is troubled with hints of secrecy and stagnation:

> The hall door was squeezed into a corner of the turret . . . as if it was in hiding from dangerous visitors, and wished to keep itself a secret—a noble door for all that—old oak, studded with great square-headed iron nails, and so thick that the iron knocker struck upon it with a muffled sound. (2)

The description of the door suggests that the nobility of the Audleys is thick and impenetrable, massive, yet somehow afraid of invasion. The door symbolizes Lord Audley—"noble," "old," "square-headed," and "thick." The feared invasion at which the opening description hints is the marriage of Lord Audley to Lucy Graham/Helen Milton. Lady Audley—a self-fashioned adventurer—uses her self-consciously constructed femininity to breach the impregnable Audley family. However, the text implies that Lady Audley's success in penetrating the Audley estate results from a weakness in the Audley family, from the values inherent in the family estate.

The estate is in a fashionable state of disrepair, it contains a juxtaposition of architectural styles, and there has been no effort to spruce up the "ancient" buildings:

> A smooth lawn lay before you, . . . and an orchard surrounded by an ancient wall . . . overgrown with trailing ivy . . . the place had been a convent. . . . The house . . . was very old, and irregular and rambling. The windows were uneven; some small, some large; some with heavy stone mullions and rich stained glass; others with frail lattices that rattled in the breeze; others so modern that they might have been added only yesterday. Tall chimneys rose here and there behind the pointed gables, broken down . . . (2)

The image of the vine-covered wall suggests that the ivy has merged with the bricks and this lack of distinction between the natural and the man-made has "naturalized" the claims of the estate. The reader is addressed ("you") and encouraged to position herself as the surveyor of the view or the "prospect. The grounds contain a "prospect" (46), and "old well" (20), a "rustic wooden bridge" (227), and the "lazy horses and the lazy waggoner . . . a flock of sheep straggling about the road . . . [and] bricklayers just released from work" (69). It is significant that even the bricklayers—indisputably a sign of productive labor—are shown after they are finished with work and are semantically linked to the "lazy waggoner" and his horses. The novel continually effaces all signs of productivity on the Audley estate, yet there still remain brief hints that Audley Court was more than just ornamental. Lord Audley is mentioned as having a steward, "a stalwart countryman, half-agriculturalist, half-lawyer" who assumedly manages the business aspect of the estate (Braddon 239). Yet that is the only mention of any agricultural production on the estate, and it is certainly overwhelmed by the constant images of stagnancy.

Robert Audley, the erstwhile heir to the Audley estate, embodies the stagnancy of the nonproductive estate. Robert Audley "was a handsome, lazy, care-for-nothing fellow of about seven and twenty," who "exhausted himself with the exertion of smoking his German pipe and reading French novels," with a "listless, dawdling, indifferent, irresolute manner" (27). In fact, Robert is described as dozing by a stream while his friend, George Talboys, is allegedly murdered. He is described by his cousin, Alicia Audley, as "a lazy, selfish, sybarite, who cares for nothing in the world but his own ease and comfort" (238).

Although Robert Audley's laziness and indifference is partly a style that covers up his detective skills, I would argue the murder of George Talboys and its aftermath is the catalyst of his detective drive. In fact, Robert's disinterest in the Audley estate or in his own class status is illustrated in his disinterest in his cousin, Alicia. Robert's concern with the fate of the ancestral estate does not occur until halfway through the novel. Until this point, he has been stridently negligent of his ancestral obligations. In fact, as Robert Audley explains to Clara Talboys, the village of Audley is named after his ancestor:

> "I have a vague recollection of hearing a story of some ancestor who was called Audley of Audley in the reign of Edward the Fourth. The Tudor tomb inside of the altar rails belongs to one of the heroes of our race, but I have never taken the trouble to post myself in history of his achievements." (221)

This passages establishes the importance of the Audley family, while at the same time demonstrating Robert Audley's (disingenuous) disinterest in the value of his own social status and the source of his family's wealth.

The novel charts Robert's growing investment in his class identity and his refusal to allow Lady Audley—an imposter, a member of the "wandering poor"—to contaminate the sanctity of his family home. Robert's uneasiness, his growing suspicion that his Uncle's wife is not who she seems, expresses itself in a dream about Audley Court:

> In those troublesome dreams he saw Audley Court, rooted up from amidst the green pastures and the shady hedgerows of Essex, standing bare and unprotected upon that desolate northern shore, threatened by the rapid raising of a boisterous sea. (210)

The "boisterous sea" refers to the "shabby seaport" of Wildersea, where Helen Maldon lived. Robert connects the social mobility that such a seatown affords pretty young women with the destruction of his family's integrity. Curiously, he blames the town itself for helping these women snare unsuspecting young men: "He comes to some place of this kind and the universe is suddenly narrowed into about half-a-dozen acres" (212). This constricted focus is the opposite of the scope and range and implicit wisdom afforded by the picturesque prospect. However, the fine prospect and picturesque landscape does not protect Audley Court from the infiltration of Lady Audley.

CONCLUSION

The responsibility for the novel's later violence and the eventual abandonment of the estate is attributed not only to Lady Audley, but to the estate itself, and the ideology of the country estate. The "peaceful" appearance of the rural landscape represents the myth of the English history as unchanging/static. However, the novel deconstructs the image of the pastoral, showing it to be stagnant and yet pregnant with violence:

> No crime has ever been committed in the worst rookeries about Seven Dials that has not had its parallel amidst that sweet rustic calm which still, in spite of all, we look on with a tender, half-mournful yearning, and associate with peace. (Braddon 46)

Although Lady Audley's crime—her attempted murder of George Talboys—fails, her true crime is that she is the catalyst for the destruction of Audley Court. Even after he has successfully exorcized Lady Audley from his family's country estate, Robert Audley does not remain on the estate. Instead, he settles his new family in a "fairy cottage . . . a fantastical dwelling-place of rustic wood-work" where the ladies "eat strawberries and cream under a noble old mulberry tree upon the lawn" (Braddon 375). This "fantastical" scene suggests a retreat into an even more remote and unrealistic vision of rural, preindustrial England.

Braddon's novel illustrates the troubled relationship between the English country estate and the middle-class tourists and readers whose desire to penetrate the estate robs it of its value. The sensational shock of the novel is not the attempted murder or Lady Audley's bigamy, it is the fact that a poor but pretty girl from Wildersea could so easily become mistress of a country estate. The abandonment of Audley Court suggests an inability to imagine a peaceful merging of classes. The novel represents all middle- or lower-class characters' desires to possess Audley Court as violent and illegitimate. What does this imply about the texts' attitude toward its own readership? That would depend, in part, on whether one reads the tone of the final passage-which describes the abandoned Audley Court—as mournful or triumphant.

NOTES

1. For a fuller discussion of the Picturesque, see John Barrell, *The Idea of Landscape and the Sense of Place: 1730–1840* (Cambridge: Cambridge UP, 1972); Ann Bermingham, *Landscape and Ideology: The English Rustic Tradition, 1740–1860* (Berkeley: U of California, 1986); Christopher Hussey, The *Picturesque: Studies in a Point of View* (London: Frank Cass, 1967); Martin Price, "The Picturesque Moment," *From Sensibility to Romanticism,* ed. Hilles and Bloom (Oxford: Oxford UP, 1965); Stephanie Ross, "The Picturesque: An Eighteenth-Century Debate," *Journal of Aesthetics and Art Criticism* (1987).

2. See James Buzzard, *The Beaten Track,* for a full discussion of the emergence of British tourism.

WORKS CITED

Barrell, John. *The Idea of Landscape and the Sense of Place: 1730–1840.* Cambridge: Cambridge UP, 1972.

Bermingham, Ann. "The Picturesque and Ready-to-Wear-Femininity," *The Politics of the Picturesque.* Ed. Stephen Copley and Peter Garside. Cambridge: Cambridge UP, 1994.

———. *Landscape and Ideology: The English Rustic Tradition, 1740–1860.* Berkeley: U of California P, 1986.

Braddon, Mary Elizabeth. *Lady Audley's Secret.* New York: Virago Modern Classics, Penguin, 1987.

Brodkey, Linda. "Writing on the Bias," *Writing Permitted in Designated Areas Only.* Minneapolis, U of Minnesota P, 1996.

Buzzard, James *The Beaten Track: European Tourism, Literature, and the Ways to 'Culture', 1800–1918.* Oxford: Clarendon P, 1993.

Fulford, Tim. *Landscape, Liberty and Authority: Poetry, Criticism and Politics from Thomson to Wordsworth.* Cambridge: Cambridge UP, 1996.

Gaskell, Elizabeth. *North and South.* Oxford: Oxford UP, 1973.

Helsinger, Elizabeth. "Turner and the Representation of England." *Landscape and Power.* Ed. W. J. T. Mitchell. Chicago: U of Chicago P, 1994.

Hussey, Christopher. *The Picturesque: Studies in a Point of View.* London: Frank Cass, 1967.

Price, Martin. "The Picturesque Moment." *From Sensibility to Romanticism.* Ed. Hilles and Bloom. Oxford: Oxford UP, 1965.

Ross, Stephanie. "The Picturesque: An Eighteenth-Century Debate." *Journal of Aesthetics and Art Criticism* 46 (Winter 1987) : 271–79.

Shivelbusch, Wolfgang. *The Railway Journey.* Berkeley: U of California P, 1977.

PART II

Aurora Floyd

Six

The "Espaliered" Girl: Pruning the Docile Body in *Aurora Floyd*

Jeni Curtis

Woman? Doesn't exist. She borrows the disguise that she is
required to assume. She mimes the role imposed upon her. The
only thing really expected of her is that she *maintain, without
fail, the circulation of pretence by enveloping herself in femininity.*
—Luce Irigaray, "Des marchandises entre elles,"
New French Feminisms

Either the woman is passive; or she doesn't exist. What is left
is unthinkable, unthought of.
—Helene Cixous, "Sorties," *The Newly Born Woman*

The general opinion of men is supposed to be, that the
natural vocation of a woman is that of a wife and mother. . . .
What is now called the nature of women is an eminently
artificial thing—the result of forced repression in some
directions, unnatural stimulation in others.
—John Stuart Mill, *The Subjection of Women*

In her novels *Lady Audley's Secret* and *Aurora Floyd,* M. E. Braddon investigates certain constructions of femininity, the apparent oppositions of
angel and demon. In *Lady Audley's Secret* the two are figured in the one

character, Lucy Audley. In *Aurora Floyd* there are two women who appear to embody the two extremes, passionate Aurora and her passionless cousin Lucy. In this novel, as in *Lady Audley's Secret,* the text unsettles the seemingly fixed oppositions of surface and depth, secrecy and knowledge, and what is natural and unnatural in women. Preceding Ruskin's "Of Queen's Gardens" by two years, *Aurora Floyd* challenges (and perhaps prompts) its construction of domestic order and harmony. It exposes the division of the separate spheres and the education of women as helpmeet as a dangerous construct for women. Even though domestic order is restored at the end of the novel and there appear to be no more secrets, for all truths are apparently revealed, the matter is not so simple. Harmony is achieved not at the cost of incarceration and death, as in *Lady Audley's Secret,* but by another kind of violence: in the reshaping of the temptress Aurora into a Madonna figure and in the mute and mutilated figure of her angelic cousin Lucy.

THE DOCILE BODY AND THE PROBLEMATICS
OF DESIRE

Michel Foucault's term "the docile body," coined to describe the strictness of military training and the disciplining of the soldier into an obedient working unit, may appear an incongruous term to apply to Victorian womanhood. However, if we look at the discourses surrounding the education of girls, and the construction of femininity, of what was "natural" for a woman to be, the idea of docility—self-abnegation, subservience, and obedience to another authority—is particularly apt. Nancy Armstrong has argued persuasively that Foucault's concepts of political power tend to concentrate on patriarchal institutions: the army, the prison, or the clinic. She would hold that:

> When we expand our concept of the political further even than Foucault's, we discover grounds on which to argue that the modern household rather than the clinic provided the proto-institutional setting where government through relentless supervision first appeared, and appeared in its most benevolent guise. (67)

Armstrong has traced the gradual evolution of the construction of domestic womanhood and the ideology of the separate spheres, through seventeenth- and eighteenth-century treatises on philosophy and economy, conduct and advice books, and literature, especially the domestic novel. These texts produced the "countless microtechniques of socialization" that the middle class deployed, by the "surveillance, observation, evaluation, and remediation" of private life, and which in the second half of the nineteenth century, became inscribed in institutions—such as the production and regulation of etiquette through manuals of correct behavior, especially women's behavior (69).

Yet the ideas of what constitutes a "natural" woman, the middle-class ideal of true womanhood, embodied in the literatures of surveillance, from conduct books to novels, are based on a fundamental paradox. If the books were written on the assumption that woman's nature is fixed and given, what then could be the need for books that also assume that women (and men) can be produced, shaped, and trained? The repressed counter-assumption, repressed because of its inherent contradiction, is that the nature of woman is suspect. The fear of woman's transgression was so great that the necessity of a surveillant discourse arose.

The most troublesome area concerned the question of women's desire, especially sexual desire. Such desire was frequently constructed in nineteenth-century texts not as physical, bodily needs (these were "unnatural"), but as a desire for maternity. Thus William Acton could write:

> I am ready to maintain that there are many females who never feel any excitement whatever. Others, again, immediately after each period, do become, to a limited degree, capable of experiencing it; but this capacity is often temporary, and may entirely cease till the next menstrual period. Many of the best mothers, wives, and managers of households, know little of or are careless about sexual indulgences. Love of home, of children, and of domestic duties, are the only passions they feel. (209)

This particular construction of women's sexuality—the fulfilment of desire through motherhood—is depicted as being natural, which infers that any other manifestation of women's sexuality is unnatural. What is remarkable in the human female is her desire to please. Central to Acton's construction of ideal womanhood was the belief in the innate desire for self-abnegation on the part of women, a trait that both reinforced and was reinforced by his construction of women's sexuality. He maintained, as a general rule, that a modest woman seldom desires any sexual gratification for herself. She submits to her husband's embraces, but principally to gratify him; and, were it not for the desire of maternity, would far rather be relieved from his attentions, and again:

> In many a human female, indeed, I believe, it is rather from the wish of pleasing or gratifying the husband than from any strong sexual feeling, that cohabitation is so habitually allowed. . . . In some exceptional cases, in-

deed, feeling has been sacrificed to duty, and the wife has endured, with all the self-martyrdom of womanhood, what was almost worse than death. (210)

Similarly W. R. Greg wrote:

> Women whose position and education have protected them from exciting causes, constantly pass through life without ever being cognizant of the promptings of the senses. Happy for them that it is so! We do not mean to say that uneasiness may not be felt—that health may not sometimes suffer; but there is no consciousness of the cause. Among all the higher and middle classes, and, to a greater extent than would commonly be believed, among the lower classes also, where they either come of virtuous parents, or have been carefully brought up, this may be affirmed as a general fact. (457)

Acton's and Greg's texts exhibit the dilemma over women's desire. They want to argue it both ways: women do and do not feel sexual desire. Women's sexual desire is a horrifying potential that environment, through ignorance and education, should silence. Yet this desire, though a possibility, is unnatural; in fact, woman's very nature appears to be unnatural. Nature, according to Greg, had made a "kind decision," which needs to be "assisted by that correctness of feeling" found in English education, to curb strong and spontaneous passion in women, and, therefore, "sexual irregularities." Natural "modesty, decency, and honour" relieve the sufferings and struggles especially of those women for whom marriage is impossible or delayed. They are (whatever their class) "the weaker sex," and Greg calls upon his (male) readers to see this as a blessing: "No! Nature has laid many heavy burdens on the delicate shoulders of the weaker sex: Let us rejoice that this at least is spared them" (457). Moreover, Greg argues, like Acton, that true desire in women is expressed in other than sexual terms, or rather women's engagement in sex springs from a something other than sexual desire—the desire to please:

> There is in the warm fond heart of woman a strange and sublime unselfishness, which men too commonly discover only to profit by,—a positive love of self-sacrifice,—an active, so to speak, an *aggressive* desire to show their affection, by giving up to those who have won it, something they hold very dear. (459)

The problem of woman's desire, therefore, could be summed up in a threefold, and most contradictory, manner: True women did not feel desire. If women did feel desire, it was the desire to please and to be a mother. Yet suspicion of the old Eve still arose, for women were suspected to possess excessive desire that must therefore be rigorously controlled or not even be seen to exist, through the social conventions of modesty and proper behavior. Their desires must be silenced. Ruth Bernard Yeazell has shown how the modest woman became a convention in fiction, and the language of modesty was a codification of certain behaviors that allowed the young woman a way to reconcile the paradoxical implications that, as a good woman, she must deny her body, while to gain a husband (and fulfil her desire for motherhood) she must display it. The period of courtship was where she had time to observe and contemplate, while at the same time her modesty imbued her with a muted eroticism in order to attract the right husband. Modesty was a virtue, and like virtue became associated almost entirely with sexuality. It entailed both the effacement and the enhancement of the body, as, for the modest woman, her simple covering clothes were deemed more attractive than blatant nakedness. The modest woman, according to Yeazell, was constructed between two opposing figures—the prude who expressed more modesty than she had, and the coquette, who did not express enough. The modest woman was the one who instinctively knew the mean, like Nancy Armstrong's domestic woman, who walked the path of frugality, discretion, and self-regulation. Her type is found in the pages of Sarah Ellis, Isabella Beeton, and John Ruskin alike.

Yet this instinctive, natural modesty was troublesome, since paradoxically it needed constant vigilance in order to preserve it. Thus woman was seen to be instinctively modest yet at the same time possessing a potentially disruptive natural lust (Yeazell). For Yeazell, the conduct books testified to the belief that instinct must be elaborately codified and endlessly discussed in order to preserve woman from her other nature (5). Modesty was inscribed upon the body—the downcast eyes, the blushing cheek—yet the literature expressed the undercurrent of fear that this was mere seeming. Like Armstrong's domestic woman, Yeazell's modest woman must be read for her depths, for "particularly when a woman's modesty is understood as a sexual virtue, the lingering fear that she has merely veiled over the original immodesty of her sex continues to trouble those who sing her praises" (11).

AURORA FLOYD—LUXURIANT NATURE, AND THE WATCHDOGS OF SOCIETY

Braddon's novel *Aurora Floyd* negotiates the paradox of the nature of womanly desire. Moreover, in raising questions of what is natural and unnatural in woman, the text exposes the way in which the oppositional construction of femininity is just that—a construction. According to different perspectives within the text, Aurora is both natural and unnatural, open and readable, and yet secretive and transgressive. Talbot Bulstrode draws on cultural stereotypes and perceives Aurora in a variety of ways that are predictably conventional descriptions of the attractive woman. To him, Aurora is an eastern drug, or an alcoholic drink, something to intoxicate, something that is exotic and forbidden (29, 40, 62). He feels "she is like everything that is beautiful and strange, and wicked and *unwomanly*, and bewitching; and she is just the sort of creature that many a fool would fall in love with" (40, emphasis added). As Robert Audley does of Lady Audley in *Lady Audley's Secret,* Bulstrode compares Aurora with notorious women in history known for their passion: Cleopatra, Nell Gwynn, Lola Montez, Charlotte Corday, all dangerous, excessive, outside of social bounds and conventionalities. But this reading of Aurora is a masculine perception of Aurora as the dangerous temptress, from the point of view of the man who is tempted, rather than the woman who may not be aware that she is tempting. The women Bulstrode is reminded of present also a male perception of women's history, or rather he draws upon those women who appear in the histories of men, by transgressing the boundaries of the private sphere and entering the public arena and yet who are still defined by their relationships to men.

The narrative voice on the other hand, when speaking of Aurora, uses imagery of nature. Braddon draws upon another recognizable stereotype, and in this reading, Aurora is constructed as natural rather than unnatural. She "was like some beautiful, noisy, boisterous waterfall; for ever dancing, rushing, sparkling, scintillating, and utterly defying you to do anything but admire it" (63). After her illness, "her own nature revived in unison with the bright revival of the genial summer weather. As the trees in the garden put forth new strength and beauty, so the glorious vitality of her constitution returned with much of its wonted power" (98). From the beginning of the novel Aurora is associated with a growing plant. Initially the metaphor appears in the sense of the family tree. Her father's firm "had been Floyd, Floyd, and Floyd for upwards of a century; for as one member of the house dropped off, some greener branch shot out from the old tree" (6). Aurora appears to have her place in this tradition. Her father "watched his daughter's growth as a child watches an acorn it hopes to rear to an oak." But for a young girl, there seems there is not the possibility of growing straight, sturdy, and strong. Instead, Aurora becomes a plant that grows wild and untrammeled:

> We do not say a flower is spoiled because it is reared in a hot-house where no breath of heaven can visit it too roughly; but then, certainly, the bright

exotic is trimmed and pruned by the gardener's merciless hand, while Aurora shot whither she would, and there was none to lop the wandering branches of that luxuriant nature. (17)

The metaphor in itself is powerful and violent and it is important to place it in the context of two other nineteenth-century texts, both concerned with the nature of woman. First, the image echoes the conduct book writer Sarah Ellis. In *Mothers of England,* written to regulate not only the conduct of mothers, but also the education of young boys and girls, Ellis writes, "If ever then the care of a judicious mother is wanted, it is in the open feelings of a young girl, when branches of the tenderest growth have to be cherished and directed, rather than checked and lopped off" (342). Ellis is, in fact, rather than prescribing passive conformity, warning against the "extinction of [a girl's] individuality" (343). Aurora's problem is that she is motherless, and so does not experience the necessary surveillance and corrective training Ellis's good mother would provide. As Lyn Pykett describes it, lacking a mother, Aurora is "improperly socialised and hence improperly feminised" (6).

Secondly, the image prefigures John Stuart Mill's metaphor of the artificiality of woman, found in "The Subjection of Women":

> in the case of women, a hot-house and stove cultivation has always been carried on of some of the capabilities of their nature, for the benefit and pleasure of their masters. Then, because certain products of the general vital force sprout luxuriantly and reach a great development in this heated atmosphere and under this active nurture and watering, while other shoots from the same root, which are left outside in the wintry air, with ice purposely heaped all around them, have a stunted growth, and soon are burnt off with fire and disappear; men, with that inability to recognise their own work which distinguishes the unanalytic mind, indolently believe that the tree grows of itself in the way they have made it grow, and that it would die if one half of it were not kept in a vapour bath and the other half in the snow. (148–49)

The implications of these passages from Braddon, Ellis, and Mill are twofold, and return us to the central paradox on the "natural woman." First, the texts presuppose an essential nature of woman that exists, prior to discourse, to be modified in some way by her entry into that discourse, be it society, education, and so on. But secondly, that nature is problematized by the very discourses with which it must engage. Can a woman be true to her "nature" if that nature is always modified in some way? On the one hand Aurora "said what she pleased; thought, spoke, acted as she pleased; learned what she pleased; and she grew into a bright impetuous being, affectionate and generous-hearted as her mother, but with some touch of native fire blended in her mould that stamped her as original." On the other hand "the end of all this was, that, in the common accepta- tion of the term, Aurora was spoiled" (17). Thus, paradoxically, in both these claims, she is at once true and untrue to nature. What is natural is shown to be a matter of perspective rather than a given truth. What makes it a "truth" is "the common acceptation of the term," that is the hegemonic discourse of the middle-class construction of womanhood. Within this discourse of social acceptability Aurora is "an original" (and the ideal is "spoiled") rather than a type like her cousin Lucy.

Lucy, in one reading, can be dismissed as the conventional well- behaved nonentity that she appears to be, the conforming heroine of the religious novels she so favors: "she was exactly the sort of woman to make a good wife. . . . She was lady-like, accomplished, well-informed; and if there were a great many others of precisely the same type of graceful womanhood, it was certainly the highest type, and the holiest, and the best" (41). Captain Bulstrode "found that she talked exactly as he had heard other young ladies talk; that she knew all they knew, and had been to the places they had visited. The ground they went over was very old indeed, but Lucy traversed it with charming propriety" (36). The Lucys of the world, then, would seem to be infinitely replaceable, their names an endless string of signifiers for one signified: or so it might seem to the "straight penetrating gaze" (33) of Bulstrode in his construction of women on purely conventional grounds: "There are so many Lucys but so few Auroras" (41). Aurora does not fit his model, whereas Lucy "was his ideal" (35):

> Talbot Bulstrode's ideal woman was some gentle and feminine creature
> crowned with an aureole of pale auburn hair; some timid shrinking being,
> as pale and prim as the mediaeval saints in his pre-Raphaelite engravings,
> spotless as her own white robes, excelling in all womanly graces and accom-
> plishments, but only exhibiting them in the narrow circle of a home. (34)

Bulstrode's model of womanhood is that of a passionless object, for he does not even think of her in terms of subjectivity. She is a "creature" and a "being." "He wanted some spontaneous exhibition of innocent feeling which might justify him in saying, 'I am beloved!' He felt little capacity for loving, on his own side; but he thought that he would be grateful to any woman who would regard him with disinterested affection, and that he would devote his life to making her happy" (34). Thus the relation- ship must be passionless on both sides—he the object of her affection, she the object of his gratitude.

It might be argued that Bulstrode's construction of womanhood should not be taken as representative. After all, he falls in love with

Aurora, despite his ideals, and marries Lucy only as second best once Aurora appears to lose her innocence and will not divulge her secret. However, in the other representative male in the novel, John Mellish, bluff and open beside Bulstrode's standoffish pride, we find a similar constraining view of womanhood. Both these men are characterized by their stereotypic views of women, and their endorsement of differing constructs of the ideal woman. Lyn Pykett has pointed out how Braddon makes "self-conscious use of stereotypes," and that "this self-consciousness foregrounds the ideological power of generic conventions." She claims that "Braddon's novels also explore, from a variety of perspectives, the hypocrisies, self-deceptions and repressions of the aristocratic, or would-be aristocratic, male, and the social codes over which he presides" (106). Mellish accepts Aurora without requiring to know her secret, thus appearing to allow her independent subjectivity. However, their marriage is described in Ruskinesque rhetoric, the bliss of domesticity undermined by the images of constraint in which it is couched:

> She was happy in the calm security of her home, happy in that pleasant *stronghold* in which she was *so fenced about and guarded* by love and devotion. I do not know that she ever felt any romantic or enthusiastic love for this big Yorkshireman; but I do know that from the first hour in which she laid her head upon his broad breast she was true to him—true as a wife should be; true in every thought; true in the merest shadow of a thought. A wide gulf yawned around the altar of her home, separating her from every other man in the universe, and leaving her alone with that one man whom she had accepted as her husband. She had accepted him in the truest and purest sense of the word. She had accepted him from the hand of God, as the *protector and shelterer* of her life; and morning and night upon her knees, she thanked the gracious Creator who had made this man for her help-meet. (119–120, emphases added)

Aurora is therefore incarcerated as effectively as Lady Audley. Her state only appears to be one of freedom. She is, in fact, domesticated, tamed. The previous imagery of the wild growing plant is extended into a metaphor of violent implications, as the womanly body is mutilated to train it into the maternal ideal, thus problematizing that ideal, since writers like Greg and Acton would hold such a desire to be woman's natural desire, in no need of training. Aurora's love for Mellish is not the romantic passion she held for Bulstrode, but both are shown as deflecting woman's nature:

> She loved you [the narrator addresses Bulstrode] with the girl's romantic fancy and reverent admiration; and tried humbly to fashion her very nature

anew, that she might be worthy of your sublime excellence. She loved you as women only love in their first youth, and as they rarely love the men they ultimately marry. The tree is perhaps all the stronger when these first frail branches are lopped away to give place to strong and spreading arms, beneath which a husband and children may shelter. (109–110)

The irony in this pronouncement is, of course, that Aurora presumably loved another man before Talbot Bulstrode, since her secret is that, at eighteen, she ran away with and married her groom, James Conyers. The implication is that if she did not love Conyers, was his attraction merely sexual? He was, after all, "wonderfully handsome—wonderfully and perfectly handsome—the very perfection of physical beauty . . . rather a sensual type of beauty" (151).[1] Aurora's secret then could be seen to be based upon her sexuality and a desire that is neither romantic nor maternal, outside of the patriarchally acceptable constructs of Victorian girlhood and womanly desire. She seems then to fulfil that older belief about woman, that she possesses hidden desires, secret passions. Yet once again, the answer is not easy. We are told that "secretiveness had no part in her organisation, and the one concealment of her life had been a perpetual pain and grief to her" (291). Similarly, "her nature, frank and open as the day, had been dwarfed and crippled by the secret that had blighted her life" (312). It would appear, paradoxically, that the most "natural" Aurora is the one who, at the end, has been suitably constrained and conventionalized, no depths and all surface, no longer an "original" but quiet and docile, "in the safe harbour of a happy home" (125), "the happy wife, secure in her own stronghold of love and confidence" (130).

WHO IS LUCY FLOYD?—HEARING IN THE MASCULINE

The metaphor of pruning "natural" desire is employed elsewhere in the novel when a "governess, companion, and chaperon" is engaged for Aurora because she was, according to her aunt,

sadly in need of some accomplished and watchful person, whose care it would be to train and prune those exuberant branches of her nature which had been suffered to grow as they would from her infancy. The beautiful shrub was no longer to trail its wild stems along the ground, or shoot upward to the blue skies at its own sweet will; it was to be trimmed, and clipped and fastened primly to the stone wall of society with cruel nails and galling strips of cloth. (42)

It would appear that the element of sacrifice does not come "naturally" as writers like Greg would have it, but is forced upon women as an act of violence and domestic imprisonment by a society that includes women like Mrs. Alexander Floyd, one of Ellis's "judicious" mothers, and Mrs. Powell, "that grim, pale-faced watch-dog" (44), to carry out its surveillance. The two metaphorical strands permeate a text that seemingly endorses the domestic ideal. Even Lucy, the epitome of perfect girlhood, is constructed in these terms. Her suitability as a wife does not come naturally. "She had been educated to that end by a careful mother. Purity and goodness had watched over her and hemmed her in from her cradle." She had been "mercilessly well educated" (22), but the process is to keep her a child in a state of infantilized purity: "She had never seen unseemly sights, or heard unseemly sounds. She was as ignorant as a baby of all the vices and horrors of the world" (41).

Nevertheless, the text undermines this seeming state of innocence. Lyn Pykett has pointed out how in certain scenes in Braddon's novels "the female body becomes a sign (or system of signs) which is imperfectly read, or misread, by characters within the text, but which is legible to the narrator, and hence to the reader—even if what is legible is finally the sign's elusiveness" (98). This is certainly true of Lucy Floyd. Lucy is far more aware than she appears to be to other characters in the novel. It is Lucy who realizes Talbot Bulstrode's love for Aurora before he does, just as John Mellish perceives Lucy's secret love for Bulstrode: "It comforted him to watch Lucy, and to read in those faint signs and tokens, which had escaped even a mother's eye, the sad history of her unrequited affection" (79). Braddon engages with discourses such as Ellis's to expose the repressive nature of their arguments, but also to endorse the idea that women may possess hidden desires—not the showy temptresses like Aurora, but the quiet docile Lucys. Ellis had written of the potential for secret desires in a young woman and the need for such desires to be controlled. Braddon's Lucy figures in Ellis's text as one of "those characters which appear in general society the most hidden, and the most reserved, [who] are struggling hard with under-currents of tumultuous feelings, of which the world has little knowledge or suspicion." Mrs. Alexander has failed therefore as an Ellis mother for "with this second life, so often hid in the bosom of her child, the mother ought to live" (340). Braddon indicates that despite the vigilance of the watchdogs of society, even women like Lucy appear to escape, but at a cost—their silence.

Passionlessness, the text implies, does not come naturally to the Lucys of the world, but as an act of repression: "Mrs Alexander's daughter had been far too well educated to betray one emotion of her heart, and she bore her girlish agonies, and concealed her hourly tortures, with the quiet patience common to these simple womanly martyrs" (47).

Bulstrode's perception of her as the perfect wife, because of her lack of passion, is merely a reflection of his own lack. She gains her heart's desire by never showing that desire. What she feels is "a tumult of wild delight," and "joyful fear and trembling." She "loved him so well, and had loved him so long." But, with true modesty, what she shows are blushes and trembling, for "she was the most undemonstrative of women." Her voice is reduced to "a low-consenting murmur which meant Yes" (134). The long discursive intrusion by the narrator that follows Bulstrode's proposal is the most overt statement in the text of the way in which the desires of women like Lucy are constrained:

> How hard it is upon such women as these that they feel so much and yet display so little feeling! The dark-eyed, impetuous creatures, who speak out fearlessly, and tell you that they love or hate you—flinging their arms round your neck or throwing the carving-knife at you, as the case may be— get full value for their emotion; but these gentle creatures love, and make no sign. They sit, like patience on a monument, smiling at grief; and no one reads the mournful meaning of that sad smile. . . . They are always at a disadvantage. Their inner life may be a tragedy, while their outer existence is some dull domestic drama of every-day life. The only outward sign Lucy Floyd gave of the condition of her heart was that one tremulous, half-whispered affirmative; and yet what a tempest of emotion was going forward within! The muslin folds of her dress rose and fell with the surging billows; but, for the very life of her, she could have uttered no better response to Talbot's pleading. (135)

Talbot's response to Lucy is to diminish her. He refers to her frequently as "poor little Lucy": "my poor little Lucy loves me after her fashion; loves me in fear and trembling, as if she and I belonged to different orders of being" (140). The misperception is ironic, since the text makes clear that they in fact *are* different, and that he will never understand the import of his words. He exemplifies "hearing in the masculine," a phrase adapted from Helene Cixous. For Cixous, even when a woman speaks her truth, she is unlikely to be heard: "her words fall almost always upon the deaf male ear, which hears in language only that which speaks in the masculine" ("Medusa" 251). Lucy has not even the chance to speak. To exist she must function within the hegemonic male discourse, as an espaliered woman "fastened primly to the stone wall of society" (42).

The text, through its metaphoric structures as well as through the intrusive narrative voice, might be said to be speaking for her. Yet the existence of Lucy's hidden inner life poses a problem of interpretation.

On the one hand, although we will never know her story in the way we are told her cousin's, the fact that Lucy has another, interior, life could be seen to allow another possibility for woman's sexuality and desire, outside of "normal" and normative discourse. On the other hand, Braddon could be seen to be merely reinforcing the patriarchal, essentialist belief that women are ever deceivers, that they have hidden secrets and desires that must be controlled.

Whether such readings are radical or reactionary, one area where the alternatives are juxtaposed is that of women's illness. The text plays upon the oppositions of the practical, everyday, "commonsense" approach of medical science and the romantic conventions of love sickness to present a masculine and a feminine reading of Lucy's condition. Denied voice, the body appears to reveal something of such women's interiorized secrets: "concealment, like the worm i' the bud, feeds on their damask cheeks; and compassionate relatives tell them that they are bilious, and recommend some homely remedy for their pallid complexions" (135). When Lucy's health declines after Aurora and Bulstrode become engaged, it is ascribed to the adverse climate which had been "too much for the young lady's strength" (63). Furthermore,

> Talbot and Aurora were both concerned to see the pale cheeks of their gentle companion; but everybody was ready to ascribe them to a cold, or a cough, or constitutional debility, or some other bodily evil, which could be cured by drugs and boluses; and no one for a moment imagined that anything could possibly be amiss with a young lady who lived in a luxurious house, went shopping in a carriage and pair, and had more pocket-money than she cared to spend. But the Lily Maid of Astalot lived in a lordly castle, and had doubtless ample pocket-money to buy gorgeous silks for her embroidery, and had little on earth to wish for, and nothing to do; whereby she fell sick for love of Sir Lancelot, and pined and died. (65)

Lucy, rather than Aurora, has the possibility of being read as the romantic heroine, but she is so docile and dull nobody else is interested enough in her to perceive it. The body has been textualized, drawn into medical or literary discourses, but both, the text implies, are open to alternative readings. Yet whatever way Lucy's textualized body might be read, the ending is either silence or death: "when people told her of her pale face, and the family doctor wondered at the failure of his quinine mixture, perhaps she nourished a vague hope that before the spring-time came back again, bringing with it the wedding-day of Talbot and Aurora, she would have escaped from all this demonstrative love and happiness, and be at rest" (66).

The novel constantly returns to the language of violation or constraint. As has been pointed out, Aurora seems to be the woman with the secret, an unacceptable transgressive sexuality. Yet, in the end, once that secret is dealt with, she returns to her "true nature," which is "frank and open as the day" (312). Secrecy, therefore, is shown as alien to her nature, another example of the paradox of what is natural and unnatural in the novel. The "unnatural," transgressive woman, passionate and secretive, is discovered to be a male construct. Her desire is disturbingly transformed into another more "natural" form, the good mother, by the end of the novel, while the third possibility, a sexuality outside the bounds of masculine discourse, disappears for her altogether: "So we leave Aurora, a little changed, a shade less defiantly bright, perhaps, but unspeakably beautiful and tender, bending over the cradle of her first-born" (384).

On the other hand, the apparently transparent, good woman, Lucy, is shown to be more opaque, less "lucid" than she seems. She is a woman in possession of a secret life, her "natural" desires and her sexuality silenced in a patriarchal society that will not allow her to exist, to find the voice of true subjectivity. Aurora, apparently rebellious, is, in fact, the conformist, complying to two different masculine constructions of womanhood, the temptress and the mother. Lucy, apparently infinitely replaceable, possesses a secret life that finds no voice in the hegemonic discourse, to be read elusively in signs of illness and suffering. For Cixous, "woman has always functioned 'within' the discourse of man, a signifier that has always referred back to the opposite signifier which annihilates its specific energy and diminishes or stifles its very different sounds" ("Medusa" 257). The last we hear of Lucy, apart from a mention of her "blue-eyed girl-baby" (384), are Bulstrode's ironic words, comparing her life with that of her cousin: "'thank Heaven, my poor little Lucy has never been forced into playing the heroine of a tragedy like this; thank Heaven, my poor little darling's life flows evenly and placidly in a smooth channel!'" (373). Lucy's tragedy (and the tragedy for the docile woman, for "there are so many Lucys but so few Auroras") is that she will always be silenced, locked within another's story, and unheard even by the object of her desire.

In constructing texts that seemingly dwelt on and prioritized plot, the sensation writers incurred the animosity of the reviewers of the time. Yet the realist myth of character, with psychological motivation and the plausibility of cause and effect, is predicated upon the idea of a fully present consciousness, of "depth," such as "depth of character." By constructing a discourse of surface, in fact highlighting surface by the implications that the truth, or the depth, is veiled in mysteries, and yet at the same time apparently revealing all by the end, uncovering the secret, the sensation writer exposed this myth of depth to be the hollow decentred destabilized absence that it is, that "character" is illusion, that "realism" masks its own production. That woman is an impossible reality if not the pathologized production of patriarchal bourgeois ideology is the textual implication of *Lady Audley's Secret.* In *Aurora Floyd,* Braddon goes even further, as she explores the contradictory discourses constructing woman's desire, exposes the dangers inherent in the division of the separate spheres and the education of women as helpmeet , and hints at the unthinkable, the secret, but silenced, voice of the docile woman.

NOTES

1. It is worth noting here that the manner in which, for example, Bulstrode "reads" Aurora as being a siren or temptress is reflected in Aurora's "reading" of Conyers, according to literary stereotypes. She perceives him, judging by his handsome appearance, as the romantic hero. Braddon ironically undercuts this: "He is thinking. His dark-blue eyes, deeper in colour by reason of the thick black lashes which fringe them, are half-closed, and have a dreamy, semi-sentimental expression, which might lead you to suppose the man was musing upon the beauty of the summer sunset. He is thinking of his losses on the Chester Cup" (152).

WORKS CITED

Acton, William. *Functions and Disorders of the Reproductive Organs in Childhood, Youth, Adult age, and Advanced Life Considered in Their Physiological, Social, and Moral Relations.* 1st ed. London: 1857; 8th ed. Philadelphia: Blakiston, 1895.

Armstrong, Nancy . "Some Call it Fiction: On the Politics of Domesticity." *The Other Perspective in Gender and Culture: Rewriting Women and the Symbolic.* Ed. Juliet Flower MacCannell. New York and Oxford: Columbia UP, 1990.

Braddon, Mary Elizabeth. *Aurora Floyd.* (1863). London: Virago, 1984.

Cixous, Helene. "The Laugh of the Medusa." *New French Feminisms.* Ed. and with an introduction by, Elaine Marks and Isabelle de Courtivron. Sussex, England: Harvester, 1981. 245–64.

———. "Sorties." *The Newly Born Woman.* Helene Cixous and Catherine Clement. Trans. Betsey Wing. Minneapolis: U of Minneapolis P, 1975.

Ellis, Sarah Stickney. *The Mothers of England, Their Influence and Responsibility.* London, 1843.

[Greg, W. R.]. "Prostitution." *Westminster Review* 53(1850): 448–506.

Irigaray, Luce. "Des marchandises entres elles." *New French Feminisms.* Ed. and with introductions by Elaine Marks and Isabelle de Courtivron. Sussex, England: Harvester, 1981. 107–10.

Mill, John Stuart. "The Subjection of Women" (1869). *John Stuart Mill and Harriet Taylor Mill: Essays on Sex Equality.* Ed. Alice S. Rossi. Chicago and London: U of Chicago P, 1970.

Pykett, Lyn. *The "Improper" Feminine: The Women's Sensation Novel and the New Woman Writing.* London and New York: Routledge, 1992.

Yeazell, Ruth Bernard. *Fictions of Modesty: Women and Courtship in the English Novel.* Chicago and London: U of Chicago P, 1991.

Seven

The Dangerous Woman:
M. E. Braddon's Sensational
(En)gendering of Domestic Law

Marlene Tromp

Aurora Floyd's first words in the novel that bears her name are: "He is [dead]." By the novel's climax, the police, her servants, her friends, and even her jovial, warm-hearted husband suspect her of shooting her first husband at point-blank range. Aurora is a bigamist, the near-ruin of her second husband's respected family name, and, most disturbingly, a suspected murderess. No one escapes the threat of death that hovers around her; both of the men to whom she later becomes engaged contemplate suicide during their courtship. Her doting father and all her lovers suffer or perish—all, seemingly, because of her presence. Though we might be tempted to dismiss Aurora's threatening demeanor as a trope of the sensation novel,[1] a genre in which *Aurora Floyd* was a landmark text, I would argue that Aurora's threat reveals much more about a culture in transition than a cursory examination might reveal.

The furor over the novel points up its importance to the Victorians and compels us to carefully examine the text and its context. One critic claimed that "half the world" knew Aurora Floyd ("Miss Braddon" 593), and another remarked that "no novelists, with the exception of Mr. Charles Dickens, [had] so completely gained and so indisputably held the public attention" as Braddon, calling *Aurora Floyd* "an event in literature" in which "everyone" participated ("Miss Braddon's Novels" 436–

37). Though she had her champions, one essay calling *Aurora Floyd* a sign of her genius ("Miss Braddon's Novels" 436–38), Braddon's reviewers were often exceedingly hostile. In fact, *Aurora Floyd* frequently drew critical attention because its popularity, superadded to its "sensational" qualities, brought it under severe scrutiny. Reviewers lamented the immorality of the "unnatural" heroine, a creature only possible in a sensation novel (Rae 93–101) and argued that this fiction had a "deteriorating effect on the mind" ("Our Novels" 424). One suggested that "the injury that these ill-toned, ill-wrought productions work on dispositions the least qualified to resist baneful influence [girls and young women] is incalculable" ("Novels in Relation to Female Education" 516–17). In the year of *Aurora Floyd*'s publication, an essay that excoriated Aurora's identity as a violent, unnatural, and dangerous creature, condemned sensation novels for their dangerous heroines and effects.

> There is nothing more violently opposed to our moral sense, in all the contradictions to custom which they present us, than the utter unrestraint in which heroines of this order are allowed to expiate and develop their impulsive, stormy, passionate characters. We believe it is one chief among their many dangers to youthful readers. ("Our Female Sensation Novelists" 353)

Clearly, the eponymous heroine was a "dangerous woman," to those inside the text and to the novel's readers—and, undoubtedly, the "law" of the day would agree.

At roughly the time of *Aurora Floyd*'s publication in 1863, Parliament was generating its own version of the dangerous woman in the Contagious Diseases Acts (CD Acts), and the similarities between the rhetoric of the novel and the debates surrounding the repeal of the acts are stunning. In these acts, the prostitute, like Aurora, was marked as a murderess and the moral and social bane of the respectable family. Furthermore, both the laws and this novel erected their figure of the dangerous woman on the grounds of colonial rhetoric, orientalizing her and providing a context for her recuperation. The CD Acts, like the novel, figured prominently in the cultural conversation, producing such social upheaval that the acts were ultimately repealed.[2] Both texts served as pivots around which fierce debates about propriety, the family, and womanhood circulated and each was persistently and pervasively present in the Victorian social framework.

Their prominence, along with the similarities in their description and critique, lends even greater weight to the parallel patterns in these texts and suggests their mutual participation in a long-standing cultural conversation. Significantly, the commentaries on the sensational qualities of the novel echo concerns about the CD Acts debates inside and outside of Parliament. Parliament believed that the acts had spawned "sensation literature" marked by "the grossest exaggeration,"[3] *precisely* the terms with which critics characterized Braddon's novel and identified them as dangerous. Indeed, Parliament expressed the same concern as the critics of Braddon's novels about the text falling into the hands of women and children—complaining that activists regularly delivered it to "the drawing-rooms and breakfast-tables of the wives and even the maiden sisters of the most respectable families." Parliament was desperate to discover the means of "stopp[ing] that stream of offensive literature which [had] flooded [their] houses."[4]

This strikingly similar discourse begs analysis.[5] The correspondence certainly indicates that both texts were products of a circulating debate that pervaded the culture, but they are more than simply products of social tensions; they participated in the production of these cultural debates, as well. I contend that the debates surrounding the Contagious Diseases Acts, which appeared only after *Aurora Floyd* had been widely circulated and digested, suggest that Braddon's contentious, exploratory fiction engaged in the revisioning of the language that created law, playing out and exposing the complex network of cultural tensions that generated the construction of the dangerous woman. Braddon's novel challenged the often unspoken beliefs that produced both the domestic angel and her dangerous "other," and more significantly for my argument, resisted the containment of violence in the home, culture, and the letter of the law within the body of this figure, anticipating and supplying a framework for the sensational anti-CD Acts literature and debates.

SENSATION AND THE DOMESTIC HEROINE

Braddon's "depraved" heroine, Aurora, draws attention to the material, unlike her "pale, prim, and saint[-like]" cousin, Lucy (1:73), whose characterization "subordinates the body to a set of mental processes that guaranteed domesticity" as Nancy Armstrong argues of domestic fiction (907). The sensation in this sensation novel lies in the bodies of Aurora and those around her, and resists the dominant novelistic and social discourse of the mid-century that operated to manage women's identities in terms of the domestic ideal. Braddon's *Aurora Floyd,* in its abundance of bodies, death, violence, and conspicuous eroticism, particularly as it surrounds the women in the novel, offers a resignification of not only middle-class women's identity, but also the material circumstances of Victorian women's lives and the law that articulated them. As Judith Butler suggests in *Bodies that Matter,* the link between bodies and politics is mutually constitutive, resulting from the "citational accumulation of and dissimulation of the law that produces material effects" (12). Yet, these citations are always fraught with instability, and the seemingly secure production of the domestic woman and the idealization of the domestic space may be contested—along with the notion that violence and danger are confined to this realm—even while it is deployed. This novel, even in its parody of "realism," serves as a "performance" of these terms whose hyperbolic nature "disrupt[s] the closeting distinction between public and private space" (233).[6] *Aurora Floyd* publicizes the functioning of the spiritually "disembodied" middle class, highlighting the management of gender and sex that cast women as the bodiless victims of impossible crimes. Physical abuse must be enacted on a body; and Aurora's body, along with the bodies of those who are beaten or murdered, materializes despite the powerful pressures that Armstrong notes domesticate women and keep their bodies invisible. *Aurora Floyd* goes further by demonstrating the ways in which the violence played out on women's bodies is obscured in the narrative: through the employment of the discourse of the colonized other, which defines and insulates her, authorizing a violent resignification of her identity, and eventually attempting to recuperate the British domestic scene. Like a Pandora's box, however, Braddon's novels reveal a host of dangers under a heavily ornamented lid that cannot be contained once they are released. My analysis begins by addressing the ornamental, and often orientalized, woman of danger, then moves to the naturalized language of social and Parliamentary law, examining the manufacture of what I call "the dangerous woman" as a screen for the production of domestically conceived violence.

THE DANGEROUS WOMAN/
THE MURDEROUS MAN

When the novel opens, Aurora has a well-kept secret: she has married and abandoned James Conyers, the deceitful family groom who had hoped to gain access to her family's wealth by beguiling Aurora into marriage. Ashamed of their illicit union and horrified by James's improprietous behavior, Aurora flees James and reports him dead to her father. Soon Aurora's great beauty and family money draw suitors, and once a newspaper account falsely reports that James has been killed in a riding accident, she agrees to marry. In a scene that marks Aurora as the link between men's love and their demise, the record of James's death literally lies at Aurora's feet while her suitor pledges his undying love. It is this account that sets off rumblings of terror in her affianced lover's imagination. Concerned about Aurora's secret past, Talbot Bulstrode, a proud

Englishman of fine family, stares at the newspaper, and despite his ignorance of its connection to Aurora, he feels overcome with a fear he
cannot name. Indeed, he wonders of any man affianced to Aurora,
"[W]ould there not always be a shuddering terror mingled with [his]
love,—a horrible dread . . . " (1:118). Once engaged, Talbot becomes
subject to precisely the fears he had prophesied and fantasizes that his
relationship with Aurora will occasion his death. Significantly, his vision
foreshadows a murder that will later be linked to Aurora—James Conyers' death by gunshot at the side of a pool:

> [Talbot] had a vague fear that he was . . . too much bound up heart and
> soul in the dark-eyed woman by his side. He turned sick and dizzy at the
> thought; and even in [the] sacred temple [of the church], the Devil whis-
> pered to him that there were *still pools, loaded pistols*, and other certain
> remedies for such calamities as those. (1:187, emphasis added).

Talbot is spared this fate, however. When Aurora refuses to tell him the
secret of her past, it "[strikes] terror to his heart," and he breaks their
engagement.

John Mellish, Aurora's next suitor, experiences the same fantasy of
death in his relationship with Aurora. Significantly this apparition arises
just before John proposes. He simultaneously contemplates marriage to
Aurora and suicide on the edge of a cliff. Aurora's self-examination reveals the drive to locate in her the failure implied in this essential Englishman's despair. She wonders, "What had she done? More wrong,
more mischief? Was her life to be one of perpetual wrong-doing? . . . Was
this John Mellish to be another sufferer by her folly?" (1:243). After
Aurora reveals to John the existence of her secret (never, however, allud-
ing to its contents), he confirms her characterization as a dangerous
woman with his telling colloquial diction: "The murder is out now"
(1:247). Finally, despite the warnings offered to John throughout the
text, he and Aurora marry.

Once installed in Mellish Park as John's bride, Aurora encounters
another man she will "endanger," Softy, a "fond" stablehand who's "a bit
touched in the upper story." When Softy brutally kicks Aurora's beloved
dog, Bow-wow, Aurora attacks and beats Softy, and the stunning scene of
her violence, quoted over and again in contemporary reviews that
marked this scene as an indication of the heroine's impropriety, serves as
a turning point in the narrative:

> Aurora sprang upon him like a beautiful tigress. . . . Taller than the stable-
> man by a foot and a half, she towered above him, her cheeks white with
> rage, her eyes flashing fury, her hat fallen off and her black hair tumbling

> about her shoulders, sublime in her passion. . . . She disengaged her right
> hand from his collar and rained a shower of blows upon his clumsy
> shoulders with her slender whip; a mere toy, with emeralds set in its golden
> head, but stinging like a rod of flexible steel in that little hand. . . . Her
> tangled hair had fallen to her waist . . . and the whip was broken in a half a
> dozen places (1:273–74)

John Mellish stumbles upon this scene and stares in horror at Aurora's behavior. His response provides a new means of reading Aurora's dangerous relationships. He selects a whip of his own "from a stand of formidable implements" and commandeers Aurora's, stowing it safely in his pants pocket (1:275). He returns to Softy, supposedly to administer his own punishment, but instead he focuses on Aurora's improprietous behavior—never mentioning Softy's attack on the dog at all. "[I]t wasn't Mrs. Mellish's business to horsewhip you, but it was her duty to let me do it for her" (1:276). Disregarding his assurances that he will see to Softy's punishment, John not only refrains from administering any beating with the whip he has displayed—suggesting that its exhibition was not for Softy at all, but for Aurora instead—he simply banishes Softy from Mellish Park, an injunction they later both ignore. Further, he literally *pays* Softy an extravagant sum, as if rewarding him for his services: "He took a handful of money from his waistcoat-pocket and threw it on the ground, sovereigns and half-crowns rolling hither and thither on the gravel-path . . . [Softy's] white face relapsed into a grin: John Mellish had given him gold and silver amounting to upwards of two years of his ordinary wages" (1:277). John's endorsement of the happily grinning Softy implicates John in Softy's behavior and suggests an implicit authorization of Softy's violence.

The narrative significance of this scene, in conjunction with the extraordinary conduct of the characters, behavior that commanded the critical attention in the reviews of the novel, calls for closer inquiry. An examination of John's "reward" of Softy for Aurora's chastisement offers us with a means of reframing all of her "dangerous" relationships with her lovers and the violence implied in their behavior, not hers. When Aurora's first suitor, Talbot, breaks his engagement with her, he abandons her in a scene he himself later describes as agonizingly cruel: She lay at his feet in a "half kneeling, half crouching attitude, her face buried in her hands," begging him for pity and trust (1:205), yet he "grievously wronged, insulted and humiliated [her]." In fact, he imagines her dead, noting "that he would rather have left Aurora lying rigidly beautiful in her coffin than as he was leaving her today" (1:206). Talbot later angrily ponders their separation as he stands alone in the fields of Bulstrode Castle. "Were his days to be misery, and his nights a burden because of her? He struck the stock of his gun violently upon the ground at the thought, and thrust the ramrod down the barrel, and loaded his fowling-piece furiously with nothing" (1:219–20). Well before Aurora's first act of violence, we see Talbot fantasizing about her death and metaphorically enacting an assault, "violently" and "furiously" performing a symbolic rape with the ramrod of his gun. Later, while discussing Aurora with her gentle and properly English cousin Lucy, he "whisked the end of his cane across a group of anemones, and decapitated the tremulous blossoms. He was thinking, rather savagely, what a shame it was that Aurora could be happy with [John]" (2:11–12). When his performance leaves Lucy in absolute subdued silence, he proposes marriage to her instead.

John also participates in the imaginative murder of Aurora. When she threatens to leave him, John informs her in graphic terms about the depth of his love: "I would rather see your coffin laid in the empty niche beside my mother's in the vault yonder . . . I would rather send a bullet into your heart, and see you lying murdered at my feet" (2:91). John's equipage suggests that he could enact this fantasy. He dedicates one whole room in his house to "whips, canes, foils, single-sticks, boxing-gloves, spurs, guns, pistols." We are also told that John could "break [his wife's] tiny wrist with one twist of his big thumb and finger." However, until "such measures *become necessary* . . . [he will] let her have her own way" (1:283, emphasis added).

In the light of her suitors' behavior, Aurora's danger begins to seems responsive and lends new meaning to Softy's attack on Bow-wow and Aurora's reaction. The beating to which Aurora responds and that John ignores mirrors the violence both her lovers imagine. Further, Bow-wow is linked to Aurora in several significant ways: he is introduced alongside Aurora and is mentioned in nearly every paragraph of Aurora's initial description, even intruding upon it with a bark. The two have grown up alongside each other and represent the "marvellous . . . sympathy which exists between some people and the brute creation" (1:90).[7] John, like Talbot before him, must court the dog as he courts his future bride. And in Aurora's married life, Bow-wow, just like Aurora, becomes a "privileged creature" at Mellish Park, "spen[ding] his declining days in luxurious repose" (1:271). I contend, based on these associations, that Softy's attack on Bow-Wow metonymically represents an attack on Aurora, representing the violence described and imagined by her lovers in a more socially palatable form.

This reading also lends significance to the identification of John and Softy. The two characters are delineated in strikingly similar terms. John, the "big, empty-headed Yorkshireman [who] babble[s] about his stud" (1:106) resembles the "soft" stablehand in several ways. Softy's size, with his gladiatorlike features and "sinews of iron" (1:268) mirror the robust and athletic John Mellish who weighs in two stones heavier than average. John considers business and scholarly thought "terrible bug-bear[s]" (1:285) but talks of horses with comfort and authority. Similarly, Softy "although a little 'fond' upon common matters, [was] a very acute judge of horseflesh" (1:285). Both characters have been life residents of Mellish Park and were favorites of John's father (1:265, 267). These similarities resonate when placed in the context of the novel's tensions. The slippage between their identities invests the threat of Aurora's potential for violence with even greater significance for John—but it also marks Softy's violence in several complex ways as well. The narrative not only depicts Aurora's presence as a deadly threat to John (as well as Talbot and James), the enactment of this threat on the body of John's double underscoring the anxiety concerning Aurora's potential for violence against her partner, it also metonymically depicts an initial assault by John that proceeds Aurora's attack.

Softy's attack on Bow-Wow, then, represents an encoded performance of intramarital violence, dramatizing the potentially menacing side of the domestic space—a husband's assault on his wife. This multi-layered performance reveals that the domestic space itself, rather than serving as a safe haven that secures and fortifies a womanhood that naturally blossoms into respectable motherhood and manufacturing men who become protectors, fathers, and providers, may be a site of danger that disrupts firmly held notions of gendered identity. An assault that Softy could have enacted on Aurora (and which he later explicitly visualizes), he redirects to Bow-Wow, deflecting the anxieties involved in the direct representation of this kind of violence and retaining the normative character of the Mellishs' union—the kind of domestic arrangement this text critiques. Softy becomes the embodiment of male violence within the home and is rewarded for his performance by John (while Aurora is punished and chastised by her husband). Although the text appears to characterize Aurora's fury as aggressive, this shift in context offers us a means of reading it as responsive, provoked by some show of potential or enacted male violence. The significance of this embedded alternative multiplies when we consider that Aurora is consistently identified as the *source* of the domestic failures.

A CUP OF BANG: THE CONSTRUCTION AND CONTAINMENT OF THE EASTERN OTHER

Aurora's portrayal in the novel suggests why this representation of marital violence is possible and why her failure, despite her position as an upper-middle-class domestic woman, is inevitable: she is cast as an Eastern figure, marked with a "touch of native fire blended in her mould" (1:31). These characteristics identify her as an appropriate target for domestic correction. In the same way that the British justified colonial invasion by suggesting that their violence responded to the savagery of the people they "reformed," the orientalization of Aurora also identifies Aurora and her "primitive nature" as the origin rather than the casualty of the imperial hero's violence; she must be civilized—a feat eventually accomplished by her husband and ex-fiancé—even if great violence is "required" to complete this task.[8]

Although many critics have seen the novel, as a genre, as acting only in concert with mainstream political repression, my argument posits that many novels, particularly sensation fiction, disrupted the operation of ideologically entrenched patterns such as these with their exposure of its administration. As Jacques Derrida notes in *Acts of Literature*, "[L]iterature seem[s] to me . . . to be the institution which allows one to *say everything [tout dire]*, in *every way*. . . . To say everything is no doubt to gather, by translating, all figures into one another, totalize by formalizing, but to say everything is also to break out of prohibitions. To *affranchise oneself*—in every field where law can lay down the law. The *law of literature tends, in principle, to defy or lift the law.* . . . It is an institution which tends to overflow the institution" (36, emphasis in original). Sensation fiction did indeed say anything and everything, the genre itself disrupting the boundaries that had been established by "proper" literary endeavors.[9] It depicted even those things that were considered intolerable in other forms of writing, it disrupted the boundaries of the genre itself. Thus, in Braddon's discussion of Aurora's identity and her capitulation to her husband and Talbot, there lies not only an articulation of an unseemly pattern, but a criticism as well.

During their courtship, Talbot describes Aurora as a cup of *bang*, an East Indian drink "which made the men who drank it half mad; and he could not help fancying that the beauty of [Aurora] was like the strength of that alcoholic preparation; barbarous, intoxicating, dangerous and maddening" (1:59). She contaminates him with the poison of her "Otherness," an effect that distorts his judgment, alters his native Englishness, and both demonizes and eroticizes Aurora. It also has the effect of drawing Talbot's attention away from the more appropriate object of affection, Aurora's very British, properly domestic cousin, Lucy. Aurora surpasses Lucy with her divine black hair "crown[ing] her an Eastern Empress" and "wonderful black eyes . . . in themselves constituting royalty" (1:76). Talbot felt "himself to be bewitched by this black-eyed siren; freely drinking of the cup of *bang* which she presented to him, and rapidly becoming intoxicated" (1:87). Talbot identifies Aurora as the seducer, enchanting him, offering him her mortal potion.

However, the novel exposes this construction as Talbot's fantasy. Aurora is not a seductress—even Talbot notes her distraction and lack of attention to his company, a "listless indifference, half-weariness, half disdain" (1:80). When Talbot plans to propose to Aurora, he describes her as a great conquering Assyrian queen, imputing the responsibility of the seduction and colonization, the control of his mind and body, to Aurora—yet she stifles a yawn in their first moments alone together (1:128). He pictures her in a conflation of Cairo and Bulstrode Castle, "clad in imperial purple, with hieroglyphics on the hem of her robe" (1:136). Talbot wants Aurora to provide the spice of the alien and exotic, as Edward Said notes of the colonized, yet he clearly wishes to maintain the power to control her as he does his fantasy. His status as an officer in the Crimean War and his skill at taming "refractory Sepoys" in India (3:308) ensure his ability—and authorization—to accomplish the task of managing, and in this case, "domesticating" Aurora.

When Talbot and Aurora's engagement fails, the pattern of Aurora's orientalization continues in her engagement to John Mellish. Like the hunter who exhibits his catch on the walls of his den, John adorns his "India" room with Aurora, displaying her among the arsenal of weapons he stores there. Despite the fact that John seems to have been mastered once they are married, the invocation of her Eastern identity ironically makes John's authority over her more entrenched. "John followed his mistress about like some big slave, who only lived to do her bidding; Aurora accepted his devotion with a Sultana-like grace, which became her amazingly" (1:254–55). This slavery, although implying a complete surrender to Aurora, mirrors Talbot's identification of Aurora as the active figure in his seduction. In John's case, this is even more suggestively depicted within the domestic space: "He was so proud of his Cleopatra-like bride . . . that he fancied he could not build a shrine rich enough for his treasure. So the house in which honest country squires and their sensible motherly wives had lived contentedly for nearly three centuries was almost pulled to pieces, before John thought it worthy of the banker's daughter" (1:259). Aurora bears the responsibility for the destruction of the Englishness of John's home, for an infiltration and reconstruction of the domestic scene, despite her absence and inactivity during the remodeling of both. In a recapitulation of the self-seduction that becomes Talbot's excuse for vilifying Aurora, the danger Aurora poses to the English home articulates her as an appropriate target of a domestically conceived violence.

In spite of the violence of which her lovers seem capable, the narrative reveals the way in which Aurora's oriental identity correlates not with her victimization, but with "her" violence. When James, Aurora's first husband, defies the newspaper report and appears alive at Mellish Park to bribe her, he is murdered, and Aurora becomes the sole suspect. She alone is identified with the crime and the weapon that kills James, although *Softy* murders James for the bribe money, and the gun originates in the room John "reserved to himself" (2:22). Though the murder finds its source in John's weapons and Softy's aggression, Aurora's Eastern characterization screens their involvement. The gun comes from the "India" room, decorated with East Indian matting and basketwork chairs, a delineation that ties it to Aurora. Further, it is Aurora's presence that leads Softy to this gun, which is "as pretty as a 'lady's toy,' and small enough to be carried in a lady's pocket" (2:221). The feminization of the murder weapon and the intoxicating "lure" that Aurora generates (as she had with the men who loved her) also links the violence to Aurora. Again, despite her inactivity and innocence, Aurora is still identified as the source of the domestic disruption, a problem that must be corrected. Thus, violence is authorized to render her fully British, purified of the native influence that makes her so uncontrollable and threatening. John will be schooled by Talbot, the imperial soldier, in the proper domestication of the Eastern figure; John will silence Aurora the way Lucy has been silenced. By the end of the narrative, Aurora has become, "Mrs. Mellish"—John's wife—though she has been referred to as "Aurora" throughout the novel.

LEGAL ANTIDOTES: THE CD ACTS AND GENDERED DISEASE

These anxieties about the dangerous woman were available to resignification because they were tensions circulating in the culture as well: tensions that the law sought to explain and contain. The Contagious Diseases Acts (CD Acts) were central in the effort to identify and remedy the problem of the dangerous women. Although the acts provoked profound controversy in the attempts for repeal, they were passed almost entirely without debate in 1864 and extended in the same fashion in 1866 and 1869, around the time of this novel's publication. So utterly naturalized that they were discursively invisible, concerns over the containment and "reformation" of dangerous women only surfaced in the debates after the publication of novels like *Aurora Floyd*. The initial uncomplicated acceptance of the CD Acts indicates a drive to constitute the dangerous/ contaminating woman and her behavior as the sole threat and, thus, as a vessel to contain cultural tensions and male misbehavior.

Concerned primarily with the registration and treatment of prostitutes infected with venereal disease, the CD Acts were designed to prevent the spread of syphilis and gonorrhea. The acts authorized the seizure of suspected prostitutes on the streets, their examination by an official physician, and their forcible detention in "lock hospitals," to suppress their "danger." Prostitutes were viewed as "dangerous women," a life-threatening peril to the men with whom they came in contact. One Member of Parliament claimed that "the [CD] Act was, in point of fact, a law to prevent murder," utterly eliding the participation of men in prostitution and their active solicitation of the "danger." As Judith Walkowitz notes in her ground-breaking study on Victorian prostitution, "[D]efenders of the patriarchal family . . . regarded prostitutes as a source of pollution and a constant temptation to middle-class sons" (34). Similar to the danger posed by women who threatened to expose another cultural infirmity, marital violence, the taint of syphilis might become a fountainhead infecting the empire's subjects throughout the age. The "subjects" in danger were definitively marked out by the legislators as men and their offspring: "Many a poor man suffered and died,—many a poor child was born to a life of misery and premature death."[10] That women were the perpetrators and men the victims of this disease was the implicit assumption of the debates. It went almost without saying that this danger was gendered, devolving solely through women, and curable only by their reappropriation to the norm. Women alone were examined under these acts—clearly an ineffective means of eliminating a disease that was primarily transmitted through heterosexual intercourse, but a very effective one of isolating women as the cause and source of it.

Similarly, Aurora bears the onus of danger within the home. The disorder created by the "dangerous women" provided a justification for their violent containment through a time-honored, eminently Victorian, method: the colonization of women's bodies and behavior. In the same way that the empire subdued the Eastern "Other," it would reclaim the savage women, retraining and purifying them. One legislator commented that the prostitutes "should be redeemed from a state of savagery to something approaching civilization."[11] Another noted that the Bishops who had supported the CD Acts were themselves "a smartish lot to go into an affair of this kind, some of them colonial." Significantly, this justified any level of violence, even what some critics of the acts later called "cruel", "brutalizing", and "violent attacks" by the police and hospital officials, productive of "great pain."

It was believed that these acts, through arrest, examination, treatment, and containment made women happier, healthier and more "civilized": "The girls came into the hospital turbulent, lawless, and godless, and it is astonishing the change that a few weeks produces in them. . . . [T]he poor creatures are apparently perfectly contented and happy."[12] The lock hospitals disciplined women by erasing their lawlessness, and contained them within the range of the cultural economy by placing them physically and socio-morally under control. The "normalized" behavior and appearance of these prostitutes became the linchpin of the Acts' success. Women were praised for bodily control, for maintaining standards of Victorian womanhood—silence and sobriety. Aurora must be domesticated as well, and through Talbot's and John's violent resignification of the domestic space (Aurora's life, marriage, and social position are mortally threatened, and Softy, the visible marker of Aurora's aggressive behavior, is murdered by Talbot), Aurora sheds the taint of her past and ascends to motherhood. Like the prostitutes in Parliament's idealized script, Aurora is saved, and in the novel's denouement, her "future belongs to [her] husband" (3:115). For the last three chapters—nearly eighty pages of the narrative—we hear the voice of this central character in the text no more. A similar silence surrounded the initial passage of the CD Acts. The "dangerous women" and their containment were so utterly normalized that they were discursively invisible for decades.

This reformation seems to suggest that Braddon's novel and the CD Acts operated only to reinforce domestic ideology. However, it is precisely the visibility of the narrative construction of the dangerous woman, the repeated citation to which Judith Butler refers, that threatens to collapse the clean distinctions offered by its binary opposition of domestic angel and her villainous counterpart. Indeed, the anxious representation of this dichotomy made apparent its inability to classify and, thus, manage women's identities. In her campaign against the CD Acts, Josephine Butler pointed out the difficulty in establishing distinctions between prostitutes and respectables "among the poor—the classes dealt with by the Contagious Diseases Acts—[because] the boundary lines between the virtuous and vicious is so gradually and imperceptibly shaded off, that there is no one part to which it would be possible to affix a distinct name or infallibly assign a class" (Walkowitz *Prostitution* 185). More complicating, Walkowitz reports in *City of Dreadful Delights* that even middle-class women shopping in the West End of London, a district frequented by prostitutes, were sometimes mistaken for their "fallen" sisters by police and the prostitutes' clientele (55, 129). Parliament feared this breakdown in terms as "a horrible thing to be avoided at any price,"[13] yet many were compelled to agree that the Acts granted police the power of "designating any woman they [chose] as a common prostitute."[14] These misrecognitions (and the fear of them) upset the functioning of the Acts in the districts of their operation, but, more significantly, they divulged the inability of the law to obliterate potentially dangerous women and exposed the profusion of social contradictions in the construction of women's identity and the framing of the dangerous woman. The increasing uncertainty that the articulation of these positions (dangerous woman/pure woman, dangerous woman/virtuous man) afforded caused the breakdown of the CD Acts and their eventual repeal in the 1883.

REVISION AND REPEAL

Only after the publication of novels like *Aurora Floyd* did these particular tensions associated with the violence against women emerge, only then was this political move brought under scrutiny. *Aurora Floyd* charted the configuration of the "dangerous woman," parodying and exposing patterns of chastisement as a means of ensuring domestic purity, and thus, opening the possibility of ideological critique. In this novel, Braddon defies the often silent and seemingly monolithic law, as Derrida suggests, by producing an excess that refigures notions of womanhood, the domestic space, and the origins of contaminating violence. This move, along with other cultural shifts, triggered a reexamination of these issues by revealing the "dangerous woman" as an ideologically charged construct designed to facilitate the purification of the domestic space and England. Braddon's "sensational" fiction explored this cultural conflict, delving into the heart of the apparently impossible and unreal. However, the pressure her sensationalism exerted on the real redefined what was possible, and more specifically, calls upon us as critics to reexamine the source of the danger in the Victorian domestic and sociocultural space.

NOTES

1. "Sensation" novels had their heyday in the 1860s and early 1870s. The term was developed by Victorian critics of Wilkie Collins's *The Woman in White*, Braddon's *Lady Audley's Secret*, and Mrs. Henry Wood's *East Lynne*, three novels considered to epitomize the genre, to describe the fiction of dramatic incident, bigamy, murder, and mystery. See below for a further discussion of this genre's place in the depiction of these issues. Henry Mansel argued that "female fiends [were] a stock article with sensation novelists" (262).

2. See Judith Walkowitz's *Prostitution and Victorian Society* for a full discussion of the debates surrounding the repeal of the CD Acts.

3. 3 Hansard 203 (20 July 1870), 576.

4. 3 Hansard 203 (20 July 1870), 1346.

5. It is important to note, however, that even in the absence of explicit signs of engagement, Braddon's express intention to tackle these issues, the correspondence of these narratives would be analytically important. As Jacques Derrida remarked, "There is a sort of paradoxical historicity in the experience of writing. The writer can be ignorant or naive in relation to the historical tradition which

bears him or her, or which s/he transforms, invents, displaces. But I wonder whether, even in the absence of historical awareness or knowledge s/he doesn't 'treat' history in the course of an experience which is more significant, more alive, more *necessary* in a word, than that of some professional 'historians'" (54– 55).

6. Here, Butler refers to drag performance and the closeting of homosexual identities. This analysis provides an apt model for conceiving of the performance of domestic identities, as well as the "closeting" of marital violence. Feminist activists have frequently borrowed the metaphors that the gay rights movement and queer theory have utilized to describe social repression and violence, to discuss the complexity of the social relations in the violent home. Although there exist profound distinctions between these sites, this essay explores Butler's articulation of gendered identity to interrogate the gendered nature of violence in the domestic space.

7. As I will later discuss, Aurora herself bears the attributes of "human" and "brute creation" in her characterization's Orientalization. Edward Said describes the phenomenon of Orientalization in his book *Orientalism*.

8. Edward Said notes in *Culture and Imperialism* that there are five characteristics to the mature British imperialism of the late nineteenth century. "One is a self-forgetting delight in the use of power—the power to observe, rule, hold, and profit from distant territories of people . . . . Another is an ideological rationale for reducing then reconstituting the native as someone to be ruled and managed . . . . Third is the idea of Western salvation and redemption through its 'civilizing mission' . . . . Fourth is the security of a situation that permits the conqueror not to look into the truth of the violence he does . . . . Fifth is the process by which, after the natives have been displaced from their historical location on their land, their history is rewritten as a function of the imperial one. This process uses narrative to dispel contradictory memories and occlude violence" (131–32). I argue that these elements are anticipated in this novel and others like it, as well as serving as a metaphor for the relative invisibility of violence in the upper- and middle-class domestic space. The appearance of these themes in the fiction of mid-century demonstrates not only the mutually constitutive nature of fiction and culture, but also, by virtue of the fate of the figures in this novel, an implicit critique of this violence.

9. Stana Nenadic constructs a lengthy argument concerning the use of novels, particularly sensation novels, for insight into Victorian culture. See "Illegitimacy, Insanity, and Insolvency: Wilkie Collins and the Victorian Nightmares." *The Arts, Literature, and Society* 133–62.

10. 3 Hansard 203 (20 July 1870), 604.

11. 3 Hansard 201 (24 May 1870), 1334.

12. 3 Hansard 203 (20 July 1870), 594.

13. 3 Hansard 201 (24 May 1870), 1318, 1326.

14. *Westminster Review* in 3 Hansard 201 (24 May 1870), 1308.

WORKS CITED

Armstrong, Nancy. "The Rise of the Domestic Woman." *Feminisms*. Ed. Robyn R. Warhol and Diane Price Herndl. New Brunswick, N.J.: Rutgers UP, 1991. 894–925.

Braddon, Mary Elizabeth. *Aurora Floyd*. New York: Garland, 1979.

Butler, Judith. *Bodies That Matter*. New York: Routledge, 1993.

Derrida, Jacuqes. *Acts of Literature*. Ed. Derik Attridge. New York: Routledge, 1992.

Hansard. *Parliamentary Debates*. 3rd series.

[Mansel, Henry.] "Sensation Novels." *London Quarterly Review* 113 (1863): 251–68.

"Miss Braddon." *The Nation* 1 (18): 593–94.

"Miss Braddon's Novels." *Dublin University Magazine* 75 (1870): 436–46.

Nenadic, Stana. "Illegitimacy, Insanity, and Insolvency: Wilkie Collins and the Victorian Nightmares." *The Arts, Literature, and Society*. 133–62.

"Novels in Relation to Female Education." *Dublin University Magazine* 85 (1875): 516–17.

"Our Female Sensation Novelists." *Living Age* 78 (1863): 352–369.

"Our Novels: The Sensational School." *Temple Bar* 29 (1870): 410–24.

[Rae, W. Fraser.] "Sensation Novelists: Miss Braddon." *North British Review* 43 (1865): 91–105.

Said, Edward W. *Culture and Imperialism*. New York: Random House, 1993.

———. *Orientalism*. New York: Pantheon, 1978.

Walkowitz, Judith. *City of Dreadful Delight*. Chicago: U of Chicago P, 1992.

———. *Prostitution and Victorian Society*. Cambridge: Cambridge UP, 1980.

PART III

Braddon in the Literary Marketplace

EIGHT

Mary Elizabeth Braddon in Australia: Queen of the Colonies

Toni Johnson-Woods

In the early nineteenth century the publishing world changed forever. The rise in literacy, improved transportation, removal of the taxation on knowledge, and improved printing technologies meant that a sixteen-page weekly periodical could be purchased for one penny. For the first time in history, publications were selling in the hundreds of thousands, and proprietors, anxious to capture readers' pennies, quickly realised an economic imperative: an exciting serial could treble sales. Australia was no different, "books and newspapers are eagerly sought after and read . . . . This is more remarkable when you get further into the Bush than it is in the towns" one observer noted (Carrington, quoted in Ward 13). The new colonists had witnessed the growth of a cheap press "back home" and no doubt wished to have access to similar reading material in their new country; they did not need to feel any more isolated than they already were. A population who had experienced the growth of the first mass media brought to the new colonies[1] the hunger for reading material.

Australian conditions were grim for book readers but ideal for weekly publications: local book publishing industry was limited, there were few libraries and fewer circulating libraries, and printed material from overseas took a long time to arrive. The colonial press responded to the need for fiction by producing a unique periodical as described by novelist/ journalist David Christie Murray in the *Contemporary Review* in 1891:

> In one respect Australian journalism surpasses the English. We have nothing to show which will at all compare with the *Australasian* or the *Leader;* but it is easy to see that they and their congeners of other cities (which are worthy of the same high praise) owe their especial excellences to local conditions. These great weekly issues give all the week's news, and all the striking articles which have appeared in the daily journals of which they are at once the growth and the compendium. They do much more than this, for they include whatever the gardener, the agriculturist, the housewife, the lady of fashion, the searcher of general literature, the chess-player, the squatter can most desire to know. They provide for all sorts of tastes and needs, and between their first sheet and their last they render their readers what we in England buy half a score of special journals to secure. The reason for their existence is simple. There is not population enough to support the specialist as we know him at home, and an eager and inquiring people will be served. (305–6)

Such compendiums resembled the English working-class penny periodicals in appearance and content, and the staple of both was the weekly serial. Though at the time Christie-Murray wrote his article the "searcher of general literature" would have found that English fiction dominated the fiction columns, it had not always been the case. Prior to the 1850s colonists exhibited a "distinctive national feeling," no doubt because many of the early immigrants left England as "convicts or assisted migrants" (2) and sought to establish a new culture in the colonies. Evidence of this flourishing patriotism was apparent in the high percentage of local fiction in new colonial publications. However, after a few years, there was a discernible shift from local to imported fiction. This movement reflected the bourgeois "calm-down" (Ward 114, 137); the wealthier immigrants who "greatly strengthened the middle class" did not demonstrate the same desire to replace their old cultural icons with new.[2] Another contributing factor to the increased overseas content was the creation of the fiction bureau. From 1872 Tillotson's Fiction Bureau offered a cheap, dependable and consistent supply of fiction.[3] Given that colonial editors now had numerous authors from whom to choose, which author appeared most frequently in Australian periodicals?

MARY ELIZABETH BRADDON

Why was Braddon so popular in Australia? With the advent of the first mass media came the first media stars; *Lady Audley's Secret* created the same press sensation Wilkie Collins and E.D.E.N. Southworth had.[4] As a consequence Braddon attracted considerable media attention, even in Australia. The Tasmanian literary journal, *Walch's* Literary Intelligencer (*Walch's*) documented her many literary milestones. In May 1863 *Walch's* recounted her early struggles and proclaimed that Braddon's "wonderful . . . *Lady Audley's Secret* has been the greatest hit . . . since the ever-famous *Pickwick Papers*" (*Walch's* 169). Later that year a laudatory review of *Lady Audley's Secret* praised Braddon's descriptions and recommended the book as "fascinating" (October 1863: 51). It continued to notice anything Braddon wrote, book and periodical appearances. Thirty-four of her titles headed *Walch's* "Reading for Winter Evenings" list (a nonalphabetical list) for a decade. Her books must have occupied considerable shelf space in Walch's bookstore. Her name also appeared in other local publications: the *Australian Journal* often contained information about her lifestyle,[5] and naturally periodicals reviewed her books.[6] Furthermore, there was a familial connection in Australia. Braddon's brother, Edward Braddon, had emigrated and was making a political name for himself in Tasmania.[7] Also one cannot discount the needs of readers who still felt cultural ties to Britain; her novels document the fashions, furnishings, and fads that appealed to colonial women both as things to emulate and as details to stave off homesickness. Braddon was more than a well-marketed author of costume melodramas with a colonial relative; her popular fiction captured some of the emerging Australian ideals.

Twenty Braddon novels appeared in major colonial periodicals between 1872 and 1895;[8] her closest rival, Wilkie Collins, had only nine novels appear. Of these 28 appearances, 17 were in Melbourne papers: eight in the *Age* and nine in the *Melbourne Leader;*[9] seven were in Sydney: five in the *Town and Country,* and one each in the *Sydney Mail* and the *Illustrated Sydney News;* four were in Queensland: three in the *Queenslander* and one in the *Brisbane Courier.*[10] It is fitting that Melbourne, especially the populist *Age,* would be the first to publish Braddon. Both the city and the woman were reinventing themselves. After the chaotic goldrush days, Melbourne was becoming more conservative.[11] Likewise, Braddon had moved up the literary feeding chain: from writing for working-class penny publications such as the *London Journal,* she now edited middle-class shilling magazines such as *Temple Bar.* No longer did her stories jostle alongside the popular thrillers of Pierce Egan and John Frederick Smith, they now resided among the more stately prose of Eliza Lynn Linton and Justin McCarthy. As Melbourne graduated from shanty town to cultural capital, Braddon moved from Bohemia to Belgravia.

In *Writing the Colonial Adventure,* Robert Dixon asserts that the "romance genre is an historically important site of contestation between contemporary discourses on gender, race, nation and empire" (Dixon 3).

Sensational fiction is an even more fractured "site of contestation" than romance. The genre evolved from the pages of the weekly press and thus responded immediately to the society in which it was produced.[12] Thrilling audiences with themes of bigamy, adultery, madness, and murder, the sensational genre demonstrates that popular fiction is not "a vehicle for the reproduction of dominant ideologies" (Dixon 9); indeed, the genre was created by the fractures in dominant ideologies, the anxieties of the Victorian age. But what happened during Braddon's "calm-down," the very years her novels were starting to appear in Australia? From the 1870s Braddon's novels lacked the hardcore sensationalism of *Lady Audley's Secret* and *Aurora Floyd;* during this time she had merely extended the textual boundaries by creating a duality in her texts. She fashioned two narratives: the primary narrative, which conformed to the dominant ideology, and a secondary one that subverted it. It is the layering of stories that allowed exploration of working-class/middle-class, imperialist/colonist, man/woman contradictions that appealed to the burgeoning Australian middle classes.

By presenting the restrictions of English life, Braddon justifies empire building. When male fictional characters leave domestic confines to either solve the mystery of domestic disharmony or recoup financial losses by exploiting the colonies, they are escaping domesticity in order to experience adventure, the adventure of empire. Whether George Talboys (*Lady Audley's Secret*), Richard Redmayne (*To the Bitter End*) or Bothwell Grahame (*Wyllard's Weird*), Braddon's males echo the same sentiments about the narrow bounds of their world and their feelings of constriction. Redmayne is typical when he is described as:

> by nature adventurous and speculative; not a man to plod on day by day contentedly . . . . Morning after morning he stared at the painted walls of his bed-chamber, bright in the glory of the summer sunshine, with a pang of disappointment, to think his life was held in by their narrow bounds. (*To the Bitter End,* 1:6–7)

It is acceptable for males to desert wives and families for months and even years because it is done in the name of furthering the British Empire.

Women and domesticity, of course, work against discourse of empire; home and hearth prevent men from empire building. While early Braddon women, such as Aurora Floyd and Lady Audley, threatened physical death to the male characters, in her later novels their menace is psychological: the threat of emasculation. Braddon confirms male's fear of domesticity by presenting the feminine succubi: women who drain men's adventurous spirit and prevent them from penetrating exotic other lands. In *Vixen* Braddon proffers two gendered views of the colonies: "[Lord Strishfogel] was in the South Seas by this time, writing a book and enjoying halcyon days among the friendly natives, swimming like a dolphin in those summery seas, and indulging in harmless flirtations with dusky princesses, whose chief attire was made of shells and flowers, and whose untutored dancing was more vigorous than refined. At the end of that second season, Jane Umleigh [who loved Lord Strishfogel] had serious thoughts of turning philanthropist, and taking a shipload of destitute young women to Queensland. Anything would be better than this sense of a wasted life and ignominious failure" (*Vixen* 21).

By juxtaposing the two visions of empire, Braddon writes the traditionally assigned gender roles of empire building: the male's eroticised pleasures of writing, swimming, and flirting, and the female's romanticised philanthropy. Not only does this juxtaposition underscore the ludicrous simplicity of both visions, more importantly, it demonstrates that for women the colonies mean hard work, while for men they mean escape.

Only after the male characters have had their adventure and tamed the bush are women allowed to come to the colonies. Women are second-wave migrants who come to domesticate the wild spaces, this is their proper and fitting role according to the male characters. For example, Redmayne left his only child, Grace, when he came to Australia because he believes "that's too rough a life for such as you. I didn't bring you up like a lady, and send you to boarding-school, to take you among such a rough lot as I must work with out yonder" (*To the Bitter End* 11). However, after some time in Australia, Redmayne changes his mind and decides that Grace should join him:

> The fact that life might be lonely [for Grace] . . . he dismissed . . . carelessly . . . . Here in these backwoods she would be a queen . . . . No doubt some handsome young emigrant would woo and win her . . . there was room enough at Bulrush Meads for a patriarchal household; and Richard Redmayne could fancy himself sitting under his vine-clad verandah, cool and spacious as a Sevillian patio, with a noisy crowd of grandchildren clambering on his knees. (*To the Bitter End* 28–29)

Redmayne's selfishness is typical of males in Braddon's texts; for though she allows them their freedom, she cannot forgive them for deserting their responsibilities, and Redmayne loses the thing he loves most, Grace.[13]

In reality the colonies offered women the promise of security. And Australian female readers could reinscribe on Braddon's female bodies their lived colonial experiences. They were more likely to understand the struggles and triumphs of Braddon's self-fashioning heroines; migrating women were as desperate as Lady Audley and as headstrong as Aurora Floyd. Immigration to Australia was not for the fainthearted: it was the furthermost colony, the one with the harshest climate and the worst reputation.[14] The women who left their homes and families to travel to the antipodes were more enterprising and courageous than history gives them credit for.[15] In Britain unemployment was high; working-class and "distressed gentlewomen" competed for the same jobs. The colonies needed labor and actively campaigned through government agents and philanthropic societies such as the Female Middle Class Emigration Society (1862). Women were particularly targeted because of their "civilising" effect and after the 1861 British census revealed that there was a "surplus" of single women, no doubt they found solace in the fact that they were wanted somewhere.[16] Thus Australia potentially offered employment and marriage.

Braddon's irregular relationship with John Maxwell no doubt increased her awareness of the social power of marriage. Her fictional bigamous marriages expose another fracture that would have appealed to the colonial reader. Away from familial and social circles, amid the social chaos of the goldfields, women decided that, as for Braddon's heroines, a new life could, and often did, mean a new partner.[17] The subversive/secondary romances not only contained the sensational elements of bigamy, adultery, and seduction, more importantly, they showed women how to trade their appearance for the security of a protector. Beautiful governesses captured old men's hearts and wallets. Popular fiction utilized Cinderella-type relationships as a narrative vehicle. The class barrier however, was rarely broken, it was only a matter of chapters before an aristocratic background was established. Braddon's characters do more than marry up; they expose a class system in transition. Even though these unequal relationships enjoy only brief successes, they reveal contemporary anxieties about the increasing power of the middle classes. Colonial women who came to Australia hoping to progress from maid to mistress witnessed the transformations caused by newly acquired wealth. As one historian noted,

> In Australia social confusion reigned after the goldrushes. Owners of many of the largest houses and some of the most expensive equipages . . . were men from the lowest class who had made fortunes on the diggings, while the scions of noble families in England, men who had won high honours at ancient universities, were driving the cabs. (Clark 312)

Evidently it was not uncommon for colonial women to marry up; the vulgar, wealthy woman became a stock character in Australian serials. Though a figure of ridicule, these women demonstrated that it was possible for a girl to better herself. Therefore, it is of little wonder that Braddon's domestics turned duchesses had more cultural currency with the currency lasses.

In her stories fictional maids and manservants represent another site of domestic disharmony and one that was particularly pertinent to Australia. Australia's domestic servants were brasher than their British counterparts—they dined, lived, and dressed like their employers.[18] Colonial immigration advertisements in the *Dundee People's Journal* in 1875 offered free passages for "agricultural labourers and domestic servants" and promised that on arrival they would be "received into Government house." Working conditions, too, demystified the master/servant relationship. In a land where "downstairs" was really the next room, the codified strata could not be maintained as maid and mistress had to work side by side. As Braddon noted in *An Open Verdict,* harmony exists when a mistress does not interfere with a maid's work. The following excerpt from an Australian serial reflects the colonial attitude:

> The table was laid for four, and Miriam [newly arrived from England] gave a little start of surprise when the servant-girl and the man of all work entered and took their places at the table. Mrs Neilson appeared serenely unconscious that anything unusual was occurring, and talked as freely before and to them as if they were honoured guests . . . . After breakfast Miriam exclaimed: "Surely, grandma, you do not take your meals with your servants."
>
> "No my dear . . . they take their meals with me."
>
> "But grandma, don't you think it lowers your dignity?"
>
> "Dignity, my dear, is an almost unknown evil in Victoria here. Jack is as good as his master, and if you see my girl going out to-day you will discover she wears a silk dress as good as mine; a better bonnet, and carries a handsome sunshade . . . . You have brought some English notions out with you, I see; but you will soon learn. We in this sunny land are totally different to the people of the mother country in many respects." (Lee 407)

Braddon, remembering her own days of servitude, often upsets the domestic hierarchy by giving her lower orders immense power in the text. In *The Day Will Come* Lord Cheriton's ex-mistress lives in his gatekeeper's lodge and is thus a constant reminder of his earlier indiscretion; in *The Fatal Three* a servant's declaration that the ward is truly the master's illegitimate daughter causes the irreparable marital breach; in *Just as I Am* a maid revenges herself by marrying her mistress's brother. For those who find actions a little too subtle, Braddon has one character state outright "your father . . . told me that he gave you [a female companion] to me as a free gift . . . and that you should be as much my own property as if you were a little negro girl bought in an African market-place" (*Just as I am*, 313) and in one scene she writes of a girl who "sat with her feet on the fender, and was regaled with strong tea and delicious home-made bread and butter, and unconsciously sold herself into bondage" (*Just as I am* 71). Braddon's depiction of domestic slavery and its discontents mirrored Australia's burgeoning egalitarian ideology, while simultaneously articulating the fears the middle class had of servant power.

Braddon exhibits the contemporary fears of the indigenous peoples and variously describes them as cannibals (*Strangers and Pilgrims* 142), as "human tigers [who] had outraged helpless women, and wallowed in the blood of infants" (*The Story of Barbara* 152), and pagans who needed converting (*Strangers and Pilgrims* and *Wyllard's Weird*), although she underwrites such assertions by reminding readers of native superiority. In *Phantom Fortune* Louis Asoph, Rajah of Bisnagar, informs Lady Maulevrier: "we were scholars and gentleman [sic], priests and soldiers, two thousand years before your British ancestors ran wild in their woods, and sacrificed to their unknown gods on rocky altars reeking with human blood!" (*Phantom Fortune* 109–10). Braddon resorts to humor to demonstrate the stupidity of contemporary fears in *To the Bitter End* when one woman contemplates life in Australia with horror:

> what leave Brierwood, and the county in which she had been born and bred, to go to associate with red Indians—people who scalped each other and lived in wigwams or if not red Indians something quite as bad— Blackamoors perhaps! She would sooner starve than taste a bit of victuals that had been touched by a Blackamoor . . . . Richard explained that the aboriginal Australian might be dark of aspect, but did not abound in the vicinity of Bulrush Meads; emigration was the order of the day, she could have plenty of stalwart Irishmen to till her lands and rear her corn. She would rather "lief have to do with Blackamoors as Irish. It's bad enough to have 'em about at hopping time." (*To the Bitter End*, 3: 57–58)

The conflation of colonial others, red Indians, Blackamoors, and Australian Aborigines, into a homogeneous group, clearly was for humorous effect. In this seemingly simple passage, Braddon reveals that emigration has robbed the Aborigines of land and that a new order of slavery exists. Australia has become civilized; it is a nation that does not need to use colonized blacks or reds for slavery it uses colonised whites. Whether Braddon was suggesting that indigenous peoples would be incapable of performing routine chores or that it was wrong to exploit them, it is impossible to say. The shocked comment about fractious Irish laborers shows Braddon's awareness of the Irish problem. The excerpt exposes the many faces of slavery, and white servants could be considered slaves. It is still a matter of some debate as to whether convicts were indentured slaves—Braddon's statement, though suggesting free labor (and not convict labor), gestures to the power relationships when the richer, stronger, aristocratic, or English, colonize land/body whether Irish, Kentish, poor relatives, or Aborigines.

As the imperial imperative was to exploit colonial resources, anyone who interfered was offending imperial order. To rape the land and steal from the indigenous was fine but to cheat the empire invited disgrace as Lord Maulevrier discovered when he returned home to a scandal because he was "rumoured to have sold the British forces in the Carnatic provinces to one of the native Princes. Yes, to have taken gold, gold to an amount which Clive in his most rapacious moments never dreamt of" (*Phantom Fortune* 7). Braddon's cynical reference to Clive indicates how she viewed the economics of imperialism. When one of the wronged Indian princes comes to England to regain his property, Lady Maulevrier refers the prince to the greatest upholder of the British Empire, its legal system, and she sneers "do you suppose that any English judge or English jury would believe so wild a story?" (*Phantom Fortune* 112). Braddon's honorable prince contrasts to the greedy Lord Maulevrier but ultimately he cannot succeed (or what would happen to an empire founded on such avarice) and the prince dies before he can reclaim his property. Property is, of course, most exploited and not just the cultural artifacts of a nation; land too is one of the richest resources—the natural beauty of Australia was not to be enjoyed for her own wild beauty, it was renarrated as a part of the sceptered isle.

Braddon's homes operate as discourses. A typical English home is the crumbling manor; the decaying outer shell reflects the inner disharmony.[19] Australian homes, by contrast, represent new beginnings and naturally were drawn with a British brush:

> There was hill as well as dale, and the site of the rough log dwelling-house was as picturesque as anything he had seen in his holiday ramble. What a king he might be here with Grace! he thought to himself. The life would not be rough for her, safe sheltered under his wing, and with honest Kentish lasses for her servants. His quick eye told him how the place might be improved: a roomy parlour built out on one side, with a wide verandah supported by rustic pillars, a pleasant shelter beneath which his darling might sit and work on sunny afternoons. And what a prospect for those gentle eyes to gaze upon! what a varied sweep of hill and valley, bright silver streamlet flashing athward greenest of meadows, a thousand sheep looking no bigger than so many daisies upon the distant uplands, a blue lake that was vast as an inland sea in the foreground, and far away on the left of the landscape a forest of almost tropical richness. (*To the Bitter End*, 2:22–23)

Braddon's description of a kingdom, complete with white servants, does not reflect the reality of the Australian countryside but reflects the Edward Gibbon Wakefield's vision that the colonies were to be little Englands. Colonizers tried to make the native countryside conform to British norms; one "marked out so many acres for wheat here, barley there . . . wide level pastures for his cattle; dotting down hedges and boundaries putting in every five-barred gate which was to impart to that fertile wilderness, the trim aspect of an English farm" (*To the Bitter End* 2:29) and echoes Henry Stanley's vision for a town in Africa "what a settlement we could have . . . pretty cottages . . . teeming with herds of cattle and fields of corn . . . how much better that its present wild and deserted aspect."[20] "Australia has been a true goldfield to the Sensation School of novelists, and many a good 'find' has it provided for them."[21] The antipodes provided Braddon with a convenient place of exile for deserting husbands (*Lady Audley's Secret*), unwanted husbands (*Aurora Floyd*), murderers (*Cloven Foot*), rejected lovers (*Wyllard's Weird*), "surplus sons" (*Strangers and Pilgrims*) and "incipient drunkards" (*Cut by the County*). Men who felt stifled in the narrow atmosphere of England could flee to the Antipodes sure that their talents, no matter how slight would earn them a fortune, people such as Bothwell Grahame, an idler and a reprobate who thinks that he might "sub-edit a colonial paper . . . [or] . . . turn parson and convert the nigger" (*Wyllard's Weird* 34). Thus Australia is a land of contradictions for Braddon; on one hand it is filled with English n'er do wells and, on the other, it provides them with an opportunity to do well. It is the place where Englishmen believed "I shall fall upon my feet, you may be sure" (*Wyllard's Weird* 34). Men fell on their feet by exploiting local resources: the goldfields and the land:

> [I went to Queensland because I had] . . . a speculative temper, and an aversion to any mode of earning my living which was open to me at home. I was not a genius like you, Cuthbert. I always hated head-work and was plucked ignominiously in every examination at Hillersley . . . . I heard of men doing wonders out yonder in the sheep-line . . . . I left Exeter with a few pounds in my pocket, and worked my way out to Australia, before the mast. I had rather a hard time of it for the first year or so, and made a nearer acquaintance with starvation than I cared about. But before the second year was over, I was manager . . . on the Darling Downs . . . . My employer made sixty thousand pounds in less than ten years, but contrived to drink himself to death in the same time. He had made me his partner a few years before he died. (*Lost for Love* 10–12)

Braddon does not reproduce the pastoral idyll; even gold comes only after "many months, toiling manfully . . . standing knee-deep in running water for hours on end, rocking the cradle with patience that surpassed the patience of maternity" (*To the Bitter End* 2:17). British readers believed that Braddon's descriptions were "real" and this led one critic to comment, "There is no faltering in the lady's firm touch. . . . Whether she is describing life in a penal settlement at the antipodes, or writing the sanguinary history of the coup d'état in *Ishmael.*"[22]

Braddon exploited Australia as a site for adventure and escape in her novels, and the new colonists no doubt relished reading stories about their burgeoning country. For though the first wave of colonists rejected things English in their earliest days, the second wave of emigrant Australians liked to read how the new colonies entertained and entered the fictional stakes in their old Home. Braddon's presentations of men, women, race, servants, and home exposed the ambiguities of colonization—the "lived experience of imperialism" (Dixon 1). William Makepeace Thackeray wrote: "if I could plot like Braddon I would be the greatest novelist who ever lived"—a talent that Australians recognized and approbated by making the Queen of the Circulating Libraries the Queen of the Colonies.

NOTES

1. Australia was not unified until 1901 and thus "the colonies" (New South Wales, Queensland, and Victoria) were treated as separate entities.

2. "Calm down" is Manning Clark's term for this period of Australian history when culture came to reflect "a society of transplanted Britons . . . who echoed the Old World of Europe rather than capture the spirit of the New." Manning Clark's *History of Australia,* abridged by Michael Cathcar (313–14).

3. Newspaper proprietor William Tillotson perceived the need for a steady source of serialised fiction. Through energetic canvassing, he signed Mary Elizabeth Braddon to his bureau. After her, many authors followed. By 1880 he had signed sixty-three writers. Fiction bureaus sent out advance sheets to editors/ proprietors throughout the world; this accounts for the almost simultaneous publication of the same serial in such diverse places as Canada, Australia, and Newcastle. Tillotson's success motivated others to set up similar bureaus such as W. C. Leng, the Authors' Syndicate, Cassell's, the National Press Agency, and the Northern Newspaper Syndicate.

4. Both authors' heroines created marketing crazes that saw hats, perfume, and fans.

5. For example, "The News and Notes" column, the *Australian Journal* August 1890: 694.

6. One tended to hyperbole: "we have always believed that there lay in her [Braddon] a very considerable amount of the literary faculty, amounting almost to genius" *Australasian,* June 1873, 616.

7. Sir Edward Braddon became the premier (1894–99) of Tasmania and helped to write the Australian Constitution. He was knighted in 1891. His descendant, Russell Braddon, is a well-known, expatriate, Australian writer.

8. My research has focused on Queensland, New South Wales, and Victorian newspapers:

Australian Appearances, Sydney Mail, Town & Country, Leader, Brisbane Courier, Age, Illustrated Sydney News, Queenslander.

9. *The Leader* was the weekly compendium of the *Age,* but *The Leader* was not merely a summarized *Age;* it maintained a separate editorial staff and published different fiction. Though both bought Braddon serials, they never used the same serial nor did the two publications run two Braddon serials concurrently.

Table 8.1 Braddon's Australian Serialization

Year	Title	Australian Appearances
1872	To the Bitter End	*Age* 20 Apr.–11 Jan. 1873
1873	Strangers and Pilgrims	*Sydney Mail* 14 Jun.–7 Feb. 1874
	Publicans and Sinners	*Town & Country* 13 Sep.–16 May 1874
	Taken at the Flood	*Leader* 25 Oct.–18 Jul. 1874
1877	An Open Verdict	*Leader* 14 Jul.–9 Mar. 1878
1878	Vixen	*Leader* 30 Nov.–2 Aug. 1879
	The Cloven Foot	*Brisbane Courier* 7 Dec.–9 Aug. 1879
		Age 28 Dec.–8 Nov. 1879
1879	The Cloven Foot	*Town & Country* 8 Feb.–1 Nov. 1879
	The Story of Barbara: Her Splendid Misery and Her Gilded Cage	*Leader* 20 Sep.–6 May 1880
1880	Just as I Am	*Age* 27 Mar.–1 Jan. 1881
	An Open Verdict	*Town & Country* 3 Apr.–18 Dec. 1880
	Vixen	*Queenslander* 19 Jan.–12 July 1880
1883	Phantom Fortune	*Illustrated Sydney News* 14 Apr.–15 Mar. 1884
1884	Ishmael	*Age* 22 Mar.–14 Mar. 1885
		Town & Country 22 Mar.–14 Mar. 1885
		Queenslander 26 Apr.–14 Mar. 1885
1884	Wyllard's Weird	*Leader* 1 Nov.–30 May 1885
1886	The Fatal Three	*Queensland* 7 Jan.–14 Jul. 1888
		Leader 28 Jan.–4 Aug. 1888
1889	Whose Was the Hand?	*Age* 11 Jan.–14 Jun. 1890
		Town & Country 1 Feb.–20 Sep. 1890
1891	The World, the Flesh & the Devil	*Leader* 24 Jan.–4 Jul. 1891
1893	All Along the River	*Leader* 4 Feb.–29 Jul. 1893
1894	Thou Art the Man	*Age* 6 Jan.–7 Jul. 1894
1895	Sons of Fire	*Leader* 23 Feb.–14 Sep. 1895

10. Unlike the *Leader/Age*, the *Queenslander/Brisbane Courier* often published the same novels, but the erratic appearances of fiction in the Brisbane Courier indicates its secondary importance; fiction was used only as a filler.

11. Paul de Serville's book *Pounds and Pedigrees: The Upper Class in Victoria 1850–80* suggests that the disappearance of the duel in the 1850s (34) and the increasing conservative stance of the once-radical *Argus* gesture to an increasing respectability (264).

12. Braddon's novels contain references to colored spectacles, railway accidents, religious fads, and cultural concerns such as the 1837 Deceased Wife's Sister Act.

13. The irony is that England has been far harsher to Grace who, without a protector, elopes and dies.

14. Australia had been long condemned as a land of prostitutes, convicts, and savages.

15. Women often took abusive employers to court, ran their own businesses, and generally displayed independence and ingenuity. See, for example, A. James Hammerton's *Emigrant Gentlewomen: Genteel Poverty and Female Emigration, 1830–1914*, Pauline Rule's "Honora and Her Sisters: Success and Sorrow among Irish Immigrant Women in Colonial Victoria," and Libby Connors's "The Politics of Ethnicity: Irish Orphan Girls at Moreton Bay."

16. Immigration agents offered bounties for single women (15 pounds) because the disproportion of the sexes was reputed to have caused immorality. The 1861 Victorian census showed that the proportion of females to males had risen to 70 percent (Sherington 65).

17. Emigrating to the colonies seemed a reasonable response to an unworkable marriage; certainly it was a cheaper option than divorce. Many inquiries, such as the one below, appeared in the weekly Australian periodicals:

> Ninety-Three writes—Suppose a woman marries, lives with her husband a short time, leaves him, and returns to the home of her parents, taking her maiden name; afterwards marries again without getting or applying for a divorce; lives with number 2 very happily several years, but to better her condition pecuniarily, leaves him and goes into a distant country, applies for and gets, divorced from him, and marries again, with numbers 1 and 2 still living, so far as known. Now, what is the condition of number 2? Can he be considered a married man or not? Does the fact of her being already a married woman when marrying her make any difference in the law and does not the divorce make him free as well, and could she rightfully and legally get a divorce without first getting a divorce from her first husband no. 1? (*Australian Journal* April 1875: 467)

Similar English periodicals (the *London Journal*, the *Family Herald*, *Reynolds' Miscellany* for instance) did not have such letters in their columns, and though this could possibly reflect an editorial decision, the fact that an Australian editor thought such letters worthwhile, suggests a perceived need for such information.

18. A Punch cartoon "Servantgalism in Australia—A Fact" (14 May 1864: 206) shows a female servant in riding habit telling her mistress "If you please, 'm, I have an hour to spare, and I'm goin' to try my new 'orse!"

19. In *An Open Verdict, Vixen, A Cloven Foot, The Day Will Come, Wyllard's Weird,* and *The Story of Barbara* the crumbling aristocratic lands bought by the newly wealthy middle class gesture to the eroding power of the upper class.

20. Dispatch to the *New York Herald,* 1871.

21. "The Sensation School" 417.

22. "Crime in Fiction" 188–89.

WORKS CITED

Braddon, Mary Elizabeth. *Aurora Floyd.* London: Tinsley Brothers, 1863.

———. *The Cloven Foot. Melbourne Leader.* Nov. 30–August 2, 1879.

———. *Cut by the County Third Volume of The One Thing Needful.* London: J. and R. Maxwell, 1886.

———. *The Day Will Come. Melbourne Age.* Jan 12–July 27, 1889.

———. *Lady Audley's Secret.* Oxford: Oxford UP, 1987.

———. *Lost for Love. Belgravia.* Nov. 1873–Feb. 1875.

———. *An Open Verdict. Melbourne Leader.* July 14–March 9, 1878.

———. *Phantom Fortune. Illustrated Sydney News.* April 14–March 15, 1884.

———. *The Story of Barbara: Her Splendid Misery, and Her Gilded Gage: A Novel.* London: Simpkin, Marshall, Hamilton, Kent, 1890.

———. *Strangers and Pilgrims. Sydney Mail.* June 14–Feb 7, 1874.

———. *To the Bitter End.* London: Simpkin, Marshall, 1872.

———. *Vixen.* London: Maxwell, 1879.

———. *Wyllard's Weird. Melbourne Leader.* Nov. 1–May 30, 1885.

Christie Murray, David. *Contemporary Review* (1891): 305–6.

Clark, Manning. *History of Australia.* abridged by Michael Cathcart. Melbourne: Melbourne UP, 1993.

Connors, Libby. "The Politics of Ethnicity: Irish Orphan Girls at Moreton Bay" in *Irish–Australian Studies: Papers Delivered at the Seventh Irish–Australian Conference.* Ed Rebecca Pelan. Sydney: Crossing P, 1994.

"Crime in Fiction" *Blackwood's* (July 1890): 188–89.

De Serville, Paul. *Pounds and Pedigrees: The Upper Class in Victoria 1850–80.* Oxford: Oxford UP, 1991.

Dixon, Robert. *Writing the Colonial Adventure: Race, Gender and Nation in Anglo–Australian Popular Fiction, 1875–1914.* Cambridge: Cambridge UP, 1995.

Hammerton, James. *Emigrant gentlewomen: genteel poverty and female emigration, 1830–1914.* London: Croom Helm; Totowa, N.J.: Rowman and Littlefield, 1979.

Lee, Mrs. Harrison. "Tempted and Tried: The Story of Two Sisters: An Australian Tale." *Australian Journal.* Apr. 1888: 407.

Letter. *Australian Journal.* Apr. 1875: 467.

"News and Notes" column. *The Australian Journal.* Aug. 1890: 694.

Rule, Pauline. "Honora and Her Sisters: Success and Sorrow among Irish Immigrant Women in Colonial Victoria" in *Irish–Australian Studies: Papers Delivered at the Seventh Irish–Australian Conference.* Ed. Rebecca Pelan. Sydney: Crossing, 1994.

"The Sensational School." *Temple Bar* 29 (1870): 417.

Sherington, Geoffrey. *Australia's immigrants, 1788–1978.* Sydney; Boston: Allen & Unwin, 1980.

Walch's Literary Intelligence and General Advertiser. 1859–1916.

Ward, Russel. *The Australian Legend.* Melbourne: Oxford UP, 1978.

NINE

"Our Author":
Braddon in the Provincial Weeklies

Jennifer Carnell and Graham Law

INTRODUCTION

The scope of Braddon's work, in its quantity, versatility, and above all in its tendency to cross boundaries, remains both surprising and disquieting. Her literary career stretched from the eve of the American Civil War to the outbreak of the Great War in Europe. Her copious literary output centered around some eighty novels, whose form ranged from melodrama to naturalism, from romance to satire, and whose ideological stance compassed both the challenging and the conformist. A similar variety can also be found in their modes of publication. The first British editions of her novels in book form varied in format from low-quality "shilling dreadfuls," at the beginning of her career, through the bulky and expensive triple-decker editions aimed largely for discount sale to the rental libraries, to the slim single-volume editions sold at low but fixed prices in book shops in increasingly large quantities from the 1890s. Moreover, the vast majority of Braddon's novels were published initially not in volume but in serial, and here the range of formats was equally varied: we find them at first in independent weekly numbers at a penny, or in cheap popular weeklies dedicated to melodramatic fiction, such as the *Halfpenny Journal;* from the early 1860s in middle-brow literary monthlies, most notably *Belgravia,* edited by Braddon herself for around a decade; and finally, from the early 1870s, syndicated in popular metropolitan and provincial weekly newspapers.[1]

This material history needs to be studied more thoroughly if we are to understand the deeper meanings of Braddon's diversity and productivity. An important underlying question is to what extent the quantity and generic form of her fiction should be seen as determined either by the general process of the commodification of fiction in the later Victorian period, or by her status as a woman in both the family and society. Authorship in the later Victorian period was undoubtedly subject to a rapid process of professionalization, so that Romantic models of literary composition as quasi-divine inspiration came increasingly to seem untenable, and many writers kicked against the indignity of becoming a "Pegasus . . . in harness."[2] In particular, female authors, though the dominant forms of popular fiction were then largely written by women for women (Flint Pt. IV), were subject to processes of production and distribution that were controlled by, precisely, "middlemen," whether book publishers, newspaper proprietors, journal editors, or library owners (Brake chap. 7; Cross chap. 5). And yet, while all this is true, to address the issues only in these terms risks presenting writers, and women writers especially, as merely passive victims of economic and ideological circumstance. Whereas we know that many authors accepted with great enterprise the challenge of writing seen as the rapid accumulation of literary capital, and several of the "Queens of the Circulating Libraries" were quite capable of using sensation and romance covertly to mock expressions of Grundyism and to question the restricted roles then assigned to women in both private and public spheres. Both statements apply with equal validity in Braddon's case.

To deal with the publication history of all Braddon's works is obviously beyond the bounds of the present essay, which limits itself largely to the question of serialization in British provincial newspapers. The narrower aim, carried out in the "Data" section, is to fill in as many as possible of the blank spaces in the bibliographic record of the publication of Braddon's work in provincial weeklies from 1873 onwards. Her novels were syndicated first by the firm of Tillotson and Son of Bolton, Lancashire, and later by W. C. Leng and Company of Sheffield, Yorkshire. Technically many of these newspaper serializations constitute first editions (Pollard 247–53). The only attempt to provide a thorough bibliographical record of Braddon's writings, that of Robert Lee Wolff, in his critical biography of 1979 and bibliography of 1981, is concerned more with Braddon's work in volume, and contains many omissions and not a few errors concerning its serialization.[3] The next section, "Discussion," tells the story of the production of the "newspaper novels" in more detail, with the aim of adding a few pieces to the general picture that is now beginning to emerge of the publication options open to popular authors in the late Victorian period, and of the pressures thus exerted on the process of composition and the formation of popular genres. A major source is the Tillotson records surviving from the last quarter of the nineteenth century.[4] These include numerous letters from the 1880s written by John Maxwell, Braddon's husband, publisher in both magazine and volume form, and literary agent, to W. F. Tillotson, the driving force behind the Bolton enterprise, that is, the two most important "middlemen" in Braddon's midcareer.[5] This correspondence offers considerable insight into both the public process of serialization and syndication, and the private regime under which "our Author," as Braddon is regularly referred to in the correspondence, composed her novels.

DATA

Here brief details are given of all Braddon novels where initial publication has been traced in British newspapers, covering the period 1873 to 1901. In each case we have given dates and number of parts in at least one journal; in cases where the novel has been located in more than one paper, priority has been given to the earliest traced. Unless otherwise stated all appearances recorded have been checked back carefully to the original journals, usually in the form of the annual volumes (or microfilms of them) held at the British Library Newspaper Library. Details of the syndicating agency, the payment Braddon received for newspaper publication rights, and details of first publication in Britain in volume are also provided where available. Details of payments derive from the Bolton archives, especially the Tillotson trade ledgers, or from the anniversary volume *Sheffield Daily Telegraph, 1855–1925*. Months or days of volume publication, where given, derive from Braddon diary entries cited by Wolff (*Sensational Victorian; Catalogue*), or from references in the Maxwell-Tillotson correspondence at Bolton, or, where hypothetical, from the month when the review of the novel appeared in the *Athenaeum*.

Wolff (*Sensational Victorian*, 238–39, 464; also *Catalogue* 136, 126) states that Tillotsons also bought rights to two further Braddon novels, *Lucius Davoren* in 1873, and *The Golden Calf* in 1882, but no mention has been discovered of these novels among the Tillotson papers at Bolton or Oxford, and no trace has been found around those periods in any of the Lancashire Journal Series, or in other likely papers. Further, *Taken at the Flood* was extensively advertised as a new departure for Tillotsons, was their first novel not to be published anonymously, and was timed to coincide with the opening on 30 August 1873 of two new Tillotson journals: the evidence is thus overwhelming that *Taken at the Flood* was the first

Table 9.1 Braddon's Working Schedules for 1874–76

BOOK TITLE Serial Title [if different]	SYNDICATOR Payment to Author	1ST WEEKLY SERIALIZATION Parts Dates	OTHER LOCATIONS TRACED	LIBRARY EDITION Number of Vols. Publication Date
A. *Taken at the Flood*	Tillotsons £450	*Western Daily Mercury* (Plymouth) Sat Supplement 33 pts Sat 30 Aug. '73–11 Apr. '74	34 pts, Sat 30 Aug. '73–18 Apr. '74: *Bolton Weekly Journal* (Dundee) *People's Journal* *Sheffield Daily Telegraph* Weekly Supplement, *Newcastle Weekly Chronicle, Portsmouth Times*, Sat edition (Cardiff) *Weekly Mail, Farnworth Journal & Observer, Tyldesley Weekly Journal* Pts 23–34, Sat 31 Jan.–18 Apr. '74: *Leigh Weekly Journal Eccles & Patricroft Journal* 35 pts, Sat 30 Aug. '73–25 Apr. '74 (Dublin) *Penny Despatch*	Maxwell 3 vols [Apr.] 1874

B. *A Strange World*	Tillotsons £600	(Dublin) *Penny Despatch* 31 pts Sat 18 Apr.–28 Nov. '74 (omitting Sat 14 Nov.)	33 pts, Sat 18 Apr.–5 Dec. '74: *Bolton Weekly Journal Tyldesley Weekly Journal Sheffield Daily Telegraph Weekly Supplement (Cardiff) Weekly Mail, Newcastle Weekly Chronicle, Western Daily Mercury* (Plymouth) Sat edition 33 pts, Wed 22 Dec.–9 Dec. '74:	Maxwell 3 vols [Feb.] 1875
C. *Dead Men's Shoes*	Tillotsons £450	*Leigh Journal & Times* 33 pts Fri 30 Jul. '75–10 Mar. '76	(Dundee) *People's Friend* 33 pts, Sat 31 Jul. '75–11 Mar. '76: *Bolton Weekly Journal Sheffield Daily Telegraph Weekly Supplement* 33 pts, Wed 4 Aug. '75–15 Mar. '76: (Dundee) *People's Friend* 37 pts, Sat 31 Jul. '75–8 Apr. '76: *Western Daily Mercury* (Plymouth) Sat edition	Maxwell 3 vols [Feb.] 1876

(*continued*)

Table 9.1 (Continued)

Book Title Serial Title [if different]	Syndicator Payment to Author	1st Weekly Serialization Parts Dates	Other Locations Traced	Library Edition Number of Vols. Publication Date
D. *Weaver's & Weft* *Weaver's & Weft: or, in* *Love's Net*	Tillotsons £300	*Bolton Weekly Journal* 16 pts Sat 26 Aug–9 Dec. '76	Same dates & parts: *Sheffield Daily Telegraph* Weekly Supplement 16 pts, Wed 30 Aug–13 Dec. '76: (Dundee) *People's Friend*	Maxwell 3 vols (final vol. short stories) [? Mar.] 1877
E. *An Open Verdict*	Tillotsons £500	*Leigh Journal & Times* 33 pts Fri 4 May–14 Dec. '77	33 parts, Sat 5 May–15 Dec. '77: *Bolton Weekly Journal* *Sheffield Daily Telegraph* Weekly Supplement (Dundee) *People's Journal*	Maxwell 3 vols [Jan.] 1878
F. *The Cloven Foot*	Tillotsons £400	*Newcastle Weekly Chronicle* 24 pts Sat 5 Oct. '78–15 Mar. '79	24 pts, Sat 30 Nov. '78–10 May '79: (Cardiff) *Weekly Mail* 25 pts, Wed 9 Oct. '78–26 Mar. '79: (Dundee) *People's Friend* Not in any Tillotson journals	J & R Maxwell 3 vols [(? Sep.) 1879]

G. *Just as I Am*	Tillotsons £500	*Newcastle Weekly Chronicle* 32 pts Sat 7 Feb.–11 Sep. '80	Same dates and parts: *Sheffield Daily Telegraph* Weekly Supplement 33 pts, Sat 7 Feb.–18 Sep. '80: *Bolton Weekly Journal*	J & R Maxwell 3 vols [(? Oct.) 1880]
H. *Phantom Fortune*	Tillotsons £750	*Leigh Journal & Times* 27 pts Fri 9 Mar.–7 Sep. '83	(Dundee) *People's Journal* 25 pts, Sat 24 Mar.–8 Sep. '83: *Liverpool Weekly Post* 26 pts, Sat 17 Mar.–8 Sep. '83: *Farnworth Journal & Observer* 27 pts, Wed 14 Mar.–12 Sep. '83	J & R Maxwell 3 vols [Sep.] 1883
I. *Wyllard's Weird*	Tillotsons £750	*Leigh Journal & Times* 27 pts Fri 19 Sep. '84–20 Mar. '85	(Dundee) *People's Friend* 20 pts, Sat 8 Nov. '84–21 Mar. '85: *Birmingham Weekly Mercury* 28 pts, Sat 20 Sep. '84–28 Mar. '85: *Newcastle Weekly Chronicle* 28 pts, Wed 24 Sep. '84–1 Apr. '85: (Dundee) *People's Friend*	J & R Maxwell 3 vols [20 Mar. 1885]
J. *Cut by the County*	Tillotsons £250	*Leigh Journal & Times* 6 pts Sat 3 Jul.–7 Aug. '85	Same dates & parts: *Bolton Weekly Journal* 9 pts, Sat 20 Jun.–15 Aug. '85: *Birmingham Weekly Mercury*	J & R Maxwell (3rd vol of *One Thing Needful*) [15 Aug 1886]

(continued)

Table 9.1 (Continued)

BOOK TITLE Serial Title [if different]	SYNDICATOR Payment to Author	1ST WEEKLY SERIALIZATION Parts Dates	OTHER LOCATIONS TRACED	LIBRARY EDITION Number of Vols. Publication Date
K. *One Thing Needful*	Tillotsons £500	*Sheffield & Rotherham Weekly Independent Budget* 20 pts Sat 27 Mar.–7 Aug. '86	18 pts, Sat 18 Sep. '86–15 Jan. '87: (Cardiff) *Weekly Mail*	J & R Maxwell 3 vols (inc *Cut by the County* as final vol) [15 Aug 1886]
L. *Like & Unlike*	Tillotsons £1000	*Leigh Journal & Times* 27 pts Fri 25 Mar.–23 Sep. '87	Not in any Tillotson journals 27 pts, Sat 26 Mar.–24 Sep. '87: *Bolton Weekly Journal* 27 pts, Wed 30 Mar.–28 Sep. '87: (Dundee) *People's Friend*	Spencer Blackett 3 vols [24 Sep. 1887]
M. *The Fatal Three*	Lengs £1250	(Sheffield) *Weekly Telegraph* 24 pts Sat 14 Jan.–23 Jun. '88	Same dates & parts: *Nottinghamshire Guardian* 24 pts, Wed 18 Jan.–27 Jun. '88 (Dundee) *People's Friend*	Simpkin, Marshall 3 vols [(? Jun.) 1888]
N. *The Day Will Come*	Lengs £1250	(Sheffield) *Weekly Telegraph* 25 pts Sat 12 Jan.–29 Jun. '89	26 pts, Mon 14 Jan.–8 Jul. '89 (Dundee) *People's Friend*	Simpkin, Marshall 3 vols [1889]
O. *One Life, One Love* *Whose was the Hand?*	Lengs £1250	(London) *Pictorial World* 24 pts Thur 2 Jan.–12 Jun. '90	23 pts, Sat 11 Jan.–14 Jun. '90 (Sheffield) *Weekly Telegraph* 24 pts, Sat 11 Jan.–21 Jun. '90 *Glasgow Weekly Mail*	Simpkin, Marshall 3 vols 1890

Title		Serial		Publication
P. Gerard: or, The World, the Flesh, & the Devil / The World, the Flesh, & the Devil / The World, the Flesh, & the Fate Reader	Lengs Unknown	As The World, the Flesh, & the Devil: (Sheffield) Weekly Telegraph 22 pts Sat 10 Jan.–6 Jun. '91	As The Fate Reader: 24 pts, Mon 5 Jan.–15 Jun. '91: (Dundee) People's Friend	Simpkin, Marshall 3 vols 1891
Q. The Venetians (The Venetians: or,) All in Honour	Lengs Unknown	(2nd serial rights to Tillotsons for £110) (Sheffield) Weekly Telegraph 23 pts Sat 9 Jan.–11 Jun. '92	23 pts, Fri 10 Mar.–11 Aug. '93: Leigh Journal & Times 23 pts, Sat 11 Mar.–12 Aug. '93: Bolton Weekly Journal	Simpkin, Marshall 3 vols 1892
R. All Along the River	Tillotsons (Serial rights bought from Lengs for £500)	Newcastle Weekly Chronicle Supplement 20 pts Sat 21 Jan.–3 Jun. '93	19 pts, Sat 8 Jun.–12 Oct. '93 Ripon Observer 21 pts, Sat 21 Jan.–10 Jun. '93 Birmingham Weekly Mercury Not in any Tillotson journals	Simpkin, Marshall 3 vols (final vol. short stories) 1893
S. Thou Art the Man	Lengs Unknown	(2nd serial rights to Tillotsons for £350) (Sheffield) Weekly Telegraph 23 pts Sat 6 Jan.–9 Jun. '94	Untraced	Simpkin, Marshall 3 vols [1894]
T. Sons of Fire	Lengs Unknown (2nd serial rights to Tillotsons for £350)	(Sheffield) Weekly Telegraph 23 pts Sat 5 Jan.–8 Jun. '95	Untraced	Simpkin, Marshall 3 vols [1895]

(continued)

Table 9.1 (Continued)

Book Title Serial Title [if different]	Syndicator Payment to Author	1st Weekly Serialization Parts Dates	Other Locations Traced	Library Edition Number of Vols. Publication Date
U. *London Pride: or, When the World Was Younger* *When the World Was Younger: A Tale of Merry England*	Tillotsons (Serial rights bought from Lengs for £850)	*Birmingham Weekly Mercury* 26 pts Sat 5 Oct. '95–28 Mar. '96		Simpkin, Marshall 1 vol 1896
V. *Under Love's Rule* *The Little Auntie*	Tillotsons (Serial rights bought from Lengs for £450)	*Newcastle Weekly Chronicle* Supplement 10 pts Sat 10 Oct.–12 Dec. '96		Simpkin, Marshall 1 vol 1897
W. *Rough Justice* *Shadowed Lives* [initially *A Shadowed Life*]	Lengs Unknown	(Sheffield) *Weekly Telegraph* 19 pts Sat 16 Jan.–22 May '97	Published in Britain exclusively in the (Sheffield) *Weekly Telegraph*	Simpkin, Marshall 1 vol 1898
X. *In High Places* *George Nameless:* *A Romance of Life in High Places*	Lengs Unknown	(Sheffield) *Weekly Telegraph* 23 pts Sat 29 Oct. '98–1 Apr. '99	Issued previously in monthly parts in the (London) *Lady's Realm,* Nov. '97–Oct. '98	Hutchinson 1 vol 1898
Y. *During Her Majesty's Pleasure*	Lengs Unknown	(Sheffield) *Weekly Telegraph* 11 pts Sat 12 Jan.–23 Mar. '01		Hurst & Blackett 1 vol 1908

Braddon work to be taken on by Tillotsons. *Lucius Davoren,* on the other hand, has been located in serial form under the title *Publicans and Sinners* both in the popular London weekly, the *Home Journal* in 1873, and in the Australian *Sydney Mail;* the arrangements were probably made between John Maxwell himself and George Street, a London agent who acted for many colonial journals (Morrison 311). In the case of *The Golden Calf,* there seems little doubt that Wolff has simply misidentified references in the Maxwell-Tillotson correspondence to *Phantom Fortune.* Wolff also makes no mention of the newspaper serialization of the final six Braddon novels shown in the table.

DISCUSSION

Publication

In 1866, when at the age of twenty-two William Frederic Tillotson was taken into partnership with his father, the family firm operated a small though thriving printing and stationery business in the Lancashire cotton town of Bolton. When he died suddenly in 1889, the Tillotsons were major newspaper proprietors. They then owned one of the first halfpenny evening papers in England, a chain of penny weeklies based on the *Bolton Weekly Journal* and known as the "Lancashire Journals Series," and a pioneering syndication agency with an international reputation, known for its specialization in novels in serial as the "Fiction Bureau" (Turner, 39–56). Such a development was obviously unthinkable without the rapid expansion of demand for popular provincial newspapers sparked by the removal of the "taxes on knowledge" (the duties on advertisements, newspapers, and paper repealed in 1853, 1855, and 1861 respectively) and fueled by the growth in popular education leading to the Forster Education Act of 1870 (Altick chaps. 7–8, 15). That this remarkable success story took place in the town of Bolton rather than a major industrial city like Sheffield or Manchester, was due almost entirely to the energy and enterprise of W. F. Tillotson himself. The publishing engagement between Tillotsons and the Maxwells covers most of this period of rapid expansion, and is linked to a number of new ventures by the Bolton firm.

From the earliest issues of the *Bolton Weekly Journal* a major attraction was short stories or novels in serial, generally reprinted works or those by local writers published anonymously for little remuneration. But when the decision was made in 1873 to expand, Tillotsons chose to invest a large sum in the newspaper serial rights of a new novel by a popular author and advertised the opening of Braddon's *Taken at the Flood* widely.

Not surprisingly, given the heavy outlay (over £1000 for *Taken at the Flood* and *A Strange World* alone), even the earliest Braddon novels appeared not only in the Lancashire Journals but in provincial weeklies covering almost the length and breadth of the United Kingdom. This is shown by the list of journals carrying *Taken at the Flood*, probably the only complete listing in table 9.1. Soon other big names such as Wilkie Collins and Margaret Oliphant were selling material regularly to the Fiction Bureau, and there were occasional appearances by such stars as Thomas Hardy and Robert Louis Stevenson. But Braddon was still the "name" author most regularly linked to Tillotsons, and several of the Bureau's standbys like Mary Cecil Hay and Frederick Talbot were novelists published and represented by John Maxwell, and who had hacked for his *Belgravia* before Chatto and Windus took over in 1876 (Edwards, 1–36). In addition Maxwell's firm acted as book publishers for the occasional author, such as Dora Russell, for whom Tillotson gained volume as well as newspaper publication rights.

The link with the Maxwells was also crucial to the expansion of the Tillotson syndication business into the colonial and American markets. As Elizabeth Morrison has shown, Maxwell had succeeded in placing several of Braddon's works in weekly newspapers in colonial Australia even before 1873; this connection continued into the 1890s, with Tillotson taking over the paperwork at some point. Though there is evidence of Tillotson already buying American serial rights in the mid-1870s (Turner 43), and though the Fiction Bureau did not open up its New York Branch until late 1888 (Turner 47–48), the marketing of Braddon's *Phantom Fortune* represented a new step. When he accepted a further Braddon work at the end of 1882 after a break of over two years, for the first time Tillotson prepared a detailed circular advertising for a "coterie" of statewide papers to take up advance proofs of Braddon's latest at £25 per journal. After having it checked by Maxwell, he mailed it to newspaper proprietors in the United States; perhaps only four journals including the *Chicago Daily News* took up the offer on this occasion and at the cost of the long-standing connection with *Harper's Weekly* (letters, telegrams, and circulars, Oct. 1882 to Feb. 1883, ZBEN/4/3). But the technique was repeated for *Wyllard's Weird* in 1884, and Tillotson wrote in 1885, during negotiations concerning Wilkie Collins's *The Evil Genius*, of having established business relations with eight American newspapers in all (letter to A. P. Watt, 23 Nov. 1886, Wilkie Collins papers, A. P. Watt Archive).[6]

The technical and economic aspects of syndication were not complex but the process required vigilant attention to detail and incurred considerable communication and transportation costs if agreements were to be kept and constant deadlines met. As later in the United States, from the mid-1870s Tillotson worked to create a stable "coterie" of half-a-dozen or more major British provincial weeklies with complementary circulations, which would pay substantial sums to serialize new novels simultaneously in advance of volume publication. In addition, back lists were maintained of fiction already published in volume but for which Tillotson retained newspaper publication rights, and these novels and short stories were sold by the column to lesser journals at much lower rates. Text was available from Tillotsons in reprint on paper slips to be reset by the local publisher or, from perhaps around 1876, in stereotype plates, that is, casts of columns of type made from molds, which could be simply mounted and locked into the form (Turner 21–38).

During the period when Braddon was engaged to Tillotsons, payments to writers increased considerably, but varied according to the author's name value and the length of the work. In the case of full-length novels, the surviving Tillotson trade ledgers reveal a minimum of £10 for early unsigned local works like J. Bradbury's *Grace Barton* in 1875, and a maximum of £1300 for Collins's *The Evil Genius* in 1885 or Walter Besant's *Herr Paulus* in 1887 (ZBEN1/2–3). But prices also depended on specific publication rights conceded, including both time and place restrictions. In Braddon's case, though volume publication rights were never conceded, soon American and colonial newspaper rights were generally granted along with British, but the period in both cases was normally limited to one year after the appearance of the first installment in the earliest journal. When, in May 1885, Maxwell negotiated to increase the price for the newspaper serial rights to *Like and Unlike,* he could only get Tillotson to agree to a price approaching that afforded to Collins by extending the period to seven years (ZBEN/4/3). There is evidence that, from the beginning, the syndication of Braddon's fiction yielded a substantial profit for the Bolton firm. For example, the Tillotson trade ledgers reveal that Braddon was paid £450 pounds for *Dead Men's Shoes* in April 1875, and from the subscribing journals Tillotson received £560 in the same month and a further series of payments totaling £220 by the end of June alone, while in the case of *The Cloven Foot* income of nearly £800 was collected during initial serialization against an outlay of only £400 (ZBEN/1/2, 421, 426). Although these figures obviously overlook the cost of wages, communications, transport, and other overheads, they suggest that Tillotson's enterprise was amply rewarded.

But for the Maxwells also the access to new markets that the Tillotson connection opened up was opportune. That Braddon produced twenty novels within less than a decade of starting to write professionally at the age of twenty-three, can largely be explained by immediate economic pressures—initially the need to support herself and her mother (Wolff, *Sensational Victorian,* chap. 1–2) and later the losses due to the

financial entanglements of John Maxwell in the mid-1860s (Sadleir).[7]
The same cannot be said of the novels she turned out at a rate of nearly
two per year throughout the 1870s and 1880s, for by then the Maxwells
were the owners of substantial literary and immovable property. In 1885
Maxwell wrote, "My wife must be occupied. It is as natural for her to write
as it is for a mountain torrent to flow" (Oct. 14, ZBEN/4/3); but there
was also a perception in the London literary world that Maxwell was a
hard taskmaster adept at exploiting female writers and appropriating
their work. This is captured precisely in a cartoon in *The Mask* of June
1868 that represents Maxwell as circus ring master forcing Braddon, a
bareback rider on a winged horse inscribed *Belgravia,* through a tight
series of paper hoops named for her novels.[8] Both images probably
contain a large grain of truth. There is also little doubt that, whatever the
reasons for Braddon's high productivity, and whatever its literary consequences (a question we will return to), in market terms there was often
an oversupply of Braddon's fiction, and equal or greater reward might
have been achieved with less output.

In the 1860s there is a sharp cleavage in Braddon's fiction between
those novels aimed at the popular market for penny and shilling dreadfuls, and those issued in the middle-brow monthlies and for the circulating libraries, which the blanket term "sensation" and the fact that both
types of journal were owned by Maxwell often serve to disguise. While this
balancing act obviously allowed Braddon's early writings to reach a very
wide audience, it inevitably incurred the displeasure of the London literary establishment, who found it difficult to "place" the author. Particular
provocations were the use of multiple pseudonyms and story titles to
disguise parallel composition and publication, and the attempt to pad
out stories written as penny-dreadful serials to triple-Decker length for
volume publication (Wolff, *Sensational Victorian* chap. 4). When, following her nervous collapse of 1868, Braddon returned to the literary grind-
stone after a gap of almost two years, her latest novels were published
entirely by the house of Maxwell, first serialized in *Belgravia* and then in
three volumes for the libraries, and reached a more limited audience
concentrated around the metropolis and among the middle class. As the
Australian adventures suggest, Maxwell was actively seeking a wider market. Syndicated publication by Tillotsons in the provinces thus served to
extend both the geographical and social range of the initial readership of
Braddon's new work in her mid-career, without compromising its status
for the libraries or reviewers; its value to the Maxwells was not only the
cash from serial rights but the stimulus to subsequent book sales of her
novels in cheaper reprints, from gaudy railway yellowbacks to elegant
collected editions.

The surviving letters from Maxwell to Tillotson reveal a fluid mixture of commercial and social intercourse. Detailed negotiations concerning rights conceded, rates or methods of payment, and publication dates stand side by side with social invitations, family news or inquiries, and personal banter. Tillotson and his wife, Mary (an avid reader of Braddon and other Tillotson authors, who took advantage of her husband's business to collect the autographs of eminent writers),[9] were both fully a generation younger than Maxwell, but so nearly was Braddon herself; despite the distance between Bolton and the Home Counties, there were occasional social engagements involving the two families, particularly at holiday times, while Tillotson himself was a frequent visitor to London. When Gerald, Braddon's eldest child, suffered a nervous breakdown near the beginning of his acting career while he was on tour in the United States in early 1887 and his parents were on holiday in the South of France, they cabled immediately to Tillotson to ask him to use his American contacts to help out (letters and telegrams, 3–10 Feb. 1887, ZBEN/4/3). Despite Maxwell's overbearing manner, the relationship that emerges with "gentle Willie" seems touchingly warm and affectionate. Following the inevitable contentions caused by differences of interest in the business negotiations, Maxwell is always quick to protest eternal trust and friendship, and there is something of the feel of lovers making up after a tiff. Braddon also was clearly fond of Tillotson and dedicated *Taken at the Flood* to him. This mutual affection and respect is in marked contrast to the distrust and disdain that another eminent Tillotson author, Wilkie Collins, seems often to have felt toward the northern newspaper proprietor, whom he once referred to as "an impudent little cad" (cited in Peters 417).

Yet Maxwell's discourse in the letters to Tillotson can also be read as an allegory of gender relations in the later Victorian literary world. The two wives represent the female author and reader: background presences, endlessly engaged in the isolated domestic activities of knitting and unraveling a garment of prose fiction, subject to the will of their masters, the middlemen. In the foreground, the two husbands, neither of whom show sign of having read the novels in question, represent the publishers and agents, nicely calculating the value of fiction in shillings to the yard, playing power games of manipulation and control. "Author writes two novels yearly, never more, never less. Shortest offered. Belgravia have longest. Wire acceptance, negotiate own property," runs one particularly pithy telegram from Maxwell (3 Nov. 1885, ZBEN/4/3). We encounter an altogether more prominent role for the author in the negotiations between Tillotson and A. P. Watt, Wilkie Collins's literary agent in the 1880s (Law, "Wilkie" 259–61), which must at least in part be accounted for in terms of gender roles. In response to Tillotson's inquiry about Braddon's attitude to the Society of Authors then in process of foundation, Maxwell dismissed the effort as a "vision conceived by Vision-aries. Nothing in it" (21 Feb. 1884, ZBEN/4/3), although other Tillotson authors such as Walter Besant and Collins were taking leading parts (Bonham-Carter chapt. 6).[10] The female roles thus figured in this corre-spondence are particularly ironic when we recall that William Tillotson's sudden death in 1889 and John Maxwell's incapacitation due to ill health shortly after, soon gave the two Marys the opportunity to show they were quite capable of, variously, running the Fiction Bureau and negotiating publication rights (Turner 48–51; Wolff, *Sensational Victorian* chap. 9).

Maxwell often complained, only half in jest, that Tillotson got his own way on terms by taking advantage of their friendship ("be happy always getting own way from us hence pleasantest relations," telegram, 23 May 1885, ZBEN/4/3), but he was always irate if payment failed to arrive on time ("No remittance! Why?" 10 Mar. 1883, ZBEN/4/3), and he more than once objected strongly to accepting deferred payment because it lowered Braddon's literary dignity ("Authors do not give credit any more than do Physicians or Barristers, if at the head of their professions," 5 Jan. 1883, ZBEN/4/3). But the contentions between the two were seldom merely questions of money. A more permanent irritation was Maxwell's fear of piracy and copyright loss. Following the British Married Women's Property Act of 1882, Maxwell declared angrily that his wife was pre-pared, under its provisions, to take action in her own right against un-authorized serialization of *Phantom Fortune* in the Canadian *Hamilton Daily Spectator* (6 Dec. 1883, ZBEN/4/3). Until the American Chace Act of 1891, works by foreign authors had no copyright protection in the United States, and there the term piracy had moral rather than legal weight. Here Maxwell's fear, expressed repeatedly in the 1880s, was that Tillotson's sending of advance proofs to the States risked allowing Ameri-can newspaper publication to occur before the first appearance in a British journal, thus in theory imperiling the entire British copyright (Nowell-Smith chap. 4).

Both men were aware that, though the Tillotsons were the front-runners in the syndication of fiction in Britain, competition was growing. From the early 1880s the pioneering literary agent A. P. Watt tried to lure well-known authors like Braddon and Collins away from Tillotsons and form his own newspaper syndicates (Law, "Wilkie" 257–59). At the same time there were American-based syndicates, like that run by the proprie-tors of the *Detroit Free Press,* who wanted Braddon on their books (letter from Robert Dennis to Maxwell, 15 Dec. 1884, ZBEN/4/3). And closer to home, there was a rival newspaper chain based in Sheffield, South York-shire, which moved aggressively into Tillotson's syndication territory sometime in the mid-1880s. The *Sheffield Daily Telegraph* had been founded in 1855, and could claim to be the oldest English daily paper outside London. The principal proprietor from the mid-1860s was W. C. Leng, who had gained his journalistic experience on the staff of the *Dundee Advertiser,* owned and edited from 1851 by his younger brother John Leng. Both the Leng brothers were long-standing members of Tillotson's syndicates, John as the founder of the Dundee weeklies the *People's Journal* and *People's Friend.*

The *Telegraph*'s Saturday supplement, under the guidance of W. C. Leng, probably carried all of Tillotson's Braddon novels up to *Just as I Am.* In the early 1880s, the editorship was taken over by C. D. Leng, W. C. Leng's elder son; the Saturday supplement soon achieved its independence as the *Sheffield Weekly Telegraph* and began to commission fiction on its own account under the banner The Editor's Syndicate. By 1887 there were ambitious plans to turn the paper into a national illustrated weekly miscellany based in London; the title was quickly changed to the *Weekly Telegraph,* and the format to that of a modern-style tabloid with bold headlines and generous graphics (*Sheffield Daily Telegraph 1855–1925* 25–33). In this C. D. Leng was perhaps following the lead of his uncle's weekly *The People's Friend,* which had by then established a similar position throughout Scotland. By the last years of the century C. D. Leng had achieved his goal of a solid nationwide circulation for the journal, which by then had been transformed into a cheap thirty-two page quarto magazine with a color cover. Around that time Leng seems to have ceased to offer his serials to other British journals and to have carried them exclusively in the *Weekly Telegraph.*[11]

Maxwell habitually forwarded to Tillotson not only requests from individual journals wishing to serialize Braddon's work, but also details of offers from rival syndicators, with ambiguous motives. He claimed that he was acting out of openness and friendship, but he often used the rival offers to influence negotiations and Tillotson was sensitive to any hint of treachery. C. D.Leng perhaps first approached the Maxwells in mid-1885 (9 June 1885, ZBEN/4/3), and renewed the attack with success in the spring of 1887, when Maxwell finally agreed to sell him the serial rights to Braddon's next three novels with an option on the succeeding three (10, 22, 26 March and 5 April 1887, ZBEN/4/3). The fundamental reason for the break with Tillotsons was a disagreement not so much over levels of remuneration as over frequency of publication. To begin with Tillotson had been happy to publish Braddon's works "back to back," with *Taken at the Flood* finishing and *A Strange World* commencing in the same issue, and until 1878 the longest Braddonless period in the Lancashire Journals was just over half a year. But by the late 1870s, when the Fiction Bureau's list of distinguished authors was growing, Tillotson clearly wanted to cut back to a Braddon every other year. But at the same time, since *Belgravia* had been sold to Chatto & Windus in 1876, serial publication in the literary monthlies was becoming more intermittent, and Maxwell kept pushing for Tillotson to take an annual novel from "our Author." In 1878 *The Cloven Foot* was accepted but did not appear in any of the Lancashire Journals. In 1885 during the negotiations for *Like and Unlike*, Maxwell was shocked when publication was offered nearly two years later ("N. B. Telegram reads 1887. I infer commencing March 1886 is date intended by you—that 7 is wrong." 21 May, ZBEN/4/3), and then forced a clearly reluctant Tillotson to accept the novelette *One Thing Needful* to fill in the gap by threatening to defect to A. P. Watt for more money.[12] Once again the work did not appear in Tillotson's own journals.

So when, in a crucial step in the marketing of the modernized *Weekly Telegraph*, C. D. Leng offered Maxwell a generous price for the next three Braddon novels, the latter again tried to force Tillotson's hand. Tillotson wrote for advice to R. E. Leader, the proprietor of the rival *Sheffield Independent*, who on Tillotson's behalf had taken over the "coterie" for *One Thing Needful*, and received the following reply, dated 25 March:

> I am much obliged to you for asking my opinion on the latest Sheffield effort to trump your best card. My feeling is that it would be most unfortunate to let Miss Braddon get "out of your hands for ever"—and yet I think Mr Maxwell far too shrewd to let anything of the kind take place. But I quite agree with you that an annual tale from her pen would be quite too much. (ZBEN/4/3)

But by then the die was cast, for Maxwell had already written on 26 March, agreeing on Braddon's behalf to a final interview before the "transfer of services" took place. So on 14 January 1888, the day that serialization of *The Fatal Three* was beginning in the *Weekly Telegraph*, Maxwell posted what amounts almost to a lover's farewell:

> as we really have a future I do not desire to lessen the confidence I have always felt in our relations; or to diminish the faith I have in your willingness to uphold, rather than degrade, our Author's Copyright under all circumstances whatsoever! So let it be! again and again so let it be.
>
> I was not to blame in our correspondence last year. Your language was firm: mine only informing: the result unavoidable. I warned but in vain! New arrangements merely succeeded. Our dearest "Willie" pronounced the Decree of severance after long years of peaceful and pleasant servitude. (ZBEN/4/3)

The commercial loss was almost certainly greater on Tillotson's side, for Wilkie Collins died in 1889, and the younger generations of

Tillotson's "eminent" authors, such as Besant and H. Rider Haggard, proved not nearly so faithful as Braddon had been. Instead the authors engaged most consistently to the Bolton firm from the 1890s were such lesser lights as the local Lancashire novelist J. Monk Forster or William Le Queux, best known for his spy thrillers. Weight shifted noticeably from fiction in serial to short stories, as the rapid decline of the market for three-volume novels reduced both the length of and the demand for serial novels in newspapers. But by 1889, of course, Tillotson was dead and Maxwell himself virtually incapacitated. From late 1892, A. P. Watt began to act as Braddon's literary agent and handled many of her serial rights until her death in 1915.[13] But for a brief period Braddon herself conducted the negotiations with C. D. Leng who continued accepting an annual Braddon novel with almost clockwork regularity until well into the 1890s. Once again Braddon quickly developed a sense of personal obligation; in 1892 she responded to a new offer from Tillotsons:

> I must confer with Mr. Leng as the representative of his Father's firm. He, like the late Mr. Tillotson, has always been particularly considerate and courteous in his dealings with me, and I am bound—after an engagement extending over six consecutive years—to study his interests in any future negotiations. (4 Nov. 1892, ZBEN/4/1/22)

In fact, in the case of a number of Braddon novels in the 1890s, C. D. Leng was happy to sell on to Tillotsons, first serial rights (*All Along the River, London Pride,* and *Under Love's Rule*), second serial rights (*The Venetians, Thou Art the Man,* and *Sons of Fire*) or various colonial rights (*The Day Will Come, One Life, One Love,* and *During Her Majesty's Pleasure*). In the case of *In High Places* exclusive serial rights were sold to the publishers Hutchinson, who then sold second rights on to Lengs and others (A. P. Watt Collection, folder 35.12). Braddon also sold newspaper publication rights to at least five short stories directly to Tillotson during the last decade of the century (notebook A, Tillotson papers, Bodleian Library). But by this time Braddon was moving nimbly from producing triple-deckers for the rapidly declining library market to single volumes for the growing bookshop trade in new novels (Wolff, *Sensational Victorian* 359– 60). *Sons of Fire* was to be her last novel in three volumes. In shifting primary allegiance from Bolton to Sheffield, she was also, consciously or unconsciously, participating in a further transformation in her initial reading public, from the local communities of readers representing a wide range of social backgrounds created up and down the country by Tillotsons "coteries," to the single but atomized audience for new mass-produced periodicals that Lengs sought to tap.

Composition

When she wrote her first novel for the newspapers, Braddon was already well used to the pressures of serial composition, as she had by then been writing in installments for well over a decade. Indeed with her work for Tillotson she was returning to the pattern of her early career; her first novel, *Three Times Dead,* was issued in weekly parts in 1860 by C. R. Empson in Beverley, Yorkshire, and this continued with the half-dozen or so anonymous melodramas she wrote for Maxwell's *Halfpenny Journal* between 1861 and 1865 (Wolff, *Sensational Victorian* chap. 4). In contrast, her novels in Maxwell's shilling magazines, *Temple Bar* and *Belgravia* were in monthly parts. While allowing a more leisurely pace of plot, composing in monthly installments in practice meant no less hectic a schedule of work. Five Braddon novels appeared back to back in *Temple Bar* from January 1862 to February 1865; and in the early years of *Belgravia,* which commenced in November 1866, she was not only editing the magazine but writing much of each issue herself under her own signature ("the author of *Lady Audley's Secret,* etc."), that of "Babington White," or anonymously, so that it was by no means unusual for three Braddon stories to run in the same issue (Edwards 40ff.). Braddon was of course not unique among Victorian women writers in her prolific output; her fellow sensationalist Florence Marryat, for example, also notched up more than eighty titles, while more sober writers like Margaret Oliphant and Charlotte M. Yonge scored over ninety and a hundred respectively, and they all also wrote generally for serial publication. But Braddon was unusual among the respectable authors serving the circulating libraries in having the formative experience of working for the proletarian penny-fiction weeklies. Doubtless the drive of her narrative style was influenced by this apprenticeship, in the need both to supply quick copy to the printers and to maintain sufficient suspense to ensure the next penny was forthcoming.

During the hectic early years of her career Braddon's facility as a story-teller allowed her to make her plots up as she went along, having only a vague idea as to how they would conclude. By the time of the newspaper novels she would have a short rough plan, which often changed during the course of composition. *Cassell's Saturday Journal* later reported on her methods in a piece entitled "Novelists 'Skeletons' ":

> Miss Braddon may be taken as a type of several lady novelists, so far as "skeletons" go. She draws up one for every story; though in some cases—that for "Dead Men's Shoes" is an example—it barely covers a couple of pages; but she has great difficulty in clinging to it faithfully to the end. (19 Mar. 1891, X 620)

By the late 1880s she was laying more emphasis on the psychological integrity of character, but maintained the same casual ease of plotting. In an interview with Joseph Hatton, another Tillotson author, in 1887, Braddon was characteristically reticent about the nature of the first of the novels she was pledged to write for Lengs:

> You know, how having settled the plot of a novel, one frequently modifies it in the course of its development; how often characters themselves take the bit and run away with one. I might say something touching the story I am writing and then later on disappoint the reader. (Hatton 29)

But despite the lack of planning, the haste of composition, and the impossibility of going back to change installments already published, the revisions that Braddon generally carried out toward the end of the period of serialization and before her new works appeared in volume form (see Wolff, *Catalogue,* e.g., 122), reveal few textual changes of note. What alterations there were appear to have been generally minor verbal and structural revisions, not only for the sake of stylistic improvement but also to reflect the different mode of publication.

Changes to chapter titles, and emendations immediately around a part break, such as the replacement of pronouns by proper names or expansions to establish more clearly a character's identity on first appearance, are among the most apparent revisions. Braddon probably gave more time to the first Tillotson novel, *Taken at the Flood,* which reveals eleven chapters retitled out of fifty-eight and a similar order of textual changes around part and chapter breaks, including two paragraphs entirely cut. More typically, the second, A *Strange World,* has only five title changes and fewer and more minor textual revisions. Among the title changes in both cases are the substitution of literary quotation for plain description, and German or French language for English. In *A Strange World,* for example, "O'er All There Hung a Shadow and a Fear" replaces "Borcel End," while "Glamour" becomes "Éveillons le Plaisir, son Aurore est la Nuit." A few of the later, shorter Tillotson novels, such as *The Cloven Foot,* reveal no changes in chapter titles and indeed few textual revisions of any kind. We should also note here a number of significant changes in chapter partitions. These often serve to illustrate how Braddon geared her narratives specifically to the psychological demands of weekly serialization. For example, *One Thing Needful* had twenty-five chapters in serial, but this was reduced to twenty-two in volume, the three extra units being subsumed within adjacent chapters; there were also seven accompanying title changes. The first serial installment concluded with the hunchback Lord Lashmar standing before a crowd of onlookers on the balcony of a burning building that he had climbed to rescue a child, whose father,

Lashmar's enemy, had perished in the same attempt. The newspaper reader thus had to wait in suspense until the following week to find out if Lashmar escaped with the child. There the descent was dealt with in the opening sentence: "Five minutes of supreme anxiety, and all was over." In the book this mechanism of suspense is avoided as Lashmar's rescue and escape are described seamlessly within the same chapter.

Changes of narrative content and style are largely restricted to changes of name. Among the earlier novels, there are a number of cases where characters are redrawn simply by being renamed. For example, in *A Strange World* once again, the amateur sleuth Humphrey Clissold becomes the more heroic Maurice Clissold, while the professional police investigator Paufoot is further diminished to Smelt. More telling still are those many cases among the later newspaper novels where the title itself was changed significantly for the book version. *Gerard, The Venetians, London Pride,* and *In High Places* ran respectively in the weeklies under the more dramatic titles *The World, the Flesh, and the Devil; All in Honour; When the World Was Younger;* and *George Nameless;* although continuity was preserved through the use of subtitles. There were cases, however, where the transformation was total. *Rough Justice* appeared in serial at first as *Shadowed Lives* and then as *A Shadowed Life,* though here the change was due largely to the fact that similar titles already existed.[14] *Under Love's Rule* started out unrecognizably as *The Little Auntie,* a title almost diametrically opposite in connotation and tone. *Whose Was the Hand?* was reborn as *One Life, One Love;* here it seems likely that Braddon decided during the course of composition that the rhetorical appeal of the serial title was inappropriate to the narrative as it developed. Although a murder is central to the plot, the form is by no means that of a whodunit; instead the psychological detail of the growth of obsession is the central interest.

The foregoing brief account is inevitably based only on a cursory examination of the texts of the twenty-five newspaper novels in serial and volume form, and doubtless a systematic collation would turn up many other detailed points of difference. However, it does seem sufficient to support the contention that Braddon had little time or inclination to revise these works at all extensively before volume publication. Nevertheless, such changes as there were do suggest both that "our Author" was sensitive to the changing constituency of her audience from the readers of cheap newspapers to "respectable" library subscribers, and that the form of her fiction in this period was significantly influenced by its initial publication in weekly parts.

Braddon wrote rapidly and efficiently under pressure, and her early critics, while generally denigrating her work, usually conceded that she was a writer with technical flair and natural ability who was wasting her potential on novels of incident rather than character, or, as an *Athenaeum* reviewer put it, a case of "great ability turned to vulgar use" (Unsigned Review of *Eleanor's Victory,* 19 Sept. 1863, 361). Indeed many reviewers during the 1860s were disturbed by her prolific output and, convinced that she would quickly exhaust her talents, advised her to write less. Whether fewer books would necessarily mean better is an open question to which we shall return, as it is arguable that those works on which she spent the most care are of less value than her more popular productions. Braddon's own thinking on this issue was ambivalent. When the editorship of *Belgravia* gave her a greater degree of independence concerning form and theme, she used the magazine as a forum not only for taking revenge on the high-brow literary reviews and for justifying sensationalism in fiction (Robinson), but also for carrying out experiments in social and historical narrative influenced by contemporary French models and relatively untouched by melodrama. These she had begun with *The Doctor's Wife* (1864) and *The Lady's Mile* (1866), both featuring as a prominent character the peripatetic and self-conscious fiction writer Sigismund Smith, and both owing much to her reading of Flaubert. ·

Throughout the 1860s we can see her attempting not only to meet the exigencies of her commercial taskmaster Maxwell, but also to placate the god of letters in the person of the elder statesman of Victorian fiction, Sir Edward Bulwer-Lytton. From 1862 until his death in 1873, Braddon wrote a series of long letters to Bulwer-Lytton as a "devoted disciple," praising the scattered works of his declining years as permanent monuments to art and deprecating her own copious but ephemeral productions (Wolff "Devoted Disciple"). In December 1862 Braddon wrote:

> I know that my writing teems with errors, absurdities and contradictions, and inconsistancies [sic]; but I have never written a line that has not been written against time—sometimes with the printer waiting outside the door. I have written as conscientiously as I could; but more with a view to the interests of my publishers than with any great regard to my own reputation. The curse of serial writing and hand to mouth composition has set its seal upon me, and I have had to write a lot of things together. (Wolff, "Devoted Disciple" 11)

Due allowance given to the psychological demands of flattery and defensiveness, it would still be a mistake to read these letters as a privileged communication of Braddon's authentic attitude to her own work. Certainly she was keen to write "serious" novels, as Bulwer-Lytton encouraged; but she was also keen to make herself and her dependents financially secure, and to please the audience who could give her the means to do so. Certainly, in moving away from the crude melodrama of her early penny dreadfuls, Braddon intended to allow her novels more complex characterization and more natural dialogue. But this by no means entailed a rejection of the mode of sensationalism *per se.* After all, the sensational can achieve depth through symbolic concentration, and functions not as a unitary genre but as a composite, transgressive mode: melodrama within domesticity, respectability rent to reveal monstrosity. In an important letter to Bulwer-Lytton of May 1863, Braddon wondered whether it might be possible at the same time to worship the God of art and the Mammon of commercial success:

> I have learnt to look at everything in a mercantile sense, and to write solely for the circulating library reader, whose palette [sic] requires strong meat, and is not very particular as to the qualities thereof. . . . I want to serve two masters. I want to be artistic and to please *you.* I want to be Sensational, and to please Mudie's subscribers. . . . Can the Sensational be elevated by art, and redeemed from all it's [sic] coarseness? (Wolff, "Devoted Disciple" 14)

While many of the shorter and later efforts among the newspaper novels seem not to set their sights above the level of superficial excitement or light entertainment, a number of the full-length works written for Tillotsons can justifiably be read as striving toward this union of opposites.

At the height of the controversy over sensation fiction in the early 1860s (see Brantlinger), in addition to the serious charges of incivility and indecency, the genre had been condemned regularly as mechanical and superficial: it sought to replace the profundities of motivation and characterization with mere speed and fluidity of incident. The sensationalists were thus accused not merely of ignorance of social propriety and moral corruption of the innocent, but further of profaning the holiness of literature. Henry Mansel summarized these objections in an unsigned essay in the *Quarterly Review:*

> A sensation novel, as a matter of course, abounds in incident. Indeed, as a general rule, it consists of nothing else. Deep knowledge of human nature, graphic delineations of individual character, vivid representations of the aspects of Nature or the workings of the soul—all the higher features of the Creative art—would be a hindrance rather than help to a work of this kind. . . . "Action, action, action!" though in a different sense from that intended by the great orator, is the first thing needful, and the second, and the third. The human actors in the piece are, for the most part, but so many lay-figures on which to exhibit a drapery of incident. . . . Each game is played with the same pieces, differing only in the moves. We watch them advancing through the intricacies of the plot, as we trace the course of an x or y through the combinations of an algebraic equation, with a similar

curiosity to know what becomes of them at the end, and with about as much consciousness of individuality in the ciphers. (Mansel 486)

This can be seen in part at least as a genuine perplexity in the face of the increasing commodification of fiction, at the time of emergence of the first distinctly modern popular genre—the detective story.[15] The first and most notorious of sensation novels, whether Wilkie Collins's *Woman in White* (1860), Ellen (Mrs. Henry) Wood's *East Lynne* (1861), or Braddon's *Lady Audley's Secret* (1862), had each provided settings for some of the earliest English literary detectives and thus helped to give them an aura of the uncanny. Although the sensation novel has often been seen as a phenomenon characteristic of and limited to the 1860s, these three major practitioners continued to use the mode well beyond the end of the decade. While Collins's work from the 1870s was characterized by the framing of an explicit social "mission" within the forms of sensation, in newspaper fiction in particular, Braddon pursued the line of development toward classical English detective fiction, playing a part in its evolution from Dickens to Doyle.[16]

Powered by the twin engines of enigma and suspense, tales prominently featuring crime and detection naturally lent themselves to weekly serialization, so it is unsurprising that almost all Braddon's novels for Tillotson and Leng feature at least one unnatural death. The plots of the first two newspaper novels, *Taken at the Flood* and *A Strange World,* both foreground crime and investigation. In *Taken at the Flood,* the heroine Sylvia forsakes an ardent lover to marry an elderly man for his money and position; when the husband is paralyzed and his brother dies, she substitutes the two identities and smuggles the survivor into a private insane asylum, secretly employing her own disgraced mother as an accomplice. The investigation is carried out by her husband's steward Bain, but the reader quickly learns the guilty secret, and the suspense rather concerns whether Sylvia will be blackmailed into marriage with Bain, or will escape to commit bigamy with her first love. In *A Strange World,* there is little attempt to leave the reader in doubt of the murderer's identity; rather the suspense lies in whether he will be caught and his crime exposed to society. And the investigator, the friend and counselor of the victim, is finally concerned less to establish the guilt of the murderer, than to refute the charge of illegitimacy against the heroine who he goes on to marry. Ten years later, in *Wyllard's Weird,* which begins when a French girl is thrown to her death from a train and goes on to point an accusing finger at each of a series of passengers, Braddon comes much closer to the classical detective enigma, though the *Athenaeum* review treated the novel as merely another tired revival of sensationalism (Unsigned Review, 21 Mar. 1885, 371–72). Among the later newspaper stories, *Cut by the*

County, Like and Unlike, The Day Will Come, Whose Was the Hand? and *Thou Art the Man* also have an explicit detective element, with the last two making use of Wilkie Collins's technique of the relation of portions of the narrative through the medium of a character's journal. However, as in the beginning with *Lady Audley's Secret,* Braddon's preference throughout is for the guilty family secret and amateur investigation behind closed doors, and it is not until *His Darling Sin* (1899) that a professional detective is allowed to take center stage and solve the crime before the public gaze.

The social and sexual deviance depicted in the newspaper novels still often offered a challenge to respectable values, though rather less consistently than in Braddon's key novels of the early 1860s, *Lady Audley's Secret* and *Aurora Floyd,* whose representations of passionate women in defiance of the bounds of law, social class, and feminine modesty so disturbed Margaret Oliphant ("Novels"). Violent crime, if described in any realistic detail, still had the capacity to repel and offend. The murder in *Like and Unlike,* for example, was "too shocking" for the *Athenaeum* reviewer (1 Oct. 1887, 435); it consisted of the bludgeoning to death of his unfaithful wife by an upper class thug, who wrapped her corpse in the blood-soaked carpet and dumped it in a river. Months pass before the decomposing body is retrieved, and it is only identifiable by the beautiful golden hair that remains. Sexual transgression still tended to excite even stronger emotions. The *Spectator,* on reviewing *Just As I Am,* found repugnant the situation of a young woman forced by her family to marry another for the sake of social position, but continuing to meet her lover while pregnant by her husband. As with Lady Audley, there was the refusal to countenance the idea that such a shameful secret life could be hidden behind the facade of angelic beauty:

> Now, is it credible that a woman, even a bad woman, just about to bear a child to her husband, should keep up a correspondence, and arrange meetings with an old lover? Is it credible that any man could be found to abet her? And this woman has a "countenance of child-like innocence and purity," as Miss Braddon tells us, without a word of comment. (22 Jan. 1881, vol. 54 126)

Though slightly later in *Like and Unlike* Braddon dared for the first time to explicitly introduce a prosititute to her readers, such extreme instances are relatively rare.

But as in her earliest novels Braddon continued to entice her readers with glimpses of exotic settings and strange lives. In *A Strange World* (1875), in addition to the murder mystery, Braddon exploits the disreputable image of the theatrical world and the young actress. Both aspects were stressed in an advertisment for the second Braddon novel in the Tillotson papers:

> "A Strange World" will reveal some curious secrets and some strange features of a sphere of life which has always been associated with mysterious and even tragic interest; and as the plot is developed the interest and curiosity of the reader will be enhanced to the close of the Story. (*Bolton Weekly Journal,* 21 Mar. 1874, 2)

A Strange World was not the only 1874 Braddon novel with a theatrical setting; however, *Hostages to Fortune,* appearing simultaneously in *Belgravia,* is a much bleaker work, whose theatrical characters display all the forms of immorality and corruption imagined by popular prejudice, and are detached from authorial sympathy. In contrast, Justina Elgood, the wholesome heroine of *A Strange World,* is authorially approved; her struggle as a young though unsuccessful provincial actress is presumably based on Braddon's own experiences. Here the treatment of the question of Justina's legitimacy unmistakably teaches the lesson that Bohemianism is by far less vicious than Grundyism. For 1874 was also the year in which Braddon attempted to gain some measure of social respectability as, following the death of his first wife, she and John Maxwell were at last able to marry. However, because of the ensuing publicity that drew attention to their previous "sinful" union, throughout the following year the Maxwells were forced by the scandal to remove from their permanent home in Richmond to live temporarily in Chelsea. *Dead Men's Shoes,* composed during this exile, and whose immediacy is concentrated by the unusual use of the narrative present tense, is her most bitter and trenchant in its criticism of small-town hypocrisy.

The theme of illegitimacy was a particularly personal one for Braddon because of the irremediable position of her own five children. The subject is returned to repeatedly in the novels written for Lengs, as her children were entering adulthood: in *Gerard,* where a young woman's lover refuses marriage even when she becomes pregnant; in *Thou Art the Man,* which contrasts a millionaire's treatment of his legitimate and illegitimate daughters; and, most interestingly, in *The Venetians* where Lisa, an Italian opera singer, is proud of her illegitimate son and openly acknowledges him. She is amazed that an English woman might contemplate suicide in a similar situation. She is rewarded by success in her career and in her business investments, and is finally able to reject an aristocrat's offer of marriage and preserve her independence. Alongside the popular elements of mystery and melodrama, in the newspaper novels Braddon thus often succeeded in drawing sympathetic attention to women marginalized or condemned by bourgeois society.[17]

An economical way to pursue the ideological orientation of Braddon's work in the newspaper novels is to survey the treatment of the contrasting pairs of heroines often featured, in terms of transgression versus submission, or the erotic against the angelic. Three of the most complex of the Tillotson sensation novels can illustrate the main variations: the heroic failure of transgression, the timid triumph of submission, or radical ambivalence. After a series of insipid female leads in domestic romances (Clarissa Lovel in *The Lovels of Arden* [1871] or Flora Chamney in *Lost for Love* [1874], for example), in *Taken at the Flood* Braddon reverted to the pattern of *Lady Audley's Secret* and *Aurora Floyd*, with the heroine as glamorous criminal. Sylvia Carew is a Pre-Raphaelite beauty condemned to the role of an impoverished schoolmaster's daughter. She constantly flouts respectable opinion, is suspected of murder, attempts bigamy, and is finally rewarded not with union with her lover but with death by typhoid. But Braddon is in large part sympathetic to her heroine's frustrations and admires her willpower and courage. She devotes a good deal of space to evoking Sylvia's alternating moods of ambition and listlessness, and her overwhelming sensations of constraint and claustrophobia, as she marries to be free of her domineering father only to find she is an even closer prisoner as the wife of an elderly man. In contrast, the minor heroine, the passive and long-suffering ward Esther Rochdale, may at last and by default win the hand of the handsome hero, but in the process she gains little sympathy or even sustained attention from the narrator.[18]

In *Phantom Fortune* the contrast is between the Maulevrier sisters Lady Lesbia and Lady Mary, the former glamorous and desperate for fast and fashionable cosmopolitan society, the latter unpretentious and unwilling to leave the valleys and hills of the English Lake District. But Lesbia's Parisian costumes and coquetry are shown to be cold and heartless, while the tomboyish Mary exudes a warm, tweedy eroticism, and it is the latter who succeeds in the marriage market. Mary wins the kindly and handsome Lord Hartfield, and is allowed to keep her country haven, while Lesbia has to make do with the paunchy city financier Mr. Goodward, and ends up a social outcast after allowing herself to be kidnapped and seduced by an adventuring scoundrel from the Caribbean. Here Braddon extends little sympathy to the transgressor. In *An Open Verdict*, two female leads are again given almost equal attention, but here the weighting of sympathy is more finely balanced. Beatrix Harefield is a detached and alabaster beauty, a wealthy heiress deprived of human warmth by a strict and jealous father. Her sole friend from childhood has been the rosy and impetuous Bella Scratchell, whose poverty forces her to earn money as a morning governess and companion. Both are attracted by the hero, the grave young socialist clergyman Cyril, but when Beatrix's father dies in suspicious circumstances, Bella's jealous actions bring suspicion of murder on Beatrix. Beatrix recoils into saintlike self-sacrifice, and Bella into greed and sensuality. The latter's profligacy leads to her death in a riding accident, while the former's patient service is finally rewarded by reconciliation with Cyril. Despite their dichotomies, both women are presented as at once victims and victors, and fairly share authorial sympathy, in marked contrast to the noble hero who hardly escapes the charge of being a bloodless prig.

A number of general points can be made on the basis of this brief and doubtless reductive survey. First, the best of the newspaper novels are complex structures not only in their plotting but also in their social and cultural symbolism. Secondly, they remain ideologically challenging to mid-Victorian social and sexual proprieties, but less uniformly and aggressively so than in the early triple-decker novels. Finally, Braddon's transgressive heroines in the 1870s and 1880s are rather more introspective than those of the early 1860s; being allowed more fully to enter the consciousness of such female protagonists perhaps encouraged in Braddon's readers a greater degree of empathy with their gestures of defiance and of understanding of the causes.

All of the newspaper novels then contain sensational elements, in the form of mystery, crime, and impropriety. That this was specifically in order to appeal to the debased taste of the provincial newspaper reader is unlikely, since these factors were precisely what most library subscribers were looking for when they borrowed a new Braddon. What does seem certain, however, is that during Braddon's engagement to Tillotson, many of the novels that were written not for the provincial syndicates but for metropolitan literary journals (not only *Belgravia,* but also, from the late 1870s, the weeklies *All the Year Round, World,* and *Whitehall Review*) were significantly less sensational. Important examples are: *Joshua Haggard's Daughter* (1876), *Vixen* (1879), *The Story of Barbara* (1880), *The Golden Calf* (1883), *Ishmael* (1884), and *Mohawks* (1886). This dichotomy is particularly clear on the many occasions where Braddon produced two novels in a year. For example: in 1876 Tillotson got the satirical *Dead Men's Shoes* while *Belgravia* had the tragedy *Joshua Haggard's Daughter,* which, unusually, Braddon spent over a year composing and revised extensively before volume publication; in 1884, the newspapers had the Devonshire detective story *Wyllard's Weird* rather than the *Ishmael,* an epic of the Paris Commune; and in 1886 the novelettes *One Thing Needful* and *Cut by the County* instead of the historical *Mohawks* (1886). During the period of her engagement to Lengs, of course, Braddon's output declined to a single novel per year, and the pattern of parallel composition finally ceased.

The "non-newspaper" novels then are often those where Braddon attempted to placate the gods of literature. Artistic "seriousness" thus implied not only an avoidance of melodrama in favor of domestic realism or Zolaesque naturalism, but also a preference for historical or foreign settings and themes. A key point is that, as in the 1860s, Braddon was regularly at work on "serious" and "popular" works at the same time. In this sense her characteristic mode of composition was to work simultaneously in series and in parallel. Figure 9.1, representing a segment from the mid-1870s shortly after Braddon's engagement to Tillotson, and based on Braddon's surviving working "Schedules" for 1874–76 (reported in Wolff *Sensational Victorian,* notes to chaps. 7–8), illustrates the basic pattern:

However, the cleavage between the two modes is far less sharp than had been the case in the 1860s. Between *Hostages to Fortune* and *Dead Men's Shoes* it is difficult to distinguish which is the heavyweight. And Braddon often veered toward the sensational even when she was attempting to write "seriously." In *The Golden Calf* (1883), which clearly shows the influence of her reading of Zola's *L'Assomoir,* there is the detailed examination of the effects on a unstable marriage of the husband's growing addiction to alcohol and mental degeneration. But toward the end of the process Braddon incongruously has the deranged husband burn down the house and end his own life, while the wife is rescued from the encroaching flames by her admirer who has disguised himself as a hermit to remain near her. Conversely, we can occasionally trace naturalistic tendencies in novels for Tillotson such as *The Cloven Foot* and *Phantom Fortune* (see Wolff, *Sensational Victorian* 289–91, 295–99).[19]

Contemporary critics also were by no means certain to evaluate Braddon's "serious" efforts above her "popular" ones. Even those London journals that had complained loudest at the impropriety and triviality of her early works, often saw things differently by the 1870s. With the first novel she wrote for Tillotson, *Taken at the Flood,* the *Athenaeum* was grateful that Braddon was returning to her earlier style after a period devoted to more "worthy" fiction:

> Miss Braddon has returned to her best style. "Taken at the Flood" is far better than "Lucius Davoren," than "Strangers and Pilgrims"—than in short, any of those books which we have both praised and blamed. A very simple story, which does not seem to have cost Miss Braddon so much pains to write as some of these which we have named. It is not a great novel, but it is a thoroughly good one. (2 May 1874, 592)

When she did take more time and trouble in plot and characterization, she was often accorded unfavorable notices by the loftier journals. Reviewers tended not to recognize the attempt at elevation, or the influence

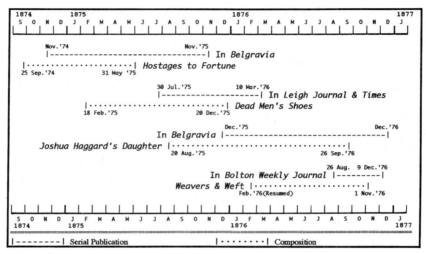

Figure 9.1 Braddon's Pattern of Dual Composition

of Flaubert and Zola, and would compare her disparagingly to George Eliot. The *Spectator,* for example, was more enthusiastic about *Wyllard's Weird* than *Ishmael* (2 May 1885, 581–82). Again the *Athenaeum* complained about the defects of the "later manner," which it defined negatively in its review of the sentimental novel *Asphodel* (1881): "It does not depend upon intricacy of plot, upon crime or mystery" (26 Feb. 1881, 245–46).

Braddon herself, not surprisingly, defended her greater labors on the "serious" works. When, in a 1911 interview she was asked to name her favorites among her own novels, *Lady Audley's Secret* headed the list, but none of the other choices were sensational works. Most were the carefully researched and revised historical works: "Of Miss Braddon's favourites amongst her own books, we gathered that the first published one, "Lady Audley's Secret," "Asphodel" and "Vixen," the historical romance "London Pride," "Mohawks" and "The Infidel," both eighteenth-century stories—which were by a strange coincidence also our favourites—stand high" (Holland 708). And, among the few modern critics who have commented on Braddon's works of the 1870s, 1880s, and 1890s, Wolff, (*Sensational Victorian* 270–77 & 304–15) comes to a similar conclusion, in regarding *Joshua Haggard's Daughter* and *Ishmael* as among her finest novels. For the present writers, however, the works of "our Author" from those decades most worthy of revival and detailed study are those in which the sensation pattern laid down by Braddon in the 1860s remains apparent: the facade of respectability of the country house ruptured by

157

the emergence of guilty secrets and suppressed passions. This would include, notably, *Taken at the Flood, An Open Verdict, Phantom Fortune,* and *The Fatal Three,* all of which were produced for the provincial syndicates.

It is only in the final years of the century that we can see a marked and irreversible decrease in the mechanisms of sensation, in part at least because material no longer needed to be stretched for three-volume publication. Braddon quickly trimmed her style to the limits of the pithier one-volume novels of the Edwardian period, and produced several interesting character studies, including *Dead Love Has Chains* (1907) and *Our Adversary* (1909). In a 1913 interview, Braddon herself explained the shift simply as a response to the demands of the literary market, reflecting the changing expectations of a new generation of readers.

> "No, no golden-haired heroines now," was the reply to a natural question. "The days for golden hair have passed away. Less detail of heroines is wanted now and more character study. Readers are not satisfied with incidents alone; they like to see character evolve as events move." ("Miss Braddon at Home," 9).

If there is a level at which we can see Braddon's writing as subject directly to appropriation by the representatives, alternately, of the older literary establishment (Bulwer-Lytton) and the newer commercial regime (Maxwell or Tillotson), it is also true that "our Author" appears personally to have been sensitive to an unusual extent to the indirect pressures exerted on her narratives by the sense of a newly constituted popular audience. In other words, Braddon felt in a rather modern way that her work belonged finally not to herself but to her readers.

The above account then suggests the perhaps surprising and decidedly unromantic conclusion that, at least in the 1870s and 1880s, and in marked contrast to Margaret Oliphant's witness on her own case (Oliphant *Autobiography;* Colby and Colby), Mary Braddon's prolific output as an author was neither necessarily in her own economic interests, nor necessarily detrimental to the literary value of her writing. If Braddon's natural talent and fluency as a storyteller was repeatedly appropriated by literary middlemen for commercial or other purposes, the author herself appears often to have been a not unwilling victim. But while Braddon was generally content to conform to the financial and ideological demands of the fiction marketplace, she was also quite capable of using popular fictional paradigms in order to challenge specific social and sexual prejudices. New readers of Braddon in the late twentieth century are generally struck by the modernity of the ironical, self-distancing tone that she tends to adopt in her writing, in marked contrast to the more dated feel of the prose of contemporary sensationalists such as Wood and Collins. Braddon's remarkable facility in adapting to successive stages in the professionalization of the role of the author and the commodification of fictional form in the later nineteenth century can be seen as a symptom of the same attitude. It is this strikingly modern mode of double consciousness that makes Braddon, in a final sense, "our Author."

NOTES

1. Generally on Victorian serial publication, see: Hughes, Pollard, and Schmidt.

2. Colby (1992) draws attention to this conceit in a passage in Thackeray's *Pendennis* vol. 1 chap 37. More generally on later Victorian publishing history, see Cross; Feltes, Modes chaps. 4–5 and *Literary;* Griest; and Keating, chap. 2.

3. Wolff appears not to have gone back to the original newspapers to confirm details of serial publication, instead relying on secondary evidence in correspondence or diaries.

4. Held principally in the *Bolton Evening News* Archive at the Central Library, Bolton, Greater Manchester. Hereafter references will use the Central Library call numbers, prefixed ZBEN. Further papers are in the possession of Michael L. Turner, Head of Conservation at the Bodleian Library, Oxford. The Tillotson papers now held at Bolton are owned by the present proprietors of the *Bolton Evening News* and *Bolton Journal,* (part of the Reed Regional Newspapers group), and our thanks are due to Mr. John B. Waters, Managing Director, for his kindness in faciliting the viewing of the papers and for permission to cite them here.

5. The surviving letters from Maxwell principally cover the years 1882 to 1887, and are contained in a file at the Central Library, Bolton, designated ZBEN/4/3, which also includes telegrams and postcards, a few documents from outside this period, occasional letters from Braddon herself, Tillotson or third parties, and some attached printed papers, altogether totaling nearly two hundred otherwise unnumbered items. Unless otherwise stated, references to ZBEN/4/3 indicate letters from Maxwell to Tillotson.

6. More generally on Tillotson's American operations, see Johanningsmeier 56–61.

7. As early as 1863, she claimed almost to have "earned enough money to keep me and mother for the rest of our lives" (letter to Sir Edward Bulwer-Lytton, 13 April, reproduced in Wolff, "Devoted Disciple" 13)

8. Reproduced in Wolff (*Sensational Victorian* Plate 25, between pages 242 and 43). See also Charles Reade's conclusion that "her taskmaster drove her too hard" in his 1874 notebook (reproduced in Wolff, *Sensational Victorian* 79–83).

9. See letter of Wilkie Collins to W. F. Tillotson of 15 Feb. 1880 (ZBEN/4/6/16), contributing a letter signed by Dickens to the collection, among other correspondence from authors held at Bolton referring to Mary Tillotson's hobby.

10. Braddon was eventually persuaded to join the Society in 1905, long after Maxwell's death (see letters from Anthony Hope Hawkins, then Secretary, of 15 October and 1 November 1905, in the Wolff Collection).

11. See the announcement in the (Sheffield) *Weekly Telegraph* of 2 Jan. 1897: "Notwithstanding the great cost, the proprietors of the 'Weekly Telegraph,' intend to try the effect of publishing Miss Braddon's 1897 story (which will begin on January 16) exclusively in in this journal."

12. Tillotson was caviling over giving £500 for *One Thing Needful,* until Maxwell revealed that Watt had already offered £900 for the same work. When Tillotson finally agreed to the £500, Maxwell peevishly suggested that he make a quick profit by immediately reselling the rights to Watt (nine letters & telegrams, 14 Oct. to 4 Nov. 1885, ZBEN/4/3).

13. Extensive business correspondence on Braddon's behalf from the 1890s onwards is also preserved in the Watt Collection at Chapel Hill, beginning with a letter of 1 October 1892 from A. P. Watt to Harpers in New York concerning the publication of the short story "The Island of Old Faces" (folder 15.15).

14. After the first part had been published in the *Weekly Telegraph,* the title was abruptly changed, with the following brief notice: "The title *Shadowed Lives* having been utilised by another author, we have decided to alter Miss Braddon's story to *A Shadowed Life.*" Unfortunately, the title A *Shadowed Life* had also been used previously by the Scottish novelist David Pae as the title of a serial published anonymously in a number of provinical weeklies from the late 1870s. A similar incident had occurred earlier, under the threat of legal action, with *The Story of Barbara* (Wolff, *Sensational Victorian* 491–92).

15. Interestingly, Mansel's terms are precisely those in which, almost a century later, writers like Raymond Chandler were to attack the British detective story of the 1920s for its neglect of character and motivation in favor of mechanism and puzzle, and to recommend the depth and authenticity of the emerging American crime novel (see Law, "Roman policier" 341–43).

16. In the 1890s, detective stories were common not only in new popular metropolitan magazines like George Newnes's *Strand Magazine,* but also syndicated in provincial weeklies. Conan Doyle's second Sherlock Holmes novel, *The Sign of the Four,* for example, was serialized in Leng's *Weekly Telegraph* in 1890, shortly after Braddon's *Whose Was the Hand?*

17. We should recall that Martha Vicinus (1981) has argued convincingly that the instability of Victorian domestic melodrama often served to articulate the insecurities of social groups in positions of powerlessness or undergoing social transformation.

18. In a rare modern instance of extended discussion of the novel, Rachel

Anderson (85–91) seems to us to entirely misread the narratorial tone in judging the moral of the story to be "the sin, and the foolishness, of marrying, not for love, but for material gain."

19. It is important to note here that the scandalous image of Zola's writings in Britain in the 1880s held a popular as well as a Bohemian attraction. Remarkably, an English translation of *Germinal* appeared in serial in both the Conservative London Sunday paper *The People* and the *Sheffield Weekly Telegraph* in mid-1885, shortly after its original issue in Paris.

WORKS CITED

Unpublished Materials

A. P. Watt Archive, Berg Collection, New York Public Library, New York City.
A. P. Watt Collection (#11036), General and Literary Manuscripts, Wilson Library, The University of North Carolina at Chapel Hill.
Bolton Evening News Archive, Bolton Central Library, Greater Manchester.
Tillotson papers, in the possession of Michael L. Turner, Bodleian Library, Oxford.
Wolff Collection, Harry Ransom Humanities Research Center, The University of Texas at Austin.

Published Materials

Altick, R. D. *The English Common Reader: A Social History of the Mass Reading Public, 1800–1900.* Chicago: U of Chicago P, 1957.
Anderson, Rachel. *The Purple Heart Throbs: The Sub-literature of Love.* London: Hodder & Stoughton, 1974.
Bonham-Carter, Victor. *Authors by Profession: Volume 1, From the Introduction of Printing until the Copyright Act 1911.* London: Society of Authors, 1978.
Brake, Laurel. *Subjugated Knowledges: Journalism, Gender, and Literature in the Nineteenth Century.* New York: New York UP, 1994.
Brantlinger, Patrick. "What is 'Sensational' about the 'Sensation Novel'?" In *Nineteenth Century Fiction* 37.1 (June 1982): 1–28.
Colby, Robert A. "Harnessing Pegasus: Walter Besant, *The Author* and the Profession of Letters." *Victorian Periodicals Review* 23.3 (Fall 1990): 111–20.
Colby, Vineta, and Robert A. Colby. *The Equivocal Virtue: Mrs. Oliphant and the Victorian Literary Market Place.* Hamden, Conn.: Archon, 1966.
Cross, Nigel. *The Common Writer: Life in Nineteenth-Century Grub Street.* Cambridge: Cambridge UP, 1985.
Edwards, P. D., I. G. Sibley, and Margaret Versteeg. *Indexes to Fiction in Belgravia.* (Victorian Fiction Research Guides 14). St. Lucia, Queensland: U of Queensland, 1990.

Feltes, N. N. *Modes of Production of Victorian Novels*. Chicago: U of Chicago P, 1986.

—————. *Literary Capital and the Late Victorian Novel*. Madison, Wis.: Univ. of Wisconsin Press, 1993.

Flint, Kate. *The Woman Reader, 1837–1914*. Oxford: Clarendon P, 1993.

Griest, Guinevere L. *Mudie's Circulating Library and the Victorian Novel*. Bloomington, Ind.: Indiana UP, 1970.

Hatton, J. "Miss Braddon At Home." *London Society* (January 1888).

Holland, C. "Fifty Years of Novel Writing. Miss Braddon at Home" *Pall Mall Magazine* (November 1911).

Hughes, Linda K., and Michael Lund. *The Victorian Serial*. Charlottesville, Vir.: UP of Virginia, 1991.

Johanningsmeier, Charles. *Fiction and the American Literary Marketplace: The Role of Newspaper Syndicates in America, 1860–1900*. Cambridge: Cambridge UP, 1997.

Johnson-Woods, Toni. "Mary Elizabeth Braddon: Queen of the Desert." Unpubl. paper delivered at the 4th Annual Conference of the Society for the History of Authorship, Readership, and Publishing (SHARP) at Worcester, Massachusetts, July 1996. [See essay this volume.]

Keating, P. J. *The Haunted Study: A Social History of the English Novel 1875– 1914*. London: Secker & Warburg, 1989.

Law, Graham. " 'Il s'agissait peut-être d'un roman policier,": Leblanc, Macdonald, and Robbe-Grillet." In *Comparative Literature* 40 (Fall 1988): 335–57.

—————. "Wilkie in the Weeklies: The Serialization and Syndication of Collins's Late Novels." *Victorian Periodicals Review* 30.3 (Fall 1997): 244–69.

[Mansel, H.L.]. "Sensation Novels." *Quarterly Review* 133 (1863): 481–514.

"Miss Braddon at Home." *The Daily Telegraph* (4 Oct. 1913): 9.

Morrison, Elizabeth. "Serial Fiction in Australian Colonial Newspapers." In *Literature in the Marketplace: Nineteenth-century British Publishing and Reading Practices*, edited by John O. Jordan and Robert L. Patten, 306–24. Cambridge: Cambridge UP, 1995.

"Novelists' 'Skeletons.' " *Cassell's Saturday Journal* (19 Mar. 1892): 10:620.

Nowell-Smith, Simon. *International Copyright Law and the Publisher in the Reign of Queen Victoria*. Oxford: Clarendon P, 1968.

Oliphant, Margaret. "Novels." *Blackwood's Edinburgh Magazine* 102 (Sept. 1867): 257–80.

—————. *The Autobiography of Margaret Oliphant: The Complete Text*. Ed. Elisabeth Jay. Oxford: Oxford UP, 1990.

Peters, Catherine. *The King of Inventors: A Life of Wilkie Collins*. London: Secker & Warburg, 1991.

Pollard, Graham. "Serial Fiction." In *New Paths in Book Collecting*, edited by John Carter, 247–77. London: Constable & Co., 1934.

Robinson, Solveig C. "Editing *Belgravia*: M. E. Braddon's Defense of 'Light Literature.' " *Victorian Periodicals Review* 28.2 (Spring 1995): 109–22.

Sadleir, Michael. "Mary Elizabeth Braddon." In *Things Past.* London: Constable, 1944, 69–83.

Schmidt, B. Q. "Novelists, Publishers, and Fiction in Middle-Class Magazines 1860–1880." *Victorian Periodicals Review* 17.4 (Winter 1984): 142–53.

Sheffield Daily Telegraph 1855–1925: A Record of Seventy Years. Sheffield: W. C. Leng & Co., n.d. [1925].

Terry, R. C. *Victorian Popular Fiction 1860–1880.* London: Macmillan, 1983.

Turner, Michael L. "The Syndication of Fiction in Provincial Newspapers, 1870–1939: The Example of the Tillotson 'Fiction Bureau.'" Unpub. B.Litt. Diss. Oxford Univ.: 1968.

Unsigned review of *Asphodel* by M. E. Braddon. In *Athenaeum* no 2784 (26 Feb. 1881) 245–6.

Unsigned review of *Eleanor's Victory* by M. E. Braddon. In *Anthenaeum* no 1873 (19 Sep. 1863) 361.

Unsigned review of *Just As I Am* by M. E. Braddon. In *Spectator* vol 54 (22 Jan. 1881) 126.

Unsigned review of *Like and Unlike* by M. E. Braddon. In *Athenaeum* no 3127 (1 Oct. 1887) 435.

Unsigned review of *Taken at the Flood* by M. E. Braddon. In *Athenaeum* no 2428 (2 May 1874) 592.

Unsigned review of *Wyllard's Weird* by M. E. Braddon. In *Athenaeum* no 2995 (21 Mar 1885) 371–2.

Unsigned review of *Wyllard's Weird* by M. E. Braddon. In *Spectator* vol 58 (2 May 1885) 581–2.

Vicinus, Martha. "'Helpless and Unfriended': Nineteenth-Century Domestic Melodrama." *New Literary History* 13 (1981): 127–43.

Wolff, Robert Lee. "Devoted Disciple: The Letters of Mary Elizabeth Braddon to Sir Edward Bulwer-Lytton, 1862–1873." *Harvard Library Bulletin* 12 (1974): 5–35; 129–61.

———. *Sensational Victorian: The Life and Fiction of Mary Elizabeth Braddon.* New York: Garland, 1979.

———. *Nineteenth-Century Fiction: A Bibliographical Catalogue.* Vol. 1. New York: Garland, 1981.

Ten

Misalliance:
M. E. Braddon's Writings for the Stage

Heidi J. Holder

Mary Elizabeth Braddon, famous as a novelist, began her professional life in the theater. Working as an actress in the regional theaters at Brighton, Hull, and Beverley in the late 1850s under the stage name Mary [or Mary Anne] Seyton, Braddon appeared in such plays as Tom Taylor's *Still Waters Run Deep* and J. B. Buckstone's *Leap Year!*.[1] She performed a wide range of roles, from melodrama to farce. Her theatrical background would provide her with material for her novels, including *Aurora Floyd, Dead Sea Fruit,* and *A Lost Eden*. What is less known, however, is that Braddon throughout her career as an author worked hard at building a career as a playwright.

An early break, courtesy of a female theater manager, afforded Braddon the chance to see one of her plays staged in the West End: *Loves of Arcadia* appeared at the Strand in 1860. Other productions would follow: *Griselda* (Princess's Theatre, 1873), *Genevieve* (also known as *The Missing Witness,* staged at the Theatre Royal, Liverpool, in 1874), and *Like or Unlike* (produced at the Westcliffe Saloon, Whitby, in 1890; and the Gaiety, Brighton, in 1891). Other plays remained unproduced: *Married Beneath Him* (published in 1882), *Marjorie Daw* and *Dross* (published in 1886), and *A Life Interest* (unpublished, written in 1893). W. B. Maxwell noted that seven unproduced plays lay in Braddon's desk at the time of her death; Robert Wolff has attempted to identify some of them from

Braddon's diary entries, but none of the texts are extant (Maxwell 281; Wolff 502–3).

Despite repeated rebuffs from theater managers, Braddon wrote dramatic pieces throughout her career, paid close attention to theatrical trends, and always composed her plays with an eye to eventual production. These were not "closet" pieces; in the published version of *Genevieve*, entitled *The Missing Witness*, Braddon has even gone to the trouble of making suggestions for cuts in a note under the Dramatic Personae listing: "All dialogue enclosed between the parenthetic marks, [], and in italic type, may be omitted to shorten piece if the theatre cannot give the time necessary to act the full play as written." If Braddon's theatrical background gave her practical advantages as a playwright, her rapid rise to fame as an author and the appearance of numerous adaptations of her plays—especially *Lady Audley's Secret* and *Aurora Floyd*—made her name a draw for audiences.

Why, then, did Braddon fail to make a place for herself as a playwright? Her plays, I believe, are as good as if not better than many pieces produced on West End stages in the latter half of the nineteenth century. One factor working against her was the fact that hers was a period in which women were very clearly not welcomed as dramatic authors in the West End. Theater historians can name female playwrights from the Romantic period (Joanna Baillie, Jane Scott, Elizabeth Inchbald) and from the early Victorian period (Catherine Gore, Eliza Planche); after that, one must jump ahead to the "New Woman" and suffragist dramatists of the nineties and the Edwardian years (Elizabeth Robins, Lady Bell, Cicely Hamilton). The largely working-class theaters of the East End proved more hospitable to women playwrights at this time, but Braddon does not seem to have aimed for productions in these venues.

Aside from the unwelcoming theatrical milieu, Braddon might well have had difficulty for another reason. Her plays reveal a decidedly combative attitude toward the theatrical conventions of their time, particularly as regards gender roles.

In her initial foray into playwriting, Braddon had found an ally in Louise Swanborough, actress and lessee of the Strand Theatre. *Loves of Arcadia* was produced at the Strand in March 1860. A "frothy and trivial" piece, as Wolff terms it, the comedy was nonetheless a pleasing vehicle for Swanborough, who played the female lead, Mademoiselle du Launay. The story—of two members of the court of Louis XV who flee an arranged marriage to one another only to meet and fall in love in the forest (where they have disguised themselves as shepherds)—is indeed slight; yet it draws considerable humor from Braddon's insistent playing upon notions of artifice and nature. The wayward groom, the Chevalier de Merrilac, seeks a pastoral existence yet is repulsed by the "coarseness" of the shepherdesses he meets. When he comes across the disguised Mademoiselle du Launay, he cries, "A Divinity! A New wild flower for Jean-Jacques Rousseau. Now this is something like a shepherdess" (16). When the King himself comes across the disguised couple, he comments on the scene to Richelieu:

> *Louis:* They are perfect. Is it not a wonderful imitation of nature?
> *Richelieu:* Pardon me, Sire, it is nature.
> *Louis:* What, are they not China?
> *Richelieu:* No Sire, see they move. (28)

The emphasis on an artificial ideal is reiterated in the play's many references to painting, to china, and to music. It reached its height in the second act, set at court, when Merrilac poses in a picture frame, causing Mlle. du Launay to wonder at the resemblance to her "shepherd."

The King, who seems a tyrant, proves a wise manipulator. When he offers his wayward courtiers a choice between marriage and death, he is fully aware of their alternate, "pastoral" identities: he has only to make those identities known to the lovers for the happy ending to take place. "You see," he says, "We are not such a tyrant as we look" (62).

This early work of Braddon's does bear some resemblance to her later, more weighty attempts at drama and comedy. In particular, the theme of the ideal that the loved one—especially the woman—must emulate would reappear in her dramatic writings with a sharper, more political edge. What would change drastically was the role of men; Louis would be the last wise, paternal figure in Braddon's drama, to be succeeded by a series of deeply flawed and misguided male characters.

The work was enough of a success to earn Braddon some attention as a playwright. *The Era Almanack* of 1869 even included her in a list of "Living Dramatic Authors":

> Although her numerous novels, which have acquired such well-deserved popularity, have furnished an abundance of material to adapters, the principle piece Miss Braddon has as yet contributed to the stage is a neat two-act comedy, called *Loves of Arcadia*, produced at the Strand Theatre . . . and which met with a most favourable reception."[2]

Braddon's theatrical writings quickly found a groove. Her favored theme was the unjustly persecuted female—particularly the wife. Her next experiment on the stage after the rather gentle *Loves of Arcadia* was *Griselda*, a version of Boccaccio's tale of the patient wife. This might seem a grim and unappetizing choice, though Braddon did soften the story, shortening the length of Griselda's "test" to two years and revising the charade of the Prince's remarriage. Essentially, though, the story remains the same: a prince falls in love with a peasant girl, marries her, and then decides to "test" her love by rejecting her, throwing her back into poverty, and taking her children from her (in this case one child, an infant boy).

Griselda, staged at the Princess's Theatre in November 1873, was a success, thanks no small part to the presence of the popular actress Mrs. Rousby in the lead role. The reviewers spent a great deal of time singing the praises of Rousby, who would soon, unfortunately, go into decline and drop out of the production. Braddon's name was prominently featured on the programs—this at a time when authors could not be certain of billing—and she was also permitted to write a historical "note" for the program detailing the history of the tale of "Patient Griselda" (programs, Theatre Museum). The management evidently considered her name marketable.

In Braddon's version Griselda is still, to be sure, the long-suffering wife. However, she displays a characteristic that would become typical of Braddon's theatrical heroines: she is more perceptive and morally just than her husband. From the outset Griselda fears Cosmo, the Iago-like courtier who will lead her husband astray. When she warns her husband of Cosmo's envy and malice, Gualtiero dismisses her, saying "Child this folly/ Would anger me, Could love be wroth with beauty/ As I perceive a speck on thy perfection" (15v). While her husband is fooled by Cosmo until the last act, Griselda understands from the first what is happening and why. The enlightenment of the play's final scene belongs to the men, and Griselda's patience has run out. When she believes her child is stolen she turns on her husband, crying "Nay I'll not look / On him that stole my child lest / I should curse him" (44). Realizing his folly, Gualtiero reconciles with Griselda, even going down on his knees to ask her forgiveness.

In a turnabout that would prove an enduring feature of her plays, Braddon rewrites the final, mock-wedding scene. While in Boccaccio's story *Griselda* is forced to make preparations for her husband's remarriage to another woman (who is eventually revealed to Griselda as her own daughter), before finally being restored to her position as wife, in Braddon's version Griselda refuses to accept any divorce:

> I have been patient, will be patient still
> But not to hear shame put upon my son.
> Let him divorce me, if the law can do it,
> Let him divorce me, if his heart can bear it;
> I have been his true wife, and yonder babe
> Is his true son. I'll take him in my arms
> Stand by the alter when my lord's new wife

Comes to be married. I will hold him up
Above the priest and throng of wedding guests
And cry aloud till the Cathedral echoes.
This is his son, this is Saluzzo's heir. (36)

In the end, Griselda herself is the veiled bride, and Cosmo is the one who is astonished at the unveiling ("Perdition!" he cries, when he sees it is Griselda). Braddon's play, while making use of the most punitive of tales, manages to transform Boccaccio's story into something close to its opposite: a lesson for men.

Buoyed by the enthusiastic response of audiences to *Griselda*, Braddon quickly moved to try her hand at the dominant genre of the day, the sensational melodrama. Playwrights such as Dion Boucicault, Watts Phillips, and Tom Taylor built their careers in the mid-century theater with dramas that put burning buildings, sinking ships, trainwrecks, and boat races on the stage. Braddon herself chose an avalanche for her sensation scene in *Genevieve* (published as *The Missing Witness*). In many respects the play lovingly follows the conventions of contemporary melodramas: the villain secretly seethes with jealousy and hatred, false messages are delivered, a life-and-death struggle takes place on a precipice.

However, Braddon's treatment of the two female leads proves unusual. The peasant girl Genevieve is the heroine of the piece—once again Braddon makes the lower-class female the focus and moral center. She is the staunch friend of Pauline de Marsac, a young woman of wealth and status. The villain desires Pauline, and plots to put her fiancé out of the way, only to be repeatedly foiled by Genevieve, who functions as a kind of "house detective" at the Chateau. At a time when female credulity and weakness were popular plot facilitators, Braddon's females stand out for their inability to be led astray. Genevieve's own fiancé, the rather dull farmer Andre, is easily coaxed into believing that she has been unfaithful to him; however, when the villain tries the same tactic with Pauline, she refuses to bend: "I cannot believe it! No, a thousand times no!" (47).

Genevieve herself appears to have near-superhuman abilities and strength. She is ever-watchful and knowing. She threatens to strangle one of the villain's flunkies (her father-in-law to be), who chastises her: "what a very violent young woman you are, Genevieve!" (28). When, after a brief struggle on a dangerous footpath the villain throws his rival off a cliff, Genevieve battles with him in turn—and is not so easily dispensed with. After wrestling with the peasant girl all the way down the footpath, the villain cries, "Loose your grasp, I say!" to which Genevieve retorts, "Never, with life." The villain wonders, "what can I do with this wildcat?" (42). His solution is to lock her in a cottage, which is promptly buried in an avalanche (an Act drop that brought the audience to its feet). After being buried alive for three weeks, Genevieve appears to her fiancé in a dream, indicating where he can find her. Once the cottage has been uncovered, her miraculous survival is explained by the fact that two goats were also trapped in the cottage, conveniently providing milk.

Genevieve, who at first seems a "feisty second-lead" female type, has by the play's conclusion become a figure of remarkable power. For a similar type, one must look to a play such as Dion Boucicault's *Jessie Brown; or, the Relief of Lucknow* (1859), in which the title character virtually wills the rescue of the residents of Lucknow, threatened by the Sepoy Rebellion. But such heroics were permitted to women in colonial or imperialist melodramas (at least in the early- and mid-Victorian era), since opponents were native peoples. To embody moral power in a woman was something less familiar in domestic melodrama.

Braddon's ambivalent approach to her theatrical models is most evident, perhaps, in her attempt at writing domestic comedy-drama. She had begun writing for the stage at a time when the drama was at one of its perennial "low" points. In the view of many nineteenth-century theater critics, the drama of the first half of the century was hopelessly degraded, and was rescued in the second half by a series of managers and playwrights who elevated the drama to a respectable status. The playwright's lot at mid-century was a hard one, as noted by the influential critic Clement Scott:

> No encouragement whatever was given to authors of talent, to rising men, to coming men, to lights that might have shown. Robertson—the best fellow in the world, once an actor, one of a splendid histrionic family, who knew the stage from boyhood,—with a heart almost broken with neglect, turned cynic in despair. (1:474)

The Robertson here held forth as a representative playwright of his time would ultimately emerge as one of the chief "rescuers" of the drama. The low-keyed domestic realism of his plays, produced under the management of Squire and Marie Bancroft at the Prince of Wales's Theatre in the 1860s–1870s, set a standard for comic drama and have since acquired near-legendary status in British theater history; Robertson's plays *Society* (1865), *Ours* (1866), *Caste* (1867), *Play* (1868), *Progress* (1869), *The M. P.* (1870) were immensely popular and successful. As their titles hint, these were plays with aspirations to intellectual seriousness (one of many things deemed lacking on the early Victorian stage by its theater critics). *Caste,* in particular, takes on the issue of social stratification, via the popular dramatic theme of the "misalliance."

Robertson's "realistic" dramas held a dual appeal for the audience: they maintained, in staging and dialogue, what was accepted as a simple, straightforward depiction of contemporary life; but these plays also exploited melodrama's focus on the problem of distinctions—particularly, in the domestic drama, those of class, although in later melodrama issues of sex roles and racial difference would become more prominent. Robertson's plays dealt obsessively, as Clement Scott noted, with "the relations of the different strata of society" (264). Robertson's best known play, *Caste* (1867), concerns the union of Esther, a poor dancer, and D'Alroy, the son of a Marquis.

After much suffering, including the false report of D'Alroy's death in India, Esther is reunited with her husband and accepted in upper-class society, while her sister Polly is to marry her beau Sam, an ambitious gas-fitter. Esther, it must be noted, always speaks and carries herself in a manner suitable to D'Alroy's class, and no transformation is required for her to fit her new role. Her sister, however, embodies a more typically high-spirited and vulgar "lower-class" type.

Robertson would have many imitators, and it seems that Braddon was among them. In 1881–82 she tried her hand at a piece in the Robertsonian vein; her play, *Married Beneath Him: A Comedy in Four Acts*, bears a remarkable resemblance to Robertson's *Caste*.[3] What is notable in Braddon's piece is her clear revision of the earlier, much-lauded play. Simply put, *Caste* is the story of the son of a Marquis who marries a dancer from the corps de ballet (this would be the dancer in a theatrical company, not a classical "ballerina"). The romantic leads, Esther Eccles and the Hon. George D'Alroy, are surrounded by classic Victorian theatrical "types": Esther's sister Polly, and Polly's suitor Sam Gerridge the Gas-fitter, provide the classic second-lead comic support; Captain Hawtree is D'Alroy's cynical and "dandyesque" friend; and the social poles are represented by the haughty Marquise, who spurns her son's wife, and the drunken Eccles, who lives off the labor of his daughters.

Braddon's play cunningly takes aim at some of the weaknesses and inconsistencies of Robertson's formula in *Caste*. In *Married Beneath Him*, her heroine—significantly named "Polly"[4]—is very much a low-comic type. Where Robertson's Polly was the comic second-lead female, Braddon makes this type her lead, her romantic heroine. Braddon's Polly is a slangy, hoydenish circus performer, whose habits of behavior and speech make her upper-class lover wince: "She reminds me of the girl in the fairy tale, out of whose mouth dropped toads and scorpions" (11). However, he offers to educate her and, between the first and second acts, marries her.[5]

The theatrical context, plot line, and character types (down to the dandy and the haughty aristocratic relatives) all clearly echo Robertson's play. But Braddon's manner of advancing the plot, and her choice of resolution, playfully invert audience expectations. Her Polly, surprisingly, doesn't change. When we meet her again at Hunstanton Hall, she is complaining about her honeymoon trip to the Italian lakes—"these dismal old ponds will give me the blues," she mutters (21)—and is hoping to enjoy herself at a good horse race or "bean-feast." While somewhat reminiscent of *Aurora Floyd* in her impulsive behavior and equestrian bent, Polly is not presented as morally flawed. During a chaotic weekend in which Polly's adoptive, circus-owner parents, snooty in-laws, and long-missing biological father all show up at Hunstanton Lodge, it is her husband who must finally change. His coaching of Polly to act the role of fine lady merely makes her seem rude and "odious" (29), he mistakes his wife's long-lost father for her lover, and he wrongly denounces her before their guests. Realizing his mistake, he must beg her forgiveness and accept her criticism of him: "don't you think, Hunstanton, that when a man marries beneath him he ought to have the courage of his opinions; and, that instead of trying to hide his wife's humble origin, it would be better for him to face society boldly and say—Yes, I found my wife in a circus." (53).

Braddon has taken the template provided by Robertson, but rearranged it in unsettling ways. Michael Booth, in analyzing *Caste,* had pointed out its limitations:

> The play is not in the least democratic and completely supports the status quo; the clash between classes is merely comic when the only militant representative of the lower orders is Eccles and the only standard-bearer of the aristocracy is the Marquise. (90)

Braddon's play locates the class conflict within the marriage itself, and makes the lower-class wife the obvious "winner." In such a context, the anticipated happy ending takes on a keen political edge. The play also gave Braddon a chance to try to put theater people on the stage, a choice that likewise reveals class interest. As Ruth Burridge Lindemann has observed, in an astute reading of dramatic adaptations of Braddon's novels, dramatists frequently downplayed or deleted the theatrical characters and settings in such novels of Braddon as *The Black Band,* *Aurora Floyd, Only a Clod,* and *The Cloven Foot.* Lindemann sees this erasure as revealing a clear class bias: As the middle classes redefined the respectability of a theater that they had previously isolated and defined as Other, it became more problematic to represent theatrical characters on the stage. At the same time, Braddon needed to justify a personal theatrical history as an actress by contesting perceptions of disreputable theatricality and immoral theatrical women. The resulting rupture between Braddon's "theater" and the theater's own (non) self-representation reveals the competing cultural interests at work in the novels and in the adaptations (288). In *Married Beneath Him,* Braddon could attempt not only to reorganize the Robertsonian model of domestic comedy-drama according to her own taste, but also to restore to the stage the theater people who had been so scrupulously deleted from adaptations of her novels.

The unjustly persecuted wife or lover would prove to be a constant theme in Braddon's playwriting, as would her interest in at once appropriating and manipulating popular genres and character types. During the same period in which she wrote *Married Beneath Him,* Braddon also authored two more domestic comedy-dramas, *Marjorie Daw; A Household Idyll* and *Dross; or, the Root of Evil.* Both plays bear resemblance to Robertsonian comedy, and to the work of James Albery (another exemplar of "quiet" domestic realism, whose *Two Roses,* staged in 1870, is an obvious precursor to *Dross*). *Marjorie Daw* revisits the themes of idealism and artifice found in *Loves of Arcadia.* A young woman entertains her beloved cousin as he recuperates from eye surgery by telling him wholly fictitious tales of a lovely and fashionable woman who has moved in next door. Of course, he falls in love with the fiction and must learn to recognize the "true" love of his quiet and modest cousin: he has "fallen in love with a shadow" and "neglected the substance" (21).

Thomas Chugg, the central figure in *Dross,* likewise must shift his attentions from a greedy, fashionable widow to his faithful friend and housekeeper (who has long loved him). This is the only one of Braddon's extant plays with a man as the focus of the plot; Chugg, a farmer, inherits an estate and is transformed from an amiable fellow into a pretentious "lord of the manor" who refuses to be "domineered over" by the female members of his household (20). He is, naturally, "lowered" to his proper place when another will is found. Interestingly, Braddon has a male character seek after fashion and divert his affections from their proper channel. This is very often the female role in Victorian drama, but Braddon has assigned it to Chugg. And when she puts a male in this role Braddon shows no desire to alter the conventional ending: Chugg is firmly put down.

Having tried her hand at domestic comic drama, Braddon moved on to the full-fledged domestic melodrama. In 1890 there was a copyright performance of *Like or Unlike* (*hereafter to be called "Hands not Hearts" or "For Better for Worse"*). In this dramatic version of her own novel *Like and Unlike* (1887), Braddon shifted the emphasis somewhat. The novel focuses on twins, Adrian and Valentine—the one bookish and virtuous, the other fashionable and self-absorbed. Valentine, having won his brother's beloved, neglects and eventually kills her when she tries to depart with her lover. On the periphery is the lower-class woman Madge, the daughter of a prostitute who runs a home for "fallen women" in London. Madge spurns Valentine's advances, but offers him a kind of redemption—in good works—in the end.

The social satire of the novel, displaying what Wolff called the "mindlessness and viciousness of the upper class" (342), might have seemed a likely source for a play in 1890. At this time Henry Arthur Jones and Arthur Wing Pinero were building their theatrical reputations with plays that revealed an intense interest in fashionable society and the crossing of social boundaries. The 1890s would carry this trend further, with the success of numerous dramas that were set exclusively among the upper classes. Braddon's play, while part of the "fallen woman" tradition that included *Still Waters Run Deep* and the many dramatic versions of Mrs. Henry Wood's *East Lynne,* offers a mix of conventionality and innovation.

Braddon's play moves the female characters to the forefront, the connections among the women forming one of the distinctive features of the play. While in such dramas as *Still Waters Run Deep* (still popular, and revived in 1887), women pose a real danger to other women, in *Like or Unlike* the character of Madge proposes an explicitly "sororal" sensibility. When Madge confronts the man who would seduce Valentine's wife Helen, he points out that she is "saving the wife of the man who tried to dishonor her"; she replies that "I am a woman; and I mean to save another woman—if I can" (act 2, p. 5). Later, in attempting to keep Helen from "bolting," she warns, "you scorn the idea of sisterhood with me, Mrs. Belfield, you may remember that in the day when no honest woman will acknowledge sisterhood with you" (act 2, p. 6).

So powerful is Madge that she ultimately changes the play's ending. After Valentine has struck his wife on the head with a stick (in a very violent confrontation scene), and forced his twin brother to help him roll the body in a carpet and throw it in the river, Madge appears at the river's edge, waits for them to leave, and then dives into the water to rescue Helen—who, in the dramatic version, is not dead. When Helen is miraculously revealed in the last act, she is a convert to Madge's view: "You shall be to me as a sister from this day," she insists (act 4, p. 8). Of obvious secondary importance is Helen's reconciliation with her husband, who is transformed into another one of Braddon's not-quite-believable cowed and repentant men.

The third female character merits noting. Mrs. Baddely, the estranged wife of an army officer and the older sister of Helen, is a very traditional character in "fallen woman" plays—the worthless, dangerous female relative or confidante. Mrs. Baddely, who flirts with men and extracts money and gifts from them, has failed as a sister and chaperon.

In fact, her relationship with her sister replicates that of Mrs. Sternhold to her niece Mrs. Mildmay in *Still Waters Run Deep,* the popular drama in which Braddon herself acted the part of the despicable aunt in 1857. Having instructed her niece in how to dominate and trick her husband, Mrs. Sternhold must submit to his correction in the end, as he commands her to "go and dress for dinner." Taylor's play is one in which the misunderstood husband reasserts his rightful role as master of his house. Such a denouement runs counter to Braddon's own tastes, and one can read the play *Like or Unlike* as her "correction" of Taylor's plotline. Having played the Sternhold/Baddely character, she turned about and created Madge, a very radical type, in seeking a counterpart for whom one must look to Shaw and the suffragist-playwright Elizabeth Robins. Madge's association with prostitutes even makes her a better counselor to Helen, as when she warns her that she is being "lightly spoken of" in the men's clubs: "The women among whom I go are women who live behind the scenes of society, Mrs. Belfield—and you and many of your friends would be startled to hear how they talk of you, and to find how much they know about you." (Act 1, p. 19)

Like or Unlike was staged only in Whitby and Brighton. That the play was licensed as written may generate surprise, given the numerous references to prostitution. One scene even takes place in "the parlour of the Forlorn Hope," the refuge run by Madge for "fallen women." Significantly, Braddon chooses this setting for Valentine's appeal to Madge for help after he is accused of murdering his missing wife. Just prior to his appearance, bedraggled and desperate, Madge and her assistant had been discussing the typical case of a seventeen-year-old girl who came to London and was unable to find work; then, instead of a miserable, degraded woman, it is Valentine who enters, full of guilt. Nowhere is Braddon's tactic of forcing men into the traditionally female role of the humbled spouse more apparent. The spinster Madge gets to play the role of "hero," rescuer, raisonneur. It is not surprising that the play, Braddon's most aggressively feminist, did not receive a West End staging (although it was staged at the Gaiety in Brighton in June 1891); yet it must have given her great pleasure to write it.

The feminist critique in Braddon's plays is supported by her backhanded use of statements derogatory to women. She persistently makes fun of conventional "Wisdom" regarding women and of the casual disparagement of the sex. In *The Missing Witness* (also known as *Genevieve*), the General spurns the worthy Genevieve's warnings about his villainous guest Varriere: "Women are made up of prejudices, and presentiments, and nerves, and hysterics, and all sorts of sentimental folly" (14); and when Genevieve chastises her fiancé for his unfounded jealousy, saying "I did not think you were capable of such a meanness," he dismisses her by claiming "that's what every woman says" (18). The villainous Cosmo in *Genevieve* is given to such utterances as "woman's sharp tongue were made to wear a gag" (38v). Braddon takes great care to put conventional criticism into the mouths of male characters who are deluded, pompous, or malicious. And when a female character proclaims traditional views of women, it somehow comes out askew, as when Mrs. Nangle, in *Married Beneath Him,* solemnly upholds the conventional view of womanhood by chiding her husband thus: "You may look down upon private life, but it's woman's proper spear [sic]" (7).

It is very tempting to see in Braddon's feminist tinkering with character and genre a response to her own sufferings in an "illicit" union with the married John Maxwell. The melodramatic quality of Braddon's own private life, and her persecution by Maxwell's brother-in-law, Richard Brinsley Knowles have been amply commented upon (Wolff's biography clearly charts the scandal). Braddon's career as a novelist survived the extended scandal, but her career in the theater did not. Theatrical managers of the time exhibited great concern about the "respectability" of their theaters, and were defensive about charges of immorality. Managers lobbied hard for an image of their theaters as exemplars of English morality and good taste—not as harmful influences. Braddon's awkward living arrangements may well have made her anathema to them. Their skittishness might explain why *Genevieve,* despite its great success in Liverpool, never made it to London.

By all accounts the Liverpool production enjoyed an excellent run, and was well-acted and expensively mounted. The chief theatrical newspaper of the time, the *Era* (London), gave the play more attention than was usual for a provincial production, and suggested that Braddon was as talented a dramatist as she was a novelist: "the development of the story, the incidental situations, and the climaxes were all characterised by the grasp, finish, and power, which are the secrets of the command she has so long held over tens of thousands of readers" (12 Apr. 1874). The reviewer for *The Daily Courier* (Liverpool) roundly praised the piece, noting that "Miss Braddon had to bow her acknowledgments several times from a private box and from the stage" (7 April 1874: 5). *The Liverpool Post* wrote a glowing review of the piece, claiming that "its sensational scene was so powerful and successful that the author received at the end of the third act the honours which are usually reserved until the fall of the curtain" (7 Apr 1874: 5). The reviewer was certain, he said, that the piece would go on to London (a belief expressed in all the reviews I have found). But in an extraordinary digression, he praises Braddon's "courage," and defends her from the "prejudice" of the press: "about no other writer of the day has so much puling and affected nonsense been written." This was in

April, 1874; in September, Maxwell's wife would die in a Dublin insane asylum and the scandal would be revived full force.

That a theater reviewer felt compelled to mount a defense of the playwright makes evident that Braddon's status was a very live issue, and part of a distracting "drama" in itself. The "peccadilloes" of a male playwright such as Dion Boucicault might cause gossip, but hardly rendered him untouchable. And Braddon must have been keenly aware that her background as an actress—something she kept quiet—would already have marked her as sexually suspect. As Tracy Davis points out, "despite the tendency for Victorian performers to be credited with increasing respectability and middle-class status and for actors to receive the highest official commendations, the popular association between actresses and prostitutes and belief in actresses' inappropriate conduct endured throughout the nineteenth century" (100). Given the illicit nature of Braddon's union with Maxwell, she had to be doubly aware of this lingering "taint" assigned to women in the theater.

While Braddon was consistent in the creation of powerful, dominant women in her plays, she seems to have released some of her hostility toward theater managers in a stunningly nasty character, the lovely, scheming actress-manager of the novel *Hostages to Fortune* (written following the scandal surrounding Mrs. Maxwell's death in 1874). A figure completely in line with traditional stage villainesses, she is even a "bad" playwright who adapts morally suspect French plays. She can be read, in fact, as a kind of representative of everything that was held up to Braddon as a possible image of herself, from her acting days to her success as a "sensation" novelist and her public shame as a married man's mistress: a morally suspect purveyor of trash.

In her dramatic writings Braddon seems moved by a desire to rework the theatrical traditions she had come to know as an insider in the theater, traditions she monitored and reworked. If Braddon suffered under the imposition and juggling of stereotypical "roles" in her private life—as wife, mother, "mistress"—she had also taken up roles in a more literal fashion, on the stage, playing disruptive women who must be put in their place in the end. Along with the odious "Mrs. Sternhold" Braddon had played "Mrs. Popples" in J. Sterling Coyne's *The Man of Many Friends* (originally staged at the Haymarket in 1855; Braddon played the role at Brighton). A foolish little woman who yearns to be fashionable, Mrs. Popples is set straight by her husband: "nature formed you for a sensible little wife, but art has well-nigh spoiled you" (32), he preaches. Braddon had similar roles in Tom Taylor's *Victims* and Charles Dance's *Delicate Ground*. Taking on such roles evidently made a long-lasting impression on Braddon, who, creating the characters she never got to play, reworked the Victorian drama from the actress's standpoint: the men learn their lessons and the women are vindicated. In Braddon's "misalliance" with the theater, however, the unappreciated, maligned, and "unsuitable" woman never quite found her place.

NOTES

1. For an overview of Braddon's acting career, see Wolff, pp. 45–54.

2. The piece also mentions "a slight commedietta from her pen, called *The Model Husband* . . . revived at the Surrey, in October 1868, and acted with success." I have been unable to locate this play; no licensing copy exists in the Lord Chamberlain's Collection.

3. Wolff lists *Married Beneath Him* as "never published," suggesting that it had "disappeared" (285). The play was in fact published by Maxwell, probably in 1882 (no date appears on the text).

4. "Polly" was also, by chance, Maxwell's nickname for Braddon.

5. There are some parallels here with Shaw's *Pygmalion*, particularly in such speeches as this one, by Polly: "I've heard people say that's the flaw in your system of modern education. You are always making ladies and gentlemen, and, when you've made 'em, you don't know what to do with 'em; so you just let 'em quietly starve" (14). For discussion of Braddon's writings as a source for Shaw, see Putzelle.

WORKS CITED

Booth, Michael R. *Prefaces to English Nineteenth Century Theatre.* Manchester, England: Manchester UP, 1979.

Braddon, Mary Elizabeth. *Dross; or, The Root of Evil. A Comedy in Four Acts.* London: John and Robert Maxwell, [1886].

———. *Griselda.* MS. LCP 53129(J). British Library.

———. *Like or Unlike;* A Drama in Four Acts. Hereafter to be Called "Hands Not Hearts" or "For Better for Worse." MS. LCP 53458C. British Library.

———. *The Loves of Arcadia.* MS. LCP 52990(N), British Library.

———. *Marjorie Daw:* A Household Idyl in Two Acts, London: John and Robert Maxwell [1886].

———. *Married Beneath Him.* A Comedy in Four Acts. London: John and Robert Maxwell, [1882].

———. *The Missing Witness:* An Original Drama in Four Acts. London: John and Robert Maxwell, [1874]

Coyne, J. Stirling. *The Man of Many Friends.* London: Dick's Drama, n.d.

The Daily Courier (Liverpool).

Davis, Tracy C. *Actresses as Working Women: Their Social Identity in Victorian Culture.* New York: Routledge, 1991.

The Era (London).

The Era Almanack. London: The Era, 1869.

Lindemann, Ruth Burridge. "Dramatic Disappearances: Mary Elizabeth Braddon and the Staging of Theatrical Character." *Victorian Literature and Culture* (1997): 279–91.

Liverpool Daily Post.

Maxwell, W. B. *Time Gathered.* London: Hutchinson, 1937.

Nicoll, Allardyce. *A History of Late Nineteenth-Century Drama 1850–1900.* 2 vols. Cambridge: Cambridge UP, 1949.

Putzell, Sara Moore. "Another Source for Pygmalion: G.B.S. and Mrs. Braddon." *Shaw Review* 22 (1979): 29–32.

Robertson, Tom. *Caste. Plays by Tom Robertson.* Ed. William Tydeman. British and American Playwrights series. Cambridge: Cambridge UP, 1982.

Scott, Clement. *The Drama of Yesterday and To-Day.* 2 vols. London: Macmillan, 1899.

Taylor, Tom. *Still Waters Run Deep.* London: Lacy's Acting Editions, n.d.

Wolff, Robert. *Sensational Victorian: The Life and Fiction of Mary Elizabeth Braddon.* New York: Garland, 1979.

PART IV

Genre and Culture

ELEVEN

Braddon and Victorian Realism:
Joshua Haggard's Daughter

Pamela K. Gilbert

M. E. Braddon is, of course, best known for her sensation novels. Literary historians seeking to resurrect Braddon as a subject of legitimate scholarly and aesthetic interest have generally deprecated the sensation novels, asserting that Braddon has been typecast as the author of *Lady Audley's Secret,* and pointing out that the balance of her large oeuvre ranges broadly in subject and form. Traditionally opposed to the sensational, or melodramatic, or popular narrative of Victorian times is that great accomplishment of the canonical novelists, the novel (as Frye termed it) of high realism. Braddon herself, although she had not Frye to name it for her, made a clear distinction between what she called "something good," a "novel of character," and her novels penned for want of money, the "sensational" novels that would fill the pages of *Belgravia.* The first and best known of these realist novels is the intriguing 1867 revision of *Madame Bovary,* entitled *The Doctor's Wife,* which has received attention elsewhere in this volume. Another often remarked novel conceived along these lines is *Joshua Haggard's Daughter* (later and more often published as *Joshua Haggard*), which Wolff describes as, "a masterpiece, a deceptively simple rural tragedy, its melodrama held well within bounds by a classic dignity of theme and treatment" (Wolff 257).

Having now nearly a century and a half of general agreement that the sensation novel/melodrama and the realist novel are quite opposite, it seems worth inquiring regarding how, precisely, the difference is to be articulated. It is a matter of some importance to make this distinction, if we consider that the realist novel continued to develop into the modern novel, while the melodrama and sensation novel, depending on whom you ask, either died a well deserved death or parented such degenerate and feminine forms as the popular romance. In both genres, the novel began as a feminine and female-produced form; however, only in one does the changeling survive as the largely male-produced and certainly masculine-identified canonical novel form of the early twentieth century. Braddon, who produced largely in both genres, is now remembered only as a sensationalist. In part, this essay aims to recuperate her work in the realist mode, but, perhaps more importantly, to trace her interrogation of the apparently "obvious" distinction between these modes, and her use of sensation fiction to "mark" the difference within the text. I have examined this pattern in *The Doctor's Wife* elsewhere; I will now take the opportunity to discuss her much more subtle and interesting reading of the gendered hierarchy of fictive forms in this, her mature and arguably "most realist" work—a work that places the inadequacies of the patriarchal body on display.

The *Athenaeum* offers some definition of the merit of *Joshua Haggard's Daughter.* It relies "upon analysis of character rather than upon complication of incident" (in Wolff, 275). *The Athenaeum* also remarks the influence of *Middlemarch* (although Wolff dissents). However, the reference to Eliot is apropos. Braddon enjoyed Eliot's work, and being like Eliot, a woman novelist with a questionable domestic history, may particularly have admired Eliot's ability to maintain a reputation for spotless morality in her fiction. *Joshua Haggard's Daughter* is very much like Eliot's work in a number of respects, all of which place it squarely in the emerging tradition of what we have come to think of as mid-Victorian realism. Placing the setting of the novel in a past of the middle distance, a time "before the present" that nevertheless holds seeds of contemporary issues (i.e., just before the '32 Reform) is very much a technique associated with Eliot. The focus also, on respectable shopkeeping and lower-middle-class rural Britons is familiar to us from Eliot and Gaskell. Finally, the emphasis on interiority and psychological reality is a trend in the period that is most fully developed in Eliot's work. Here are fairly clear distinctions of between the sensation novel, with its focus on the present, on the grand bourgeoisie and the aristocracy, and its oft remarked reliance on plot rather than character, as the mainspring of the story. As Brooks remarks "Plot has been disdained as the element of narrative that least defines and sets off high art—indeed, plot is that which especially characterizes popular mass-consumption literature" (*Reading for the Plot* 4).

With these distinctions in mind—and leaving aside the very interesting question of how and why "realist" characteristics came, apparently arbitrarily, to be prized above "sensational" ones—I would like to briefly suggest that the differences between Braddon's novels are not as clear as they are held to be. Wolff cites the "Euripidean" theme that underpins *Joshua Haggard's Daughter* (i.e., Naomi's Electra-like love and jealousy of her father) as a mark of the novel's quality. Yet all of Braddon's novels abound with classical themes and allusions; *Lady Audley's Secret* contrasts the theme of Ulysses with frequent references to Jason and Medea to highlight the male selfishness and betrayal that incites female murderousness. Although *Lady Audley's Secret* arguably ends with a return to a melodramatic splitting in which good vanquishes evil (and banishes it from the domestic space), the novel overall, as essays in this collection attest, is not so simple. *Lady Audley's Secret*'s plot is not more complex than that of *Joshua Haggard's Daughter,* and there are parallels between the plots that suggest that Braddon is, as she so often does, playing with an ironic revision of her earlier novel. Braddon herself suggests, in *The Doctor's Wife,* that the differences between respectable and hack writing is more a distinction of class tastes than of topic or theme; her character Sigismund Smith, a sensation novelist who himself makes the transition into respectability, remarks that the difference between penny-sensation and the respectable middle-class novel is simply the number of bodies it takes to sate their appetites: his three-volume bestseller is *The Mystery of Mowbray Manor,* a "legitimate three volume romance, with all the interest concentrated on one body."

Braddon uses revisions of and references to popular literature both to position her "realist" novel and to critique attitudes toward popular literature and reading itself. Braddon uses references to popular literature to cue reader expectations—expectations that will be overturned one by one, as "reality" is not the stuff of novels. In a scene echoing a famous moment in *East Lynne,* Joshua's new and very young wife comes for the first time to take her place at Joshua's home, which is managed by his sharp-tongued spinster sister Judith, a character very similar to Wood's Miss Corny. Judith makes great show of giving up her place at the head of table to the new mistress of the house, who, unused to preside at table and hoping to win over the formidable sister-in-law, begs Judith to retain her place—whereupon Judith resumes it and never offers to relinquish it again. In *East Lynne,* as in *Joshua Haggard's Daughter,* this inaugurates a regime of persecution of the young wife that undermines the happiness of the marriage. As in *East Lynne,* the husband is culpably ignorant of the workings of his own household. In *East Lynne,* however, the wife's misery leads eventually to her adulterous elopement. In *Joshua Haggard's Daughter,* Judith's carping will eventually contribute to Joshua's false suspicions of his wife's infidelity, and his decision to turn her out of the house, which leads to her death. The reader is early invited to misconstrue the reference to *East Lynne* as foreshadowing; by the time Joshua misreads the signs of his wife's "guilt," we know better than he because we have learned earlier to suspect our own reading abilities.

Braddon also refers to her own bestselling sensation, *Lady Audley's Secret.* The similarities are clearly drawn. Like Sir Michael, Joshua takes a young girl of unknown origin to wed. Cynthia is described in much the same physical terms as Lady Audley, with her flaxen curls and melting blue eyes. Unlike Lady Audley, Cynthia is exactly the innocent child she looks, and the self-centered cruelty of Sir Michael and Robert, which goes unremarked and is offset by Lady Audley's criminality, is clearly foregrounded in Joshua's treatment of his wife. Finally, Joshua's wife, Cynthia, and his daughter's fiancé, Oswald, meet in a wooded area by an old mine shaft. It is an echo of the meeting of Lady Audley and her first husband, and we suspect, as Oswald's subsequent mysterious absence continues, that he is dead at the bottom of the shaft. However, while George is in fact alive, having escaped his murderous wife, Oswald is indeed dead, killed and concealed there by Joshua.

The eponymous Joshua Haggard, a very pious evangelical dissenting minister and grocer, rules his family and his village flock with unquestioned authority. Although fiercely proud with a tendency toward fanaticism, Joshua is a kind and sympathetic character, whose faults do not become damaging until he faces, for the first time in a fairly sheltered life, challenges that test his self control. Interestingly, it is Joshua who, having forbidden his daughter to read novels, consistently misreads the circumstances surrounding him. "I have forbidden my daughter to read novels . . . lest the unrealities she should find in them should give her a false picture of life, and encourage her to form baseless hopes or foolish desires" (226), states Joshua, yet it is he who encourages a courtship between his daughter and the squire's son, confident in his own social eminence. It is also he who, a middle-aged man, will choose an untutored wife scarcely out of her teens for her beauty and childishness, and refuse to consider that her love may principally reflect inexperience and gratitude. "Joshua had never been a great reader," (263) the narrator informs us.

Naomi, his daughter, has perforce grown up an inexperienced reader, but is able to recognize the grain of truth in "minor" literature. When she asks about a book of "forgotten" poets, her lover, Oswald, who favors the Romantic poets who are contemporaries of the characters (the novel is set in the late 1820s and early 1830s), laughs, and says that Byron has sent them all to Hades. After all, there is no true feeling in such poetry, "unreal as a stage play" (264). Yet when he reads from this book a selection from Waller in which the poet addresses his love for two women at once, Naomi intuitively grasps its potential application to her own relationship with Oswald, who is to conceive a passion for his future mother-in-law.

In short, although women in the Victorian period are traditionally the ones who are likely to be affected badly by their reading,[1] Braddon reverses that trend. In her earlier realist work, *The Doctor's Wife,* Isabel, the protagonist, is led to an illicit, but not quite actually adulterous love by her too- credulous readings of romances. However, it is her male lover who "misreads" Isabel as a Byronic adulteress ready to throw over all social restraint. In *Joshua Haggard's Daughter,* Oswald is the type of the worrisome reader. Although a man, and therefore presumably immune to the deleterious effects of light reading, he is described as feminine, a "weak vessel." Oswald's tastes do not run to sensational literature (which would be an anachronism anyway in a novel set in the early '30s), but to those other dangerous writers, the Romantics, especially Byron, Scott, and Goethe. His attitude toward these texts is contrasted with the prosaic or "realistic" activity of his feminine audience, as he reads Scott aloud: " 'What women you are for plain needlework!' he exclaimed one warm morning in a sudden burst of impatience, wearied by the rhythmical movement of the two needles methodically stitching on, no matter how passionate the subject of his reading—whether Rebecca was standing on the castle parapet, or Constance de Beverly left to perish in her living grave" (2:45). Keenly alive to the potential dangers of literature, it is Oswald who reads Goethe's *Werther* to Cynthia, Joshua Haggard's young wife, in order to declare his passion for her. Although she shares his feelings, Cynthia remains the voice of moral reason.

However, it is the most masculine character in the novel who proves the most dangerous reader of all. Joshua is the very type of the powerful masculine body, with his "gladiator's" physique and "noble brow." Following Oswald's declaration, Joshua enters his house to find his wife upset with the copy of *Werther.* What follows is a lesson on the dangers of novel reading—or the dangers of not reading well enough: " 'There's too much novel reading in this family,' snapped Judith [Joshua's sister]. 'You mustn't expect things to go on as they ought, if you let the young squire bring bad books into your house' " (2:61). Cynthia protests that it is not a bad book, and Joshua examines it briefly:

> "Joshua took the book and glanced at it helplessly. He was not able to take a bird's-eye view of plot and style, swoop upon a catchword here and there, and straightway make up his mind that the book was altogether vile, after the manner of some modern critics. . . . 'I do not think, my dear Judith, that you are a very acute judge of literature,' he said mildly.

'Perhaps not, . . . But I hope I am a tolerable judge of human nature' "
(2:62). [Joshua concludes that] " 'Oswald . . . must bring you only pleasant
books. In a world where there is so much real sorrow, it is foolish and even
wrong to waste our tears on story books. . . . I do not like to see you low-
spirited about a foolish book, written by some weak-minded German,' said
Joshua with a sublime ignorance." (2:64–65)

Had Judith read Shakespeare, the narrator hints, she might have found
words to tell her brother what she thinks rather than relying on "dark
hints," "[b]ut as her sole notion of the poet was that he had been a rather
low and loose-lived person who wrote plays, and glorified much drinking
of sack" (2:65), she does not. The narrator's many references to Othello,
and Joshua's language, taken directly from Othello's, operate both to
underscore the themes of jealousy and wronged innocence and as an
apologia for the value of cautionary tales: had Joshua been more of a
reader, perhaps he might have been less quick to believe ill of his wife. It
is not until Judith has poisoned his mind with Iago-like suspicions that
Joshua reads Werther, understands its message, but believes it means
more than it does. Experienced readers, Braddon warns, in a theme that
runs through many of her novels, are better trained to interpret reality
than those who have been kept from books.

Further, although Joshua is always at least reading the Bible and
other religious texts, he is the type of what Flynn has called the "dominat-
ing reader," the reader who reacts to uncertainty by imposing his own
concerns on the text and refusing to be open to material that does not
reinforce his own sense of mastery. As his misreadings of the texts and
contexts around him proliferate, and his vulnerability to jealousy in-
creases, he moves closer to the crisis both of the story and of his life as a
yet-untried Christian. When the great test comes, he fails, falling into sin
through his misreading. He kills Oswald, and violently rejects his wife.
Joshua's guilt causes his subsequent descent into madness, a madness
characterized by egomania, in which he continues to preach, sure of his
own primacy and correctness in his interpretation of the Scripture. He is
able to use the text as a refection of his own madness and sin, disregarding whatever does not fit his own interpretation. "Joshua conjured up
those visions of horror with a strange uncanny power. . . . He dwelt on
these horrors with a gloomy relish, and spoke of hell and doom with a
familiar knowledge" (2:250). Yet "[e]ven in the troubled state of his brain
. . . that book [the Bible] was his rock of defense, his sheet-anchor. He
looked into those pages for justification, for assurance of redemption
and grace, and he seldom looked in vain. If he had sinned, had not David
sinned also, and yet retained his exalted place in the love of God and
men? Was he to humble himself more than David had humbled himself?

Had David ever ceased to be King, and Priest, and teacher, chief and supreme among the people?" (2:258).

Braddon also compares him to a barrister: "He used the Scriptures for their [his congregation's] benefit, as as skillful barrister uses precedents for the extrication of his clients. He found bounteous promises that they had never dreamed of in those familiar words of Holy Writ . . . he held a golden key, with which he opened the treasury of heaven" (2:248). This reference, which evokes Robert Audley's detective scrutiny of Lady Audley, reminds us that Joshua has indeed "played detective," following his wife, observing her unseen, reading her copy of Werther and drawing mistaken conclusions from it. Like Robert Audley, he too has acted as judge, jury, and executioner. Unlike Robert, however, whose journey from uncertainty to certainty is slow and beset by self-doubt, Joshua never doubts his ability to read truly and judge appropriately— and he is wrong.

Braddon's indictment of Joshua's self-absorption, however, begins much earlier in the novel, in his high-handed treatment of his children and especially the women of his household. This already strong tendency intensifies in madness, and is linked most specifically to his cruelty to his wife and inability to recognize her needs or her pain. He considers the brutal way in which he has turned his wife out of doors, and concedes that she is probably innocent of wrongdoing, "And I thrust her from me with violence and contumely, and sent her back to servitude and dependence. . . . Surely that was a sacrifice which Heaven must approve" (2:261). Braddon explains that the "intense egotism which is one of the characteristics of a mind off its balance had taken possession of him. He felt himself the centre of the universe. The Bible had been written for him. He stood face to face with his creator and felt himself worthy to be saved " (2:261). The narrator's appraisal of the lessons of the Bible, however, is less subjective and more critical, and isolates specifically the prerogatives of patriarchy as blameable and subject to abuse. "He had almost forgotten that bitter day of parting, the day when he had driven her into banishment, with more cruelty than Abraham has shown to ill-used Hagar; and it can hardly be said that the patriarch was a pattern to all future husbands in that transaction" (2:278).

Braddon emphasizes pride and the will to dominate as Joshua's character flaws. Although he is genuinely concerned with being good and kind, his absolute confidence in his own interpretation of events and lack of openness to the views of others lead to disaster. In a further ironic rewriting of *Lady Audley's Secret*, it is Joshua who attempts—and commits—murder, Joshua who both marries a young wife out of season, as does Sir Michael, and throws the true lover down the well/mineshaft. It is not the tainted biology of female madness, but the jealous rage of the patriarch that leads to insanity, and it is insanity that leads, not only to attempted and faked deaths, but to the actual deaths of Oswald, Cynthia, and finally Joshua himself.

The mid-Victorian economies of gender that, feminists have argued, Braddon critiques slyly in her sensation novels are starkly revealed in her realist fiction. If in *Lady Audley's Secret,* women's irrationality, weakness, and greed seem to threaten patriarchal order, it can certainly be argued that it is the bad decisions and irresponsibility of the male characters that ultimately undermine it—Sir Michael, who marries a young beauty knowing she does not love him, old Lt. Graham, who drinks and gambles away his own and his daughter's fortunes, George Talboys, who abandons his wife and son for three years. But in *Joshua Haggard's Daughter,* there can be no question of where responsbility lies. The delicate, childish, angelic wife is exactly what she seems. It is the patriarchal leader of the community in whom sin and madness are concealed—and the community cannot be righted simply by containing or erasing a femme fatale.

Brooks suggests that the huge production of plot-oriented literature, such as the sensation novel, in the nineteenth and early twentieth centuries may be an expression of anxiety regarding the loss of master narratives (6). Certainly the master-narrative of gender that had been developed in the mid-nineteenth century was in perpetual crisis and dislocation—and perhaps even more crucially, that of the family. In his earlier work, Brooks suggests that melodrama, described in strikingly similar terms as those applied to sensation, functions to contain anxieties by reducing complex conflicts to simple, Manichaean oppositions in which virtue and justice always triumph.[2] It is an appeal to absolute values, in which the social order is always purged and normalized.[3] The sum of Brooks's work, then, would seem to indicate the following relationship between realism and melodrama: both forms narrativize anxieties about the loss of moral certainty and master narratives in a post-sacred world. Melodrama contains these anxieties by appealing to an overarching moral dualism that succeeds in righting the wrongs displayed in the melodrama, and realism explores the complexities evoked by loss of moral certainty. All of the above offer the spectacle of woman's body as the final symbol of both the desire and terror evoked by the (im)possibility of absolute moral knowledge. As Brooks notes, drawing on film theory, the female nude emerges as The type of the nude in modernity; "precisely because it is the norm, the male body is veiled . . . the gaze is 'phallic,' its object is not" (*Body Work* 15). Citing Barthes, he remarks that the body of the patriarch, (or indeed, any eroticized male body) meanwhile, remains hidden, the horror of phallic lack only exceeded by the threat of its certainty. I am particularly interested in

Brooks's work, not only because it represents fine and influential scholarship in this area, but because his work has persistently engaged "popular" forms and practices of reading (melodrama, reading for the plot), while declining to provide detailed readings of popular literature below a certain level of canonicity. He also has rarely addressed literature by women, or literature written for women. Perhaps as a supplement to this lack, I would like to finish by suggesting a reading of *Joshua Haggard's Daughter* through and against some of Brooks's observations.[4]

It has been argued that the sensation novel is a novel that places the body of a woman at the center of the text. It is her secret, and her affect, that engages the reader (Cvetkovich, Pykett). Peter Brooks has argued that the art of modernity, and especially its principal literary form, the novel, is defined by its quest to "know" the truth of the woman's body; this "epistemophilic urge" drives the plot. The man's body, on the other hand, has been unrepresentable; the patriarch's genitals must remain veiled, as the lack of the phallus (and presence, merely, of the vulnerable penis) is intolerable (*Body Work*). *Joshua Haggard's Daughter*, however, is a novel that places the patriarch's penis—and its inadequacies—very much on display. It is Joshua's suffering body and psychological crisis that engages us. As in other Braddon novels, we are made to see the inadequacies of a beloved father; as in Gaskell's *Mary Barton* we see a daughter protecting a murderous father against the claims of her lover. However, here the criminal's motive is clearly sexual jealousy—the jealousy of an aging husband for a wife attracted to a man her own age. Having delayed his daughter's marriage by two years, Joshua himself comes home with his stunningly inappropriate choice, calmly remarking to his daughter's suitor "I have stolen a march upon you" (2:294). Braddon takes pains to show the congregation's disapproval of Joshua's choice and his reaction of offended pride. He wins them back over, and the interlude serves no useful plot function except to highlight Joshua's amour-propre—unless we read it as setting a stage for a heightened sense of his sexual humiliation. The language surrounding the murder is rife with phallic imagery. When Joshua sees a letter from Oswald to Cynthia that is to goad him into fury, "every word [is] like a knife thrust" (2:123). Although he describes his wife as daughter, and his love for her as "almost fatherly," and although both his daughter and sister have sacrificed their lovers to his patriarchal authority, Joshua in this instance is described as the wronged son: "What was he to do? How find revenge great enough for this gigantic wrong? . . . justice . . . was what he demanded. He felt himself like Orestes, privileged, nay, appointed to slay" (2:124). The balance of power between the weak, effeminate "boy" Oswald— whom Joshua cradles in his arms at the beginning of the novel—and strong paternal Joshua, has evidently shifted (perhaps not coincidentally just as Oswald's father has died and he has come into his estate as Squire, the "real" patriarch of Combhaven—Oswald falls in love with Cynthia over his father's death-bed). Although Joshua escaped the legal vengeance of Oswald's brother by his explanation that the men duelled, and that therefore he is not a murderer, later, on Joshua's deathbed, the truth is revealed:

> "Some kind of struggle—whether bodily or mental . . . —was racking him. His nether lip worked convulsively; the veins stood up darkly purple from the broad strong brow. . . . 'We stood up, face to face, each with a pistol in his hand. . . . But as I lifted my hand to take aim at his heart I saw his arm flung up, his pistol pointed to the sky. It was but an instant . . . before I fired straight at his breast. . . . This was the crime that weighed upon my soul and dragged me down to the pit. O God, I can see him now, with his face lifted up, the sun shining on it, his arm raised to fire in the air.'" (2:300)

Twice, Joshua, who, although suffused with blood, struggles, but will never "rise" again, emphasizes Oswald's erectness, which signifies also his generosity and power, even in death. Although it is Joshua who throws Oswald's body down into the vaginal mineshaft, it is in fact Joshua who is emasculated, "dragged . . . down to the pit." Castration of the other cannot win back the lost phallus.

Wolff remarks the original publication of the novel as *Joshua Haggard's Daughter,* and its subsequent transformation to *Joshua Haggard* as Braddon's need to avert public attention from what he reads as the novel's primary theme: Naomi's love, incestuous in intensity, for her father. Certainly that is a theme in the novel, and Naomi's suffering is foregrounded in the first title—a traditional title in an era in which either a family name or a woman's name was often designated as title. I would argue, however, that the renaming reflects a more accurate read-ing of the real subject of the novel. Further, I would argue that if the respectable three decker's interest must concentrate "on one body," Braddon's realist novel chooses that body shall be the masculine body of Joshua, rather than the sensationalized bodies of his wife-like daughter or his daughter-like wife.

Wolff regrets that the critics largely "misread" the novel, and offers what he sees as a particularly egregious example, Charles Kent's belief that Braddon had been writing in defense of "a celibate clergy" (in Wolff 276). Wolff continues, "Taken by surprise, MEB was not prepared to dispute him: 'I think you have hit the right nail on the head, . . . the only critic who has noticed the point. . . . A man who has the souls of his fellow men in his keeping should keep his own soul unclouded by pas-sion'" (Wolff 276). Wolff believes Braddon's agreement is false, that she is simply "not prepared to dispute" Kent. Possibly. However, it is quite possible also that Braddon is expressing here a real recognition of Kent's idiosyncratically framed but not wholly inaccurate reading. Braddon's later fiction is rarely in the first instance about what people should do; it is about what people actually do from various motives, and the reader is left to draw the appropriate moral if s/he wishes. Tracing backwards from the moral Kent discovers and that Braddon cautiously approves, we might restate the point this way: people with authority and power over others are particularly dangerous when human weakness, especially sexual weakness, threatens to expose their authority as spurious. But Joshua's culpable weakness, as the narrator is careful to point out, is not his passion for Cynthia, but his overweening pride that will not allow him to accept the challenge to his virility/authority, and leads to the actual murder/symbolic castration of his rival. If viewed in this light, the nature of the "misreading" is most interesting, even though it is clearly in part motivated by Kent's political agenda. Pride as the tragic flaw is both clearly cued in the novel and a traditional theme. Yet Kent bypasses that obvious reading to one that targets the exposure of the patriarch's sexuality to scrutiny—better that the use of the patriarchal penis should be literally sacrificed than his phallic authority be exposed as lacking.

Although sensation novels like *Lady Audley's Secret* and *East Lynne* suggest masculine inadequacy, their normative plot endings function to contain female transgression. Feminists reading "against the grain"— that is, against the plot but often with theme, have recuperated the critique of male domination to be found in those texts. *Joshua Haggard's Daughter* (or *Joshua Haggard*), however, the first of Braddon's novels, according to Wolff, written at her own pace and in a period of financial security and consequent experimentation, is used to anatomize phallic inadequacy at length. Although it can be argued that Arnold, Oswald's much more masculine and energetic brother, reinstates phallic authority both as Squire and as mate for Naomi after Joshua's death, it is a phallic authority appropriately circumscribed by maternal realism. Bound to duel with Joshua in vengeance for his brother's life, Arnold is persuaded by Naomi to forgive. From phallic absolutism and melodrama, we are brought into the realm of the realist, the circumstantial, and the pragmatic: "'What am I to do, Naomi? Counsel me . . . I am like a child in your hands'" (2:274), as he moves from the simple logic of offended honor to the "dark problem" (275) of correct retribution for the complex interweaving of multiple responsibility for sin that Naomi's analysis of the problem offers: "'I can do nothing; I feel myself tied and bound. Either way there is wrong and misery. . . . What can I do?'" (2:274). Naomi leads Oswald—the one man in the text who has read *Werther* correctly and without danger—from the logic of melodrama to the pragmatism of realism, a logic in which regardless of sensationalized female peril like

Charlotte's or Rebecca's, real women must stitch monotonously onward. Braddon suggests that good readers will find the truth of any narrative, and that within any text, sacred or secular, major or minor, there is a truth to be found, or a falsehood to be imposed, depending on the reader. In her "realist" novel, she explicitly identifies the abuse of patriarchal authority with poor reading skills and the tendency to dominate the text, and those tendencies, in turn, with anxieties about phallic authority. By placing the male body at the center of her text, and taking male sexual jealousy as a central theme, she makes open display of the topic that, though central to her sensation novels, is displaced by and hidden behind the sensationalized female body used as a shield for male anxiety. It might be said that, for Braddon, the ideal realist novel engages precisely the sensational secret that melodrama strives to cover with the veiling power of the female body to engage the gaze—a pervasive masculine sense of exposure and inadequacy in the imperial decade of the seventies.

NOTES

1. For a detailed discussion, see, for example, Kate Flint's *The Woman Reader.*

2. See *The Melodramatic Imagination.* Brooks also develops at length his sense of the melodrama's democratic nature, its disregard of *Lady Audley's Secret's* divisions. Brooks is most concerned with French melodrama, emerging in the post-revolutionary period—*Lady Audley's Secret's* concerns play out quite differently in English melodrama, a point that critics have not always keep in mind in applying Brooks's insights.

3. Melodrama, therefore, although it has come to be a feminine—identified form, operates according to a masculine, rule—governed ethics, rather than a "feminine" situational ethics of care. I am thinking here of Carol Gilligan's, Margaret Walker's, and Nel Nodding's work in particular.

4. As any categorical analysis such as Brooks's is vulnerable to specific exceptions, my use of a very condensed (and reductive) version of his argument is to some extent unfair. My purpose here, however, is not to refute Brooks, but to illuminate a certain aspect of Braddon's "realism," which, I would argue, carries over into her sensation novels. A secondary purpose is to suggest how Brooks's reading might be productively complicated by attention to fictive forms produced by and for women.

WORKS CITED

Braddon, M. E. *The Doctor's Wife.* London: Ward, Lock, and Tyler, [nd. 1864?].

———. *Joshua Haggard's Daughter.* Liepzig: Tauchnitz, 1877.

———. *Lady Audley's Secret.* Ed. David Skilton. New York: Oxford UP, 1987.

Brooks, Peter. *Body Work: Objects of Desire in Modern Narrative.* London and Cambridge, Mass.: Harvard UP, 1993.

———. *Reading for the Plot: Design and Intention in Narrative.* Cambridge, Mass: Harvard UP, 1984.

———. *The Melodramatic Imagination: Balzac, Henry James, Melodrama and the Mode of Excess.* New Haven: Yale UP, 1973.

Cvetkovich, Ann. *Mixed Feelings: Feminism, Mass Culture and Victorian Sensationalism.* New Brunswick, N.J.: Rutgers, 1992.

Flint, Kate. *The Woman Reader: 1837–1914.* Oxford: Oxford Clarendon, 1993.

Flynn, Elizabeth. "Gender and Reading." In *Gender and Reading: Essays, Texts, and Contexts.* Ed. Elizabeth A. Flynn and Patrocinio Schweickart. Baltimore: Johns Hopkins UP, 1986: 267–88.

Gilligan, Carol. *In a Different Voice: Psychological Theory and Women's Development.* Cambridge, Mass.: Harvard UP, 1982.

Noddings, Nel. *Caring. a Feminine Approach to Ethics and Moral Education.* Berkeley and Los Angeles: U of California P, 1984. Pykett, Lyn. *The "Improper" Feminine:The Women's Sensation Novel and the New Woman Writing.* London; New York: Routledge, 1995.

Walker, Margaret Urban. "Moral Understandings: Alternative 'Epistemology' for a Feminist Ethics." In *Explorations in Feminist Ethics: Theory and Practice.* Ed. Eve Browning Cole and Susan Coultrap McQuin. Bloomington: Indiana UP, 1992. 165–75.

Wolff, Robert Lee. *Sensational Victorian: The Life and Fiction of Mary Elizabeth Braddon.* New York: Garland, 1979.

Wood, Mrs. Henry. *East Lynne.* Ed. Sally Mitchell. New Brunswick, N.J.: Rutgers UP, 1984.

TWELVE

Fiction Becomes Her: Representations of Female Character in Mary Braddon's *The Doctor's Wife*

Tabitha Sparks

I

This is not a sensation novel, the narrator insists in sensation author Mary Braddon's 1864 novel, *The Doctor's Wife*. This assertion interrupts the account of a forger, the shadowy Jack-the-Scribe, who upon reentering the life of his daughter, the titular Isabel Gilbert, both entreats her for money and murders her beloved. To complicate circumstances further, it is not Isabel's husband who is murdered, but her Byronic love-interest, the squire-poet Roland Lansdell. Amidst these gothic conspiracies of murder, criminality, and illicit love, what can we make of the narrator's denial? While Braddon's novels typically figure intrigue and passion as the dysfunctional tenants of the country estates that populate her imaginative terrain, she determinedly resists such sensationalism in *The Doctor's Wife* but only with partial success.

According to her letters, *The Doctor's Wife* was Braddon's Anglicization of Flaubert's *Madame Bovary* (Wolff 162). Like her fictional counterpart, *Emma Bovary*, Isabel betrays an apprehension of the world that is overdetermined by novel reading, for, disenchanted with her prosaic life as a doctor's wife, she wanted to be a heroine, "unhappy, perhaps, and dying early" (14). By articulating the distance between her heroine's naivete and the narrator's omniscient wisdom, Braddon's mockery of Isabel constitutes one of her most conspicuous realist techniques, one of her best efforts at writing a novel more concerned with interior psychology than with sensationalism. However, quite apart from the fact that she dispenses with Flaubert's themes of adultery and suicide, Braddon complies with the plot determinations of the sensation genre in a number of familiar ways, including the portrayal of violent murder and extramarital passion. She further obscures her efforts at psychological realism, after the manner of Flaubert, by employing the narrative conventions of a third genre of fiction, the sentimental novel, which diverges from sensationalism and realism in its idealized female characters. Braddon's multi-faceted, but ultimately confused compendium of three types of popular Victorian literature, sensationalism, sentimentalism, and realism, makes *The Doctor's Wife* an extraordinary document of the competing epistemologies at work in 1860s fiction. Braddon's use of these contrasting narrative styles allows us insight into her understanding of the representation of women, as the often convoluted portrait of Isabel provides an unusual perspective into the wildly divergent characterizations of heroines in this decade. For despite the flaws in *The Doctor's Wife*, Braddon's ability to trouble the generic conventions of each of these categories of fiction attests to her canny insight into the limiting and insufficient representations of women in all types of Victorian fiction.

The relative obscurity of *The Doctor's Wife* prompts the inclusion of a brief plot summary. At the start of the novel, Isabel Sleaford is a fey young woman whose only pastime consists of reading romance novels. When her family's boarder, hack-novelist Sigismund Smith, introduces Isabel to Dr. George Gilbert, he unintentionally links the destinies of two diametrically opposed characters. But first, without warning and under mysterious circumstances, the Sleaford family abruptly moves, and when Isabel eventually contacts Smith in hopes of finding a governess position, he places her with a relative, Mr. Raymond, who turns out to be Dr. Gilbert's neighbor. Shortly following their reunion, Gilbert proposes to and is accepted by Isabel, only to situate her in a monotonous lifestyle that she deeply resents. Soon, Isabel meets the dashing Roland Lansdell, and, in the fashion of her favorite literary heroines, falls in love with him—though when Lansdell asks Isabel to elope, she refuses him. Isabel's domestic imprisonment comes to an end when Dr. Gilbert dies of typhoid, a day before her father, supposed to be dead, returns in disguise and delivers a fatal blow to Lansdell, his old nemesis. Despite these tragic circumstances, Lansdell has bequeathed to Isabel the bulk of his considerable fortune, as a gesture of his love for her, ironically transforming her into a sophisticated lady-with-a-past. Isabel's final installment in the

Lansdell estate thus fulfills her girlish fantasy of becoming a heroine after the sensational fashion of her literary familiars.

II

Henry Mansel's 1863 review of twenty-four sensation novels, published in the *Quarterly Review,* indicts superficial character development as one of the shortcomings of the genre. The narrative conventions of sensation novels, he writes, are wholly determined by the commercial character of their production. Perhaps purchased at a railway stall, to provide entertainment for a train journey, these books are

> written to meet an ephemeral demand, aspiring only to ephemeral existence, [so that] it is natural that [sensation novels] should have recourse to rapid and ephemeral methods of awakening the interest of their readers, striving to act as the dram or the dose, rather than as solid food, because the effect is more immediately perceptible (Mansel 485)

Mansel's identification of perceptibility as one of the sensation novel's major projects must be properly contextualized within a genre that simultaneously values the obfuscation of character identity as a primary method of awakening the interest of its readers. Analysis of the typical sensation novel's portrayal of women, particularly by way of this genre's fascination with the capriciousness of legal identity, can convey how *The Doctor's Wife* transcends such superficial evaluation of female identity.

Why do sensation novels so often figure characters that suffer a dislocation from their proper name and legal identity? The answer to this question lies in the fact that the sensation genre emerged in the mid-Victorian period alongside an almost palpable anxiety over the increasingly disrupted signification of class rank. Social realist novels dedicated to pondering the question, What makes a gentleman? abounded, and novelists like Dickens, Gaskell, and Dinah Mulock Craik offered answers that only partially succeeded in upholding the traditional equation between birth and character.[1] In Robert Surtees's popular novel, *Ask Mamma* (1858), we see how modern fashion could obscure (if not unambiguously transform) the status of a servant-girl: "[The] speedy influx of fashion and abundance of cheap tawdry finery has well nigh destroyed the primitive simplicity of country churches. The housemaid now dresses better—finer at all events—than her mistress did twenty-years ago, and it is almost impossible to recognize working people in their Sunday dresses" (Surtees 332).

The unreliability and ambiguity of social significations such as finery epitomize the lack of confidence wrought by this transforming material society. Confusing appearances in sensation novels often express what is terrifying about these fictions: the moral chaos effected by this class confusion. In their study of the literary and artistic representations of nineteenth-century women, *Victorian Heroines*, Kimberly Reynolds and Nicola Humble contend that

> the fears tapped by the sensation genre are those of an outsider within—
> and the danger of the insider becoming an outsider: the intense scrutiny of
> class and economic status that afflicted the Victorian bourgeois in their
> rapidly changing society is reflected in the many plots that revolve around a
> sudden loss of fortune or revelation of illegitimacy. (Reynolds and Humble
> 102)[2]

Indeed, inasmuch as most sensation novels feature plots involving mistaken identities or clandestine relationships, they are confirming the danger of deceptive surfaces. For instance, in Wilkie Collins's *The Woman in White* (1864), a novel deeply concerned with the vulnerability of the upper-class domestic order, young heiress Laura Fairlie falls into a marital trap whereby her villainous husband threatens to usurp her inheritance. What endangers Laura is a striking resemblance to her half-sister, the dubiously sane Anne Catherick, and Laura's husband Sir Percival uses this likeness to trap his wife in an asylum. The significance of this plot is that Laura's consequence in the novel is wholly based upon a correct identification of her body; her characterization is important insofar as it records her exterior, with little emphasis upon her subjectivity, and her increasingly fragile physical constitution comes to represent the disturbingly weak infrastructure of her class. Even Walter Hartright, the man who loves her, rhapsodizes about Laura by speaking of her in symbolic, abstract terms that underscore his psychic appropriation of her:

> The woman who first gives life, light and form to our shadowy conceptions
> of beauty, fills a void in our spiritual nature that has remained unknown to
> us till she appeared. . . . Take her as the visionary nursling of your own
> fancy; and she will grow upon you, all the more clearly, as the living woman
> who dwells in mine. (61)

Walter's arrogation of Laura operates similarly to Sir Percival's, but where Percival fetishizes her class status (and takes on the false title of Sir), Walter revels in Laura's beauty as a surface for which he provides the inner text. That both men desire Laura for surface features links *The Woman in White* to Mansel's description of sensation novels as capitalizing upon effect at the expense of real substance or character development. The definitive role of Laura's body that subsumes the notion of woman as character extends to another woman in the book, Marian Halcombe, whose masculine will is distinctly marked by her mustache. Attention to the sensation novel's typical characterization of women as beautiful surfaces to be possessed or dispossessed by men and social castes demonstrates how *The Doctor's Wife* diverges from the genre critiqued and defined by Mansel. Collins's Laura Fairlie remains an immutable character despite the traumas she experiences. Her vulnerable legal identity resembles a possession rather than a psychological foundation, formulating her wealth and beauty to be the defining facets of her character; all traces of Laura are lost, the novel reveals, once she is separated from her legal name:

> [T]o all the world she was dead. Dead to her uncle who had renounced her; dead to the servants of the house, who had failed to recognize her; dead to the persons in authority who had transmitted her fortune to her husband and her aunt; . . . socially, morally, legally—dead. (380)

Laura's psychological identity is negligible if the social, moral, and legal offices that decree her existence so emphatically bury her. Braddon's Lucy Audley follows a similarly nonsubjective characterization. At the close of *Lady Audley's Secret*, Lucy remains steadfastly "bad," never once lamenting her crimes and deceptions; like Laura, her character is constant, and the plot of the novel is devoted to uncovering its constitution. The possibility that Lucy may change in response to her circumstances is not explored, for in ironic contrast to the repeated mutations of her name, Lucy herself remains permanently depraved (Mansel 486). But in *The Doctor's Wife*, change is an essential facet of Isabel Gilbert's characterization. Braddon's refusal to codify Isabel along the legible lines of the sensation novel heroine, remarkable for her beauty, wealth, or in Lucy's case, consistent immorality, results in the portrait of a woman that exceeds the finite boundaries of the sensation genre's allegiance to "perceptability." Indeed, Isabel's somewhat ambivalent characterization departs from the sensational theme of dislocated identity (i.e., loss or alteration of legal name) because its ambiguity reflects Isabel's difficulty in knowing her self rather than illustrates a public (mis)recognition of her family name or social position, as in the case of Laura Fairlie or Lucy Audley.

Braddon does invoke sensational attention to the significance of female beauty insofar as Isabel's appearance is constantly debated. Public consensus differs as widely as to argue that Isabel is elegant and striking, or "cheap" and insignificant. But the arguments over her beauty (or lack thereof) do not classify a threat to the social order, as they do in *The Woman in White* or *Lady Audley's Secret.* Isabel's imperfect mien predicates no specific class. Repeatedly praised for her haunted "great black eyes," Isabel's "melancholy" aspect marks her for a quixotic future, one befitting an inveterate reader: "Isabel's beauty was of a poetic kind, which could only be fully comprehended by a poet; but Mr. Gilbert arrived at a vague conviction that she was what he called pretty" (12). More aptly, sensation novelist Sigismund Smith finds Isabel "gorgeous" and "lovely," and declares that he "does her for all [his] dark heroines—the good heroines, not the wicked ones" (15). Isabel's alliance to characters in fiction and to the genre of poetry suggests that her appearance is dominated by her subjectivity. Internal dissatisfaction characterizes Isabel's melancholy aspect, in direct contrast to Mansel's reproach that the sensation novel lacks "deep knowledge of human nature, graphic delineations of individual character, vivid representations of the aspects of Nature of the workings of the soul" (Huskey 5).

The public discordance over Isabel's appearance falls neatly into a gendered argument. Men see Isabel as romantic-looking, and women emphasize her affectedness; Roland Lansdell, upon first meeting Isabel, finds her "a lovely nonentity," and his cousin Lady Gwendolin dismisses her instantly as "a very dowdy-looking person" (73). Isabel's female neighbors in Greybridge, where she moves after her marriage to George Gilbert, find her decidedly ignoble in appearance.

> She was not pretty—when you looked into her. That was the point upon which feminine critics laid great stress. At a distance, certainly, Mrs. Gilbert might look showy. The lady who hit upon the adjective "showy" was very much applauded by her friends. At a distance Isabel might be called showy; . . . but look into Mrs. Gilbert, and even this show of beauty vanished, and you only saw a sickly young person, with insignificant features, and coarse black hair—so coarse and common in texture, that its abnormal length and thickness—of which Isabel was no doubt inordinately proud—were very little to boast of. (57)

While the men in the novel are impressed by Isabel's outer charms, these ladies choose to accentuate character rather than exterior: "look into Mrs. Gilbert," they insist. Refusing to take Isabel's surface charms for anything real, they exemplify the project of the sentimental novel, which dismantles the sensation novel's fascination with perceptible facets of identity, and delves into the subjective arena of character. The sentimental novel, largely read by middle- class Victorian women, and devoted to the explication of morals rather than to the unraveling of suspenseful, florid plots, is a genre not associated with Mary Braddon. But Isabel's ambiguous beauty and its signification of a complex, inner life, represents Braddon's attempt to abandon sensationalism and its conventions of characterization and move into more introspective modes of character development.

III

When Isabel rejects Roland's proposal that she elope with him, the novel undergoes a curious transformation of genre. At this point, Isabel seems primed to fall in the ignoble footsteps of other sensation heroines who sin: women, like Lucy Audley or Isabel Vane of Mrs. Henry Wood's *East Lynne* (1861) who succumb to the temptation of adultery. Isabel's fascination with another fictional adulteress, Edith Dombey, further anticipates her infidelity and thus her adherence to a pattern of sensation fiction whereby, in Melynda Huskey's words, the "novel (and its readers) gets its thrills from the spectacle of woman on the verge of an irretrievable fall" (in Mitchell 34). But Braddon upsets this expectation of infidelity abruptly when Isabel casts off Roland's offer as morally contemptible, and the narrator tells us that "not for one minute did the doctor's wife contemplate the possibility of taking the step which Roland Lansdell had proposed to her" (133). Isabel here begins (almost halfway through the novel) to resemble the suffering but virtuous heroines from the sentimental novel, also popular in the 1860s, but diametrically opposite to the sensation novel in both formal features and ethical design. Sally Mitchell, in "Sentiment and Suffering: Women's Recreational Reading in the 1860s," defines the ideologies behind this popular genre, including among its major authors Rhoda Broughton, Ouida, Charlotte Yonge, Caroline Norton, and Florence Marryat. The sentimental novel, she writes, "gratifies common needs; it provides a mode of distancing which gives repressed emotions a form that is publicly acceptable and that makes them a source of pleasure" (31). The sentimental novel as an authorization of emotion more closely resembles Isabel's experience in reading than it does the text of *The Doctor's Wife* itself, which in dramatic plot elements like suspense and coincidence, falls under the category of sensationalism. Similarly, Mitchell's definition of the sentimental novel heroine sounds less like Isabel than it does like the literary characters with whom Isabel confuses her own reality and experience:

> The characters are virtually indistinguishable: the Dorothys, the Helens, and Isabellas all fade into one another. The plot is a series of events, often repetitive. The language is at best unobtrusive. . . . There is little satire or humor or overt social comment. . . . Furthermore, and most crucially,

women's novels are highly emotional. "Sentimental" is the term most frequently used, and by the mid-nineteenth century, "sentimental" was becoming a pejorative word. (35)

Braddon makes clear that Isabel reads novels explicitly desiring this formula, whereby she can be assured of both a happy ending, and a temporary escape from her own life. But the text of *The Doctor's Wife* does not
consistently correspond to these criteria, for in particular, Isabel is herself
an idiosyncratic heroine, partly because her "true" identity and integrity
is largely concealed until her rejection of Lansdell. The sentimental
heroine, continues Mitchell,

> feels a vague but pressing sense of discontent, which is expressed in a series
> of scenes of victimization, being alone, taken advantage of, misunderstood
> and being the one who is right when everyone else is wrong and not having
> one's rightness recognized until almost too late. (45)

In contrast to this explication, Isabel is decidedly in the wrong when she
cavorts—however innocently—with Lansdell, and consequently neglects
and mistreats George. Rather than feel sorry for Isabel during the first
half of the novel, we are incited to judge her according to the sensational
standards that she so provocatively seems to follow, and we are implicitly
cautioned not to identify with Isabel. Instead, we look upon her mistakes
with the eye of the seasoned reader, and understand her poor judgments
as those practiced by a young woman inadequately prepared for reality by
the romantic tracts of sentimental literature.

The closest textual link between *The Doctor's Wife* and the sentimental narrative is the ending of the novel, which plucks Isabel out of her
grief for George and Lansdell and situates her in the aristocratic Lansdell
estate—exactly the scenario she fantasized about during her youthful
reading. There, repenting for her previous selfishness, she devotes her
life to philanthropy, and finally reveals the characteristic most exemplary
of the sentimental heroine: the wisdom achieved by suffering (Mitchell
44). At the end of the novel, Isabel has learned that "no grief, however
bitter, can entirely obscure the beauty of the universe" (195). The narrator affirms that Isabel "passes away from me into a higher region than
that which my story has lain" (196), and her newly developed charitable
impulse is exemplified by the good works she performs on the Lansdell
estate, which include the construction of "pretty Elizabethan cottages,
with peaked gables and dormer windows," (195) for the Lansdell tenants.
Mitchell confirms that sentimental novels show a predilection for "utopian" endings, which "remake society not through revolution but by
magic" (12). While this "utopia" usually takes the form of an idealized

marriage, the linchpin of that marriage is a measure of female control, which is certainly evident in Isabel's situation as the single proprietor of a grand, country estate.

IV

But complicating once again the link between *The Doctor's Wife* and the sentimental genre, Braddon's social critique that allows us to identify Isabel's improvident marriage as the consequence of the narrow life of a lower-middle class girl firmly places the novel's social conscience outside of the territory of the sentimental novel, which in Mitchell's estimation, typically divulges little "overt social comment."[3] Indeed, analysis of the cultural environment responsible for Isabel's poor decisions and devotion to sentimental literature is evident from the very start of the novel. As a girl in her family's ramshackle house in Camberwell, London, Isabel reads in the back garden, where the overgrown plants reflect her fertile but undisciplined imagination, as well as her tenuous membership in the lower periphery of the middle class.

> It was a dear, old, untidy place, where the odour of distant pigsties mingled faintly with the perfume of the roses; and it was in this neglected garden that Isabel Sleaford spent the best part of her idle, useless, life . . . lolling in the low basket-chair, with a book on her lap, and her chin resting on the palm of her hand. (12)

The earthy stench of the Cockney animal pens here encroaches upon Isabel's withdrawal from the mundane realities of her "vulgar and commonplace life," and while it functions as a reminder of how near the Sleaford family is to their lower-class neighbors, the smell of the roses offers a compensatory gesture toward more desirable surroundings. The weedy garden here suggests a social critique of Isabel's idleness and her taste in reading materials, which threaten to sprout beyond the strictly tamed limits of respectable literature and thereby fertilize her incipient romantic impulses. Even the school where Isabel receives her haphazard education figures her contingent middle-class status: "She had been taught a smattering of everything at a day-school in the Albany road; rather a stylish seminary in the opinion of the Camberwellians. She knew a little Italian, enough French to serve for the reading of novels that she might have better left unread" (14). Isabel's mental self-indulgence is also the effect of inadequate education and guidance:

> If there had been anyone to take this lonely girl in hand and organize her education, Heaven only knows what might have been made of her; but

> there was no friendly finger to point a pathway in the intellectual forest, and Isabel rambled as her inclination led her . . . living as much alone as if she had resided in a balloon, forever suspended in mid-air, and never coming down in serious earnest to the common joys and sorrow of the vulgar life about her. (15)

If we plant class ideology in Isabel's garden of earthly delights, the terrain of *The Doctor's Wife* proves to cultivate the same kind of "social problem" narrative familiar to the works of Dickens, Gaskell, and George Eliot. While Braddon's narrator regrets the superficiality of Isabel's fantasy world, he also admits to the vulgarity of that which she is trying to elude, which allows us to sympathize with her habits of literary escapism. Viewing Isabel's reading practice through the lens of social commentary less familiarly applied to Mary Braddon's novels than to those of the Victorian realists helps explain Isabel's propensity to misread, and puts her in the company of a heroine like Maggie Tulliver in George Eliot's *The Mill on the Floss* (1860). The tension between Maggie's self-interested desire for a more intellectual and spiritual existence, and the earthly realities that she must contend with, presents a dynamic similar to Isabel's more prosaic conflict between reality and fantasy, and the cravings of her individual subjectivity in a bourgeois state that prepares and expects its women to be "angels in-the-house." But when Maggie complains about fiction's propensity for fair women in the literature she reads, she divulges an aptitude for critical insight seemingly beyond Isabel. She says,

> I'm determined to read no more books where the blond-haired women carry away all the happiness. I should begin to have a prejudice against them. If you could give me some story, now, where the dark woman triumphs, it would restore the balance. I want to avenge Rebecca and Flora MacIvor, and Minna and all the rest of the dark haired unhappy ones. (270)

While Isabel never questions the internal designs that reward certain heroines and not other ones, she shares Maggie's blurred distinction between art and life. In choosing to forego novels that don't end according to her own sense of fairness, Maggie here attests to the degree of influence that they have over her own self-identification as a dark-haired "heroine." Anticipating her future (and semi-autobiographical) portrait of Maggie and reflecting on her own early experience with novel reading, George Eliot writes as a young girl about the temptations of getting lost in fictional worlds:

> I shall carry to my grave the mental diseases with which [novels] have contaminated me. When I was quite a little child I could not be satisfied

with the things around me; I was constantly living in a world of my own creation, and was quite contented to not have companions that I might be left to my own musings and imagine scenes in which I was the chief actress. (Haight 1.22)

Novels have certainly contaminated Isabel's powers of reckoning, and her repeated fantasies about being an actress make her a viable symbol of the damaging influences of fiction that here worries the young Marian Evans. Isabel's inability to distinguish between fiction and reality offers, in Kate Flint's opinion, the most sustained investigation in Victorian literature of reading in relation to sensation fiction (Flint 288). Far from condemning Isabel's reading habits, Braddon's novel critiques instead the ideological conditions of bourgeois domesticity that inspire and enable Isabel's narcissistic imaginings and compulsive visits to the lending library and the looking glass. The very possibility that allows Isabel to spend her days reading novels can be seen as a critique of her empty social and intellectual environment, the absence from her life of meaningful work, and the narrowness of her daily activities that inspires her obsessive fantasizing and self-delusion (Gerrard 10). But however conscientiously Braddon labored to make *The Doctor's Wife* a "psychological" and socially critical novel, various plot elements (the dependence on coincidence, the dramatic reappearance of Isabel's father and his murder of Lansdell, for instance) reveal Braddon's familiar, sensational techniques. The sentimental "utopian" ending, too, is a major weakness in Braddon's project to make *The Doctor's Wife* realistic. As Braddon wrote to her mentor, Edward Bulwer-Lytton, her original intentions for the novel included an ending to Isabel's story more consistent with the hard lessons illustrated in Flaubert:

> My original intention was to have left [George Gilbert] alive, and Isabel reconciled to a commonplace life doing her duty bravely, and suppressing all outward evidence of her deep grief for Roland. Thus the love story would have been an episode in a woman's life, succeeded by an after-existence of quiet work and duty. . . . I might have done much better with the story in this way, but I am so apt to be influenced by little scraps of newspaper criticism, and by what people say to me. (Wolff 165).

Braddon's plans for a story illustrating the wisdom born of experience and youthful recklessness were interrupted by the anxiety of what other people thought of her work. Her sensitivity to public opinion, in fact, seems to provide an explanation for why *The Doctor's Wife* is a novel burdened by too many disparate narrative ideologies. In the interest of pleasing her public, Braddon attempted to meet the requirements of three incompatible fictional genres.

V

Thus far I have identified narrative conventions in *The Doctor's Wife* conforming to and diverging from sensationalism, sentimentalism, and realism. Examination of all of these genres provides useful insight into the sometimes conflicted representation of Isabel, who at various points in the novel fits the criteria of the facile sensation heroine, the morally scrupulous sentimental heroine, and the culturally disadvantaged heroine of social realism. Needless to say, these genres do not seamlessly cohere, but the epistemological transformations behind these various characterizations of Isabel do make *The Doctor's Wife* a fascinating exposition of the ideological crosscurrents of popular fiction at work in the 1860s. Sensation novels focus on a woman's social value, which is represented by her appearance and class. Sentimental novels probe the innate morality of a female character, often pitting a woman's piety and respectability against the corrupting influences of society. Realist novels consider what makes a woman (character) what she is, by investigating the social circumstances that construct behavior. But by emphasizing Isabel as a reader who is constructively looking to create herself out of the novels she reads, ("She wanted her life to be like her books" [14]) Braddon underscores the conflicts produced by these three methods of portraying women. If these representations are taken as blueprints for fashioning one's best self, the result—as the characterization of Isabel reveals—is almost hopelessly confused.

However, what Braddon does achieve in her integration of the three narrative genres is a deceptively realistic portrait of a Victorian woman reader. In fact, Isabel's character as a reader almost completely obscures her status as a heroine, so that when Sigismund Smith muses to George Gilbert that "Novels are only dangerous for these poor foolish girls, who read nothing else, and think that their lives are to be a paraphrase of their favorite books," (15) we do recognize Isabel in his description, but it is Isabel the reader, not the subject of romantic fiction, that we identify. Isabel's claim that she wants to be a heroine corresponds to Braddon's own claim that she wants to be a realist writer. Both character and author already are what they aspire to be. Isabel exists securely within a fictional world, and Braddon achieves in *The Doctor's Wife* an apt portrait of a woman's life that is overdetermined by the conflicting ideologies of popular fiction.

NOTES

1. While Craik's *John Halifax, Gentleman* (1855) tentatively affirms that a man who makes his own fortune can be considered a gentleman, the novel under-

mines this claim by revealing that Halifax is the orphaned son of a gentleman. We must supplement his rise to fortune with the knowledge that the class he eventually reaches is in fact his birthright, at least in the traditional logic of pre-bourgeois society. Craik's capitulation to the convention of the noble man exiled from his familial privileges thus divulges that she is uncertain about whether a gentleman is made or born.

2. See also Jonathan Loesberg's essay, "The Ideology of Narrative Form in Sensation Fiction."

3. In *Family Fortunes, Men and Women of the English Middle-Class, 1780–1850*, Lenore Davidoff and Catherine Hall note that "smaller, non-utilitarian gardens surrounding a separate house became [in Victorian England] an integral part of the romantic, anti-urban individualism of the middle-class." Isabel's precarious hold on middle-class respectability finds an appropriate context in the family garden, albeit one connected to a rented house, and desperately untidy.

WORKS CITED

Braddon, M. E. *The Doctor's Wife*. NY: Dick and Fitzerald [no date].

Collins, Wilkie. *The Woman in White*. New York: Penguin, 1988.

Davidoff, Lenore, and Catherine Hall. *Family Fortunes, Men and Women of the English Middle-Class, 1780–1850*. Chicago: U of Chicago P, 1991.

Eliot, George. *The Mill on the Floss*. New York: Norton, 1994.

Flint, Kate. *The Woman Reader, 1837–1914*. Oxford: Oxford UP,

Gerrard, Lisa. "Romantic Heroines and the 19th Century Novel." *International Journal of Women's Studies* 7 (1984): 10–16.

Haight, Gordon, ed. *The Letters of George Eliot*. New Haven: Yale UP, 1955.

Huskey, Melynda. "No Name: Embodying the Sensation Heroine." *Victorian Newsletter* 8 (1992): 5–13.

Loesberg, Jonathan. "The Ideology of Narrative Form in Sensation Fiction." *Representations* 12 (1986): 115–38.

Mansel, Henry. "Sensation Novels." *Quarterly Review* 113 (1863): 481–514.

Mitchell, Sally. "Sentiment and Suffering: Women's Recreational Reading in the 1860s." *Victorian Studies* 21 (1977): 29–45.

Reynolds, Kimberly, and Nicola Humble. *Victorian Heroines*. New York: New York UP, 1993.

Surtees, Robert. *Ask Mamma*. London: Methuen, 1911.

Wolff, Robert. *Sensational Victorian*. New York: Garland P, 1979.

THIRTEEN

"Go and Marry Your Doctor": Fetishism and "Redundance" at the *Fin de Siècle* and the Vampires of "Good Lady Ducayne"

Lauren M. E. Goodlad

O! let us have women doctors, women lawyers, women
parsons, women stone-breakers—anything rather than these
dependent creatures who sit in other people's houses
working prie-dieu chairs and pining for freedom.
—M. E. Braddon, *Birds of Prey*

In a novel recently published the supply of marriageable
maidens . . . is described as so plentiful that brides were "two
a penny, . . . while bridegrooms were like snakes in Ireland."
Here is our miserable superfluity again thrown in our teeth!
. . . In country towns the poor, dear girls outnumber the
marriageable men by about six to one."
—Mrs. Humphry, *Manners for Women*

In mid-Victorian novels such as *Lady Audley's Secret* (1862) and *Birds of Prey* (1867), Mary Elizabeth Braddon exposed the dangers of female dependence in an increasingly materialistic Victorian society. But for the fact that Lucy Audley's aberrant femininity is mystified as innate evil and hereditary madness, the novel would be a trenchant critique of the duplicity and violence to which impoverished middle-class women are desperately driven. It is clearly no coincidence that these novels were published in the same decade as W. R. Greg's controversial essay on "redundant" women (unmarried women forced to work for a living). Woman's "natural" role, Greg insists, is "completing, sweetening, and embellishing the existence" of others; especially of the *men* upon whose earnings it is their "essential" function to depend. Yet, rather than women's work in general, Greg's primary object is to condemn *middle-class* women's increasing access to traditionally male *professional* labor (Greg 436). Thus, at a time when professional alternatives to middle-class careers in trade and industry were achieving unprecedented socioeconomic and symbolic importance—a historical transition that provides an important context for this essay—Greg intervenes to establish the unquestionable *masculinity* of professional vocation.

That neither Greg's article nor the problem it describes had ceased to be at issue more than thirty years later is evident in a range of *fin-de-siècle* texts, from Mrs. Humphry's 1897 conduct manual (cited above), to George Gissing's somber novel on the very same theme, *The Odd Women* (1893). It is also demonstrable in the consistently popular works of Braddon, whose mid-Victorian focus on female "redundance" resurfaces in "Good Lady Ducayne," a story published in *The Strand* in 1896. Indeed, as I shall demonstrate, the mid-Victorian debate over "redundant" middle-class women and the professional employment to which they arguably warrant access, is reproduced in two of the most notorious categories of fin-de-siècle femininity: the Odd Woman and the New Woman.

One important difference, however, is the fin de siècle's especial penchant for gothic representations of the feminine. Braddon's 1896 tale of vampirism was published a year after such popular narratives of monstrous femininity as Marie Corelli's *Sorrows of Satan* and George MacDonald's *Lilith*. Braddon's friend Bram Stoker published *Dracula* a year after "Good Lady Ducayne"—the same year in which Philip Burne-Jones unveiled his scandalous portrait of female vampirism. In this essay, however, I aim to do more than tease out Braddon's relation to late-century gothic genres while comparing her fin-de-siècle social critique to its mid-Victorian antecedents. Braddon's position as a popular writer whose works dramatize ("sensationalize," "gothicize") women's lives without articulating any obvious "feminist" position is in itself immensely interesting. That the author was herself both the exemplary helpmeet of Victorian domestic ideology and the resourceful professional provider who threatened the latter's stability, cannot but enhance our fascination. Braddon's ability to adapt to and capitalize on various trends in the market for popular literature over a period of more than thirty years—including "penny dreadfuls," "sensation" novels, serial publications, three-volume novels for the circulating library, one-volume "bestsellers," and short "gothic" fiction—is perhaps unequaled.

For all of these reasons, I suggest, Braddon poses a singular challenge to the materialist critic of literature and culture. Perhaps the overarching motive of the following attempt to "historicize" "Good Lady Ducayne," a largely forgotten minor work, is to demonstrate the unexpected complexity of what would appear to be the most modest of scholarly projects. Even were she writing in a genre less "overdetermined" than the vampire genre at the end of the nineteenth century, Braddon's inclination to allegorize cultural history in popular form without, in any final sense, diminishing its complexity, would, I believe, demand the fullest attention from the critical historiographer. In reply to the concern that historicist scholarship refrain from a methodological tendency "to drain the heterogeneity and conflict out of culture, and with them the possibility of change" (Patterson 261), I offer these readings of "Good Lady Ducayne" as a work of literature *about* historical change in which fin-de-siècle England materializes as a heterogeneous culture in conflict with its own innovations and the legacies of its mid-Victorian past.

In this way, the series of readings that follows aims to exemplify the critical (historicizing) process as a continuous multidisciplinary endeavor (rather than to provide a veritable menu, as it were, of alternative critical approaches). I begin (in section II) with a classical Marxist reading of "Good Lady Ducayne," locating Braddon's fiction alongside contemporaneous socialist writings and demonstrating that Braddon's vampirism is more responsive to Engels's Great Depression–era socialism than to Marx's famous mid-Victorian evocation of the vampire in *Capital.* In the next two sections, I introduce a less familiar but equally proximate sociohistorical context—the complicated ideological contest between "entrepreneurial" and "professional" ways of conceptualizing English national and middle-class identity. On the surface, I argue, Braddon's tale celebrates a new professional social relation, the historical origins of which overlap with mid-Victorian Britain's quest to define and authorize the "gentleman." But Braddon's enthusiasm for that end is considerably undermined by contradictions between professionalism's professed gentility and its ever-expanding disciplinary ambitions. Section V, influenced by postmodernist cultural theory, demonstrates the historicist's obligation to read the tale at yet another level—as an allegory *about* representation in an increasingly mass (and, consequently, increasingly feminized) culture. The final section contrasts Irigaray's feminist analysis of "Women on the Market" with Braddon's fin de siècle fictional critique. Braddon's "redundant" vampire, I argue, is ultimately an anti patriarchal figure of woman's uncanny power to signify in a still alien mass culture. Influenced by psychoanalytic as well as Marxist theories of fetishism, this section posits an important historical shift between mid-Victorian and fin-de-siècle constructions of sexual difference, in relation to which Braddon's contribution to late-century gothic fiction is especially instructive.

I. BRADDON'S "GOOD LADY DUCAYNE"

The plot of "Good Lady Ducayne" is deceptively simple. Like Braddon— compelled to take up acting and then writing to support herself and her mother—the heroine of "Good Lady Ducayne" is the daughter of an educated gentlewoman deserted by a "scoundrel" husband. Less resourceful than her creator, eighteen-year-old Bella Rolleston sews mantles with her mother before deciding to pursue employment as a hired companion. After enlisting the (exorbitant) services of a London employment agency, Bella is placed as the companion of "good" Lady Ducayne, an antiquated noblewoman who resides in an Italian hotel, attended by an insidious physician, Dr. Parravinici. There, while living in the "lap of luxury," and literally closeted within Lady Ducayne's opulent bedchamber, Bella reports strange dreams and an increasing lassitude suggestive of (technologically assisted) vampirism. In spite of increasing ill-health, and the knowledge that Lady Ducayne's last two companions died of mysterious illness, Bella oscillates between a vague but "invincible horror," and the conviction that her "uncanny" employer is "so very kind" and "venerable" (149).

Bella has, meanwhile, befriended Dr. Herbert Stafford, a young English physician, and his "respectable" sister, Lotta. Noting his increasing attraction to Lady Ducayne's pretty companion, Lotta advises her brother of the unsuitability of marrying the daughter of a seamstress. Herbert eventually detects Lady Ducayne's vampiric activity and confronts her and Dr. Parravinci, threatening to expose them. In reply Lady Ducayne releases Bella from her service with a check for a thousand pounds, advising her to *"Go and marry your doctor."* Lady Ducayne's money, we learn, is to be invested in debenture stock in Mrs. Rolleston's name, "to be her very own" for life. The story closes with a letter between mother and daughter in which the bride-to-be explains that "It is all good Lady Ducayne's doing." She adds Herbert's promise that the "word 'mother-in-law' has no terrors for him" (162).

II. BRADDON'S CRITIQUE OF
ENTREPRENEURIAL CAPITALISM

Capital is dead labour which, vampire-like, lives only by sucking
living labour, and lives the more, the more labour it sucks.
—Marx, *Capital*

In his illuminating essay on *Dracula*, Franco Moretti argues that Stoker's
vampire, despite his aristocratic title, represents *capital;* for, like capital,
Dracula is impelled toward growth, expansion, and accumulation (Moretti 91). The fact that Braddon's century-old Lady Ducayne was born in
1793, on "the day Louis XVI was guillotined" (158), symbolically con-
nects her "vampire thirst" to the emergence of capitalism. In fact, more
so even than Dracula's (ambiguously amorous and familial) relation to
his victims, Lady Ducayne's vamping of hired companions emblematizes
the same predatory relation between capitalist and laborer that Carlyle
had named the "cash nexus." Yet that the vampirism she practices is
decadent and lethargic rather than, like Dracula's, aggressively monopo-
listic and imperial is equally crucial to the kind of capitalist critique
Braddon is articulating. Written at the tail end of a "Great Depression" of
almost twenty years' duration, Lady Ducayne's vampirism, I want to argue, specifically represents the enfeebled position of entrepreneurial
capitalism at the fin de siècle.

In this respect Braddon's capitalist allegory tallies with the chronic
socioeconomic dysfunction depicted in Engels's *Socialism:Utopian and
Scientific* (1880) even more than with Marx's mid-Victorian *Capital*. Marx
introduces the figure of the labor-sucking vampire to describe the
capitalist's artificial extension of the "natural" working day. *Capital* thus
describes a highly productive stage of capitalism in which the monstrous
acquisitive drive of the vampire-capitalist eventually incites the rebellion
of his living victim. Indeed, confronting the capitalist, Marx's laborer
resembles the protagonist of a gothic fiction as she recognizes the inhu-
man fiend that preys on her: *"the thing that you represent face to face with me,
has no heart in its breast"* (Marx 256). By contrast, Engels's and Braddon's
Great-Depression-era texts have a different gothic tale to tell in which
both laborer and capitalist are comparatively agency-less. The 1880s was
the decade in which the term "unemployment" first came into use (*Sexual Anarchy* 5). In this unprecedented context Engels indicts capitalism's
failure to *produce* maximally and to *circulate* effectively. In contrast to
Marx's insatiable entrepreneurial monster, Engels's late-century capitalist is the inept beneficiary of an exploitative and unstable system of
exchange over which he exercises little or no control. More decadent

epicure than acquisitive vampire, this capitalist passively feeds off a dys-functional status quo until it self-destructs, and the *"mode of production rises in rebellion against"* a manifestly contradictory and inoperative *"form of exchange"* (Engels 433, emphasis added). This is precisely the condition allegorized in "Good Lady Ducayne." Decadent, aristocratic, otiose and—with implications that will be elaborated further—foreign and female, Lady Ducayne's lust for "a few more years in the sunshine" retains the self-interest of Marx's vampire-capitalist, while further representing the prodigality, artificiality, and near-obsolescence of Engels's anach-ronistic bourgeoisie. Yet, despite her pungent critique of contemporary capitalism, Braddon's sympathies with socialism must not be overstated. Instead, the vampire theme of "Good Lady Ducayne" demands a more nuanced and historical contextualization.

III. *"GO AND MARRY YOUR DOCTOR"*: BRADDON'S MID-VICTORIAN-ERA PROFESSIONAL CHALLENGE TO THE ENTREPRENEURIAL IDEAL OF ENGLISHNESS

> It may appear paradoxical, but it is strictly true, that the
> manners of an English gentleman have much more in
> common with the manners of a labourer than with the
> manners of a mercantile clerk or a small shopkeeper"
> —*Cornhill Magazine* (1862), quoted in Palmer 277

In *The Rise of Professional Society* (1989), Harold Perkin distinguishes be-tween two competing ideologies or "ideals" of Victorian middle-class identity: the "entrepreneurial" and the "professional." Against the entre-preneur's reflexive identification with capitalist competition, the Vic-torian professional propounded the putative superiority of "trained ex-pertise" and meritorious service. Perkin demonstrates how this anti-capitalist rhetoric enabled professionalism's "massive expansion in size and influence" at the fin de siècle, and its eventual "triumph" in the twentieth century.[17] Integral to the increasing predominance of pro-fessionalism and to entrepreneurialism's corresponding decline was a new emphasis on *human* capital. Indeed, by the fin de siècle, Perkin declares, "the most important kind of waste had come to be recognized as the waste of *human* resources"—precisely the kind perpetuated by Lady Ducayne's vampiric consumption of one "idle" companion after another (155).

As we shall see, the implications of Perkin's thesis profoundly com-plicate Braddon's critique of capitalism. In addition to Marxist tensions between capitalist and working classes, Braddon's tale intervenes in a longstanding ideological contest between two antithetical versions of middle-class identity. While the *entrepreneurial* view of (male) middle-class character concentrates on business and industry, in apparent opposition to the "feminine" domestic sphere, its *professional* counterpart, concentrating on such areas as medicine and letters, established institutions like the Church, and the expanding civil service, is—in many respects—self-consciously *aligned* with domesticity. This split *within* middle-class identity explains why Lady Ducayne's figurative ownership of the means of production—her declining "entrepreneurial" vampirism—is answered neither by a reassertion of individualist Englishness (Moretti), a rebellious recognition on the part of her working-class victim (Marx), nor a collapse of the unstable "form of exchange" off of which she battens (Engels). Instead, Lady Ducayne's late-century capitalism-as-vampirism is brought to a halt, almost anticlimactically, by an exemplary English *professional:* Dr. Herbert Stafford.

To make this point more clear, I want to elaborate on the mid-Victorian-era rhetorical distinctions so crucial to professionalism's increasing influence. In a seminal essay on the Victorian literary professional, Mary Poovey demonstrates how the mid-century "literary man" represents an ideal of "selfless" labor. Like the middle-class housewife whose uncompensated domestic labor is the prototype for his "selflessness," the male literary professional neutralizes the material inequalities of bourgeois capitalism by creating a basis of *symbolical* equality—a crucial realm "outside the inexorable logic" of competitive "market relations" (Poovey 115–22). Poovey's distinction between "domesticated" literary enterprise and "undomesticated" market activity is analogous to Perkin's distinction between professional service and entrepreneurial competition. In either case, I suggest, the purport of the contrast is radically to revise the logic through which *value* is defined and determined. To the entrepreneur's assertion that "use-value" is inherent in acquisition and efficiently distributed through competitive market relations, the professional responds with an appeal to *human* capital and the nonmaterial registers (including service, reputation, and expertise) by which its merits are assessed. Even more fundamentally, to the entrepreneur's implicit assumption that *self-interest* is both the motive and "natural" justification for capitalist exchange, the professional responds with the *disinterested* service, or "selflessness," upon which his alternative system of value is predicated.

Here, I suggest, professionalism avails itself of two distinct epistemological registers within which value is determined. From within a modern, scientific and empiricist frame, the professional offers consultative expertise as an advanced form of rationalized endeavor superseding the cruder, manifestly Darwinian form of capitalist competition. But, by further invoking a romantic and arguably premodern frame, the professional also offers service as a presumptively non-commodified and non-commodifiable form of quasichivalric labor within a community reconstituted as professionals and their clientele. The "fee" for professional service is neither the industrial worker's wage, nor the capitalist's exploitative extraction of surplus value. It is instead "a guaranteed reward" (Perkin xii) for meritorious service, actuated independently of the *logic* of capitalism. Consequently, what the professional offers is not so much expressed as a new system of exchange (which is why private ownership of property is rarely at issue), but, instead, as *a new and superior social relation*. From this perspective, Lady Ducayne's declaration, *"Go and marry your doctor,"* is not only a specific injunction to Bella, but an emblematic prescription for an entire society.

Professionalism's new social relation, moreover, is inextricably tied to what is perhaps the most hotly contested form of symbolic capital in the nineteenth century: the status of the "gentleman." Whether understood in terms of morals, breeding, education, blood, or national character, what the ontological basis of the Victorian gentleman invariably excludes are the self-interest and acquisitive drive of the entrepreneurial capitalist. That is why the *Cornhill* writer (see epigraph) links the manners of the gentleman to the manners of the common laborer while opposing both to the manners of the *commercial* middle classes. This is but one example of the crucial mid-Victorian rhetorical nexus between professionalism's investments in "human" capital and its proliferation of anti-capitalist definitions of the gentleman—a nexus that, in texts such as Ruskin's *Unto this Last* (1860) and Arnold's *Culture and Anarchy* (1867), present the gentlemanly professional and the relations he engenders as vehicles of social redress. Here, I am arguing—contemporaneous with the launch of Braddon's literary career—are the historicocultural foundations of Dr. Herbert Stafford's narrative authority, and the key to his role in ostensibly resolving a vampire plot representing the social crisis of fin-de-siècle capitalism. For in lieu of either working-class rebellion, or bourgeois-capitalist collapse, Braddon's "professional" response to late-century capitalism-as-vampirism imagines a new social relation by rewriting, without fundamentally transforming, the extant system of exchange.

But, it is also important to recognize that Herbert's professional potency is *not* primarily founded on his technical expertise or—to invoke Foucauldian genealogy—on his deployment of modern medicine's disciplinary power/knowledge, a problem to which I will return. Tactically speaking, moreover, Herbert's "professional" refusal of Lady Ducayne's acquisitive logic is in itself insufficient, for it fails to provide a lasting resolution to the social problem of Bella's "redundancy." Here is where Bella's ambiguous social status—the significance of her being a *déclassé* gentlewoman rather than a born-and-bred seamstress—becomes especially important. For, in the end, Herbert Stafford's provenance of a new social relation must be authorized by (what is strictly speaking) extraprofessional means. Just as he proved his professional and gentlemanly credentials by rejecting the terms of the capitalist *labor* market, so Herbert must further dismiss the concomitant commercialism of the *marriage* market.

Although in most respects a stunningly obtuse heroine, Bella is shrewd on one telling point: *"No young man can afford to marry a penniless girl nowadays"* (147), she writes. In counseling him to dismiss Bella as "an absolute pauper" (152), Herbert's "thoroughly respectable" sister exemplifies a prevailing logic in which marriageability (a kind of use-value) is determined by the same standards that dictate the advisibility of entrepreneurial investment. When Herbert replies that he "shouldn't think any less" of Bella "if her mother made matchboxes," Lotta responds, "Not in the abstract—of course not. Matchboxes are honest labor. *But you couldn't marry a girl whose mother makes mantles"* (152, emphasis added). Lotta's reply glaringly exposes the same bourgeois "contradiction" that Poovey's homemakers and literary professionals are invoked to conceal (Poovey 98, 114–15). Paying lipservice to one of capitalism's chief mythological mainstays, she affirms the "abstract" equality between a suitable (middle-class) wife and the daughter of an honest matchbox-maker. Mythical abstractions aside, Lotta knows that bourgeois society depends upon the kind of material (class) *in*equalities that mandate the impossibility of a rising young doctor's marriage to "a girl whose mother makes mantles."

Yet it is precisely this impossibility that Braddon's physician rejects. When Herbert sentimentally remarks upon Bella's "heart," Lotta attempts to separate the gentleman from the professional, protesting, "What have you to do with hearts, except for dissection?" (152). But Herbert's professional "service" claims to comprehend a shift in consciousness that Lotta's bourgeois provincialism cannot fathom: not the disciplinary power/knowledge of modern medicine, but the antirationalist transcendentalism of the professional's new social relation. On these phenomenological grounds, Herbert reclaims capitalism's illusory freedom to follow the "heart," asserting it as the epiphanic insight of a postentrepreneurial social relation. "[I]f ever I love a woman well enough to think of marrying her," he assures Lotta, "riches or rank will count for nothing with me" (154).

As though first to emphasize but, ultimately, to undermine professionalism's homologous relation to domesticity, Bella's eventual removal from the vampiric labor market is effected by Herbert's assumption of a series of transformative professional *and* familial roles. It is no surprise to find the hero dexterously performing the professional services of doctor, clergyman, and detective/barrister as he deals with Lady Ducayne. What is more remarkable are his dealings with Bella. Rather than inform her that she has been victimized and, so, appeal to her own *self-interest,* Herbert again assumes a professional role, "treating Bella as coolly *as if he'd been the family physician, and she had been given over wholly to his care"* (161; emphasis added). But, in the end, professionalism's new social relation is fully mobilized only when its connections to domestic ideology are pushed to their logical extreme. To manage Bella's removal from Italy, Herbert must "take upon [him]self the privileges of an elder brother" and eventually of her betrothed (161). Braddon's response to capitalism is thus radically distinguished from Marx's, since Bella *never* fully apprehends the circumstances of her vamping; never, like Marx's laborer, recognizes her exploiter as "the thing . . . [with] no heart in its breast." Even more significantly, Bella never becomes the owner of her own human capital. Rather than achieving professional independence (in the manner urged upon "redundant" women by protofeminist Victorians), Bella "completes" herself in the manner urged by W. R. Greg—by becoming the dependant of male (professional) labor. Nevertheless, the ostensibly antifeminist and reactionary implications of this professional critique of late-century capitalism are confounded, not least by Lady Ducayne's figurative but powerful role as the marriage broker between Bella and Herbert.

"Good Lady Ducayne," I have so far suggested, details an anticapitalist rhetoric, especially prevalent in mid-Victorian middle-class culture, in which professionalism asserts its merits less by reference to its technological capabilities than to its putative monopoly over gentlemanliness. After 1870, factors such as the dramatic expansion of the British state, the acceleration of empire, the institution of national education and, more generally, the increasing massification of English culture, altered the symbolic position of the professional in ways that tended to emphasize technological expertise and specialized knowledge. By these lights, Herbert Stafford's brand of gentleman-professional manifestly verges toward the obsolescence of the entrepreneurial capitalism he symbolically overthrows.

IV. BRADDON'S CRITIQUE OF
MEDICAL AUTHORITY

No group of men so truly interprets, comprehends, and
sympathizes with woman as do physicians, who know how
near to disorder and how close to misfortune she is brought
by the peculiarities of her nature
—S. Weir Mitchell, *Doctor and Patient*

Hence, it will not, perhaps, be surprising to find that problems *within* Braddon's professional-*cum*-domestic plot tell upon the viability of the new social relation it superficially celebrates. Because the social merits of his professionalism must be demonstrated by his (presumably homologous) domestic activities, Herbert's performance as brother and husband should be unambiguous and irreproachable. On the contrary, however, in the exercise of these crucial relations Herbert veers toward an orthodox paternalism, resembling the regulatory power of modern medicine, but failing to achieve even this dubious agency. Upon Lotta's confiding to her that Herbert *"treats [Lotta] like a child"* Bella tellingly reflects, *"Perhaps this is what makes some girls so eager to marry—the want of someone . . . to care for them and order them about"* (146). Bella's supposition superficially recalls W. R. Greg's "wretched" old maid, pining for want of someone "to love, cherish, and obey." Yet, like John Ruskin's paradigmatic lecture on Victorian femininity, Greg himself insists that woman's economic dependence on men is not only "natural" but also *useful* (Greg 437). In "Of Queen's Gardens" (1864), Ruskin specifies that "A woman in any rank of life ought to know whatever her husband is likely to know"— (rather than be oblivious to his arcane disciplinary knowledge)— *"but to know it in a different way."* By thus constructing an incommensurable difference between the sexes, discourses like Ruskin's, of course, enable the pacification of women and the regulation of their bodies. But, I want to emphasize, they do so by way of establishing—as well as mystifying, sacralizing, and romanticizing—women's (uniquely "feminine") *use.* Indeed, the purport of the gentleman-professional's homology with domesticity is to appropriate the special symbolic capital of the "feminine"; to sieze woman's exceptional capacity to *"know . . . in a different way"* and transform it into the basis of a new (male) social relation.

By contrast, Herbert's mode of relating to his sister and future bride, as though they were constitutionally feeble and mentally childlike, constructs them as (to borrow a term popularized by the New Poor Law) "non-able"—capable neither of creating nor managing "use," but only of *consuming* it. This tendency to treat women as though they were patients, epitomized by S. Weir Mitchell in 1887 (cited above), *reverses* the homology upon which Braddon's professional social relation depends. Braddon's ideal professional is superior to the entrepeneurial capitalist because, as a gentleman, he is inherently domesticated—*not* because he professionializes (much less pathologizes) domesticity. Fragile, ailing, and indolent, and requiring constant medical supervision, the woman represented by Victorian medical authorities resembles the childless Lady Ducayne more than Ruskin's "helpmate." Thus, medicine's male regulatory authority—originating in early-Victorian specialist discourse but, by the fin-de-siècle diffused into mainstream culture—clashes with the popular image of the gentleman-professional, whose enduring legitimacy enables Herbert's apparent triumph over vampire-capitalism. Whereas the latter looked forward to a new social relation by constructing homologies between gentleman-professionals and the selflessness of homemakers, the former—from the vantage point of Braddon's tale— threatens to turn women into *vampires;* that is, into "a leisured class of consumers" (Shuttleworth 53).

Even as they diminish the credibility of his new professional social relation, Herbert's subtle disciplinary complicities point to Braddon's multipronged attack on male medical authority. Because the indolent consumption that medicine prescribes evokes the horror of Lady Ducayne, Braddon invidiously connects modern medicine's will-to-knowledge to the foreign "quackery" of Parravinici. Moreover, as embodied in Herbert Stafford, medicine's regulatory will-to-power fails conspicuously. The truth is that while Lotta Stafford unquestionably belongs to a "leisured class of consumers," she is manifestly *un*-childlike, hardly passive, and no more the ingenue of Bella's false impression than she is the invalid of Herbert's.

But if Lotta thus flouts modern medical authority, in Bella we find a comparatively unresisting patient for the medical man. That Bella's relation to Herbert unmomentously shifts from doctor/patient, to (intended) husband/wife in the space of a few lines, suggests a literal reading of the prescription to *"Go and marry your doctor."* It is even possible to argue that the story narrates the ironic displacement of Lady Ducayne's acquisitive vampire-*capitalism* by Mrs. Herbert Stafford's passive, parasitic but medically authorized vampire-*consumption.* There is, after all, little evidence of the "helpmate," or expert housekeeper in Bella's makeup. And yet, without entirely discounting the tenability of such a reading, I want to suggest that Bella is too vacuous, too passive a heroine to represent even the limited agency of the parasite. Never fully the agent but chiefly the passive *object* of consumption, Bella most convincingly represents woman as *commodity:* what Marie Corelli's bestselling 1895 novel described as "a piece of goods," "for the buying" of marriage-minded men (Corelli 160).

Indeed, the main obstacle to Bella's marriage prospects is, ultimately, not her *own* pennilessness, but her mother's: the story's most problematic "redundant" woman is not the "Odd Woman" whom Bella might become, but the abandoned wife and indigent mother-in-law-to-be that Mrs. Rolleston threatens to remain. Hence, Bella's complete repression of having been victimized by the employer she was wont to regard as "a funny old grandmother" (146), her oblivious insistence that Lady Ducayne "really is the dearest old thing" (161), points to the underlying irony of "good" Lady Ducayne's crucial providence. And, while woman's commodification and redundancy are linked to medicine's disciplinary ambitions, they are not reducible to its effect. Instead, the position of women in Braddon's tale redirects our gaze from the ostensible heroics of male professionalism to the ostensible fall of female monstrosity. For "Good Lady Ducayne" leaves no doubt as to the fact that the "fairy godmother" (142) of this Cinderella story is a *vampire*.

V. BRADDON'S "POSTMODERN" ALLEGORY OF REPRESENTATION

> She read a good deal of that kind of literature which may be
> defined as specialism popularised; writing which addresses
> itself to educated, but not strictly studious, persons, and
> which forms the reservoir of conversation for society above
> the sphere of turf and west-endism. Thus, for instance,
> though she could not undertake the volumes of Herbert
> Spencer, she was intelligently acquainted with the tenor of
> their contents; and though she had never opened one of
> Darwin's books, her knowledge of his main theories and
> illustrations was respectable. She was becoming a typical
> woman of the new time, the woman who has developed
> concurrently with journalistic enterprise.
> —George Gissing, *New Grub Street*

I have argued that irreconcilable conflicts between Herbert's gentlemanly professionalism and his "regulatory" paternalism seriously undermine the credibility of the social alternative he represents. At the same time, I now want to emphasize, the tale's ostensible resolution is a marriage that has been brokered by a *vampire*—a vampire, moreover, whose "capitalist" form of exchange constitutes the bride as a commodity form. Lady Ducayne's symbolic centrality, I suggest, points to an important textual "meta"-level. Here Braddon's "professional" critique is rescripted as an allegory in which representation itself—the exchange of signifiers through which meaning is generated—is logically prior to the material social relations we have so far considered. Thus, Herbert's wholesome, English, and masculine professionalism becomes dependent upon a signifying exchange that—as metonymically represented by Lady Ducayne—is monstrous, feminine, un-English, and mass.

To make this point more clear, I want first to demonstrate Braddon's particular relation to fin-de-siècle England's increasingly and self-consciously mass culture. The post-1870 introduction of mass literacy expanded the literary market while intensifying the split between "popular" and cultivated tastes (Gagnier 25–26). George Gissing, for example, scathingly satirized commercial literature in *New Grub Street* (1891), describing the "quarter-educated" audience as "that great new generation" of "young men and women who can just read, but are incapable of sustained attention" (Gissing 496). Rather less contemptuous than Gissing, Braddon had long been a master of popular and, arguably, proto–mass fiction. In 1866 Braddon began editing *Belgravia*—the first Victorian publication to suggest to lower-middle-class readers that when they "opened its pages" they entered "the fashionable world of the aristocratic rich" (Wolff 179). Braddon's proficiency in thus manipulating the constitutive relationship between image and identity points to another defining feature of fin de siècle mass culture. As Regenia Gagnier explains, the 1890s, "a time of overproduction," "initiated modern practices of advertising," identifying commodities with "desired modes of living" and, most significantly, "initiat[ing] an ideology of choice dependent on *the proliferation of images*" (54). A consumerist society of this kind is structured not only by the reigning mode of *production,* but also (or, as Baudrillard argues, even more fundamentally) by the reigning mode of *signification* on which *all* meaning—including that which structures capitalist production—is contingent.

Gissing's *New Grub Street* exemplifies the priority of fin-de-siècle representational systems, linking the vulgarity of the "masses" to popular education and literature, and depicting such figures as the "new" middle-class woman, whose "typicality" is attributable to a certain (classed and gendered) form of "journalistic enterprise" (see epigraph). But rather than, like Gissing, condemn mass culture, in "Good Lady Ducayne," Braddon exposes her own complicities, offering, on the one hand, a critique of late-century social realities, and, on the other, a metalevel allegory about the process by which such "realities"—including her critique—are actuated. Like a palimpsest in which mid-Victorian social "truths" are visibly overwritten by fin-de-siècle representational shifts, Braddon's text at once figures Lady Ducayne as the emblem of an antiquated mode of capitalist production, *and* of a thriving late-capitalist mode of representation—an exchange of signifiers through which all values and meanings are mediated.

Reading "Good Lady Ducayne" this way, as though the vampire were a late-century spin-doctor of sorts, directs us away from exploitative practices per se and toward underlying representational effects. It becomes clear, for example, that by insisting that her brother "couldn't marry a girl whose mother makes mantles," Lotta produces a rhetorical distinction between her own bourgeois values and Herbert's disdain for "riches and rank." Herbert's professional credentials are further legitimated by his "disinterested" advocacy of Bella, and authoritative challenge to Lady Ducayne. But as Herbert shifts from selfless professional to self-interested suitor, Lady Ducayne responds by turning from vampirism to matchmaking. Portioning off her erstwhile victim with a check for a thousand pounds, she instructs Herbert to take his "girl" and marry her if he likes (160). It is, then, quite literally *"all good Lady Ducayne's doing."* The vampire's dramatic capitulation to Herbert's professionalism diverts attention from the fact that, in actuality, Lotta's commercial values reign supreme: a rising young doctor, that is to say, *doesn't* "marry a girl whose mother makes mantles." Thus, Lady Ducayne's "goodness"—her conclusive provenance of the necessary sum—is the ineradicable relic of what remains, despite pretense to the contrary, a commodifying capitalist exchange. However much gentlemanly professionalism might play *within* the reigning mode of signification, distinguishing between its own "disinterest" and capitalism's will-to-acquisition, Lady Ducayne's "goodness" remains to testify to professionalism's profound complicities.

This analysis indicates why and how Lady Ducayne both helps to create the illusion of Herbert's oppositionality, and potentially undermines it. But what does it suggest about Lady Ducayne herself—about the uncanny, "feminine" power to signify that she represents? The answer points to the extent to which the massification of fin-de-siècle culture was defined and experienced as a process of *feminization*. Even while masterfully manipulating the popular market, Braddon herself aspired to—but never achieved—the modernist "authenticity" attributed to male writers such as Flaubert. Consequently, Braddon was uniquely positioned to discern the late-nineteenth-century's determination to *feminize* the mass, while reserving "real, authentic culture" as a *masculine* "prerogative" (Huyssen 47–49). Male figures such as Herbert thrive off the fin de siècle's propensities to deploy gender (as well as nationality) in making invidious distinctions between "high" culture and "low"; for example, authorizing Herbert's English, masculine professionalism at the expense of Lady Ducayne's feminine and Continental vampirism. Yet, insofar as Lady Ducayne personifies a totalizing mass culture—that is, insofar as she brokers all meanings and relationships in a tale in which she is ostensibly the antagonist—Herbert's authority is but the effect of symbolic exchanges that *she* puts into play. *His* "modernist" pretensions to social authenticity are but the alibi for *her* ever-surer hold over the power to signify.

To be sure, Lady Ducayne is recognizably aberrant and ominous: like many gothic monsters, she awes readers and manipulates their perceptions without eliciting their sympathy or conscious identification. To this extent Braddon seems to have shared Gissing's repugnance to the massifying tendencies of the fin de siècle. Nevertheless, the demystifying powers with which she invests "feminine" mass culture— particularly, its power both to manipulate and unmask the mythos of "masculine" authenticity (professional or otherwise)—are Braddon's definitive comment on a culture that situates women as consumers of pulp, while positing men as artists of the beautiful. As the professional and popular female writer, in other words, Braddon both authoritatively identifies with and recoils from "vampiric" signification—from a mass culture at once experienced as monstrous, feminine, and (increasingly) ubiquitous.

VI. WOMEN *IN* THE MARKET: ODD WOMEN, NEW WOMEN, AND THE FETISHIZATION OF SEXUAL DIFFERENCE

> The woman is to the man as the producing class is
> to the possessing.
> —Eleanor Marx

> So many *odd* women—no making a pair with them.
> The pessimists call them useless, lost futile lives.
> I, naturally—being one of them myself—take another view.
> I look on them as a great reserve. When one woman
> vanishes in matrimony, the reserve offers a substitute
> for the world's work.
> —George Gissing, *The Odd Women*

> Hence women's role as fetish-objects inasmuch as, in
> exchanges, they are the manifestation and the circulation of
> a power of the Phallus, establishing relationships of
> men with each other?
> —Luce Irigaray, "Women on the Market"

We are now prepared to consider the crucial role of gender in Braddon's overlapping narratives of capitalist, professional, and representational modes of exchange. Eleanor Marx's (above-cited) fin-de-siècle equation between male-female and capitalist-labor relations anticipates by nearly a century Luce Irigaray's conclusion that women are the "one 'class' of producers" upon whose exploitation "all the social regimes of 'History' are based." A fascinating model against which to read "Good Lady Ducayne," Irigaray's seminal feminist critique takes the commodification of women to its logical extreme, applying Karl Marx's analysis of the commodity form to the position of women in patriarchal society. Like the Marxist commodity, Irigaray argues, women function as objects of exchange *between* men. As Mothers ("Red Blood"), women's socially crucial *use-value* is the reproduction of the labor force. But as Virgins ("White Blood") women are but commodities to be exchanged *on* the market. In this form women bear a purely representational value, antithetical to reproductive use, determined wholly by men's labor/needs/desire, and tantamount to the (fetishized) *exchange-value* of Marx's commodity (Irigaray 175–85).

In "Good Lady Ducayne" Bella's disturbing vacuity, the semi-consciousness with which she transits from one dependent function to another, mark her as the archetypal woman-commodity. Like Irigaray's Virgin, Bella *"is pure exchange value"*; a reflection less commodity, mirroring the desires of others while "lack[ing] specific qualities of her own" (Irigaray 185–87). Nevertheless, Braddon's tale poses a problem for Irigaray, foregrounding a traffic *between* as well as a traffic *in* women. While Braddon's professional critique is decidedly antifeminist (subjecting Bella to Herbert's authority), and arguably misogynistic (vilifying aberrant bourgeois femininities in order to legitimate masculine professionalism), her "postmodern" allegory of representation, I have suggested, works through a very different and profoundly antipatriarchal narrative logic. Indeed, at this metalevel, Braddon's tale tellingly diverges from Irigaray's formulation of "Women on the Market," narrating a tale in which female "redundance"—now embodied in the fin de siècle's "Odd" and "New" women—portentously operates as a vampiric returned that will no longer be repressed.

Whereas the exchange-value of Irigaray's woman *on* the market is wholly determined by male activities, *Bella's* exchange-value is, by contrast, greatly determined by women's operations *in* the market. Foremost among these is, of course, Lady Ducayne's value-investing interest in (what is, for Irigaray) the cardinal sign of Bella's "reproductive" use: her youthful "Red Blood." As her future husband, Herbert Stafford might be the ultimate proprietor of Bella's "utility." But even insofar as their marriage will convert her into his "private property," the crucial "third term" that has constituted Bella's value on the market will have always been supplied by Lady Ducyane. What this suggests is the omission of at least one female role intrinsic to the logic of nineteenth-century England. Irigaray writes, *"Mother, virgin, prostitute: these are the social roles imposed on women"* (Irigaray 187). Of these, only the prostitute readily harmonizes with Victorian anxieties over female "redundance." But can the reproductive use of Victorian mothers safely be consigned to patriarchal ownership when men like Braddon's father, Bella's father, and (in *Lady Audley's Secret*) George Talboys leave their wives without adequate male provision? And what of another sort of "virgin" whose performance *on* the market is insufficient to constitute her as the "fetish-object" of men? By either W. R. Greg's or Irigaray's lights *this* woman is deprived of her "natural" (maternal) function. Yet her consequent "social" role is not the "pure exchange value" of the Virgin, but its negation as the *unexchangeable* or "Odd" Woman. Worse still, as epitomized by the declaration of Gissing's heroine (see epigraph), the Odd Woman's "redundance" threatens to assume the uncanny social form of woman *in* the market: a "New" sort of woman who competes with men rather than mirrors their labor/needs/desire. Thus, to omit the Odd Woman—the woman who is neither reproductive *nor* exchangeable—is ultimately to omit the New Woman, who functions *in* the market as the broker of other women/commodities; as the competitor of men. The ghostly prototype of Lady Ducayne is, from this vantage point, Dickens's Miss Havisham—another monstrous Odd Woman whose manipulation of female exchange-value constitutes a challenge to the phallic power of men.

It is important, therefore, to recognize that all of the women who contribute to Bella's "value" are, in one form or another, "redundant": that is, single women living independently of male earnings. And, for the very same reason, all are in some form, arguably, *vampires*. Hence, the key to the incompatibilities between Braddon's women *in* the market, and Irigaray's women *on* the market, is, I suggest, Braddon's acutely perceptive engagement with fin de siècle representation—her anticipation of recent postmodernist critiques of Marx. Just as, according to Baudrillard, Marx (unwarrantably) exempts "use" from the otherwise ubiquitous reign of capitalist exchange, so Irigaray privileges female reproductive capacity, overlooking the degree to which mother's "Red Blood"—one of the premier fetishes of Victorian domestic ideology (and medical inquiry)—is but another aspect of patriarchal *"semblance."* Precisely what Braddon's vampirism so vividly exemplifies is the uninvited side-effect of this fetishization of woman's reproductive "nature": the uncanny power of "redundant" femininity as it literally *redounds* in a form—the "New" form of woman *in* the market—for which fin de siècle patriarchy has (as yet) no effective rationalization. What "returns" with a vengeance in the late-nineteenth-century female vampire is the full measure of everything repressed by the commodification of women (including the fetishization of women's reproductive "use"): female need, desire, and, perhaps above all, female signification. The she-vampire's monstrosity is, in other words, but the effect of woman's long-fetishized reproductive power once it is cathected neither as Mother nor as Virgin but, instead, as woman's economic, sexual, and symbolical aggression. Thus, Braddon's allegory of representation also operates as an antipatriarchal feminist critique. For the power that it wrests from male subjects such as Herbert—the "power of the Phallus"—is the power to signify; a power that, given the fin de siècle's hostility toward its own mass culture, is frequently imagined as both feminine and monstrous.

This point becomes even clearer once we shift from Marxist to psychoanalytic theories of fetishism. In her powerful feminist revision of Freud, Elizabeth Grosz describes the classical Freudian fetishist as the pre-Oedipal boy who *"wants to have his cake and eat it too";* to retain both "his most precious object" (his mother), and "his most precious organ" (his penis) (144). To accomplish this end, he endows women with a symbolic phallus—the fetish object—in order to resolve his own sexual crisis (the fear of castration). This fetish, Grosz emphasizes, is not a substitute for his *own* phallus (the one he fears losing), but for the one that introduced the very possibility of loss—*the phallus his mother never had.* Thus, by endowing his mother with a substitute for the sign of power that she lacks, the fetishist "disavows" knowledge of all possible lack, including (especially) his own.

Although it will not do to liken the "psyche" of an entire culture to that of its archetypal individual—the (pre-Oedipal) boy of psychoanalysis—I want, nevertheless, to establish what I believe is an important identification between Victorian patriarchy—armed with its notion of "incommensurable" sexual difference—and the Freudian fetishist who "wants to have his cake and eat it too." Like the pre-Oedipal boy, Victorian patriarchy must indemnify its masculine identity by differentiating itself from its female (m)other—a process that involves minimizing the threat of anatomical difference (physical "castration" and the loss of power it symbolizes). Unable simply to deny or to tolerate a threatening physiological difference upon which society's reproduction depends, Victorian patriarchy "endows" women with a "talisman" by *fetishizing woman's reproductive use.* Like the Freudian "substitute," this fetishization of one aspect of woman's (social) body *"both* affirms *and* denies"—that is to say, *disavows*—the disempowering implications of sexual difference. Because the difference is "incommensurable"—endowing masculinity with a *"power of the Phallus"* it denies to women, while simultaneously

229

phallicizing (that is, mystifying and fetishizing) the singular power of the womb—Victorian patriarchy *has its cake and eats it too.* Thus, by virtue of a ubiquitous masculinist logic of fetishism, woman's "phallus"—her unique, maternal, and useful "femininity"—remains intact, while phallic power per se remains the exclusive province of men.

Of course, Victorian patriarchy's fetishistic strategy is destabilized by any challenge to the myth of "incommensurability." Insofar as she (inevitably) raises questions about the "use" of *un*harnessed, *un*exchanged reproductive power, the Odd Woman is troublesome, uncanny—liminally monstrous. When, as happened with increasing frequency in the turbulent decades between Greg's essay and the fin de siècle's cult of female vampirism, the Odd Woman becomes *also* the New Woman—a woman *in* the market—the fetish becomes apparent; its strategic disavowal falters. The substitutive relation between fetishized reproductive femininity and missing female "phallus," in other words, becomes dangerously visible. In this way the New Woman demands either that Victorian patriarchy acknowledge the "phallic" power with which it has long invested women (in fetishized form), *or* that it divest women entirely of "power and authority," and face the consequent threat of its *own* "castration." What the reader of fin de siècle gothic immediately recognizes is the familiarity of these horrors: for "phallic" women and "castrated" men are precisely what recur with obsessive frequency in narratives of female vampirism.

Mary Elizabeth Braddon, I am suggesting, apprehended the fetishistic and commodifying logic of Victorian England and allegorized it in her popular fiction. Read in this way, Lucy Audley—who, in violation of patriarchal law, transmutes herself from privately held Mother to Virgin-commodity—is a prototype for the she-vampires of the *fin de siècle*. Lucy's irresistible femininity is but the "talisman" of male fetishism; its lurid underside, the murderous "beautiful fiend," is poised at any moment to turn (*un*reproductive) phallicized power against men. Yet, in the various ways I have described, "Good Lady Ducayne" does not, like *Lady Audley's Secret*, rehearse this familiar paradox, but, instead, shrewdly revises it by the lights of fin de siècle mass culture. Whether by arranging marriages, authorizing male professionalism, or otherwise advising her contemporaries to *"Go and marry [their] doctors,"* what Braddon's tale unwaveringly insists is that *"It is all good Lady Ducayne's doing."* As the woman writer, capitalizing upon the latest trends in popular literature to meet the demands of an expanding mass audience—while both trends and audience were being feminized and denigrated by the emerging masculinist "high" culture of the fin de siècle—Braddon clearly allies *herself* with Lady Ducayne: vilified, female, but, in the final analysis, ascendant. If, by the end of Braddon's tale, the word "mother-in-law" has no longer any "terrors" for Herbert Stafford, it is only because a professional woman has first manipulated the signs.

WORKS CITED

Auerbach, Nina. *Woman and the Demon.* Cambridge: Harvard UP, 1982.

Baudrillard, Jean. *The Mirror of Production.* Trans. Mark Poster. St. Louis: Telos P, 1975. Extended in *For a Critique of the Political Economy of the Sign.* Trans. Charles Levin. St. Louis: Telos, 1981.

Braddon, M. E. "Good Lady Ducayne." *The Penguin Book of Vampire Stories.* Ed. Alan Ryan, NY: Penguin, 1987, 138–62.

Carlyle, Thomas. *Past and Present.* New York: New York UP, 1965.

Colley, Linda. *Britons: Forging the Nation, 1707–1837.* London: Vintage, 1996.

Corelli, Marie. *The Sorrows of Satan.* Oxford: Oxford UP, 1996.

Engels, Frederick. *Socialism: Utopian and Scientific.* In *Karl Marx and Frederick Engels; Selected Works.* New York: International, 1968.

Fraser, Derek. *The Evolution of the British Welfare State.* 2nd ed. Houndmills: Macmillan, 1984.

Gagnier, Regenia. *Idylls of the Marketplace: Oscar Wilde and the Victorian Public.* Stanford, Calif.: Stanford UP, 1986.

Gissing, George. *New Grub Street.* Harmondsworth, England: Penguin, 1987.

Greg, W. R. "Why are Women Redundant?" *National Review* (April 1862).

Grosz, Elizabeth. "Lesbian Fetishism." *Space, Time, and Perversion: Essays on the Politics of Bodies.* New York: Routledge, 1995.

Haight, Gordon S., ed. *The Victorian Portable Reader.* Harmondsworth, England: Penguin, 1972.

Hall, Jasmine Yong. "Solicitors Soliciting: The Dangerous Circulations of Professionalism in *Dracula* (1897)." *The New Nineteenth Century: Feminist Readings of Underread Victorian Fiction.* ed. Barbara Leah Harman and Susan Meyer. New York: Garland, 1996.

Heller, Tamar. "The Vampire in the House: Hysteria, Female Sexuality, and Female Knowledge in Le Fanu's 'Carmilla' (1872)." *The New Nineteenth Century: Feminist Readings of Underread Victorian Fiction.* Ed. Barbara Harman and Susan Meyer. New York : Garland, 1996. 77–95

Mrs. Humphry. *Manners for Women.* Rpt. London: Ward, Lock & Co., 1987. London: Kent, 1993. 56.

Huyssen, Andreas. *After the Great Divide: Modernism, Mass Culture, Postmodernism.* Bloomington: Indiana UP, 1986.

Irigaray, Luce. "Women on the Market." *This Sex Which Is Not One.* Trans. Catherine Porter. Ithaca, N.Y.: Cornell UP, 1985.

Langland, Elizabeth. *Nobody's Angels: Middle-Class Women and Domestic Ideology in Victorian Culture.* Ithaca: Cornell UP, 1995.

Laqueur, Thomas. "Orgasm, Generation and the Politics of Reproduction." *The Making of the Modern Body*. Ed. Catherine Gallagher and Thomas Laqueur. Berkeley: U of California P, 1987.

Ledger, Sally. "The New Woman and the Crisis of Victorianism." *Culture and Politics at the Fin de Siècle*. Ed. Sally Ledger and Scott McCracken. Cambridge: Cambridge UP, 1987. 1–41.

Marx, Karl. *Capital*, vol. 1. ed. Frederick Engels. Trans. Samuel Moore and Edward Aveling. New York: International Publishers, 1967.

McNally, Raymond. *Dracula Was a Woman*. New York: McGraw-Hill, 1983.

Mill, John Stuart. "Civilization," *Collected Works*, vol 18. Ed. J. M. Robson. Toronto: U of Toronto P, 1965–1977.

Mitchell, Sally. "Sentiment and Suffering: Women's Recreational Reading in the 1860s." *Victorian Studies* 21.1 (1977): 29–30.

Moretti, Franco. *Signs Taken for Wonders*. London: Verso, 1983.

Mueller, Hans-Eberhard. *Bureaucracy, Education and Monopoly: Civil Service Reforms in Prussia and England*. Berkeley: U of Calif P, 1984.

Palmer, A. Smythe. *The Ideal of A Gentleman* London: Routledge, 1908.

Patterson, Lee. "Literary History." *Critical Terms for Literary Study*, 2nd ed. Ed. Frank Lentricchia and Thomas McLaughlin. Chicago: U of Chicago P, 1995.

Perkin, Harold. *The Rise of Professional Society: England Since 1880*. London: Routledge, 1989.

Peterson, Audrey. *Victorian Masters of Mystery: From Wilkie Collins to Conan Doyle*. New York: Ungar, 1984.

Poovey, Mary. *Uneven Developments: The Ideological Work of Gender in Mid-Victorian England*. Chicago: U of Chicago P, 1988.

Ruskin, John. "Of Queens Gardens." *Sesame and Lilies*. London: Dent, 1944.

———. *Unto this Last and Other Writings*. Harmondsworth, England: Peguin, 1985.

Senf, Carol A. "Women and Power in 'Carmilla.'" *Gothic* 3 (1986): 29–31.

Shorter, Edward. *Bedside Manners: The Troubled History of Doctors and Patients*. New York: Simon and Schuster, 1985.

Showalter, Elaine. "Desperate Remedies: Sensation Novels of the 1860s." *The Victorian Newsletter* 49 (1976): 1–5.

———. *Sexual Anarchy: Gender and Culture at the Fin de Siècle*. New York: Viking, 1990.

Shuttleworth, Sally. "Female Circulation: Medical Discourse and Popular Advertising in the Mid-Victorian Era." *Body/Politics*. Ed. Mary Jacobus, Evelyn Fox Keller, and Sally Shuttleworth. New York: Routledge, 1990.

Todorov, Tzvetan. *The Fantastic: A Structural Approach to a Literary Genre*. Trans. Richard Howard. Cleveland: Press of Case Western Reserve U, 1973.

Walkowitz, Judith R. "Male Vice and Female Virtue: Feminism and the Politics of Prostitution in Nineteenth-Century Britain." *Powers of Desire: The Politics of Sexuality*. Ed. Ann Snitow, C. Stangell, and S. Thompson. New York: Monthly Review P, 1983.

Warwick, Alexandra. "Vampires and the Empire: Fears and Fictions of the 1890s," *Cultural Politics at the Fin de Siècle.* Ed by Sally Ledger and Scott McCracken, Cambridge: Cambridge UP, 1995. 202–20.

Wolff, Robert Lee. *Sensational Victorian: The Life and Fiction of Mary Elizabeth Braddon.* New York: Garland, 1979.

FOURTEEN

Spectral Politics: M. E. Braddon and the Spirits of Social Reform

Eve M. Lynch

In Mary Elizabeth Braddon's 1864 novel, *The Doctor's Wife,* her character Sigismund Smith, a writer of serial penny fiction, ruminates on the restrictive boundaries of producing for a sensation-hungry weekly audience when he yearns to write "a great novel." Hemmed in by the voracious demands of the plot-driven tale of crime and woe, Sigismund chafes at the necessity of maintaining temporal and factual realism in his narrative, scoffing, "If you tie me down to facts . . . I can't write at all." This brief protest serves as a reigning principle for his literary creator, Braddon herself, whose talent for writing sensational, outlandish fiction kept Victorian audiences enraptured while it made her rich. Yet the crime-filled penny dreadfuls and novels she serialized in low-brow magazines posed a problem for Braddon because they confirmed her writings as plot-driven page-turners, tied to the "facts" of highly paced, intricate schemes and allowing little room for developing overt critical commentary. Like her mouthpiece Sigismund, Braddon agitated to experiment with fiction that considered more pressing social issues, particularly in the problems she saw arising out of Victorian reform policies that ignored the private domestic trials of women and the poor. Braddon repeatedly returned in her fiction to exposing the laissez-faire individualism and complacency that allowed the wealthy and the middle classes to desert the poor and dependent women in the prosperous mid-century.

   Braddon experimented in 1866 with writing a social novel not tied to mystery and murder sensation in *The Lady's Mile,* a novel that examines the tight circumference around women's restricted lives in its trope of the celebrated carriage and bridle path in Hyde Park. The boredom of this fashionable treadmill the women traverse is likened to the dull adherence to convention, luxury and extravagant gaiety that dictate the women's narrow lives: "They go as far as they can, and then go back again." The woman who strays beyond the "palpable iron railing" that defines the Lady's Mile becomes lost in the "impenetrable forest depth" of Kensington Gardens: "But on the highway of life the boundary-line is not so clearly defined. There are women who lose themselves in some unknown region beyond the Lady's Mile, and whom we never hear of more." (13–14). Braddon's interest in women who "lose themselves in some unknown region beyond" drew her past the idle women of *The Lady's Mile* and into a broad acquaintance with the political, social and economic issues directing the lives of Victorian women of all classes.

   Braddon's use of the "unknown region" metaphor borrowed from a widely recognized image explaining economic and social divisions in England as a business of national boundaries. Gertrude Himmelfarb has noted that Victorian authors frequently testified to a chasm supposedly separating the "two nations" of England, the "low" and the "high," and located the "other" nation in a "foreign" or "unknown" country: "With predictable and monotonous regularity every parliamentary report, social novel, and journalistic exposé announced itself, and was hailed by reviewers, as an excursion into 'distant lands,' 'dark and unknown regions,' . . ." (Himmelfarb 404). For Braddon, that "unknown region beyond" increasingly came to serve as a metaphor for an "impenetrable" English domestic space that lurked side-by-side with respectable society but was silently isolated by convention, shame, and secrecy, covering up the despair of social ills haunting Victorian life.

   Robert Wolff has argued that *The Lady's Mile* was an early, singular experiment in serious social commentary, with Braddon returning to sensational murder plots in the face of her own social ostracism for her unorthodox liaison with John Maxwell. Wolff asserts that Braddon set aside her desire to protest social conventionalities when savage personal criticism was leveled at her own life, returning instead to writing the popular fiction of graphic and incidental sensation until the mid-seventies, when she once again sounded an insistent radical note. I argue, however, that Braddon did not abandon her radical social criticism during this period, as can be seen in numerous short stories that turn their interest on the plight of characters caught in social and economic, rather than criminal, desperation. If her novels returned to the lurid and improbable tales of murder, her social writing transmuted into a newly popularized form that could carry the weight of her critical examination while appearing to deliver the quick thrills of popular sensation that brought her audiences and income. Throughout the sixties, and particularly after she took over the editing and writing of *Belgravia* in 1866, Braddon was able to indulge her desire for exploring the undercurrents of social problems within a genre ideally suited to adapting a double effect, the uncanny ghost story. The sudden and enormous popularity of supernatural tales, especially the Christmas ghost stories, provided Braddon with a venue for exploiting the sentimental genre of the social/ psychological tale while maintaining her audience's desire for ghastly effect. This vehicle allowed Braddon to deflect the sensational aura of murder, criminal scheming, insanity, and violence into an arena of obscure supernatural agency, one not bound by the facts of everyday life and journalistic sensation, thus retaining the intrigue and suspense of a good murder story while paradoxically suppressing the expected emphasis on crime and detection. Discovery and exposure continued to drive the plot toward a satisfaction of psychological tension, but the effect was enhanced by suspending and subverting the sensation over the course of the story, rather than producing a series of dramatic, revelatory climaxes.

With her audience satisfied that the chill would still arrive in the dénouement, Braddon could indulge her exploration of the unmarked "boundary-line" dividing the public world of societal conventions from the "unknown region beyond" that lay hidden in private frustration as a reminder of English social and psychological dislocation. Those murky regions were the ambiguous and fluctuating outlines of inequities Braddon saw persisting in the affluent decades of high Victorianism in spite of political reform, economic expansion, and philanthropic volunteerism. Braddon's ghostly tales repeatedly expose social inequalities from within the apparent comfort of home and hearth, suggesting that the parameters of the unknown regions shadowing Victorian life are more familiarly and cannily drawn than the spatial metaphor implies: in the ghost story, the "other side" typically conjoins the mysterious and the material, the visible and the invisible, in the same enclosed, domestic arena. To this end, Braddon's tales are filled with characters culled from the lower orders, especially servants from the regions "below stairs" whose social position in the house was analogous to the spectral apparition that haunted it: like the ghost, the servant was *in* the home but not *of* it, occupying a position tied to the workings of the house itself, isolated from the free bonds of communication and felicity of the family. Like the spectral spirit, servants were outsiders in the home secretly observing the forbidden world of respectability. And like the supernatural influence quietly imposing its own order on the will of the domestic inhabitants, the servant in the house suggested a bilateral, silent estate of discontent and dis-ease cohabiting the same physical space as the family but imagined by that family as immaterial and invisible.

The class and spiritual discontinuity represented in the household relationships gave Braddon a domestic population through which she could survey the disturbing landscape of English social reform. Freed from the "facts" of realism, crime, and detection, Braddon could conjure the spirits of social crime that continued to haunt women and the poor dispossessed of equal standing and a voice in the affairs of the nation that affected their lives. Supernatural stories turning on ghosts, mesmerism, fantastical occurrences, and inexplicable omens—the stock in trade of tales of domestic "possession"—were readily paired with the dilemmas of those dispossessed members of the household lacking property, education, social standing, and independence. It is a mark of her commitment to social critique that Braddon's ghostly tales often refuse to resolve themselves in easy spectral explanation: in the end, Braddon frequently remains ambiguous about whether the fantastical element that seems to haunt each story is adequate to account for the devastation that ensues. Rather, she suggests that more worldly and human forces, such as poverty, greed, pride, and complacency, are what haunt the characters and reform their fates.

That Braddon turned to this genre in the years surrounding the second Reform Bill of 1867 speaks to the ways in which a spirit of national social reform, one that could give voice to the outer regions of the politically disenfranchised, enacts a "spirit" of literary reformulation that voices her social conscience. It is not surprising that the decades in which this ghostly genre exploded in popularity also saw an overhaul of social reform leading to the Education Act of 1870, the Married Women's Property Acts of 1870 and 1874, the Custody of Infants Act of 1873, the Matrimonial Causes Act of 1878, the act of 1875 enabling universities to admit women, the Medical Education Act of 1876, and the acts of 1869 and 1870 granting some women the franchise at local government levels. A host of legislative statutes responded to insistent voices that haunted England over national education, the rights of married women, the rights of mothers, and, on various levels, the enfranchisement of a broader, more democratic spectrum of the country. The Reform Bill of 1867 became a national centerpiece for generating support for social improvement and political action, philanthropic, and educative projects. In taking up the ghost-story genre in the 1860s and 1870s, Braddon found a home for her criticism that could coexist with—and even enhance—the sensational plot. The ghosts that haunt her stories from this period serve for Braddon as emblems of what Victorian society is unwilling to "see" in its social condition: laissez-faire liberalism in home policy divides the Victorian social realm into isolated "worlds" of rich and poor, dependent and independent, public and private, visible and invisible. The supernatural spirits in her ghost stories function as insistent memory of what is being suppressed socially or repressed psychologically in Victorian society. Schelling's definition of *das Unheimliche* as the "name for everything that *ought* to have remained . . . hidden and secret and has become visible" identifies the process through which societal problems continued to surface: social reform in the first half of the century that *ought* to have resolved England's problems had merely suppressed them, Braddon warns, and like the spectral hauntings of the house, the problems arise with untimely and forbidding insistence.

Braddon's ghost stories from the 1860s delineate the anxiety of dispossession that permeated the estate of dependent women and domestic workers. The theme of the woman detached from communal help, dependent and helpless to direct her own fate, is most fully developed in "Ralph the Bailiff," a novelette that ran serially in *St. James's Magazine* in 1861 and formed the lead story in Braddon's first collection of short stories published in 1867. In this tale, the woman must face the demon that haunts her because of earlier hidden crimes of her husband. Her isolation in the home becomes a form of terror that magnifies her desperation, threatening to drive her to madness. The husband, a weak-willed Lincolnshire farmer who had secretly poisoned his elder brother to inherit the family property, Grey Farm, falls prey to his ubiquitous servant, Ralph, the bailiff, who blackmails his master for his crime. The bailiff shadows his employer's every move, eavesdropping on his conversations, taking on the office of butler to control the dining room, taking over the accounting books for the farm to control the money, and insinuating himself into every decision made until the master falls "under the thrall of his inseparable retainer." When the farmer marries a young orphan, Jenny Trevor, a rector's ward, she becomes haunted by hallucinations in the dead of the night and hissing whispers of her husband's guilt. Extending the realm of his power, the bailiff overwhelms the young wife with his sinister demeanor and his insolent rejection of her authority as mistress. Under the pressure of this influence and lacking trust in her husband, Jenny sickens in feverish despair and determines to run away from home. Instead, she finds herself imprisoned on the lonely farm by the bailiff and descends into madness.

Alarmed by a dream one night in which she imagines herself holding a wailing infant who is strangling her and dragging her down, the young wife awakens to hear the low wail of a baby in the house, recalling to her mind the ghost stories attached to Grey Farm. Following the wail of the child through the house, Jenny eavesdrops through a keyhole to hear her husband's conversation with the bailiff and Martha, Ralph's sister and Grey Farm's former housekeeper, and learns the source of the servant's power: he has blackmailed his master with the knowledge of the old murder; but even more destructive to Jenny's security is the bailiff's revelation of his master's secret earlier marriage to his servant Martha, who has borne him a son. For their continued silence, Ralph demands full entitlement to the farm as well as the dowry that Jenny Trevor had brought into her marriage. Devastated by this betrayal that leaves her status as wife null, her home lost, and her dowry confiscated, Jenny flees the farm and is taken back into her old home at the rector's, where she soon learns of her husband's suicide the night of her escape. Grey Farm, now in Ralph's possession with the rest of the estate, is sold by the bailiff, who emigrates to Australia to set up his own farm, complete with servants, his sister, and his former master's infant son.

This story turns on reversals of authority and possession between husband and wife and between master and servant. In fact, Braddon interweaves the theme of "possession"—both in its spectral and material senses—between the seemingly supernatural, metaphysical authority characters hold over each other, and the legally sanctioned authority they hold over the physical and economic properties of the estate. Jenny becomes "possessed" by hallucinations and the supernatural "hissing whispers reminding her of her husband's guilt." But it is her possession by him *as her husband* that most confounds her:

> "Why had she married Dudley Carleon?"
>
> She sometimes asked herself this question, as if she had suddenly awoke from a long sleep to find herself in a strange country.
>
> She did not love him, she did not even admire him, but she had allowed him to gain so strong an influence over her, that it was only now and then she remembered this. (23)

In the somnolent "strange country" of her marriage, that "unknown region beyond" that she belatedly awakens to, the wife is mesmerized by the "influence" of her pernicious husband, an influence that borders on the demonic. His psychological hold over her, however, is made more concrete in the bailiff's control over her movements, confining her to the home and, finally, to her room, until she feels herself under an "unseen influence" that is "sapping" her very life. The marital "strange country" she inhabits is cut off from communal security by the bailiff, who becomes an "impassable barrier between the mistress of Grey Farm and the world without."

Complicating this theme of domestic possession is a reversal of power in the relationship between master and servant that deranges the barriers separating the classes and defining the family: the farmer's secret marriage to the housekeeper and the existence of her son as legitimate heir to his father's property adumbrates the division between these two parallel domestic worlds. The revelation that Martha the housekeeper—and not Jenny—is actually the legally sanctioned wife transposes the mistress-servant relationship: significantly, it is Jenny who is "crouching at the threshold of the door," spying through the keyhole to observe her fall from authority, while the housekeeper sits inside by the fireplace with the master, holding his infant son (37). This reversal of domestic portraits reveals the maternal economy of the woman's place at the hearth: aggravated by her dream of the infant strangling her that had brought her to his keyhole discovery, Jenny is confronted in the fireside scene by her own childlessness and loss of authority. With her dowry left in her husband's hands, Jenny sees her assets slipping out of his control, to be passed on to the housekeeper's son if the bailiff doesn't appropriate it sooner. Dispossessed of her husband and familial position, Jenny is finally deprived of the only property she has brought into her marriage.

Braddon's tale of possession and dispossession offers little sympathy to the lower orders, who are here portrayed as sinister, malevolent demons corrupting the household and destroying her economic position. That Braddon allows the bailiff to escape with his master's property to Australia underscores her portrait of him as criminal and social outcast. At the same time, however, Braddon clearly shows the husband's weakness as haunting Jenny's marriage and devastating the family: he, after all, has killed his own brother and abrogated the power of head of household, thereby threatening not just his own position, but his wife's as well. For Jenny, who already suspects her husband's crime of murder, the social crime of secretly marrying his housekeeper and bigamously remarrying to obscure the status of mistress and wife has more devastating consequences. With both the physically intrusive bailiff and the secretly invasive housekeeper reformulating the terms of familial structure, the foundations of lineage and inheritance are distorted, corrupting the children of marriage into terrifying incubi that strangle the legal rights of the woman. Braddon directs her sympathies into the plight of the woman with no marital property rights and no familial control, dependent on her husband and a fragile legal footing that can shift in the dead of the night to leave her destitute and stripped of all domestic posture. In the insanity that descends on the mistress locked in domestic impotence Braddon suggests that the secret crime of marriage is the madness of possession that conjures the wife into an unknown region isolated from community, robbing her of the protection of society, and dispossessing her of property, authority, and her own mind.

Braddon's criticism of the possession and dispossession threatening women is given a more satirical twist in a related ghost story published the same year in *Temple Bar,* "The Mystery at Fernwood." The plot of this tale stems from the vexed inheritance of two aristocratic brothers, twins who have been separated since an accident early in infancy. One brother, William Wendale, had been brain-damaged when his nurse dropped him from her arms; kept hidden in a remote wing of the family mansion, he is passed off by his parents and devoted sister Lucy as a distant, poor, mad relative. His twin brother Laurence has been kept sheltered from knowledge of their relationship. It is only when Laurence's fiancée, Isabel, comes to meet the family that the twin double emerges from his isolated quarters, slipping past his caretakers to wreak havoc on the domestic tranquillity. Once free, the lunatic brother murders his twin for whom, the doctors speculate, he felt "some morbid feeling respecting the likeness between the two boys" (95). Blame for this lapse in guardianship that terminates an aristocratic line comes to rest on the valet who guards William and on Lucy, who has consigned her life to caring for her invalid brother and guarding the secret from his healthy twin.

As in "Ralph the Bailiff," Braddon shows the household haunted by an uncanny influence that turns out to have foundation in the family itself. Laurence Wendale is indifferent to his familial connections, paying virtually no attention to his mysterious relative and portraying him as an "unseen presence in the house," as insignificant as the nurse and valet who watch over him like colorless, wan phantoms. To fiancée Isabel, who unexpectedly is visited by William one night in her room, the mysterious man is a "weird" and "horrible shadow," a contorted and "phantom" image of her lover, one she half-consciously suspects of rivaling the heir to the ancestral estate. For the future master and mistress of Fernwood, this domestic interloper is an eerie and mortifying vestige of familial discontinuity buried away in the house, uncomfortably estranged by fraternal indifference and pride.

But if William is the spectral reminder of too many heirs, it is Lucy, the twins' half-sister, who occupies Braddon's attention as the "redundant" sibling. Lucy is devoted to caring for William and keeps constant attendance on him—"nothing will induce her to leave the house for fear his nurse or his valet should fail in their care of him" (75). Bound to serving the family secret, Lucy's life has been sacrificed to watching over her ruined brother and protecting his healthy sibling from knowledge of this defect in the Wendale ancestry. Her self-effacement in this task becomes a model for Isabel's future role as wife, suggesting that the position of all family women, as Jenny finds in "Ralph the Bailiff," is built on secrecy and deception. As the marriage approaches, Lucy decides the time has arrived to bring her new "sister" into the dark secret so that Isabel may also become a protector of the heir: "'We found that, by constant care and watchfulness, it was possible to conceal all from Laurence, and up to this hour we have done so. But it is perhaps better that you should know all; for you will be able to aid us in keeping the knowledge from Laurence.'" (89). Braddon suggests in this arrangement the extraordinary amount of regulatory fuss and labor—attendants, parents, siblings, wife—that it takes to produce a viable successor to the family seat.

Braddon reserves her sympathy, however, to probe the cost of this practice to the unmarried sister, whose role in the home fades into a shadowy background. Physical and psychological guardian of her brothers, Lucy seems to the future mistress of Fernwood as a benevolent but ghostly presence in the house: she is the "ruling spirit of the house" who keeps everything from "fall[ing] utterly to decay" (78). To Laurence, his sister is a "banished angel treading this earth in human form," a "guardian spirit" of the home (72); he has trouble assigning to her a substantial, corporeal significance: she is as immaterial as his other mysterious relation who inexplicably comes with the home. Isabel's aunt reminds her niece that this "old maid" will become part of the estate inheritance one day: "You will find her of inestimable use when you are married—that is to say, if you ever have to manage this great rambling place'" (78). Dispossessed of her own life and independence, "possessing" the house and bound to it like an ethereal guardian, Lucy is in turn a possession to be inherited, a fixture that goes with the house like the nurse and the valet, all of them watching over the threshold to the mysterious region beyond the family quarters where William is hidden. Just as the valet has "grown grey" in his servitude, Lucy will also fade into the background of the family and household, furnishing a spectral domestic realm until, as with William, the family ceases to think of her at all. Braddon exposes the pathetic self-denial needed to sustain this absent presence in the house: in the end, Lucy blames her brother's death on "the imprudent absence" of the valet and herself (95). Prudence dictates these homely, spectral guardians never actually give up the post, only that they *appear invisible*—like ghosts—in their duty.

At the heart of the mystery of Fernwood and the Wendales lies a hollow core, a vacancy that is only fleetingly detected in the shades of rivalry and neglect that quietly eat away at the family. Like Lucy, "extra" women serve to hold together the family, devoting their lives and their resources to shoring up the flagging patriarchal estate. Fernwood, a decrepit estate neglected by the noble Wendales, will come with a meager yearly allowance, but it will take the forty-thousand-pound inheritance from a maiden aunt to bring it back to life. The present master is "sinking slowly into decay" (73) and his wife has neglected her position in favor of reading novels and sneaking in to see her invalid son each day, "as stealthily as if she were paying a secret visit to some condemned criminal" (75).

The future heir promises his fiancée to devote himself to "reforming this dreary household, which has sunk into habitual despondency from sheer easy fortune and want of vexation" (73). But Laurence is a "spoilt boy" and "dissipated," and his indifference to his distant relative belies a commitment to regenerating familial vitality. Braddon quietly points her finger at the abstracted and exploitative notions of family that have directed too much care into the hands of peripheral dependents: the trusteeship of the Wendales rests in the single women and servants who warrant capital and custody, tending the secrets and replenishing the fortunes to secure the privileges of the patriarchy. Braddon suggests the family estate in England is riding on the laurels of its dependents and "extra" women. At the center of the problem she sees a complex web of psychological and social misappropriation of privilege: inheritance practices that favor one male heir and render siblings dependent; parental indifference and laziness that squander the responsibility of family custody; dissipation of wealth in a suffocatingly enclosed, decaying world; and overreliance on unmarried women to secure the fortunes for men.

Braddon's spectral tales in the decade of the 1860s give way gradually to more vividly constructed apparitions while at the same time sharpening the focus of her social criticism that lies in wait behind those shadows. Where her stories from the sixties construct a mortified sense of dispossession that faced middle- and upper-class women in the home, her tales from the next decade examine the travails of women in service and the poor. This is not to say that Braddon comfortably left the manorial hearth to scour the ghosts and skeletons lurking in the pantries of peasant cottages: she continued to view her spectacles, if not always from the safe distance of the estate grounds, at least from the fireplace of the comfortable Victorian home. But her concern that the wealthy ranks of society were deserting their responsibility to the poor and dependents, became more deeply entrenched and caustic. In "At Chrighton Abbey," first published in *Belgravia* in 1871, Braddon links the theme of charity for the poor to the fragile position of the governess who is only charitably placed in the home. Braddon critiques systems of private philanthropy that are dependent on the integrity of the landed rich: she shows a spirit of voluntary responsibility for the poor carried on by the disinherited governess and servants while a rising mood of arrogance, indifference, and economic isolationism plagues the rich. Her 1879 tale, "The Shadow in the Corner," shows an incisive exposition of the educational and class factors quite literally forcing poor women into a corner. In this story an impoverished orphan is hired as drudge in a research scientist's lonely house, where her own intelligence is compressed between the ignorant and superstitious jealousy of the old servant couple who supervise her and the self-absorbed, elite rationality of her educated master. That she has no way out of this corner becomes Braddon's most dire criticism of class prejudice that undercuts national education and employment of poor women. Both stories subtly convert their ghostly themes into overt censure of English class exclusivity and intellectual complacency.

"At Chrighton Abbey" is narrated by Sarah Chrighton, who had been orphaned twelve years earlier and forced into earning her living abroad as a governess. A distant relative of the Chrighton family, Sarah had been reared by her father, a rector in the parish church within the park walls, but his death had left his educated daughter penniless and homeless. Sparing the family the "degradation" of a relative sent "out to service," Sarah had obtained situations far off in Vienna and St. Petersburg so as not to "inflict shame upon the ancient house to which I belonged." Sarah's only close relative, a brother, was also sent out to foreign regions, where he is employed in the Indian Civil Service. Desiring to revisit England and her "dear old country home" once more, Sarah accepts an invitation from the Squire's wife to spend the Christmas holiday at the Abbey, where she is welcomed into the house by the familiar old butler and housekeeper.

The Squire's household celebrates the festive holiday under a strain of domestic tension: the Chrighton heir, Edward, has engaged to marry a proud, disdainful young heiress, Julia Tremaine. When the servants and family join together in the spirit of yuletide charity to prepare and disperse gifts of clothing and food to the neighboring poor, Miss Tremaine refuses this duty, scorning active engagement with the lives of the local poor who depend on the Squire's bounty and causing a rift in her impending marital union. Irritated at her misanthropy, Edward accepts a hunting invitation at a friend's estate to effect a temporary separation; the governess unsuccessfully attempts to bring the dispute to an end, but the headstrong Edward and the obstinate Miss Tremaine refuse to yield their pride and positions. Discouraged, Sarah retires to her room and falls into a reverie in front of the fire. Startled awake by an "unearthly" sound of a huntsman's horn, Sarah sees in the courtyard below a noiseless, ghostly parade of scarlet coats and hounds, gentlemen and grooms, riding into the stables that have not been used for more than half a century. Anticipating that the housekeeper, Mrs. Marjorum, will understand the meaning of the ghostly apparition, Sarah runs down the back staircase to the servants' quarters, where she learns that the spectral appearance of the ancestral Squire and his hunting pack always warns of the impending death of the next Chrighton heir. Chagrined by her willingness to believe the housekeeper, Sarah chides herself for being swayed by the superstition, telling herself: " 'It is natural enough for an old servant to believe in such things . . . but for me—an educated woman of the world—preposterous folly' " (182). Yet fearing for Edward, Sarah subdues her pride and discloses the ghostly omen to his fiancée, suffering the young woman's "unconcealed disdain" for Sarah's superstitious inclination and failing to effect a reconciliation of the couple. Edward departs for his hunting engagement and when he fails to return at New Years, the Chrightons learn of Edward's death that day in a steeplechase. Chastened by this unyielding result of her pride, Julia Tremaine retires to her father's home to become a "very angel of mercy and compassion amongst the poor of the neighbourhood" (188). Through the years, the governess returns on occasion to visit her distant family and her ancestral home.

Braddon begins this story by extending her earlier theme of dispossession, updated here in the governess who has lost her home and must earn her living abroad. Like her brother in the Indian Civil Service, Sarah has lost both hearth and native country, returning as a visitor from her expatriation in the outer regions beyond English society. Braddon directly critiques the Victorian practice of promoting the emigration of governesses to reduce the ranks of single women in England. From the middle of the century, benevolent organizations such as the National Benevolent Emigration Society, the Society for the Employment of Women, and the Female Middle-Class Emigration Society regularly sent women out to the colonies to improve employment and marriage prospects (Peterson 16–17). As part of a larger mission to dispose of "redundant" women in England, the project receives Braddon's quiet censure for securing "respectable" and "invisible" employment of women—much as the Indian Civil Service employs "extra" men like Sarah's brother—that selectively culls the ranks of an impoverished and disinherited middle class. Throughout the story Braddon juxtaposes the noble spirit of the governess to the idle foolishness of the young heiress, pointing up the arbitrary fortunes that mark some women as marriageable, and therefore worth keeping in England, and less fortunate women as "extra," to be banished from sight like spectral wanderers.

Crossing and recrossing the British border, negotiating between visibility and invisibility, Sarah Chrighton inhabits a ghostly realm of English consciousness. Patrick Brantlinger has argued that this policy of emigration has "complex, unconscious interconnections" with British imperialist ideology and the rage of occultism that thrived in the latter part of the Victorian era: conquering the borderland between the "foreign" realms of territory and death posited a way of controlling frontiers as English anxiety about empire became more shrill (Brantlinger 249). Certainly Sarah's exile out to the eastern edges of European culture signals an English desire to harbor its "excess" populations in a world commerce. But Sarah's dislocation is not only physical and commercial, it is also social: she has lost her standing in the English home. When she returns to Chrighton Abbey, she is welcomed by the old butler and the housekeeper, not the Abbey's mistress, indicating Sarah's warm but precarious place in the Chrighton household. Sarah is settled in to her room by the housekeeper and listens to the old woman's foreboding concern about the haughty Miss Tremaine before dining alone in the breakfast room. Only after this lengthy reinduction into Chrighton Abbey is Sarah greeted by her relation and hostess, Fanny Chrighton, and brought to meet the family in the drawing-room. The extended entrance into the heart of both the story and the family domain allows Braddon to point up Sarah's position in the household as tenuously poised between the family and the household domestics. In her exile she has acquired the subnatural characteristics of other ex-centric figures in the home. Like the housekeeper who can see into the impending family strife, Sarah also "sees" the family's fate in the ghostly apparition that appears below her bedroom window. As outsiders with a peripheral view into the family, these domestic onlookers are placed like ghosts themselves, inhabiting the ancient passageways and watching the fortunes of the family, but remaining like Sarah, "quiet spectator[s] of life's great drama, disturbed by no feverish desire for an active part in the play" (165).

From her particular position as governess and "foreign" outsider, Sarah has crossed over both social and national barriers into the unknown region beyond English society and then returned to the family hold, securing a position that allows her to "mediate," both supernaturally and socially, between the world of the household servants and that of the established gentry. Her outsider status as emigrant and servant in foreign families allows her to see into the English home from a more distant lens that is at once worldly and domestic. It is the governess to whom the ghostly omen appears because she can break through class reserve and turn to the servants below stairs to uncover the meaning of the spectral warning. Braddon explores the class conflict of this mediation through the focus of Sarah's "careful" education (161). The governess insists that she is an "utter unbeliever in all ghostly things—ready to credit any possibility rather than suppose that I had been looking upon shadows" (178). Yet she still breaks out in a "cold sweat" upon seeing the apparition and turns to the housekeeper "below stairs" for help. That her fear leads her to the servants' stairwell and Mrs. Marjorum's room, rather than to the front stairs and the family, underscores the class boundaries drawn around types of knowledge, with superstition and the irrational seen as outmoded, ignorant belief systems coveted by the lowest classes: as Miss Tremaine disdainfully reminds her, "'[Y]ou don't mean to tell me that you believe in such nonsense—ghosts and omens, and old woman's folly like that!'" (182).

But Sarah also "despise[s]" herself for "such weakness" that allows her "mind and nerves" to overwhelm how rationally she interprets the scene. It may be "natural enough" for the old housekeeper to credit ghosts, but an "educated woman of the world" cannot be seen to accept such "preposterous folly" (181–82). After all, Sarah's independent living had been earned off of her "industriously cultivated"—and therefore *not* natural—education in the "usual modern accomplishments" (161). But in her attenuated posture at the Abbey, those drawing room credentials remain inadequate to account to Sarah for more than class bias and discretion: "I had a lurking conviction that it would be well for me not to mention that scene to any member of the family till I had taken counsel with some one who knew the secrets of Chrighton Abbey" (178). The secret knowledge of the house is cordoned off by the condescension and pride of "cultivated" knowledge that represents Sarah's only familial inheritance.

The governess' willingness to risk humiliation by exposing her social weakness is juxtaposed with Julia Tremaine's unbending arrogance. Her uncharitable attitude toward the poor who depend on the *largesse* of the Squire's family reveals a myopic willfulness innate in the upper classes that threatens to blind them to the surrounding social body, fading the poor into disinherited souls spectrally inhabiting the estate of the rich. Julia is set to one day replace Fanny Chrighton as *châtelaine* of the Abbey, and her pride would end a tradition of economic responsibility filtered through communal involvement. Braddon critiques the young woman's petulant, snobbish remove that detaches personal obligation and transforms social responsibility into a bureaucratic civility:

> "I don't like poor people. . . . I am not *simpatica,* I suppose. And then I cannot endure their stifling rooms. The close faint odour of their houses gives me a fever. And again, what is the use of visiting them? It is only an inducement to them to become hypocrites. Surely it is better to arrange on a sheet of paper what it is just and fair for them to have . . . and let them receive the things from some trustworthy servant. In that case, there need be no cringing on one side, and no endurance on the other." (173)

Braddon would not have a tradition of private philanthropy and social responsibility transfer from the hands of the wealthy into an anonymous, institutional system of welfare that solidifies further alienation between the classes.

Joining the recurrent debate about "two nations" isolated from each other and reduced to an impersonal cash nexus, Braddon comes down clearly on the Tory side of maintaining class connections through human relations and social involvement between classes. The author sees the active and humanized involvement of patronage as part of a long-standing and mutually constitutive social exchange that would be broken down by institutional, detached modes of public charity that absolve the wealthy of personally engaging their poorer neighbors. Julia Tremaine's scorn for looking in on the lives of the Abbey tenants is subtly balanced against the generosity of the Chrighton household domestics who unflinchingly—and sympathetically—watch over the weary secrets of the upper class. The young woman's reaction against the annual "point of union between the cottage and the great house" (173) may be honest, Braddon suggests, but it is cruel and inhumane, and those qualities will erode the foundations not only of estate and State, but of family as well. In contrast to Julia's detachment that blinds her to the lower orders, Sarah's ability to cross over crucial social boundaries allows her to "see" the fate of the wealthy English family fatally isolating itself from its dependent neighbors and the poor. Braddon suggests in the governess' view down from her window to the ghostly scene that it is only by crossing over the borders of class and national ideologies that the shadowy body of humanity below can be "seen."

Braddon again returns to the class distinctions isolating ways of seeing and forms of knowledge in her 1879 story, "The Shadow in the Corner." In this ghost story, she critiques a system that reserves educational resources to the wealthy while ignoring those who must earn their own living in miserable domestic labor. Michael Bascom, a retired university professor of natural science who lives for his quiet and lonely research labors, occupies the old house at Wildheath Grange with his two elderly servants, Daniel Skegg and his wife. Skegg hires a "waif and stray," Maria, the recently orphaned daughter of a small tradesman, to help his wife out as a maid-of-all-work. When Maria turns out to be a pleasant, intelligent young woman, the master takes an interest in the "pretty thing" (4) dusting and straightening his books. But after her first night in the house, Maria begins to sicken and grow pale and attributes the problem to a nightmarish shadow of a hanged man that arises in the predawn hours on the wall of her lonely attic room, awakening her early each day and disappearing at broad daylight. The master determines to expose Maria's fears as irrational by sleeping in the room himself. When he is awakened by the shadow that appears in the corner, he too feels weighted down by an "agonising memory of a life wasted; the stings of humiliation and disgrace, shame, ruin" (9). In the full morning light, however, he despises himself for succumbing to the strange sensation, and when Skegg suspects that his master has also seen the phantom, Bascom boasts of an uninterrupted, restful night's sleep and retreats to his solitary studies in proud embarrassment, loath to let his servant think that he is also superstitious. Maria, informed by the jealous servant that her master denies seeing the apparition and thinks her a fool, returns to her garret room and in the early morning hangs herself in the corner.

In this tale Braddon criticizes the way education continues, in spite of national reforms, to be the narrow reserve of the wealthy, isolating classes and endangering poor young women. Further, she suggests that the scientific rationality that underlies educative ideology is an unfeeling, cold basis for categorizing and controlling knowledge, and that in the end this rationality is just as open to prejudice and self-serving application as the superstitious belief systems it replaces. The airy elitism of Bascom's "fanatic" love of scientific research is shown to be wholly inadequate when the scientist faces the inexplicable shadow in the corner: he ultimately denies his own eyes and experience in the attic in order to uphold his authority over his servants and maintain a strict division of knowledge and rank between classes. At the same time Braddon suggests that the obtuse ignorance of the selfish old servants abuses the plight of rural girls who have few opportunities to get out from under the drudgery of serving other people.

Maria's education and work life are paired in this story with her master's to suggest the "heavy burden of care" that weighs her down and contrasts her "wasted" life toiling in Wildheath Grange with the comfortable ease of her employer: the "stings of humiliation and disgrace, shame, [and] ruin" (9) that worry Bascom in his night in the garret room seem self-pitying echoes of the real humiliation and ruin a life of drudgery causes Maria. The deathly shadow that forms on the wall in the early predawn recalls the dreary hours of the Victorian maid-of-all-work: like her real-life counterpart, Maria is also up early cleaning in Bascom's study and then "disappearing" in broad daylight: "Whatever work she did there was done early in the morning, before the scholar's breakfast" (4). As the Victorian maidservant, Maria labors out of sight, like a ghostly agency moving the tables and chairs, tidying the books and emptying the grates, and disappearing to the "other side" of the house for most of the day. Braddon asks us to compare the days of these two workers, the scholar and the drudge, to see the common waste that confronts each: Maria's dusting of the volumes of books in Bascom's library is immediately compared to Bascom's "dry-as-dust career" as a natural scientist (3–4). But it is Maria who is finally worked into the deadly corner; Bascom, fleeing from the "melancholy fate" that meets Maria, ends his days at Oxford, "where he found the society of congenial minds, and the books he loved" (11). Braddon suggests that the consequences of a wasted life take their toll more brutally on the poor working girl whose "corner" is not a cloistered shelter of intellectual retreat, but a numbing boredom and exhaustion caused by tedious days that begin at unholy, and unhealthy, hours.

Maria's modest education is shown to be the crux of the problems she faces making a living. She had been educated by her father, who "spared no expense" in giving her "as good an education as a tradesman's daughter need wish for" (4). Yet both Bascom and the servant Skegg agree that her education is an impediment to her domestic work: Skegg growls that Maria's father was a "fool" to educate her "above her station" and Bascom concedes that this makes a "bad bargain" for Skegg and his wife: "'You don't want a young lady to clean kettles and pans,'" Bascom tells his servant (3). Education, it seems, is fine for the master, but neither man wants the charwoman to entertain such lofty pursuits. Writing at the end of the first decade of compulsory education, Braddon sharply exposes the lingering effects of a national ambivalence about educating young girls whose prospects remain tied to domestic labor. In rural England, Braddon suggests, little has changed since passage of the Education Act of 1870. The fate of serving girls remained dismally unchanged since the prior decade when, as one commentator had noted, rural complaints about the "weakness" of girls in domestic service was directly attributed to their education:

> Farmers' wives complain that girls of the present day are weaker than they used to be twenty or thirty years ago. They attribute this weakness, whether rightly or wrongly, to the effects of "schooling;" and in some parts of the country a pound a year extra wages is given to a girl who cannot read, as that is a security that her constitution has not been injured by too much study. It must be allowed, that five hours a day of sedentary work, even in a well-ventilated school room, is a bad preparation for a life of incessant activity. (*Englishwoman's Review* 18)

Without a purpose for her education, Maria's careful preparation can only end in futile desperation. But if Maria's background is perceived as overeducating her for work, her belief in the ghost is also seen by the men as ruinous, an annoying sign of undereducation and rural ignorance: Bascom admonishes her to get "these silly notions" out of her head or she "will never do for the work-a-day world" (5). For rural women, the "work-a-day world" wants neither superstition nor education: her body is all that is required of her—her mind is best left empty.

Yet if Maria is caught in an untenable position between her mind and her body, her education and her labors, Braddon suggests that Bascom's own education has failed to prepare him for the world he inhabits as well. A professor at the university for ten years before retiring to his aloof studies at Wildheath Grange, Bascom is absorbed in work that seem as barren as Maria's. If her lot employs her body and wastes her mind, he is unable to return from the intellectual desert he inhabits to fully comprehend the living body next to him. Confused by the "fair" and "delicate" girl with "translucent skin" and "soft and pleasing accents issu[ing] from those rose-tinted lips," he cannot respond humanely and retreats to his "considerations about dry bones," wondering about her as "a creature of a species hitherto unknown to him" (4). His training and disposition as a "stern materialist" living among his books restrict his view so that Maria is to him a "fellow-creature" to be dissected, studied, and finally "conquered":

> For him the universe, with all its inhabitants, was a great machine, governed by inexorable laws. To such a man the idea of a ghost was simply absurd—as absurd as the assertion that two and two make five, or that a circle can be formed of a straight line. Yet he had a kind of dilettante interest in the idea of a mind which could believe in ghosts. The subject offered an amusing psychological study. This poor little pale girl, now, had evidently got some supernatural terror into her head, which could only be conquered by rational treatment. (7)

Braddon shows little tolerance for the fixed laws and "rational treatment" that categorize and conquer with indifference, ignoring the corporeal and emotional qualities of human experience. She portrays such rationality as a cooler but equally brusque version of the "perpetual warfare with spiders and beetles" that Mrs. Skegg carries out in the solitude of the kitchen she "rules over" (3). The lowly species of creatures that enter each of these private, enclosed empires—both Mrs. Skegg's and Bascom's—meet equally indifferent and arbitrary authority that witlessly destroys them.

Braddon shows in Maria's plight the futility of educating young women if they are to remain locked into drudge work surrounded by both high and low ignorance. Without gainful employment that considered them as more than mere bodies to be exhausted in despairing conditions, orphaned girls and dependent women—regardless of education—would not find a way out of the corner in which they were trapped. The jealous servant Skegg ironically cuts to Braddon's point when he complains, "Education might be hanged for him, if this was all it led to" (8). Clearly for Maria, whose life is wasted in dreary, menial work, education *is hanged* in the lonely garret corner of the scholar's home.

Braddon's ghost stories served during this period to provide her with a successful outlet for directing her growing discontent with social conditions in England. By 1882 and publication of her Christmas story,

"Flower and Weed," in *Mistletoe Bough,* Braddon had moved into social commentary that, as Wolff notes, "barely conceals its bitter social commentary on the behavior of the upper classes" (288). Her writing career increasingly continued to explicate the need for well-planned reform of philanthropic, educational, and economic conditions. If the earlier years of her career had been haunted by her own precarious social position that left her open to attack, she quite made up for it in her later career when she no longer feared recrimination could spoil her success. But her commitment to reforming the outlines of those "unknown regions beyond" the visible realm of Victorian society had remained a constant, provocative motivation for her commentary. The ghostly tales of these years had served as a fantastic arena for Braddon to cut herself loose from the "facts," as Sigismund Smith had remonstrated, so that she could write the truth of the stories that haunted her imagination.

WORKS CITED

Braddon, Mary Elizabeth. "At Chrighton Abbey." *Milly Darrell, and Other Tales* (1871; London, 1873). Rpt. *Victorian Ghost Stories: An Oxford Anthology,* ed. Michael Cox and R. A. Gilbert Oxford: Oxford UP, 1991. 163. References are to this edition.

———. *The Doctor's Wife.* 1864. London: Ward, Lock & Tyler, 1890.

———. "The Mystery at Fernwood." *Temple Bar* (Nov.–Dec. 1861). Rpt. *Ralph the Bailiff and Other Stories.* London: Ward, Lock & Tyler, 1867. References are to this edition.

———. *The Lady's Mile.* London: Ward, Lock & Tyler, 1866.

———. "Ralph the Bailiff." *St. James's Magazine* (April, May, June, 1861). Rpt. *Ralph the Bailiff and Other Stories.* London: Ward, Lock & Tyler, 1867. References are to this edition.

———. "The Shadow in the Corner." *All the Year Round* (Summer 1879):1–11. References are to this edition.

Brantlinger, Patrick. *Rule of Darkness: British Literature and Imperialism, 1830–1914.* Ithaca, N.Y.: Cornell UP, 1988.

Himmelfarb, Gertrude. *The Idea of Poverty: England in the Early Industrial Age.* NewYork: Vintage, 1985.

"On the Scarcity of Good Maid-Servants." *The Englishwoman's Review: A Journal of Woman's Work.* (London). October 1866. 12–26.

Peterson, M. Jeanne. "The Victorian Governess: Status Incongruence in Family and Society." *Suffer and Be Still: Women in the Victorian Age.* Ed. Martha Vicinus. Bloomington: Indiana UP, 1972.

Wolff, Robert Lee. *Sensational Victorian: The Life and Fiction of Mary Elizabeth Braddon.* New York: Garland, 1979.

FIFTEEN

Electra-fying the Female Sleuth: Detecting the Father in *Eleanor's Victory* and *Thou Art the Man*

Heidi H. Johnson

When the "crime" that Anne Humpherys identifies in modern scholarship on Victorian detective fiction is finally redressed, Mary Elizabeth Braddon's name will be writ large in that crime's list of victims. As Humpherys observes, burgeoning critical interest in the subgenre has typically meant "an obsessive return to a handful of canonized texts by three male writers—Charles Dickens, Wilkie Collins, and Arthur Conan Doyle"—while "the majority of such fiction (a good deal written by women)" (259) still awaits reclamation from the long shadows cast by this select canon. It has become commonplace to recognize Robert Audley in *Lady Audley's Secret* as an amateur sleuth; however, many of Braddon's later plots of detection only briefly, if ever, surface in twentieth-century generic studies and, even then, most often for the purposes of disparagement.[1] Perhaps the deepest obscurity and the one that most deserves to be dispelled lies over Braddon's narratives of female sleuths who detect on their fathers' behalfs in *Eleanor's Victory* (1863) and *Thou Art the Man* (1894).[2] Fuller attention to these novels, written near the poles of Braddon's career, provides testimony to the centrality of the father/daughter bond in her work as a whole. Moreover, the two texts signal Braddon's participation in a broader trend within popular fiction of her era, thereby hinting at a Victorian preoccupation with this bond that has similarly intrigued current theorists of a feminist psychoanalysis.

Recent critics may, for instance, have too willingly concurred with Lady Audley in dismissing her father Maldon as a dependent and "weak, tipsy father" (232) while laying full credit for her transgressions to maternal "inheritance" (230) whether it be the "invisible, hereditary taint" of her mother's madness (233) or, as Jill Matus has persuasively argued, an ambition to circumvent the "social and psychic inheritance" of her mother's powerlessness (192). Far greater evidence exists to implicate Maldon as both the source of marital ambitions she inaccurately attributes to her own scheming and a pander who, Robert Talboys recalls, demonstrated more agency than Helen Maldon herself in concocting for Talboys's cavalry regiment "shallow tricks to catch one of us for his pretty daughter" (13). When Helen refuses to identify her father as the origin of a self-construction that left her willing "to sell [herself] to the highest bidder" (13) and a worthy teacher of the "shallow tricks" she later refines to an art form she shields the fact that her multiple crimes arose from becoming not what her mother, but instead what her father, made her.

Though the protagonists of *Eleanor's Victory* and *Thou Art the Man* are not criminals but women who identify that criminality in others, their sleuthing leads them to the same psychic hurdle in the father, and one they surmount in a way Lady Audley never does. A frequently recapitulated scenario of the daughter who detects to discover the secret of her father's death or, conversely, whose detection reveals his culpability serves as an archetype for a daughterly and womanly desire seen as vital by a number of mid- and late-Victorian authors even as they overtly condemn their protagonists' quests. The central enigma to be investigated in these novels is something quite different from and even more mysteriously hidden than the solution to a single guilty act or unexplained death. What the female sleuth seeks is the secret of the father's power, as her act of detection demystifies his primacy and allows her to reinaugurate through her own agency a process of psychosexual growth arrested by her protracted attachment to the father. If, as Lynda Zwinger asserts in *Daughters, Fathers, and the Novel,* the "sentimental daughter" of eighteenth- and nineteenth-century fiction is "sympathetic to and complicitous with the father," identifying with his desires while repressing her own (122), then the "sensational daughter" of the Victorian detective plot proffers a paradigm for the transformation of that sentiment into selfhood. This essay, then, is a double act of recovery: of the fictional trend that gives a context for Braddon's own female sleuthing narratives, and of the complex psychological inquiries and answers provided by her unjustly overshadowed plots of the daughter's detection.

The dubious character of George Mowbray Vandeleur Vane, the

father whose influence lingers long after his death midway through the first volume of *Eleanor's Victory,* is made plain to a reader from the first in a way that it never fully is to his daughter. His early history, divulged by the narrator early in the story, is contextualized within the reign of George IV, who imparted his own frivolity and "unmanly weakness" (1:41) to the culture at large; Vane takes his life's blood from the Regency as George IV's spectral successor, for he is George V in name if not in station. Profligate with what little money he does have and forever scheming to obtain more, Vane pins his hopes for future riches on his youthful friendship with a bachelor invalid, Maurice de Crespigny. His relationship with de Crespigny, characterized as a "romantic alliance" (1:55), hints at a homoerotic bond that underscores Vane's "unmanly" nature. His talent at manipulation becomes clear when, characterizing himself as a Lear-like figure, Vane rails against his older daughter, Eleanor's half-sister, who provides him with a small allowance despite the fact that he squandered the fortune she was to inherit (1:24). Vane's self-construction foists upon Eleanor her role as a Cordelia while, as the narrator points out, making clear how little Vane understands either his Shakespeare or himself.[3] Vane repeatedly suggests to Eleanor that her future role will be as a tool for "avenging himself upon his ungrateful elder children" (1:57) when, together, the father and daughter can live off the fruits of his mercenary friendship with de Crespigny.

By positioning readers at a critical distance from Vane, Braddon casts an immediate ominous aura over Eleanor's sanguine expectations after she is reunited in Paris with the father she has not seen for several years. Eleanor perceives their reunion as "the natal day of her new life" (1:92), her conjunction with the father unimpeded by the long-deceased mother who would triangulate the dyad. This prospect is shortly demolished when Vane is lured away by two acquaintances to a game of cards and later found dead in the gaming house, probably a result of suicide after he lost at écarté money his daughter Hortensia had reluctantly advanced to fund Eleanor's education at a French finishing school. When Eleanor is given a note that Vane penned to her before his death, she takes upon herself this self-pitying note's call for revenge and initiates a quest to fulfill her appointed role in the father's fiction. With only vague memories of the two men who accompanied Vane to the écarté table, Eleanor stores this remembrance away for future use, along with a partial name appearing in the note.

The position Hortensia eventually finds for Eleanor after she returns to England, as companion to a girl living on the estate of her father's former friend de Crespigny, coincidentally puts her on the track of Vane's supposed murderer. There she meets and is courted by two men, each in his own way a paternal double: the lawyer Monckton, guardian of Eleanor's charge Laura Mason, and de Crespigny's great-nephew, Launcelot Darrell. Eleanor first identifies Monckton in a paternal role to Laura when she notes that "he was old enough to be [Laura's] father" (1:274), and Monckton has in truth become Laura's guardian through a sort of masculine parthenogenesis, since Eleanor later learns that this ward is the child of Monckton's former fiancée, who jilted the lawyer to marry another man but then proved incapable of competent mothering. What Eleanor avoids recognizing is that he could just as easily be her own father, which Laura does not fail to discern when, after Eleanor and Monckton later announce their plans to marry, she observes to her guardian, "Why you must be old enough to be her father!" (2:153). Even before this marriage, Monckton's benevolently paternal influence extends from Laura to Eleanor, as "Eleanor's intellect expanded" and "her plastic mind, so ready to take any impression, was newly moulded by its contact with this stronger brain" (1:274).

Launcelot Darrell, conversely, is invariably identified as a younger version of Eleanor's own faulty father. The "unmanliness" that characterized Vane emerges physically in the "almost feminine softness" (1:292) of Launcelot's facial features and his "womanish" fingers (2:234). The resemblance extends from appearance to manner, for Launcelot, an artistic dabbler, blames others for his failure to thrive and expects that future financial independence will come from inheriting his great-uncle's fortune. The associative link between father and suitor is most directly signaled at the moment of Launcelot's proposal, when the narrator muses, "He had something of George Vane's nature, perhaps" (2:38). It is at this point, too, when Eleanor's rationale for rejecting Launcelot suggests the emotional parallel she draws between filial and romantic love: "I remember how I loved my father and looking back at my feelings for him, I know that I do not love Mr. Darrell" (2:46).

Eleanor's refusal proves a fortunate decision on multiple levels, for she also realizes that he is one of the men who accompanied her father to the French gaming house on the night of his death. Her latent drive for vengeance is spurred as she attempts to confirm her suspicion and muster the proofs that might convince others. However, this impulse toward daughterly detection is immediately impugned. A surrogate brother, Richard Thornton, with whose aunt Eleanor had lodged for many years in London, warns that her desire for revenge and the act of sleuthing itself will "waste your life, blight your girlhood, unsex your mind, and transform you from a candid and confiding woman into an amateur detective" (2:87). An uncompromising narrative voice further endorses Richard's sentiment, stating that "every natural womanly feeling" lies in direct opposition to "the girl's devotion to her dead father" (3:19) and comparing her to both Medea (3:173) and, repeatedly, to Nemesis (see, for example, 2:232, 2:292, and 3:64). As if in confirmation, Eleanor moves from neglecting her housework to coldheartedly accepting Monckton's offer of marriage because it will allow her to remain near her quarry, Launcelot, while further cloaking with her married name the identity she earlier veiled under a pseudonym.

Morally dubious stratagems, flirting with a shipping clerk, for instance, and invading Launcelot's private sketchbook to find a drawing of her father at the Parisian card table, allow Eleanor to gain preliminary proof of Launcelot's guilt. Moreover, the transgressive nature of her role is confirmed by departures from familial and marital configurations that Braddon is gradually defining as suitable. Eleanor too readily replicates her parents' own marital history, for instance, by marrying a paternally identified and much older employer, since Eleanor's mother was governess to Vane's children from his first marriage. In so doing, she instantly gains a daughter only a few years younger than herself in Laura Mason.

More importantly, in this second chance at a family headed by a man who does at least perform ably in his roles as father and husband, Eleanor's covert quest troubles the family by disrupting appropriate patterns of desire. Monckton wrongly interprets her continuing interest in Launcelot as infidelity, though he is oddly correct in his belief that a third term, the father, has been present in their marriage from the start, given Eleanor's belief that any love for a man before her vengeance is achieved would be "false to the memory of her father" (2:113). When Laura falls in love with Launcelot, she too perceives a seeming rivalry for Launcelot's attention, and Eleanor's justifiable objections to the couple's marriage only reinforce Laura's suspicions. Eleanor's warring allegiances and split identity as daughter and wife are also signaled when Braddon increasingly attributes the character's inner thoughts to "Eleanor" and her outward behaviors to "Mrs. Monckton." The marriage is finally pushed to the point of rupture when de Crespigny is on his deathbed, and Eleanor sees Launcelot and an accomplice exchange a forged will for the correct one. Because she cannot prove it, Monckton refuses to believe her, imagining that the accusation is born of desire for vengeance springing from a disappointed illicit passion for Launcelot.

Eleanor's ascent to normalcy begins with a threat that the family romance will repeat itself in her own marriage, as a marital separation sends Eleanor to London and the father/daughter dyad of Monckton and Laura off to Torquay to recover from their romantic wounds. Thrown upon her own resources, Eleanor takes a position as companion to a Mrs. Lennard, who wants a "sister" (3:182) to join her and her husband in Paris. Both Lennards, however, soon prove to be more like "two overgrown children of forty years of age" (3:197) than equals. While

Eleanor is a full generation younger than Mrs. Lennard, their positions in a maternal economy are inverted, as Eleanor assumes the role of mother to these irresponsible exemplars of arrested development, leaving her far too busy to think about either her misfortunes or her vengeance.

The likeness that Eleanor observes between Laura Mason and Mrs. Lennard leads her to realize that the latter is Laura's mother, the woman who had jilted Monckton years earlier; the same similarities between mother and daughter insinuate that Eleanor's new responsibilities present her with an opportunity to repeat and reform her earlier poor mothering of Laura. The paternal influence that led to Mrs. Lennard's faulty marital choices and inadequacies as a mother, too, suggests parallels between her and Eleanor as well, along with a predetermined life script that Eleanor can only evade by renouncing the father's psychic legacy.

Her Parisian sojourn serendipitously puts Eleanor in the path of Launcelot's companion the night of her father's death, who is also his accomplice in the exchange of wills that permitted Launcelot to inherit de Crespigny's property. Persuaded to forgive his wife when Eleanor's friend Richard Thornton tells him Eleanor's story, Monckton joins Eleanor in Paris, where together they obtain the real will and return to England but not to take possession of the estate to which Eleanor is entitled by the terms of the newfound will, written by de Crespigny in compliance with his promise to Vane. Instead, the reinscription of Eleanor within a more regularized feminine role promotes a "victory" that relinquishes both the father's dictum and his ambitions. Moreover, Eleanor's rationale for renouncing vengeance against Launcelot, guilty of cheating her father at cards and profiting from a forged will but not of murder, makes it "a properly womanly conquest" in which "the tender woman's heart triumphed over the girl's rash vow" (3:312), as the novel's closing lines insist. Launcelot's mother appeals to her to consider how she would want her own children to be treated under similar circumstances, and Eleanor responds to this plea. Instead, Eleanor takes only part of the fortune and makes the provisions that allow Launcelot to maintain his previous status and, finally, to marry Laura. Nature steps in to confirm the expulsion of Eleanor's father from her marriage to Monckton, as the novel's closing paragraphs suggest children, in the plural, born to them in the years shortly after the titular "victory."

Narrative design thus reinforces the derogatory estimations of Eleanor's sleuthing expressed by the narrator and characters she aligns with her own position. Yet on a less superficial level, the text also displays ambivalence about detection's multiple functions since it serves as a corrective to father/daughter attachment that complicates the daughter's own marital and maternal functions. The truths she has learned about her father through the detecting process lead Eleanor to a less idealized vision of him, for she justifies stepping aside from the promised vengeance with the admission, "Oh, my dear, dead father! you did wrong yourself, sometimes" (3:305). Further, without the chain of events set in motion by Eleanor's quest, Monckton would have remained in an unnatural role as Laura's sole parental figure, for through Eleanor's intercession, Laura is ultimately allowed to establish a relationship with her natural parents, the Lennards.

Only through the process of sleuthing and achieving full separation from the father, too, can Eleanor avoid all manner of incestuous unions, like the one that would have resulted from marriage to her father's double, Launcelot. A further prospect of wedlock based in an intra-familial bond is presented and evaded with the brotherly figure Richard. Eleanor's obsession prompts her to misinterpret his proposal early in the novel as an offer of his help, not his hand, as she tells him, "I know you love me, Dick, quite as much as if I were your real sister" (1:228). In a culture where a woman's continuing state as a legal possession altered only so far as she transferred her dependence and her allegiance from her father to her husband, Braddon appears to find something uncomfortably close in the similar relationships. The act of detection disrupts this conjunction of roles and desires, allowing a different pattern of desire to be formulated that escapes the trap of emotional incest. *Lady Audley's Secret* provides still further evidence of this theme's enduring importance to Braddon, since Robert Audley indifferently imagines that he will succumb to his cousin Alicia Audley's nuptial designs until sleuthing brings him into Clara Talboys's path and redirects both his own and Alicia's marital trajectories outside the family.[4]

Contemporary reviews of *Eleanor's Victory* are, in some respects, attuned to the contradictions with which the novel is riddled regarding the pejorative and positive functions of sleuthing. Much as an *Athenaeum* critic finds the novel's final volume "ineffective" (362), a writer for the *Saturday Review* suspects that the wish "not to offend the moral sense of a Christian public" led to a "weak" tacked-on ending cleansing Eleanor of the "entertaining and Pagan principles" undergirding her pursuit of revenge (397). Indeed, as W. Fraser Rae argues in an 1865 *North British Review* essay, vengeance would have been an entirely appropriate outcome, for the renunciation of it means that "the moral of the story seems to be, that to cheat an old man at cards and to forge a will are no impediments to attaining distinction in the world, and, indeed, are rather venial offences" (191). These judgments point to the dissonance of closure if the text's structuring principle is seen only as a woman's quest to achieve justice but in this, Eleanor's and Braddon's aims might be seen to differ. When releasing the daughter from the father's psychic control is instead viewed as the novel's modus operandi, the conclusion achieves greater coherence not so much as a last-minute conversion to decorous femininity but as a signifier of the daughter's liberation from the prescribed role assigned to her in serving her father's expectations and fantasies.

Additionally, the reviewers' dissatisfaction points to their suspicion that there is something wrong with the choice of roles offered to Eleanor. As Rae complains, Eleanor is "a heroine who is at once unnatural and namby-pamby" (190), a criticism foregrounding inconsistency in characterization but also a telling commentary on the limited arenas of action available to the Victorian woman. Eleanor is only "entertaining," as the *Saturday Review* writer observed (397), during the periods when she is, in Rae's terms, "unnatural" that is, during the period of her quest, and "namby-pamby" when she is gradually inserted within an appropriate marital and maternal sphere in the last half of the novel's third volume. The process of sleuthing offers a pretext for evading the only "natural" roles offered to women first as daughter, then as wife and mother, and the possibility for ensuring that the two are not essentially the same. To dub this process unnatural suggests that it can be pursued only in fiction; the notion that it might be a necessary psychological operation is confirmed by the proliferation of similarly unnatural female sleuths in the years following *Eleanor's Victory.*

Both the timeliness and tenacious mystique of Braddon's motif of daughterly detection can be surmised from its near-duplication in R. D. Blackmore's anonymously published first novel *Clara Vaughan,* which when it appeared in 1864 was described by a *Saturday Review* critic as "belonging to the same class of fiction as *Eleanor's Victory,* and in the outset provoking no little comparison with that exciting composition" (539). Blackmore felt compelled to quash suspicions that he might have been influenced by *Eleanor's Victory,* emphatically stating in the introduction to an 1872 edition of his novel that he had actually begun writing *Clara Vaughan* in the early 1850s.[5] The novels' plots are sufficiently different to put the question of plagiarism to rest. However, their similar emphases on the daughter who attempts to ascertain the secret surrounding her father's death, and the simultaneous obstruction and promotion of psychosexual development that results, point to the texts' kinship on a more profound level.

The mysterious murder of her father sends Clara on a path of vengeance that finally leads to her discovery that he was killed in error, mistaken for his half-brother by a Sicilian villain and vivisectionist who believed Vaughan had bigamously married the Italian beauty long intended as his own wife. Blackmore extends Braddon's equation of detection and abnormality with a near-lesbian attachment between Clara and a young woman, Isola, who later turns out to be her estranged cousin. As in *Eleanor's Victory*, too, autonomy from the father, signaled by renunciation of the quest at the moment truth is revealed, must be fully achieved before the sleuth's desires can be redirected into normalcy and marriage. In this case, marriage remains within the family, as Clara weds Isola's older brother Conrad, to whom she is attracted throughout much of the novel. Given that at different points in the narrative Clara has believed this young man to be either the son of her father's murderer or even her own half-brother, though, marriage to a cousin pales by comparison. Obsessive devotion to the father as a motive for sleuthing, in many respects anathematized by Blackmore, is nonetheless the sole route the text offers by which desires can eventually be regularized, identities clarified, and a fragmented family reconsolidated. Furthermore, sleuthing exonerates the father of the moral dubieties ascribed to him by his murderer while allowing the daughter to gain distance from her adoration because she was temporarily forced to doubt her father's worthiness as idol.

The father/daughter sleuthing plot takes on still greater depth and relevance when it not only unseats the father as icon but deflates this ideal and leads the sleuth to a more nuanced view of the father and, hence, of all men. Though *Eleanor's Victory* hinted at this outcome, a more vociferous call for father/daughter individuation characterizes Wilkie Collins's 1884 *I Say No*, in which the message promoted by the narrative of the daughter's detection is the danger of sheltering young women from knowledge of the father and his own desires. Bereaved at fourteen when her father suddenly dies of a heart ailment, or so Emily Brown has been told, Emily resurrects the clouded past four years later when she unearths evidence that her father was actually murdered. Though her quest leads to the final revelation that James Brown committed suicide, Emily learns en route to this conclusion that further information was being withheld from her by her guardian, a recently deceased aunt who abetted a family plan to withhold from her the inaccurate but prevailing judgment that Brown had been murdered. The prudish aunt also made a secret of Brown's liaison with a fallen woman, Sara Jethro, who Emily later learns nobly rejected her father's offer of marriage immediately before the suicide.

While the deception of Emily was well-intentioned, its effects are insidious, allowing moral if not legal guilt in several characters to go unrecognized before the truth is revealed. Emily's sheltered state even allows her to entertain the possibility of marrying an effeminate and golden-tressed charismatic preacher, Miles Mirabel, whose cowardly actions at the time of Brown's death allowed it to be wrongly considered murder. Emily's investigation, however, leads "the feeble little clergy-man" to faint at her feet and her perceptive servant, Mrs. Ellmother, instantly to mutter of Emily's suitor-in-the-wings, Alban Morris, "I call him a Man!" (426). Significantly, Emily's love for Morris can only lead to marriage once Emily ascertains that he has not been part of the "conspiracy to deceive" (388) and the act that wins Morris Emily's hand is his interview with Miss Jethro that puts the last piece of the puzzle in place to account for her father's death.

Fully worthy of his daughter's devotion, Collins's James Brown is simply a more complicated and fallible man than Emily had been allowed to recognize. Nonetheless, *I Say No* paves the way for Braddon's ne plus ultra of filial detection—the daughter's discovery of her father's crimi-nality in the 1894 novel, *Thou Art the Man*. The title this novel shares with an 1844 short story by Edgar Allan Poe points to their similar source in the Old Testament narrative of David and Bathsheba, wherein David's apportioning of guilt in response to an allegory told to him by Nathan forces him to recognize, through Nathan's pronouncement of "*Thou Art the Man*," his own analogous treachery (2 Sam. 12.7). With the biblical resonance, however, is joined the classical, since it was not uncommon for English translations of Sophocles' *Oedipus Rex* to seize upon the same phrase at the moment when the blind priest Tiresias charges Oedipus with patricide.[6] Like Poe's " *Thou Art the Man*,' " Braddon's novel is a classic case of the criminal who remains undetected because he so com-petently diverts attention to another suspect, even giving apparently well-intentioned aid that does more harm than good to this suspect. Poe's story relies upon an unnamed narrator, an "Oedipus," as he dubs himself in the story's first sentence (566) who, from the start, makes the mur-derer's guilt transparent to any minimally careful reader so that this reader can appreciate not only the ingenuity of the criminal but also the adroitness of the sleuth in perceiving guilt and prompting a confession. Conversely, Braddon's third-person narrator allows her readers to suspect guilt but only confirms it when the novel's sleuth, Coralie Urquhart, penetrates to a truth that remains concealed outside the closed circle of author, sleuth, criminal, and reader.

As a combined result of her growing observational skills and un-welcome knowledge of her father's character, Coralie learns that ten years earlier he had murdered Marie Arnold, the illegitimate daughter of mine-owner Sir Joseph Higginson, after she responded coldly to his mar-riage proposal. In a concurrent ill-fated romantic plot, Higginson's legiti-mate daughter, Sibyl, and another young man visiting Higginson's estate, Brandon Mountford, confess their mutual love. Mountford, however, admits to her that marriage would be impossible because of hereditary epilepsy that he lives in constant fear might lead to the same insanity that earlier claimed his mother. When Marie is found stabbed to death, all evidence points to Mountford's guilt because he is discovered bloody-handed near the body, recovering from an epileptic seizure, and suffering from a memory lapse.

Since it appears almost certain that Mountford will be found guilty when he is brought to trial, the unusually helpful Urquhart suggests to Sibyl a plan to extract Mountford from his cell and then spirit him away in a fishing craft. When a storm destroys the vessel, Sibyl is uncertain if Mountford arrived at his destination or, as is commonly believed, drowned. She begins vaguely to suspect Urquhart's motives, and she blames herself for colluding in a scheme that may have killed her lover. Urquhart's dual strategy to escape detection by making Mountford's guilt seem a foregone conclusion, and to win both Sibyl's hand and the Higginson fortune goes awry when he attempts to coerce Sibyl into marriage. He warns her that "marriage is your only escape from the scandal" that might occur if her romance with the universally vilified Mountford becomes public (2:167), and she promptly thwarts his plan by agreeing to marry Urquhart's icy older brother, Lord Penrith, instead.

Ten years later, Urquhart's culpability threatens to surface when Sibyl receives a cryptic note from Mountford, who was never aboard the fishing craft at all but was instead spirited away by Urquhart to a secluded retreat. This place of asylum has now become a virtual prison, with enforced captivity and poor treatment hastening Mountford's descent into madness. Urquhart's legal and moral crimes are augmented by further murder, when late in the novel he shoots Sibyl's husband, disguises the crime as a hunting accident, and, as Lord Penrith's only surviving brother, inherits his title and estate. Sibyl's attempts to locate and rescue Mountford represent a sleuthing of sorts, and in so doing, she learns a portion of her brother-in-law's guilt. But she does not explicitly set out to decipher this truth; moreover, she never suspects and never learns that he is also her husband's murderer. For the novel's most fully developed sleuth, we must turn to Coralie Urquhart, whose detection on the father's behalf becomes a source of both salvation and separation.

In each of the aforementioned novels, the daughter's "paternal monogamy," to borrow Lynda Zwinger's apt phrase for protracted attachment in sentimental novels (51), is further promoted by maternal absence. Though the mother of Blackmore's Clara Vaughan is an exception and lingers for several years after her husband's murder, this is for Clara only the physical manifestation of a death that occurred in the daughter's psyche much earlier; Clara admits, "And yet I loved dear mother truly, and pitied her sometimes with tears; but the shadow-love [for the dead father] was far the deeper" (10). *Thou Art the Man*'s Coralie Urquhart demonstrates more overtly the repudiation of the mother that allows the daughter's monogamous union with the father. A penniless parson's daughter whom the aristocratic Urquhart had largely abandoned after their marriage, this mother who goes nameless throughout the novel died in childbirth several years after Coralie's birth. The daughter's rejection of the mother is primarily signaled through her determined class snobbery, which functions as a denial of her maternal lineage. She dismisses as "unpatrician maiden aunts" (38), for instance, the mother's relations with whom she lived during much of her childhood before being taken into the home of the former Sibyl Higginson, now Lady Penrith.

Instead, Coralie allies herself exclusively with her father, naming herself "my father's daughter" (1:19) and relishing the times that other characters not always appreciatively echo her self-estimation (see, for instance, 2:199). A sexual tinge always shades their relationship, with Urquhart assessing her as a woman and not as a daughter, particularly regarding her physical appearance; the erotic subtext is accentuated when we learn near the novel's conclusion that he named Coralie after a burlesque actress with whom he was having an affair at the time of his daughter's birth (3:214–16). Coralie responds to his expectations by performing the role of "her father's daughter" publicly and, more sigificantly, within the private journal Urquhart requests she write for his perusal. Though Coralie is constructed as a character certain to strike most readers as largely unlikeable, it gradually becomes evident that her most distasteful qualities and ideological stances are really Urquhart's, mimicked by the daughter to gain her father's approval.

Indeed, the father harnesses Coralie's desire, along with observational skills she has cultivated in learning to read him so she might better please him, after Coralie is taken into Lord Penrith's home, placing Coralie in the middle of intrigue on the verge of eruption, as Urquhart suspects. Though Urquhart claims that only the "purest motives" (1:31) propel a chivalric wish to gain information about Sibyl's activities so he might help her, he orders that Coralie begin writing a detailed journal informing him of Sibyl's movements "in such a manner as will admit of your allowing me to read it" (1:30). Coralie's skepticism of his motive is evidenced by her decision to adopt "a system of diary-keeping by double entry," with separate volumes for her father's reading and for "my own little reveries" (1:38). As Coralie carries out her father's wishes in one text while covertly querying them in the other, the escalating distance between the personae constructed in each volume hints at the increasing difference between the static Coralie of her father's making and an individuated Coralie emerging from this family romance.

By empowering his daughter as a sleuth and fostering in her the hermeneutic skills that make her so able in this pursuit, Urquhart has given her tools that she finally, although at first unwittingly, turns upon him. An overheard argument between her father and Lord Penrith leaves Coralie feeling disgusted by her father's behavior, prompting a dark night of the soul during which she recognizes "she had never really loved her father" (3:56) and instantly acquires a newfound ability to perceive him disinterestedly. What she sees is a man with "all the indications of a debased character stamped upon his countenance" (3:66), a "beggar" (3:77) willing to live off his wealthier relations and a man guilty of murder. But the side effect of her extreme father-identification leads Coralie, as *Thou Art the Man*'s Electra, to stop short of the same truth-telling function assumed by Poe's "Oedipus." Noting in her own diary Urquhart's stealthy behavior while he crossed the moors on the afternoon of Lord Penrith's death, she cannot inscribe the words that would tell his guilt. With a trembling hand, she merely notes the facts that make that conclusion inescapable and ends the entry with the words, "I shall write no more in this journal" (3:122). Although at the moment of her final parting from her father Coralie insinuates that she has guessed his secret, it remains forever unwritten and unspoken.

Braddon is mute in assessing the morality of Coralie's own silence, although a similar reluctance in the novel's female paragon, Sibyl, to speak her knowledge of Urquhart's earlier crime except to Urquhart himself, shortly before he is claimed by a disfiguring cancer provides a sanction of sorts for Coralie. Braddon is little concerned with the father's legal guilt or its public identification and punishment; instead, as in *Eleanor's Victory*, she focuses on the more insidious psychological crimes that take place within the family and can only be resolved with the transformation of familial dynamics. Nonetheless, redefinition of Coralie's identity in opposition to the father, rather than in conjunction with him, initially proves just as debilitating. Status as "her father's daughter" is now less an aspiration than a burden, as she signals in disparaging herself to Sibyl as "a very Urquhart a sordid, selfish creature" (3:189) and vowing "to live a clean life to hold no companionship with a man I cannot respect as a father should be respected" (3:190). Images of the father's blood as the father's pollution recur, with Coralie attributing her treacherous spying upon Sibyl to a "venom in my blood" arising from "the hereditary taint" of the father's "bad blood" (3:210).

Coralie only emerges from the lengthy melancholy prompted by this near-erasure of self when she can winnow through the traits cultivated in her quest for paternal approval to assess their varied worths and modify them accordingly. Her ability to puncture pretenses within her social milieu, for instance, shifts from the sarcastic tone that amused her father to a more humorous tenor that diverts Lady Penrith, and she rejects her father's conventional definition of female worth by capitalizing upon the physical strength he disparaged and becoming an avid sportswoman. More crucially, she reclaims a connection with the mother that she had earlier denied. Though Sibyl Penrith functions throughout the novel as a maternal surrogate for the younger woman, Coralie discards her earlier concept that an inherent and overdetermined rivalry must necessarily obstruct such a relationship, and the two women forge a true and mutually satisfying friendship. Less conspicuously, too, Coralie's lessening class snobbery when Sibyl teaches her to recognize "strong individualities among the masses" (3:218) suggests a softening of the criterion that prohibited Coralie from claiming kinship, either real or emotional, with her mother.

Further, Coralie avoids a marital model that, as Eleanor Vane's initially did, simply substitutes a good father for a bad. Her pursuit throughout the novel of a peripheral character, the virtuous Reverend Coverdale, ultimately leads her to still further condemnation of the father because in truly recognizing the "pure atmosphere" of Coverdale's "noble thought and lofty aspiration how foul and grim her father's character looked" (3:81). Yet Braddon rejects marriage between Coralie and Coverdale as an appropriate outcome, instead bringing about a union of comparable virtue in the marriage of Sibyl and Coverdale at the novel's conclusion. The potential hazards of a different pairing are implied when Coralie muses that, with marriage to Coverdale, she "would have cast off this slough of wickedness which has gradually grown over my mind and heart, and would have emerged from the dismal swamp of past experience a good woman, purified by his love, ennobled by sympathy with his noble nature" (3:108). Coverdale, in effect, would become Coralie's super-ego. Though such a situation might be morally advantageous, the measure of Braddon's insight into its personal effects appears in her rejection of the scenario. If anyone is to purify and ennoble Coralie, it must be Coralie herself.

Eleanor's Victory less problematically and perhaps less convincingly represented the process by which its central character grows toward an integrated identity. Three decades later in a revisitation of the female sleuthing plot, Braddon approaches the same topic with more intricate strategies, as she delves more deeply into the psychological mystery of identity formation and explores ways that traces of both father and mother might be productively incorporated into the individuated daughter. This is chiefly what allows Coralie Urquhart, as both a character and a psychological profile, finally to escape the poles of feminine behavior labeled "unnatural" and "namby-pamby" by the reviewer of *Eleanor's Victory*. When, in the novel's final "postscript," the narrator informs us of Coralie's marriage to a character external to the foregoing narrative, the sheer brevity of this reference suggests that marriage is less the culmination of the individuation process than a step that must necessarily follow it. Indeed, the peripheral nature of the postscript suggests that it is a sop thrown to a reader interested only in the marriage plot but irrelevant to those who might instead perceive *Thou Art the Man*'s crucial narrative thread in the daughter's plot.

The novel's conclusion does not, however, represent the unequivocal "revitalization" of its central female characters, especially Coralie, attributed to it by critic Kathleen L. Maio (94). The pleasure Coralie took in writing the secret personal diary once led her to confide in its pages, "I find an undiminishing interest in this volume, and the facility with which my pen runs along the page makes me think that I shall some day blossom into a novelist" (3:110). When Coralie decides to "write no more in this journal," she also rejects other uses for her mind and her pen; the father's role in literally ushering Coralie into the symbolic order through his directive that she begin the diary forever taints the activity, mitigating the full recovery of Coralie from both her extended attachment and the trauma that hastened separation but can only be imperfectly resolved. Though Braddon surprisingly dismisses Coralie in the novel's concluding sentence as "mundane to the tips of her fingers" (3:253), such an evaluation stands as an assertion that attaining the commonplace might in some cases be no small achievement. The narrator's evaluation, furthermore, perhaps applies more to this psychologically complicated character's outward role as Lady Coralie Hildrop, while the inward scars that remain on the psyche might be intuited by the reader of Coralie's twin diaries and the surrounding narrative. It is tempting to stretch both Braddon's biography and these texts to the point of congruence, given the many invitations this biography proffers. By such a reading, the prototypes for both George Vane and Hubert Urquhart lie in Braddon's profligate and adulterous father Henry, largely absent from Braddon's life after she reached the age of four and described in her unpublished memoir as "a careless and happy-go-lucky gentleman who is nobody's enemy but his own" (qtd. in Wolff, *Sensational Victorian* 24). The difficulty in distinguishing between father and husband might owe something to Braddon's liaison with and then marriage to John Maxwell. Fifteen years Braddon's senior, Maxwell was not quite, like Eleanor's Monckton, "old enough to be her father," but might certainly represent a paternal figure since he eventually made her, at the age of thirty-two, "head of a grown up family who I think love me almost as well as if I were indeed their mother" (Wolff, "Devoted Disciple" 145). The fatherly hand that directs the course of the daughter's narrative figuratively in *Eleanor*, and literally in *Coralie* finds its type in Braddon's manipulative early patron, John Gilby, whose excerpted letters to Braddon in *Sensational Victorian* lend credence to Robert Lee Wolff's characterization of him as "an anxious authoritarian father" (92) who had to be cast off for Braddon to forge her own fictional and actual plots.

The pressure to produce not justice but manuscript pages to please a masculine authority might also reflect some ambivalence toward Braddon's merged personal and professional relationships with Maxwell. Autobiographical parallels are most alluring in the case of Coralie, whose system of "double entry" may replicate the series of apparent divisions that marked Braddon's career: first, her early vacillation between poetry and fiction; later, occasionally using a pseudonym at the same time that other novels appeared under her own name; and in the 1890s, her persistent and largely thwarted desire to complement her success as a novelist with triumph as a playwright. Coralie's bifurcated voice may even express Braddon's persistent frustration in harmonizing the economic and artistic aims that motivated her writing. As she explained in an 1864 letter to Bulwer-Lytton, "I am always divided between a noble desire to attain something like excellence and a very ignoble wish to earn plenty of money" (Wolff, "Devoted Disciple" 25).

As part of a broader Victorian impulse toward novels of the daughter's detection, though, Braddon's novels suggest less individual although no less intimate pre-Freudian insights into a process of female identity-formation centered in the protracted Oedipal conflict. Although Freud himself rejected the Jungian term "Electra complex" as a too-symmetrical equation of the masculine and feminine processes,[7] this Greek archetype nevertheless serves as a rough analogy for Freud's theorization of the girl's rejection of her mother, to whom she later ambivalently returns for a source of feminized identity, and her eroticized attachment to an often-idealized father. Indeed, the father in Euripedes's *Electra* is more readily exalted because he is dead, just as the fathers in each narrative of filial sleuthing discussed in this essay take similarly static positions because they are either deceased or, in *Thou Art the Man*, emotionally distant and physically absent. In Freud's model, the continuation of the daughter's Oedipal attachment into adulthood was not only almost a given but relatively unproblematic as well, since "she will in that case choose her husband for his paternal characteristics and be ready to recognize his authority. Her longing to possess a penis, which is in fact unappeasable, may find satisfaction if she can succeed in completing her love for the organ by extending it to the bearer of the organ" (Outline 194). Further, Freud located in this equation of father and husband the source of a woman's maternal desires, since producing a child compensates for her ongoing and "unappeasable" phallic lack.

Though *Eleanor's Victory* and *Thou Art the Man* in part provide fictional illustrations of the Freudian psychoanalytic models, they also prefigure late-twentieth-century criticism of such models as inadequate in either accounting for women's relationships with their mothers or suggesting ways that women can arrive at healthy identities that escape a sort of Freudian determinism. For Braddon, sleuthing becomes a means to these ends. Each daughter begins her quest by perceiving it as a way of achieving the desired union with her father—for Eleanor psychically, and for Coralie literally—while at some point she recognizes that this oneness is not only unattainable but also undesirable. Both novels affirm the need for, and the difficulty of, severing or at least attenuating attachment to the father to gain the power for self-determination, although its end is most often in Braddon the assumption of a conventional feminine role. Nevertheless, Braddon anticipates Nancy Chodorow's reinterpretation of women's psychological development as possibly beginning in the daughter's perceived competition for the phallus but, as she matures, culminating in a less conflict-ridden relational dynamic that allows her to "oscillate emotionally between mother and father" and form later relationships, particularly as wife and mother, "in addition to and not as replacements for" the original ties (193).

In both of Braddon's novels, the daughters' attachments to their fathers also recall current psychoanalytic insistence that such a dynamic not be construed as an immutable master narrative. Instead, excessive identification might better be interpreted as the daughter's understanding that biology is, however unfairly, the cultural basis of power. Sleuthing at the father's behest gives her a taste of this power, her identification with him making possible her entrance into an outer world that she learns to understand on her own terms with the skills she has cultivated in his service. Social and psychoanalytic theorist Jessica Benjamin maintains that only cultural prohibitions and biases, rather than innate gendered essences or unavoidable developmental courses, prevent children and adolescents from the most constructive identificatory strategies in which they "ideally integrate and express both male and female aspects of self-hood (as culturally defined)" (113); she further argues that this is the end toward which not only individuals but society as a whole should move. Although neither protagonist fully attains this utopian aim, sleuthing promotes their fortunate falls from innocence and too-complete paternal attachment, leading to the resolution of Oedipal or Electra conflicts that allow less confused gender identities and affective ties to emerge in each novel's resolution. Both sleuthing plots, and especially *Thou Art the Man*, also hint at the psychological effects to the daughter when maternal influence is deemed unnecessary, even denigrated, and the need for reconnection with the mother as the precondition for avoiding an "unnatural" adult identity.

Further attesting to the distinctively cultural rather than inexorably universal basis of Freudian theories,[8] early feminists discerned a parallel to Oedipal attachment in the perpetual dependence that not only shaped but impeded women's development. *In A Vindication of the Rights of Woman,* Mary Wollstonecraft contended that the roles women played as daughters and as wives were fundamentally the same and equally inhibiting, given that when women are "taught slavishly to submit to their parents, they are prepared for the slavery of marriage" (155). Such analogies became a staple by the mid-nineteenth century. In the same era as *Eleanor's Victory,* for instance, activist Bessie Rayner Parkes suggested in 1859 that the typical paradigm in which "women of the upper and middle classes are supported by their male relatives: daughters by their fathers, wives by their husbands" posed a real danger to the security of women if they failed to marry or their male protectors proved inadequate (qtd. in Bauer and Ritt 142).[9]

These writers were approaching by another route conclusions similar to those of *Eleanor's Victory* and *Thou Art the Man* that the daughter's relationship with the father sets a critical pattern for her future relationships and for her emotional, rather than specifically financial, integrity. In *Cassandra,* Florence Nightingale's denunciation of the cultural and familial shackles that bound middle- and upper-class women within the Victorian home, Nightingale hinted at the dream of liberation secretly harbored in the young woman's mind and fostered by her reading of popular fiction. "What is the secret of the charm of every romance that ever was written?" she asks. In penetrating this secret, she observes "that the heroine has generally no family ties (almost invariably no mother), or, if she has, these do not interfere with her entire independence" (28). Mary Elizabeth Braddon's plots of the daughter's detection respond to this hidden fantasy, while revealing the oversimplicity of narratives in which a parent's death alone brings the fantasy to fruition. Instead, as Braddon and others writing in a similar tradition demonstrate, the most liberatory deaths may be the lingering ones that occur in the daughter's psyche, the corpses that most matter, the psychological ones that must be detected and then finally and lovingly interred for an individuated identity to take shape.

NOTES

1. See, for example, Alma E. Murch and Ian Ousby, both of whom rely upon strict structural formulae to find Braddon's narratives wanting on such grounds as frequent recourse to coincidence in the solving of a case (Murch 155), use of more than one character to perform a sleuthing function (156), and the blending of romance with a sleuthing plot (Ousby 135). Less rigid in their application

of genre definitions, though still dismissive, are R. F. Stewart and Martin A. Kayman. Stewart provides a useful discussion of professional detectives in several lesser-known novels by Braddon (181), while Jeanne F. Bedell's essay, though it mentions neither *Eleanor's Victory* nor *Thou Art the Man*, is a serviceable catalog and summary of eighteen Braddon novels in which some form of detection occurs.

2. The novels have received only scant critical attention. Winifred Hughes argues that *Eleanor's Victory* was written as a response to Wilkie Collins's 1862 novel *No Name* (153), while both Fay M. Blake (30–31) and Kathleen L. Maio (94) refer to *Thou Art the Man* in their essays on British and American turn-of-the-century women sleuths.

3. Braddon's debt to Shakespeare, in her estimation, "a kind of God" (Wolff, "Devoted Disciple" 154), through frequent Shakespearean allusions and plots is a fascinating and underexamined facet of her fiction. Robert Lee Wolff points to parallels between Braddon's *Aurora Floyd* and *Othello* (*Sensational Victorian* 150–51), and Ellen Miller Casey to Shakespearean references in *Vixen* (76–77). Although this is not Casey's argument, *Vixen* can be read as a gender-reversed revision of the Hamlet-plot that demonstrates Braddon's ongoing interest in the father/daughter relationship that I identify in her female sleuthing novels.

4. See, for instance, Ann Cvetkovich 45–70 for an illuminating discussion of detection in *Lady Audley's Secret* as a means of playing out an Oedipal drama. The physically and psychically less consanguineous marriage between Robert Audley and Clara Talboys is, of course, complicated by numerous textual references to Clara and George Talboys's likeness that lead Cvetkovich to discern a homoerotic tinge to Robert and Clara's relationship.

5. See Dunn 111–12. Blackmore's concern that *Clara Vaughan*'s originality be properly estimated, and his willingness to proclaim that originality at Braddon's expense, also surfaced in an 1871 letter to his publisher in which he asserted, "It was wholly shaped and partly written before Miss Braddon was heard of, but not being published until after *Eleanor's Victory* (which I had then never seen) some critics declared it to be an imitation of that poor work! Miss Braddon is the very last writer I would ever think of imitating" (qtd. in Dunn 132–33).

6. See both F. Storr's (35) and Arthur S. Way's (20) early twentieth-century translations, for instance. This fascinating instance of intertextuality and, most immediately, Poe's influence on Braddon has gone previously unrecognized. Wolff, in *Sensational Victorian,* turns only to her earlier work to cite a potential source in *The Fatal Three* (473).

7. See Mitchell on this point (12–13).

8. Freud does, in one notable case, trace a lack of differentiation between the father and husband to the modern Western family in which young women are both sheltered from sexual information and taught to repress their desires ("'Civilized' Sexual Morality; see especially 194–204).

9. Parkes's essay, titled "The Market for Educated Female Labor," originally appeared in *English Woman's Journal* 4 (1859): 145–52.

WORKS CITED

Bauer, Carol, and Lawrence Ritt. *Free and Ennobled: Source Readings in the Development of Victorian Feminism.* Oxford: Pergamon, 1979.

Bedell, Jeanne F. "Amateur and Professional Detectives in the Fiction of Mary Elizabeth Braddon." *Clues: A Journal of Detection* 4 (1983): 19–34.

Benjamin, Jessica. *The Bonds of Love: Psychoanalysis, Feminism, and the Problem of Domination.* New York: Pantheon, 1988.

Blackmore, R. D. *Clara Vaughan.* London: Sampson Low, Marston, 1864.

Blake, Fay M. "Lady Sleuths and Women Detectives." *Turn of the Century Women* 3 (1986): 29–42.

Braddon, Mary Elizabeth. *Eleanor's Victory.* 3 vols. London: Tinsley, 1863.

———. *Lady Audley's Secret.* 1862. New York: Dover, 1974.

———. *Thou Art the Man.* 1894. 3 vols. London: Simkin, Marshall, Hamilton, Kent and Co., n.d.

Casey, Ellen Miller. "Other People's Prudery: Mary Elizabeth Braddon." Tennessee Studies in Literature 27 (1984): 72–82.

Chodorow, Nancy. *The Reproduction of Mothering: Psychoanalysis and the Sociology of Gender.* Berkeley: U of California P, 1978.

Rev. of *Clara Vaughan,* by R. D. Blackmore. *Saturday Review* 30 April 1864: 539–41.

Collins, Wilkie. I Say No. 1884. New York: AMS, 1970.

Cvetkovich, Ann. *Mixed Feelings: Feminism, Mass Culture, and Victorian Sensationalism.* New Brunswick, N.J.: Rutgers UP, 1992.

Dunn, Waldo Hilary. *R. D. Blackmore: A Biography.* New York: Longmans, Green, 1956.

Rev. of *Eleanor's Victory,* by Mary Elizabeth Braddon. *Athenaeum* 19 Sept. 1863: 361–62.

Rev. of *Eleanor's Victory,* by Mary Elizabeth Braddon. *Saturday Review* 19 Sept. 1863: 396–97.

Freud, Sigmund. "'Civilized' Sexual Morality and Modern Nervous Illness." 1908. Standard Edition. Vol. 9. 181–204.

———. *An Outline of Psychoanalysis.* 1940. Standard Edition. Vol. 23. 144–207.

———. *The Standard Edition of the Complete Psychological Works of Sigmund Freud.* Trans. and ed. James Strachey. 24 vols. London: Hogarth P and Institute of Psycho-analysis, 1953–72.

Hughes, Winifred. *The Maniac in the Cellar: Sensation Novels of the 1860s.* Princeton, N.J.: Princeton UP, 1980.

Humpherys, Anne. "Who's Doing It? Fifteen Years of Work on Victorian Detective Fiction." *Dickens Studies Annual* 24 (1996): 259–74.

Kayman, Martin A. *From Bow Street to Baker Street: Mystery, Detection and Narrative.* New York: St. Martin's, 1992.

Maio, Kathleen L. " A Strange and Fierce Delight: The Early Days of Women's Mystery Fiction." *Chrysalis* 10 (n.d.): 93–105.

Matus, Jill L. *Unstable Bodies: Victorian Representations of Sexuality and Maternity.* Manchester: Manchester UP, 1995.

Mitchell, Juliet. *Introduction I. Feminine Sexuality: Jacques Lacan and the Ecole Freudienne.* Trans. Jacqueline Rose. Ed. Juliet Mitchell and Jacqueline Rose. London: Macmillan, 1982. 1–26.

Murch, Alma E. *The Development of the Detective Novel.* 1958. Port Washington, N.Y.: Kennikat, 1968.

Nightingale, Florence. *Cassandra.* 1860. New York: Feminist, 1979.

Ousby, Ian. *Bloodhounds of Heaven: The Detective in English Fiction from Godwin to Doyle.* Cambridge: Harvard UP, 1976.

Poe, Edgar Allan. *"Thou Art the Man."* 1844. *The Complete Poems and Stories of Edgar Allan Poe.* Ed. Arthur Hobson Quinn and Edward H. O'Neill. Vol. 2. New York: Knopf, 1982. 566–77.

[Rae, W. Fraser]. "Sensation Novelists: Miss Braddon." *North British Review* 43 (1865): 180–204.

Stewart, R. F. *And Always a Detective: Chapters on the History of Detective Fiction.* Newton Abbot: David and Charles, 1980.

Storr, F., trans. *Oedipus the King.* By Sophocles. *Sophocles* vol. I. London: Heinemann, 1916. 1–139.

Rev. of *Thou Art the Man,* by Mary Elizabeth Braddon. *Athenaeum* 30 June 1894: 833–34.

Rev. of *Thou Art the Man,* by Mary Elizabeth Braddon. *Spectator* 28 July 1894: 118.

Way, Arthur S., trans. *Oedipus the King.* By Sophocles. Sophocles in English Verse. Vol. 1. London: Macmillan, 1917. 1–79.

Wolff, Robert Lee. "Devoted Disciple: The Letters of Mary Elizabeth Braddon to Sir Edward Bulwer-Lytton, 1862–1873." *Harvard Library Bulletin* 22 (1974): 2–35, 129–61.

———. *Sensational Victorian: The Life and Fiction of Mary Elizabeth Braddon.* New York:
Garland, 1979.

Wollstonecraft, Mary. *A Vindication of the Rights of Woman.* 1792. Ed. Carol H. Poston. 2nd ed. New York: Norton, 1988.

Zwinger, Lynda. *Daughters, Fathers, and the Novel: The Sentimental Romance of Heterosexuality.* Madison: U of Wisconsin P, 1991.

AFTERWORD

Lyn Pykett

This collection of essays marks a kind of coming of age in Braddon studies. Since Kathleen Tillotson and Philip Edwards first redirected attention to the work of Mary Elizabeth Braddon in 1969 and 1971 respectively, Braddon has been subjected to intense scrutiny as a female sensationalist. By the early 1990s her bestselling sensation novels, *Lady Audley's Secret* and *Aurora Floyd,* had taken their place in the alternative canons of female-authored literature and popular genre fiction constructed by feminist and cultural studies–influenced literary historians. Inevitably, the present volume bears traces of this recent history. *Lady Audley's Secret,* the 1860s, and the sensation genre dominate these pages, as they have most recent reconsiderations of Braddon's work. However, without underestimating the importance of the contribution this collection makes to advancing the debates on these relatively frequently scrutinized texts and topics, it is particularly pleasing to see its well-informed and detailed examination of hitherto little-discussed texts in a range of modes, genres, and publishing formats, and spanning the whole of Braddon's lengthy and prolific career. It is indeed salutary to be reminded, as we are by Jennifer Carnell and Graham Law, that Braddon's literary career stretched from the eve of the American Civil War to the outbreak of the Great War in Europe.

This volume both revisits Braddon the sensation novelist and extends her sensationalist project beyond the confines of the 1860s, but it also reinserts her fiction into the history of the emerging genre of detective fiction, directing attention to her female as well as her male amateur sleuths. We are reminded that Braddon was also a prolific writer of short stories, and made her own contribution to the nineteenth-century development of the ghost story, a form she used (it is argued here) as an instrument of social critique. Braddon's place in the repertoire of the melodramatic theater has long been assured through successful stage adaptations (by other writers) of her novels, but here we are invited to reconsider Braddon's own place in nineteenth-century theater, both as an actress and, more importantly, as a writer of plays. In several essays Braddon is viewed not simply as a practitioner of sensation, melodrama, or the sentimental, but also as a writer whose complex interweaving of these modes demonstrates or interrogates, as Tabitha Sparks puts it, "the competing epistemologies at work" in 1860s fiction. Braddon's relationship to realism is also reassessed, for example, in Pamela Gilbert's discussion of her (now) little-known novel of 1876, *Joshua Haggard's Daughter.* Hitherto it has been more usual to look at Braddon's fiction in relation to Eliza Lynn Linton's "Girl of the Period" than Sarah Grand's "New Woman," so it is particularly interesting to see Braddon considered as a fin de siècle writer, and her vampire story, "Good Lady Ducayne" (1896) treated as (among other things) a possible source for Bram Stoker's *Dracula.*

In *Beyond Sensation,* as in so many recent discussions of Braddon, the contexts in which her fiction is located are those of nineteenth-century discourses on femininity, female sexuality and domestic ideology, and contemporary debates and anxieties about changing class and gender roles. Several contributors have given fresh insights into the ways in which Braddon's novels both illuminate and are illuminated by contemporary medical and legal discourses, and how these interconnect and interact, particularly in relation to marriage and divorce laws, the Contagious Diseases Acts, and the medical and legal definition—as well as the moral and legal management—of female insanity. One new context for Braddon's work considered in this volume is the historical phenomenon of British imperialism and the discourses of empire it generated; for example in Lillian Nayder's attempt to link Braddon's responses to divorce law reform and the uprising of the Indian Sepoys in 1857. It is particularly interesting to be offered a glimpse of Braddon as writer *for* the colonies, and Toni Johnson-Woods's speculations on the reasons for Braddon's popularity in Australia suggest that there is a great deal of useful work of this kind that might be done on other writers in other places.

A concern for historical specificity is evident throughout the collection, not least for the historical specificities of the conditions of production and dissemination of Braddon's work. Braddon's fiction output was very much the product of contemporary developments in the material and structural organization of the literary marketplace, from the explosion in the penny newspaper press following the repeal of the stamp tax on newspapers in 1856, through the proliferation of inexpensive miscellanies and magazines in the 1860s (large numbers of which were founded and then abandoned by John Maxwell, Braddon's partner and later husband). Braddon was also closely associated with another major development in nineteenth-century publishing: newspaper syndicalization. Carnell and Law's exploration of Braddon's connections with Tillotson's Fiction Bureau and the widespread syndicalization of her novels and stories in the provincial English papers from 1873 onwards sheds new light on a fascinating episode in the history of the development of a modern mass-consumer culture, and helps us to rethink the question of whether Braddon is the woman writer as victim of the nineteenth-century commodification of literature, or the woman writer as an entrepreneurial agent exploiting market conditions.

In their modes of production and dissemination Braddon's novels are representative products of a modern mass-consumer culture. They also mobilize and, it can be argued, interrogate the symbols and signifying system of such a culture. Braddon's novels are consumer products that also market consumer products, for example, through their lavish display of fashion and the accoutrements of the English country house. Like the modern culture of advertising that developed contemporaneously with her career as a novelist, Braddon's fiction not only (as Katherine Montwieler puts it) "markets self-indulgence," it also educates social aspirants in the manners and taste of the upper middle classes. What is at stake here? Is this a "conservative" or a "subversive" move? In *Lady Audley's Secret*, for example, does Braddon mobilize the subversive potential of advertisements to make women (or indeed anyone) dissatisfied with their lot and question their assigned place in society, or does she mobilize consumer desire as a way of managing and containing the gendered social subject? This brings me to the big question that haunts this volume, as it does so many studies of the cultural history of the nineteenth century in recent years. Is the writer or genre (or any other cultural phenomenon one might care to substitute) that is "recovered" by the modern (or postmodern) cultural historian a radical or a conservative, an interrogator or a reinscriber, part of the problem or part of the solution (however one is minded to define both "problem" and "solution")? Something of the nature of the conservative/radical dilemma was illustrated in successive essays in which Gail Houston offers *Lady Audley's Secret* as "a penetrating early example of feminist jurisprudence," that "proves the self-interestedness of the law and male law makers," and Lillian Nayder argues that the same novel reveals Braddon as a conservative who, for the most part, "defends the institution of marriage against subversion and reform." On the whole the broad focus of this volume, and its eclectic methodologies, work to suggest that Braddon is both a radical and a conservative, and that she is neither. Indeed, on the evidence of this collection Braddon is a more complex and shifting entity than these labels would allow.

Select Bibliography

MARY ELIZABETH BRADDON

(See also essays herein)

"Loves of Arcadia" ("Comedietta"). Unpublished 1860.

Three Times Dead. London: W. & M. Clark and Beverley: Empson (1860). Re-published 1861.

Garibaldi (verse). London: Bosworth & Harrison, 1861.

The Black Band. London: Halfpenny Journal, 1861. Vickers, as book 1877.

The Lady Lisle. London: Ward, Lock & Tyler, 1862.

Lady Audley's Secret. London: Tinsley, 1862.

Captain of the Vulture. London: Ward, Lock & Tyler, 1863.

Aurora Floyd. London: Tinsley, 1863.

Eleanor's Victory. London: Tinsley, 1863.

John Marchmont's Legacy. London: Tinsley, 1863.

Henry Dunbar. London: Maxwell, 1864.

The Doctor's Wife. London: Maxwell, 1864.

Only a Clod. London: Maxwell, 1865.

Sir Jasper's Tenant. London: Maxwell, 1865.

The Lady's Mile. London: Ward, Lock & Tyler, 1866.

Ralph the Bailiff &c. London: Ward, Lock & Tyler, 1867.

Circe (2 vols.) as by "Babington White". London: Ward, Lock & Tyler, 1867.

Rupert Godwin. London: Ward, Lock & Tyler, 1867.

Birds of Prey. London: Ward, Lock & Tyler, 1867.

Charlotte's Inheritance. London: Ward, Lock & Tyler, 1868.

Run to Earth. London: Ward, Lock & Tyler, 1868.

Dead Sea Fruit. London: Ward, Lock & Tyler, 1868.

Fenton's Quest. London: Ward, Lock & Tyler, 1871.

The Lovels of Arden. London: Maxwell, 1871.

Robert Ainsleigh. London: Maxwell, 1872.

To the Bitter End. London: Maxwell, 1872.

Select Bibliography

Milly Darrell &c. London: Maxwell, 1873.
"Griselda" (drama). London: Unpublished, 1873.
Strangers & Pilgrims. London: Maxwell, 1873.
Lucius Davoren. London: Maxwell, 1873.
Taken at the Flood. London: Maxwell, 1874.
Lost for Love. London: Chatto & Windus, 1874.
A Strange World. London: Maxwell, 1875.
Hostages to Fortune. London: Maxwell, 1875.
Dead Men's Shoes. London: Maxwell, 1876.
Joshua Haggard's Daughter. London: Maxwell, 1876.
Weavers and Weft &c. London: Maxwell, 1877
An Open Verdict. London: Maxwell, 1878.
Vixen. London: Maxwell, 1879.
The Cloven Foot. London: Maxwell, 1879.
Aladdin &c. (juvenile). London: Maxwell, 1880.
"The Missing Witness" (drama). London: Maxwell, 1880.
The Story of Barbara. London: Maxwell, 1880.
Just As I Am. London: Maxwell, 1880.
Asphodel. London: Maxwell, 1881.
Mount Royal. London: Maxwell, 1882.
Ishmael. London: Maxwell, 1882.
The Golden Calf. London: Maxwell, 1883.
Phantom Fortune. London: Maxwell, 1883.
Flower & Weed Mistletoe Bough (with other stories). London: Maxwell, 1884.
Wyllard's Weird. London: Maxwell, 1885.
Under the Red Flag (with other stories). London: Maxwell, 1886.
The Good Hermione (juvenile) by "Aunt Belinda." London: Maxwell, 1886.
One Thing Needful. London: Maxwell, 1886.
Cut by the County. London: Maxwell, 1886.
Mohawks. London: Maxwell, 1886.
Like and Unlike. London: Spencer Blackett, 1887.
The Fatal Three. London: Simpkin, Marshall, 1888.
The Day Will Come. London: Simpkin, Marshall, 1889.
One Life, One Love. London: Simpkin, Marshall, 1890.
Gerard. London: Simpkin, Marshall, 1891.
The Venetians. London: Simpkin, Marshall, 1892.
"A Life Interest" (drama). Unpublished 1893.
All Along the River. London: Simpkin, Marshall, 1893.
The Christmas Hirelings (juvenile). London: Simpkin, Marshall, 1894.
Thou Art the Man. London: Simpkin, Marshall, 1894.
Sons of Fire. London: Simpkin, Marshall, 1895.
London Pride. London: Simpkin, Marshall, 1896.
Under Love's Rule. London: Simpkin, Marshall, 1897.

In High Places. London: Hutchinson, 1898.
Rough Justice. London: Simpkin, Marshall, 1898.
His Darling Sin. London: Simpkin, Marshall, 1899.
The Infidel. London: Simpkin, Marshall, 1900.
The Conflict. London: Simpkin, Marshall, 1903.
A Lost Eden. London: Hutchinson, 1904.
The Rose of Life. London: Hutchinson, 1905.
The White House. London: Hurst & Blackett, 1906.
Dead Love Has Chains. London: Hurst & Blackett, 1907.
Her Convict. London: Hurst & Blackett, 1907.
During Her Majesty's Pleasure. London: Hurst & Blackett, 1908.
Our Adversary. London: Hutchinson, 1909.
Beyond These Voices. London: Hutchinson, 1910.
The Green Curtain. London: Hutchinson, 1911.
Miranda. London: Hutchinson, 1913.
Mary. London: Hutchinson, 1916.

CRITICISM

Altick, Richard D. *The English Common Reader: A Social History of the Mass Reading Public 1800–1900.* Chicago: U of Chicago P, 1957.

Bedell, Jeanne F. "Amateur and Professional Detectives in the Fiction of Mary Elizabeth Braddon." *Clues: A Journal of Detection* 4 (1983): 19–34.

Boyle, Thomas. *Black Swine in the Sewers of Hampstead: Beneath the Surface of Victorian Sensationalism.* New York: Viking, 1989.

Brantlinger, Patrick. "What is 'Sensational' about the 'Sensation Novel?'" *Nineteenth-Century Fiction* 37 (1982.): 1–28.

Briganti, Chiara. "Gothic Maidens and Sensation Women: Lady Audley's Journey from the Ruined Mansion to the Madhouse." *Victorian Literature and Culture* 19 (1991): 189–211.

Casey, Ellen Miller. "Other People's Prudery: Mary Elizabeth Braddon." *Sexuality and Victorian Literature,* Ed. Don Richard Cox. *Tennessee Studies in Literature* 27 (1984): 72–82.

Cvetkovich, Ann. *Mixed Feelings: Feminism, Mass Culture, and Victorian Sensationalism.* New Brunswick, N.J.: Rutgers UP, 1992.

Flint, Kate. *The Woman Reader, 1837–1914.* Oxford: Clarendon P, 1993.

Gilbert, Pamela K. *Disease, Desire and the Body in Victorian Women's Popular Novels.* Cambridge: Cambridge UP, 1997.

Hart, Lynda. "The Victorian Villainess and the Patriarchal Unconscious." *Literature and Psychology* 40 (1994) 1–25.

Hazelwood, C. H. "Aurora Floyd"; *Or, The Dark Deed in the Wood. A Drama in Three Acts.* London: Thomas Hailes Lacy [n.d.: first performed 21 April 1863 at the Royal Brittania Theatre].

Hughes, Winifred. *The Maniac in the Cellar: Sensation Novels in the 1860s*. Princeton, N.J.: Princeton UP, 1980.

Kalikoff, Beth. *Murder and Moral Decay in Victorian Popular Literature*. Ann Arbor, : UMI Research, 1986.

Kaplan, Joel H. "Exhuming Lady Audley: Period Melodrama for the 1990s." *Melodrama*. Ed. James Redmond. Cambridge: Cambridge UP, 1992 143–60.

Keith, Sara. "The *Athenaeum* as a Bibliographical Aid: Illustrated by *Lady Audley's Secret* and Other Novels." *Victorian Periodicals Newsletter* 8 (1975): 25–28.

Loesberg, Jonathon. "The Ideology of Narrative Form in Sensation Fiction." *Representations* 13 (1986): 115–38.

Marks, Patricia. "'The Boy on the Wooden Horse: Robert Audley and the Failure of Reason." *Clues: A Journal of Detection*. 15 (1994): 1–14.

Matus, Jill L. "Disclosure as 'Cover Up': The Discourse of Madness in *Lady Audley's Secret*." *University of Toronto Quarterly* 62 (1993): 334–55.

Miller, D. A. *The Novel and the Police*. Berkeley: U of California P, 1988.

Mitchell, Sally. *The Fallen Angel: Chastity, Class, and Women's Reading, 1835–1880*. Bowling Green, Ohio: Bowling Green State U Popular Press, 1981.

Nemesvari, Richard. "Robert Audley's Secret: Male Homosocial Desire in *Lady Audley's Secret*." *Studies in the Novel* 27 (1995): 515–28.

Nemesvari, Richard, and Lisa Surridge. Ed. *Aurora Floyd*. Ontario, Canada: Broadview, 1998.

Peterson, Audrey. *Victorian Masters of Mystery: From Wilkie Collins to Conan Doyle*. New York: Ungar, 1984.

Pykett, Lyn. *The Sensation Novel: From "The Woman in White" to "The Moonstone."* Plymouth, U.K. : Northcote House in association with The British Council, 1994.

Pykett, Lyn. *The "Improper" Feminine: The Women's Sensation Novel and the New Woman Writing*. London; New York: Routledge, 1995.

Robinson, Solveig C. "Editing *Belgravia*: M. E. Braddon's Defense of 'Light Literature.'" *Victorian Periodicals Review* 28 (1995): 109–22.

Schroeder, Natalie. "Feminine Sensationalism, Eroticism, and Self-Assertion: M. E. Braddon and Ouida." *Tulsa Studies in Women's Literature* 7 (1988): 87–103.

Showalter, Elaine. *A Literature of Their Own: British Women Novelists from Brontë to Lessing*. Princeton, N.J.: Princeton UP, 1977.

Showalter, Elaine. "Desperate Remedies: Sensation Novels of the 1860s." *Victorian Newsletter* 49 (1976): 1–5.

Taylor, Jenny Bourne. *In the Secret Theater of Home: Wilkie Collins, Sensation Narrative and Nineteenth Century Psychology*. London: Routledge, 1988.

Tillotson, Kathleen. "The Lighter Reading of the Eighteen-Sixties." Introduction. *The Woman in White*. Boston: Houghton Mifflin, 1969.

Tintner, Adeline R. "Henry James and Miss Braddon: 'Georgina's Reasons' and the Victorian Sensation Novel." *Essays in Literature* 10 (1983): 119–24.

Trodd, Anthea. *Domestic Crime in the Victorian Novel*. London: Macmillan, 1989.

Wiesenthal, C. S. "'Ghost Haunted': A Trace of Wilkie Collins in Mary Elizabeth Braddon's *Lady Audley's Secret*." *English Language Notes* 28 (1991): 42–44.

Wolff, Robert L. "Devoted Disciple: The Letters of Mary Elizabeth Braddon to Sir Edward Bulwer-Lytton, 1862–1873." *Harvard Library Bulletin* 22 (1974): 5–35, 129–61.

Wolff, Robert Lee. *Sensational Victorian: The Life and Fiction of Mary Elizabeth Braddon*. New York: Garland, 1979.

CONTEMPORARY CRITICISM

"The Archbishop of York on Works of Fiction." *The Times* (2 November 1864): 9.

"Aurora Floyd." *Athenaeum*. 1840.

Austin, Alfred. "Our Novels (Part II): The Sensation School." *Temple Bar* 29 (June 1870): 410–24.

T. A. "Recent Novel Writing." *Macmillans*. 13 (January 1866): 202–9.

E. B. "The Sensation Novel." *Argosy* 18 (August 1874): 137–43.

James, Henry. "Miss Braddon." *The Nation* (9 November 1865): 593–94.

[Mansel, H. L.] "Sensation Novels." *Quarterly Review* 113 (April 1863): 481–514.

Oliphant, Margaret. "Novels." *Blackwood's Edinburgh Magazine* 102 (September 1867): 257–80.

"Our Female Sensation Novelists." *Living Age* 78 (August 1863): 352–69.

"Our Survey of Literature and Science." *Cornhill Magazine* 8 (January–June 1863): 132–39.

"The Popular Novels of the Year." *Fraser's Magazine* 68 (August 1863): 253–69.

[Rae, W. Fraser]. "Sensation Novelists: Miss Braddon." *North British Review* 43 (1865): 180–204.

"Recent Novels: Their Moral and Religious Teaching." *London Quarterly Review* 27 (October 1866): 100–124.

Sala, George Augustus. "The Cant of Modern Criticism." *Belgravia* 4 (November 1867): 45–55.

———. "On the 'Sensational' in Literature and Art." *Belgravia* 4 (February 1868): 449–58.

"Sensational Novels." *Medical Critic and Psychological Journal* 3 (1863): 513–19

Untitled Article. *Living Age* 77 (April 1863): 99–103.

Untitled Review. *Christian Remembrancer* 46 (1863): 209–36.

CONTRIBUTORS

Jennifer Carnell received her PhD from Birbeck College, University of London, in autumn 1998, with her doctoral thesis on "The Literary Lives of Mary Elizabeth Braddon." She is the author of a detective novel and has recently edited a volume of Braddon's early melodrama entitled *The Black Band; or the Mysteries of Midnight.*

Jeni Curtis currently teaches at St. Andrew's College, Christchurch, New Zealand. She contributes to the Victorian Studies program at Canterbury University, Christchurch, and to distance education in English for Massey University, Palmerston North, New Zealand. She is working on representations of illness in the writing of Elizabeth Gaskell.

Pamela K. Gilbert is an Associate Professor of English at the University of Florida. Her work has appeared in several journals, including *English, LIT: Literature/Interpretation/Theory, Essays in Arts and Sciences, Essays in Literature, Victorian Newsletter,* and others. Her book, *Disease, Desire and the Body in Victorian Women's Newsletter,* and was published in 1997 by Cambridge University Press. She is currently working on a second book which traces the construction of the social body through the cholera epidemics in England, especially London, 1832–1866.

Lauren M. E. Goodlad is an Assistant Professor of English at University of Washington in Seattle. She is currently finishing a book, tentatively entitled *Respectable and Rough: Disciplinary Individualism and the New Poor Law, a Critical and Literary History, 1833–1910.* She also works on gothic literature and culture, on contemporary popular culture, and on feminist issues.

Aeron Haynie is an Assistant Professor of English at University of Wisconsin—Green Bay. She is currently working on a book-length manuscript on travel and tourism in literature.

Heidi J. Holder is an Assistant Professor of English at Central Michigan University. She has published articles on J. M. Synge, Victorian theater and imperialism, the dramas of Harley Granville Barker, Victorian women playwrights, and twentieth-century Canadian theater. She is currently completing a book-length manuscript on the connections among genre, realism, and censorship in the Victorian and Edwardian theaters, and is engaged in research on the Victorian theater of London's East End.

Gail Turley Houston is an Assistant Professor of English at the University of New Mexico. The author of *Consuming Fictions: Gender, Class, and Hunger in Dicken's Novels* (Southern Illinois University Press, 1994) and *Trading Places: Queen Victoria, the Victorian Writer, and Competing Representations* (University Press of Virginia 1999), she is currently working on a book on the Arts and Crafts Movement, in particular, Victorian artist Phoebe Anna Traquair.

Heidi H. Johnson, a Ph.D. candidate at the University of Iowa, is completing a dissertation on the legal and social contexts that promoted the emergence of the female sleuth in nineteenth-century British fiction. Her articles on popular Victorian poetry and fiction have appeared in *Victorian Poetry* and *Victorians Institute Journal.*

Toni Johnson-Woods is a lecturer in Contemporary Studies at the University of Queensland in Australia. She has published in the area of popular nineteenth-century journals and popular nineteenth-century literature and is currently finishing a book that documents serialization in major nineteenth-century Australian journals.

Elizabeth Langland, Dean and Professor of English at the University of California-Davis, is the author of *Nobody's Angels: Middle-Class Women and Domestic Ideology in Victorian Culture, Anne Brontë: The Other One,* and *Society in the Novel.* She has also published numerous articles and edited books on women in literature, feminist theory, Victorian literature and culture, and narrative theory. She is currently at work on a book tentatively entitled *Imagined Geographies: The Representation of Space in Victorian Literature.*

Graham Law has taught in Japan since 1981, and is now Professor in English Studies at Waseda University, Tokyo. He has edited a number of works by Dickens and Wilkie Collins, and is joint editor of the *Wilkie Collins Society Journal.* He is working on a book entitled *Novels in Newspapers: The Serialization and Syndication of Fiction in the Victorian Press,* forthcoming in 2000.

Eve M. Lynch teaches English literature at California State University, Hayward. She has published articles on various British women writers in *Pacific Coast Philology* (September 1996), *Virginia Woolf: Themes and Variations,* ed. Vara Neverow-Turk and Mark Hussey, (Pace University Press 1993), as well as essays on Elizabeth Hands, Susanna Rowson, and Catherine Cookson in *An Encyclopedia of British Women Writers,* second edition, edited by Paul and June Schlueter (Rutgers University Press 1998). She is currently completing a book-length manuscript on literary representations of domestic servants. In addition, Dr. Lynch has chaired several panels and presented papers on nineteenth-century British literature at the annual conventions of the Modern Language Association, including a panel on Victorian ghost stories from which her essay on Braddon is developed.

Katherine Montwieler is a doctoral candidate at the University of Georgia. Her dissertation focuses on the work of nineteenth-century British women poets.

Lillian Nayder is an Associate Professor of English at Bates College, where she teaches courses on nineteenth-century fiction and the English novel. Her essays on Dickens, Collins, Stoker, and Conrad have appeared in various journals and collections, and her book, *Wilkie Collins*, was published by Twayne in 1997.

Tabitha Sparks is a graduate student in English at the University of Washington, Seattle, where she teaches in the departments of English and Comparative History of Ideas. Her research interests include noncanonical Victorian novelists, Victorian political economics, and the development of the medical field in the nineteenth century. Currently she is writing her dissertation, which investigates and historicizes the ways that Victorian novels define the relationship between domestic and medical authority.

Marlene Tromp is an Assistant Professor at Denison University. Her forthcoming book is entitled *The Private Rod: Martial Violence, Sensation, and the Law in Victorian Britian* (University of Virginia Press, 2000) and is currently working on Spiritualism and women's sexuality in the mid-Victorian period.

INDEX